# The Dynamics of Confucianism and Modernization in Korean History

# The Dynamics of Confucianism
# and Modernization in Korean History

By Yi Tae-jin

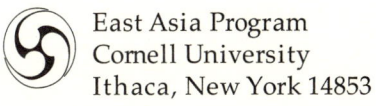
East Asia Program
Cornell University
Ithaca, New York 14853

The Cornell East Asia Series is published by the Cornell University East Asia Program (distinct from Cornell University Press). We publish affordably priced books on a variety of scholarly topics relating to East Asia as a service to the academic community and the general public. Standing orders, which provide for automatic notification and invoicing of each title in the series upon publication, are accepted.

If after review by internal and external readers a manuscript is accepted for publication, it is published on the basis of camera-ready copy provided by the volume author. Each author is thus responsible for any necessary copy-editing and for manuscript formatting. Address submission inquiries to CEAS Editorial Board, East Asia Program, Cornell University, Ithaca, New York 14853-7601.

The publication of this book was made possible by a donation from Mr. and Mrs. I.H. Cho and a publication grant from the Korea Foundation.

Number 136 in the Cornell East Asia Series
Copyright © 2007 by Yi Tae-jin. All rights reserved
ISSN 1050-2955
ISBN-13: 978-1-933947-06-8 hc / ISBN-10: 1-933947-06-3 hc
ISBN-13: 978-1-933947-36-5 pb / ISBN-10: 1-933947-36-5 pb
Library of Congress Control Number: 2007940024
Printed in the United States of America
24 23 22 21 20 19 18 17 16 15 14 13 12 11 10 09 06     9 8 7 6 5 4 3 2 1

Cover images: (1) A woodblock print portrait of Confucius, the Minister of Justice in his home state of Lu. The portrait is from "Nosakusang," a Korean compendium of Confucian works (Sin'gan sowang sagi) printed mainly with movable type from a font cast in 1455. (2) A photograph of the Hansŏng Electric Company, Chongno, Seoul, taken in 1902, showing the changes to the city streets as a result of the urban renovation project that began in September 1896. The company was a joint project of Emperor Kojong and the American company Collbran & Bostwick. Cover design by Claudia Yeo. Book layout and format by Yoon Sun Yi.

♾ The paper in this book meets the requirements for permanence of ISO 9706:1994.

CAUTION: Except for brief quotations in a review, no part of this book may be reproduced or utilized in any form without permission in writing from the author. Please address inquiries to Yi Tae-jin in care of the East Asia Program, Cornell University, 140 Uris Hall, Ithaca, NY 14853-7601.

# Contents

Preface     vii
Notes on Romanization     xi
List of Illustrations     xii

PART I: SOCIOECONOMIC DEVELOPMENT AND NEO-CONFUCIANISM

1. Social Change during the Koryŏ-Chosŏn Transition     3

2. The Socioeconomic Background of Neo-Confucianism in Fifteenth- and Sixteenth-Century Korea     23

3. New Socioeconomic Trends in Fifteenth- and Sixteenth-Century Korea: Population Increase and Cultivation of the Lowlands     49

4. The Influence of Neo-Confucianism on Population Growth in Fourteenth- to Sixteenth-Century Korea     67

PART II: INTERNATIONAL RELATIONS IN A PERIOD OF HISTORICAL TRANSITION

5. Economic Transformation and Sociopolitical Trends in Sixteenth-Century East Asia     93

6. Separating Fact from Fiction about Pre-Modern Sino-Korean Trade     121

7. Chosŏn's Adoption of International Law and Its Conflicts with China in the 1880s     139

8. Forced Treaties and Japan's Annexation of the Great Han Empire: An Argument for the Illegality of the Annexation — 165

PART III: MODERNIZATION AND CONFUCIANISM

9. King Chŏngjo: Confucianism, Enlightenment, and Absolute Rule — 207

10. Seoul's Modern Urban Development During the Eighteenth and Nineteenth Centuries — 235

11. The Leaders and Objectives of the Seoul Urban Renovation Project of 1896–1904 — 269

PART IV: OVERCOMING THE DISTORTIONS OF KOREAN HISTORY

12. Why Has Yangban Culture Been Denounced? — 295

13. Was Early Modern Korea Really a "Hermit Kingdom"? — 325

14. Korean Historiography's Escape from Modernism — 351

Notes on Original Appearance — 371
Translators — 373
Glossary of Names — 375
Glossary of Terms — 379
Index — 391

# Preface

I DO NOT EXPECT the topic of this book, Neo-Confucianism, to elicit a great deal of interest from readers in English-speaking countries. Currently, even scholars and students who study Asian cultures and history are mainly interested in modern Asian history. It is difficult to expect interest even from them in Confucianism, a pre-modern ideology. This ideology, which emphasized moral values, is now dead, and almost no student pays it any attention.

However, as the Chinese economy continues to thrive and the Japanese, South Korean, and Taiwanese economies continue to play a greater global role, this attitude toward Confucianism may change. When the economies of South Korea, Taiwan, Hong Kong, and Singapore took off about twenty years ago, the world nicknamed them Asia's "four little dragons." People noticed that all were culturally moored in Confucianism and started using popular bywords such as "Confucian renaissance" and "Asian values" to describe their successes. As the Chinese economy continues to grow, interest in traditional culture may resurge. Recently, there has been a strong trend of even sinologists reinterpreting traditional Confucian ideology in a positive light. However, this book is not about how current events relate to Confucianism.

Most of the content in this book comes from presentations that I have made at international academic conferences since 1980. This volume differs from the typical book, which is usually written over a shorter period of time and tightly organized around a central theme. However, all the content revolves around Neo-Confucianism, and in this sense, the chapters are consistent with one another. I have organized the book into sections by category, to reflect the breadth of research I have carried out over the last twenty-five years.

In the 1960s I entered academia as an undergraduate student and questioned whether Confucianism, the ideology that dominated pre-modern Korean history, was simply a mode of thought with no practical application. At the time, East Asian specialists widely believed the East was unable to develop science and commerce like the West due to the ideological bonds imposed by Confucianism. In Korea, the failure of Chosŏn to modernize and the loss of the country's sovereignty to Japan were blamed solely on Confucian thought, and the theory of the "failed Confucian state" was accepted as common sense. Although the Korean society did not purposely try to stamp out Confucianism like communist Chinese society had via the Cultural Revolution, the Korean people did make a conscious effort to bury this ideology. I think this notion of cultural defeatism is undesirable for the future of East Asia.

I became engrossed with researching whether Chosŏn dynasty Neo-Confucianism as an ideology was truly divorced from reality. The majority of my research focused on community contracts, medical and agricultural policies, and commerce-related matters. I was interested in seeing how Neo-Confucianism as an ideology had supported agriculture and developed the agricultural economy, which naturally led to analyzing how commerce and international trade had developed. My conclusion was that Neo-Confucianism, far from being an ideology devoid of real-world application, was actually a mode of thought responsible for greatly improving the lives of the people. I am not suggesting that Neo-Confucianism led to a great revolution in the East on the scale of the Industrial Revolution in the West, but I do believe that when the East was incorporated into the Western capitalist economy, Confucianism's ability to meld with and readily accept capitalism provided the impetus for twentieth-century East Asia to carry out an economic revolution.

Through my research on eighteenth-century Chosŏn Neo-Confucianism, I have discovered that when the social status system was breaking down, Neo-Confucianism adapted to deal with this new situation. When the Chosŏn state had originally devised the social status system out of a sense of duty to improve the lives of the people, it utilized the concept of *minbon* (the people as the foundation). In the eighteenth century, this base was changed to incorporate the king as well, leading to a new concept encompassing both the people and their sovereign, which was termed a *minguk* (republic). I regard this as one of the great developments of Korean history.

This ability of Confucianism to change with the times, what I term its "elasticity," is exemplified by the Chosŏn state's daring resolution to adopt the strong points of Western culture and technology in response to the "Western shock" of the mid-nineteenth century. Contrary to popular belief, the Confucian state of Chosŏn was not an isolated country. In early 1887, Pak Chŏng-yang, the first Korean diplomatic minister dispatched to the United States, began working in Washington, D.C. Just ten years later, he and his legation staff displayed remarkable cultural adaptability by initiating plans to transform Seoul into a modern city based on the model of the American national capital. This shows how willing Pak and his cohorts were to push for cultural changes in their country. The most important thing that I have gained from nearly thirty years of research on Confucian history is the ability to write convincingly that the demagoguery of Japanese military aggression is behind the theory of the "failed Confucian state."

The Korean economy has undergone rapid expansion over the last forty years and presently even leads the world in the information technology industry. One hundred years ago, the country exhibited the same progressive spirit in adopting Western culture and technology. Plans to modernize Seoul were initiated in 1896, and within three years the first electric streetcars started operation, three years earlier than in Tokyo. Korea's revolution was unable to proceed smoothly due to external pressure from China in the 1880s and Japan in the 1890s. In the 1900s, Japan seized national sovereignty from Korea by military force and crushed any further possibility of progress. The theory of the "failed Confucian state" is but one of many kinds of propaganda devised by the Japanese state. For thirty-six years Korea suffered under Japanese rule, and Koreans were relentlessly brainwashed, leading them to have no interest in their own traditional culture. Since the economic development of the 1960s, Koreans have not been able to understand the uniqueness of their own culture. While studying the role of Chosŏn Confucianism in developing an agrarian economy, I was struck by how similar the economic activities of Koreans since the 1960s have been to those of their ancestors. The nation's predisposition to hunt down opportunity and the people's strong will to improve their quality of life remained virtually unchanged.

The chapters included in this book have all been translated from Korean. Since I have not had the opportunity to study in an English-speaking country, writing directly in English poses quite a challenge. Therefore, I have relied on many people to translate my works into English and gave due credit by including their names at the end of each chapter. Since the translations were done by a number of different people, a final proofreading and revision of the book was necessary. Toward this end, Christopher Liao has done a splendid job.

Professor Milan Hetjmanek also translated one of my papers into English when he visited Seoul in the 1980s. I am also grateful to two anonymous reviewers for their helpful comments and excellent advice on the organization of this book.

Professor Michael Shin of Cornell University has played the largest role in bringing this book to publication. When he came to Seoul in 1990s, he often visited me, and I asked him to read over papers I planned to present at international conferences. As he gained familiarity with my research, he suggested that I organize all these papers into a single volume, saying such a work would be valuable to students of Korean history at American universities. His repeated assertions to this effect eventually led to the birth of this book. I am indebted to Professor Shin and express my deepest thanks here. Yoon Sun Yi of Cornell University formatted the manuscript and prepared the index. Kurt Nason, also of Cornell University, proofread the entire manuscript. I must also deliver a final word of thanks to Karen K. Smith, Mai Shaikhanuar-Cota, and Evangeline Ray of the Cornell East Asia Series for their help in publishing this volume. Special thanks goes to Evangeline for her copyediting of the entire manuscript.

# Notes on Romanization

KOREAN WORDS AND NAMES have been romanized by the McCune-Reischauer system. Some well-known names and place names have been romanized according to standard usage, such as Seoul and Pyongyang. Korean and Japanese names have been written in East Asian order with the surname coming first.

Macrons have not been used to indicate long vowels in Japanese. Such symbols are of little use to those unfamiliar with the language. Chinese words and names have been romanized by the Pinyin system.

# List of Illustrations

Figure 1a. Original document of the First Japanese-Korean Agreement (August 1904).
Figure 1b. English version of the First Japanese-Korean Agreement.
Figure 2a. Proxy statement issued by King Kojong for the representative to the Treaty of Amity between Chosŏn and Japan.
Figure 2b. Ratification statement by the Japanese emperor Meiji for the 1876 Treaty of Amity between Chosŏn and Japan.
Figure 3a. The "Convention of 1905" between Korea and Japan.
Figure 3b. English version of the Second Japanese-Korean Agreement (Convention of 1905).
Figure 4. The Korean-Japanese Agreement of 1907.
Figure 5. Proxy statement issued by Emperor Sunjong to Prime Minister Yi Wanyong.
Figure 6. Emperor Sunjong's royal edict to announce the annexation of Korea.
Figure 7. The royal edicts of the emperors of Korea and Japan announcing the annexation of Korea.

Map 1: Urban Development Projects in Seoul, 1896–1902.
Map 2: Western Quarter of Central Seoul (September 1901).

Photo 1: Unjong Street (present-day Chongno) after the urban improvement projects.
Photo 2: Monument commemorating the 40th year of Kojong's reign.
Photo 3-1, 3-2, 3-3: Thirteen-story pagoda on the site of Wŏn'gak Temple.
Photo 4: Street going from Kwanghwamun to Hyejŏng Bridge (Yukcho Street).

*List of Illustrations* xiii

Photo 5: Taean Gate of Kyŏng'un Palace (present-day Tŏksu Palace).
Photo 6: Funeral procession for Empress Min (November 1897).
Photo 7-1, 7-2, 7-3: Funeral for Emperor Kojong (1919).
Photo 8: A crowd in front of Taean Gate after Korea's liberation in August 15, 1945.

PART I

# Socioeconomic Development and Neo-Confucianism

CHAPTER 1

# Social Change during the Koryŏ-Chosŏn Transition

IN GENERAL, SCHOLARS AGREE that the late-Koryŏ to early-Chosŏn period represents an important transition in Korean history. Scholarly work has identified five major changes during this period. First, scholar-officials (*sinhŭng sadaebu*) from the small- to medium-sized landlord class emerged as a new ruling class. Second, this new class established a political system based on a centralized bureaucracy. Third, the economy saw the development of the landlord-tenant system. Fourth, these political and economic changes brought about a shift in the social-status system. Fifth, Neo-Confucianism was adopted as the ruling ideology. In addition, historical studies have examined the significance of these changes on the development of Korea. In debates on the periodization of Korean history, some scholars believe these changes marked the beginning of the medieval age, while others maintain they formed just one stage within the medieval period. Still others believe that these developments indicate that Korea at the time was a more advanced society than medieval Europe. These scholars assert that developments in this period actually mark the beginning of the so-called early-modern age (*kŭnse*). Such differences of opinion allow room for further discussion, illustrating the significance of this period as an era of transition.

Although scholars have made considerable progress in understanding the social changes during the late-Koryŏ to early-Chosŏn period, they are still unable to explain their origins and causes sufficiently. In particular, there has been a tendency to view the emergence of the scholar-officials as a new political force behind the changes. Such research, however, has not examined the issue of what made possible the emergence of this new scholar-official class. Moreover, it has not clarified whether the transition during the late-Koryŏ to early-Chosŏn period started with the Military Coup of 1170 or at a later point in time. In this chapter, I aim to contribute to the understanding of developments during this transitional period while supplementing what previous studies have covered.

OVERCOMING THE LIMITATIONS OF FALLOW-FIELD CULTIVATION

The first question to examine is: When did the transition period actually begin? In previous studies, only the Military Coup of 1170 has been offered as the beginning. Researchers who focus on the significance of this date argue that literati "well versed in letters and competent as officials" (nŭngmun and nŭngni) who emerged under the military regime formed the basis for the "newly rising scholar-officials."[1]

When discussing economic changes, scholars have merely noted that agricultural estates originated with the ownership of private land, but they have made no clear distinctions between the two. Koryŏ continuously suffered from internal disturbances and foreign invasions after the Military Coup of 1170, and the existence of such political unrest has made it difficult to examine the qualitative social changes of the period. I believe that the coup came to be considered the starting point for the social change largely because of the difficulties in examining this period.

The theory of the coup as starting date, however, raises several questions. First, more than 220 years passed between the Military Coup of 1170 and the establishment of the Chosŏn dynasty in 1392, a period too long to constitute one stage of social evolution. Second, there were few similarities between the literati "well versed in letters and competent as officials" under the military regime and the newly rising scholar-officials (sinhŭng sadaebu). Although both were literati, the latter differed from the former in their interest in Neo-Confucianism.

The scholar-officials emerged as a new political force toward the end of the Koryŏ period, during the reign of King Kongmin (1352–

---

1. Yi Usŏng, "Koryŏjo ŭi i e daehayo" (Concerning officials during the Koryŏ dynasty), Yŏksa hakpo 21 (1964).

1374). Though it overemphasizes politics, one method of examining the changes in this period is to study the activities of the officials connected to the new power groups during the reign of King Kongmin. The political activities of the scholar-officials focused on eliminating the pro-Yuan group and reforming the abuses in the administration of land and people. However, studies have revealed that similar reforms had already been attempted during the reigns of both King Ch'ungsŏn (1309–1313) and King Ch'ungmok (1344–1348). The Sarim-wŏn (Secretariat of Letters) attempted to implement anti-Yuan political reforms during the reign of King Ch'ungsŏn, and the Chŏngch'i togam (Directorate of Readjustment) tried to do the same during the reign of King Ch'ungmok.[2] The content of these two reform efforts were similar to the reform politics of King Kongmin's reign, and they also occurred in the same time period. On the basis of these facts, it seems possible to regard the early fourteenth century as the beginning of the late-Koryŏ to early-Chosŏn period.

The next topic to examine is the causes of the social changes and the process of their emergence. Widespread peasant rebellions during the military coups demonstrate that Koryŏ society had already undergone one great change. This change, however, took place during the fifty-year military regime of the Ch'oe clan after it had established political stability. The interval of these events can be said to constitute a distinctive period on its own. The situation at the beginning of the fourteenth century differed greatly from that of the military-regime period. After the Ch'oe regime fell, the Mongols finalized a treaty with the pro-Yuan aristocrats, whose social system endured for half a century. Because it was important for society to root out the structural contradictions brought about by foreign pressure, it was possible for anti-Yuan reform politics to be carried out in the fourteenth century. These facts show that the strong desire for political reform served as the basic motivating force for social change at that time. It is also important to examine what ultimately allowed reform to succeed.

Scholars have done much research on the anti-Yuan reforms during the last years of the Koryŏ dynasty because they not only succeeded after many setbacks but also brought about social development.

---

2. Yi Ki–nam, "Ch'ungsŏnwang ŭi kaehyŏk kwa sarimwŏn ŭi sŏlch'i" (The reform of King Ch'ungsŏn and the establishment of Sarimwŏn), *Yŏksa hakpo* 52 (1971). Min Hyŏn'gu, "Chŏngch'i togam ŭi sŏlch'i kyŏngwi" (The process of establishing Chŏngch'i togam), *Kukmindae nonmunjip* 11 (1977); "Chŏngch'i togam ŭi sŏnggyŏk" (The nature of the Chŏngch'i togam), *Tongbang hakji* 23–24 (combined issue, 1980).

## 6    Chapter One

Their research focused on improvements related to the agricultural-estate system, including issues related to the ownership and distribution of land. However, researchers generally recognize that these improvements were possible because the new ruling class emerged from the small and medium landlord class rather than the large landlord class. On the other hand, scholars have also directed their attention to the efforts of the ruling classes to elevate their status.

Improvements in agricultural techniques served as a catalyst for change as well. At this point in the late-Koryŏ to early-Chosŏn period, the technique of allowing land to lie fallow marked an important stage in agricultural development.[3] Another scholar corroborates this view as well.[4]

The book *Nongsa chiksŏl* (Straight Talk on Farming), which was published during this period, enables a close examination of agricultural techniques during the early Chosŏn period. It is well known that agriculture, as discussed by this book, was not restricted by fallow farming. According to the *kongbŏp*, a new law concerning land rents and taxes enacted during the reign of King Sejong, fallow farming was not permitted in *chŏngjŏn* (land which was once registered in the land register or cadastre). This represents a departure from the practice common until the mid-Koryŏ period of allowing widely scattered farms to have fallow fields throughout the country. According to farmland regulations passed in March of the eighth year of King Munjong's reign, farms cultivated every year were regarded as the best quality, farms cultivated after lying fallow for one year medium quality, and farms cultivated after two years of lying fallow lowest. According to the same regulations, one *kyŏl* of farmland on mountain slopes that did not lie fallow was equivalent to one *kyŏl* of farmland on the plains, two *kyŏl* of mountain farmland on the mountains lying fallow for one year corresponded to one *kyŏl* of farmland on the plains, and three *kyŏl* of mountain farmland lying fallow for two

---

3. Yi Tae-jin (Yi T'aejin), "Sipsa-o segi nong'ŏp kisul ŭi paldal kwa sinhŭng sajok" (Development of agricultural technology and the newly emerging scholar-officials during the fourteenth and fifteenth centuries), *Tongyanghak* 9 (1978); "Sipnyuk segi ŭi ch'ŏnbang kwangae ŭi paldal" (Development of river embankments and irrigation during the sixteenth century), *Han Ugun paksa chŏngnyŏn kinyŏm* nonch'ong (Festschrift in commemoration of the retirement of Dr. Han Ugŭn), (Seoul: Chisik san'ŏpsa, 1981).

4. Miyajima Hiroshi, "Chosen nogyoshi ni okeru jyugo seiki" (The fifteenth century in the history of Chosŏn agriculture), *Chosen shiso* 3 (1980). Kim T'aeyŏng, "Kwajŏnbŏp ha ŭi toji saengsannyŏk kwa yangjŏn" (Land productivity and land survey under the status land system), *Han'guksa yŏn'gu* 35 (1981).

years corresponded to one *kyŏl* of farmland on the plains.⁵ That the majority of farmland was rated low- or medium-quality due to the necessity of lying fallow every year or two indicates that the practice of fallow farming was common. In his commentaries, Yi Chehyŏn, a scholar from the first half of the fourteenth century, mentioned the initiation of a system of providing land and firewood for officials during the reign of King Kyŏngjong (976–981): "the areas south of the Amnok River ["Yalu" in Chinese] are generally filled with mountains, with land so poor such that almost none is kept fallow" (*Ikchae nan'go*, Remarks on the Section of King Kyŏngjong). An official, while debating the land-tax law during the reign of King Sejong, said that "the fact that there were lands that lay fallow a year or two in old times tells us that it was necessary to raise the productivity of the land" (*Sejong sillok*, Vol. 112, the section on June, the 28th reign year of King Sejong). These quotes are good illustrations of the agricultural techniques of the earlier era. Originally, fallow farming became necessary because fertilization techniques were underdeveloped; it is impossible to fertilize an entire farm when weeding techniques have not fully developed. As a consequence, it was inevitable that land had to lie fallow every other year to restore fertility. The agricultural technique of the early-Chosŏn period, when farms were free from the restriction of fallowing, was characterized by detailed studies on fertilization techniques shown in *Nongsa chiksŏl*.⁶

It is impossible to determine exactly when agricultural techniques became free from the restrictions of fallow farming. However, because the practice of cultivating crops in successive years was common in the early-Chosŏn period, it can be assumed that the shift to successive planting took place toward the end of the Koryŏ period. Let us examine several facts indirectly related to this change in agricultural methods in the final years of Koryŏ.

In a memorial to the throne, Cho Chun pointed out the great evils resulting from the development of the agricultural-estate system in the fourteenth century, "Wicked people hold large estates which sometimes reach the boundaries of countries and are demarcated by natural features such as mountains and rivers, claiming them as bequeathed by their ancestors. Thus, five or six people laid claim to a small tract of land, with one preying upon another." He also wrote that in a fixed system of land rents, "one *kyŏl* of land is assessed to be as many as

---

5. *Koryŏsa* (The history of Koryŏ), Vol. 77, *Sikhwa*, section 1, *Kyongni*.
6. Yi Tae-jin, "Sipsa-o segi nong'ŏp kisul ŭi paldal kwa sinhŭng sajok," pp. 337–38.

three or four *kyŏl*."⁷ As a result, systematic exploitation and inequality marked land ownership during this period. This phenomenon can be seen as proof of the overcoming of fallow-field agriculture.

As mentioned above, fallow farming was overcome through the improvement of fertilization techniques. Such improvements not only eliminated the need to let fields lie fallow but also greatly increased the productivity of the land. The increase in productivity can be demonstrated by comparing the output per *kyŏl* in the early-Koryŏ period with that of the early-Chosŏn period. Based on the fact that one-fourth of the harvest was paid as land tax on public land in the 11th year of King Songjong's reign (992), it is estimated that the output per *kyŏl* ranged from six to eleven *sok*.⁸ According to a discussion in 1430 (the 12th year of King Sejong's reign), "the paddies along the Kyŏngsang and Chŏlla coastal areas had an output from one *kyŏl* that produced a maximum of 50 to 60 *sok* and a minimum of 20 to 30 *sok*; even dry fields, which were extremely fertile, produced a great amount."⁹

Although farming methods were the same, there was a difference in productivity between the fourteenth century, when nonfallow planting was first tested, and the fifteenth century, when it was put into practice. In view of the wide disparity in output when the method of fallow farming was practiced and when it was not, the fact that the same farm was owned by five or six people in the fourteenth century and the fact that one *kyŏl* of land came to be assessed as three or four *kyŏl* can both be regarded as examples of exploitation by powerful figures.¹⁰

If the above interpretation is correct, we must examine the fact that lawsuits involving land ownership emerged as a great problem

7. *Koryŏsa*, Vol. 78, *Sikhwa*, Section 1, *Nokkwa-jŏn*.
8. There is a more detailed explanation in Yi Tae-jin, "Sipsa-o segi nong'ŏp kisul ŭi paldal kwa sinhŭng sajok," p. 332. The uppermost ceiling of eleven *sok* and two *hop* in the original text in Kang Chinch'ŏl, "Koryŏ chŏn'gi ŭi kongjŏn-sajŏn kwa kŭ ŭi ch'aryul sujoryul e taehayŏ" (Public and private farmland in the first half of the Koryŏ period and their graded rates of taxation), *Yŏksa hakpo* 29 (1965). Here the original text was used.
9. *Sejong sillok*, Vol. 49, the section on August, the 12th year of Sejong (1430).
10. Kim Yongsŏp, "Koryŏ sigi ŭi yangjŏnje" (The system of land survey during the Koryŏ period), *Tongbang hakji* 16 (1975), p. 84. Kim presents an almost identical explanation. However, his dissertation is based on the opinion that cultivation of other kinds of crops was limited to a small number of farms on mountain slopes and that most other farms did not shift to other kinds of crops. In this respect there is a wide disparity between his opinion and mine.

during this period. Although most of the suits were motivated by the seizure of land by large-scale landlords, according to the aforementioned memorial by Cho Chun, the problem was serious enough that "the *p'andosa* and the *chŏnbŏpsa* in the central government and the provincial magistrates and supervisors must hear so many land suits everyday that they cannot carry out their main duties." This record indicates that the whole country was affected by this problem. If fallow farming was overcome as a result of improvements in agricultural technology, the drawback was that it created disputes over land ownership. When a period of lying fallow was no longer necessary to restore fertility, it became natural for a household to ask others to cultivate the part of its land that could not be handled by family members. As a result, disputes concerning land ownership arose frequently.

In this context, another interesting issue is the disappearance of systems such as *chokjŏng* and *panjŏng* (remunerations to soldiers and local officials for services to the state, respectively) during this period. In return for their service, they were given seventeen *kyŏl* per person. This was considered a large sum in the early part of the Chosŏn period when "petty farmers, in most cases, owned one or two *kyŏl* of farmland"[11] and "farmers who tilled more than ten *kyŏl* of farmland could be considered wealthy. Not a small number of farmers owned a mere three or four *kyŏl* each."[12] It can be assumed that the generosity of the grant was meant to compensate for the year or two when the land would have to lie fallow. However, through the advancement of agricultural techniques in the fourteenth century, there was no longer a need to continue such a system. As the system of the earlier era began to break down, the distribution of the surplus generated by agricultural labor created the potential for lawsuits. The development of private land also occurred in the same period—partly due to reclamation and partly due to the elimination of idle land. An increased consciousness of ownership, together with quantitative expansion, was another contributing factor. Constant cultivation may have exerted great influence on such an increased consciousness.

---

11. *Sejong sillok*, Vol. 112, the section on June, the 28th year of Sejong.
12. *Sejong sillok*, Vol. 83, the section on November, the 20th year of Sejong.

## AGRICULTURAL DEVELOPMENT AND SOCIAL CHANGE

As I have examined so far, a change in agricultural techniques took place in the fourteenth century through the elimination of fallow-field cultivation. Considering the magnitude of the change, its social impact must have been great. The disappearance of remunerations and the development of private land, as well as other changes, must be considered in this context.

The improvement of agricultural techniques, an impetus for the development of private land, provided an important foundation for the growth of owner-cultivators—a notable phenomenon of this period. Landlord-tenant relations stabilized because the level of productivity increased due to the advancement in agricultural techniques. It is on the basis of the development of agricultural techniques that the Chosŏn period, from a macroscopic point of view, could strengthen its state conscription system and strictly enforce a policy of conscripting commoners. The elimination of special administrative units such as *hyang, so,* and *pugok* were important social changes of this period. The inhabitants of *hyang* and *pugok* made their living by farming just like commoners living in *kun* (county) and *hyŏn* (sub-county). The only difference was that in the former, heavier taxes were imposed, the areas were treated as special administrative units, and their inhabitants were treated as low-born. With the improvement of agricultural techniques, it was no longer necessary to retain this kind of discrimination since the economic power of society as a whole increased, and discrimination would only have resulted in a loss of production. A clear example of social change is the elimination of *so* as places where specific tribute-supplies were levied. With the new developments in agriculture, the situation changed so that it became more profitable or people to devote their labor to agriculture rather than other traditional occupations.

An important change associated with agricultural development also took place in the local administrative system. During the early- and mid-Koryŏ periods, improving agricultural production was among the many duties of the *allyonsa* (governors in seven provinces) and the *kamch'angsa* (superintendents of granaries in five provinces). In the *Koryŏsa*, the section on *kwŏnnongsa* (agriculture encouragement supervisors) only mentioned that "though a separate system of *kwŏnnongsa* was created," the previous system was restored in the 13th year of King Ch'ungyŏl (1287) because of the great number of abuses that harmed the people.[13] It became a rule during the Chosŏn period to appoint a man of *hallyang* rank (outside of government service) to the post of Officer for Encouragement of Farming in each *myŏn* (township) and in all subcounties, counties, cities, and provinces.[14] This change is evidence of the growing importance during this time of the encouragement of farming. A change also took place in the official duties of local officials. The six duties of magistrates of the Koryŏ dynasty were, as is well known, based on the T'ang system and mentioned nothing about agriculture.[15] In the Chosŏn dynasty, however, "encouragement of agriculture and sericulture" was the most important among the seven duties of the magistrate.[16] During the Koryŏ period, when there was no clear prospect for agricultural development under conditions of fallow-field cultivation, the central government paid no special attention to farming-related affairs and entrusted them to the *hyangni* (regional clerks).

Because of internal and external unrest, the development of farming techniques did not proceed smoothly in the fourteenth century. It seems that although changes had already begun, there was no opportunity to address them at the policy level. The intrusions of *wako* (Japanese pirates) after the mid-fourteenth century seem to have dealt a blow to the progress made up to that time. After the establishment of the Chosŏn dynasty, the government encouraged reclamation and began a land survey. These efforts indicated the desire to restart past

13. *Koryŏsa*, Vol. 77, *Paikkwan* 2, the section on Kwŏnnongsa or agriculture encouragement supervisors.
14. *T'aejo sillok*, Vol. 8, the section on July, in the 4th year of King T'aejo. "Chŏng Pun-jin said that an essential thing for encouraging agriculture is to build embankments and asked that governors order city, county, and subcounty chiefs to appoint gentlemen out of government service to the Office of Encouragement for Farming." *Sŏngjong sillok*, Vol. 245, the section on September, in the 21st year of King Sŏngjong, "Yun Hyosŏn submitted a memorial to the throne asking to unite every five households and fix a chief to administer the unit ... and to station one agriculture encouragement supervisor at each *myon* or township."
15. The six articles that were newly legislated in the 9th year of King Kyongjong: 1. Investigate diseases and sufferings of the people; 2. Investigate the competency of officials; 3. Investigate theft, robbery, and adultery; 4. Investigate whether the people violate prohibitions; 5. Investigate whether the people are faithful to their parents, friendly with their brothers, and honest; and 6. Investigate whether officials embezzle government money and grain (*Koryŏsa*, Vol. 75, Sŏn'gŏji, 3).
16. *Kyongguk taejŏn*, Vol. 1, Yi-jŏn, Kokwa (Provisions for officials). The seven articles are as follows: (1) Promotion of agriculture and sericulture; (2) increasement of households; (3) expansion of schools; (4) arrangement of the military administration; (5) making the labor conscription fair; (6) making the procedure of trials simple; and (7) elimination of wicked practices.

progress as the situation stabilized, and policy measures began to be adopted during Sejong's reign.

As is well known, *Nongsa chiksŏl* was compiled in 1428–1429 (the 11th and 12th years of King Sejong's reign) and described existing farming techniques in the three southern provinces. This text, in addition to compiling the advances in farming techniques, was designed to propagate the most advanced techniques in the northern regions of the country, especially P'yŏng'an and Hamgyŏng provinces. Since these two provinces had not yet adopted fallow-field cultivation while the Kyŏnggi and Kangwŏn provinces had, the northern regions had a great disparity in agricultural output with that of the three southern provinces. *Nongsa chiksŏl* was compiled in an effort to eliminate the disparity in farming techniques. It is also notable that the aim of the project was to standardize farming methods and to revise the taxation system. When *Nongsa chiksŏl* was published in December 1429, King Sejong asked his officials to consider adopting the *kongbŏp* as a new law of taxation. A final decision was made on the draft law in 1443 (the 26th year of his reign) after fourteen years of deliberation and trials. The law is well known for lowering the tax rate from one-tenth to one-twentieth of the harvest, reflecting the progress in farming techniques. Now it became standard practice not to recognize the practice of fallow-field cultivation in registered farms, and the subdivisions for grades of land were increased from three to six as necessitated by the widening disparity in farm productivity due to advances in farming methods. In short, the government was successful in the task of reorganizing the land system in accordance with the developments in farming technique since the fourteenth century.

The changes in agricultural technique had a tremendous impact on the constitution of society. The communal organization of the *hyangdo* (or bier-bearers' union) occupied a very significant position in village communities in pre-modern Korea. I once studied examples of the *hyangdo* of early eleventh-century Koryŏ by examining an inscription on a pagoda in Kaesim Temple in Yech'ŏn.[17] According to the inscription, two groups of bier bearers—one in the county of Yech'ŏn and the other in the subcounty of Tain within Yech'ŏn—were

---

17. Yi Tae-jin, "Yech'ŏn Kaesimsa sŏktapgi ŭi punsŏk—Koryŏ chŏn'gi hyangdo ŭi illye" (An analysis of the inscription of a pagoda in Kaesim Temple in Yech'ŏn—an example of the *hyangdo* in the first half of the Koryŏ period), *Yŏksa hakpo* 53–54 (combined issue, 1972).

the prime movers behind the erection of a pagoda of such a scale that they were embraced by all the inhabitants. According to the *Koryŏsa*, "There is in the country a custom that lanterns are lit [by two bierbearer unions] for two nights beginning on the fifteenth day of the first lunar month in all places, ranging from the royal palaces and the capital to local towns."[18] Thus, it is clear that the *hyangdo* performed rituals such as the *Yŏndŭnghoe* and *P'alkwanhoe* which were prevalent at the time. These rituals were continued by the *sangdu-gun* (members of a burial society), the descendants of the *hyangdo*.

On the other hand, according to a royal message issued in 1168 (22nd year of King Ŭijong), just a few years before the military revolt of 1170, "the *P'alkwanhoe* festivals at the two capitals [Kaegyŏng and Sŏgyŏng] have recently been losing their original dignity, and the inherited ancient custom has gradually been declining."[19] This record demonstrates that customs dating back to the early Koryŏ period were beginning to change in this period. Because of the lack of relevant historical sources, we know nothing about how the custom transformed and developed under the military regime. Nevertheless, the *hyangdo* unions revealed an aspect of Korean society after the fourteenth century that was entirely different from that of the previous era. Members of the unions generally gathered for services to honor the guardian deities of natural villages (villages that have evolved naturally, as opposed to those which were organized to conform with regional or national administrative systems) after the fourteenth century. Membership shrank greatly as the *hyangdo* became societies for natural-village rituals.[20] The transformation of the *hyangdo* indicated the increased importance of the natural-village level in Korean society, as did the designation of natural villages with the administrative unit of *ri* beginning in this period.

What was the significance of changes in the *hyangdo* organization, which can be regarded as the center of village communal life? Their transformation reflects a transition from large to small social units. It could be said that the most fundamental factor behind this transition was the development in agricultural techniques beginning in the fourteenth century.

18. *Koryŏsa*, Vol. 69, Yeji 2, the section on *Karye chabŭi*.
19. *Koryŏsa*, Vol. 18, the section on March, the 22nd year of King Ŭijong.
20. Yi Tae-jin, "Sarimp'a ŭi yuhyangso pongnip undong" (The sarim faction's movement to reestablishment the *yuhyangso*—the social background of the establishment of Neo-Confucianism in the Early Chosŏn Period) (1), *Chindan hakbo* 34 (1972), pp. 9–12.

Since the productivity of extensive farming under the method of fallow farming was low, the reclamation of a larger acreage of land was required to secure the same amount of product as would result from intensive agriculture. Under this type of agriculture, a great amount of manpower had to be mobilized at one time, and the mobilization was strongly collective in nature. It seems that the large scale of *hyangdo* groups in the first half of the Koryŏ period may have reflected this state of agriculture. The fact that local officials led *kun* (county) and *hyŏn* (subcounty) organizations during the early- and mid-Koryŏ periods demonstrates that local administration was centered heavily on counties and subcounties. In this system, community villages were ranked higher as a unit within the administrative hierarchy than natural villages.[21] It seems obvious that the development of a social structure with these characteristics would have been the result, at least in part, of the large scale of *hyangdo* organizations. The authority to mobilize local soldiers was directly entrusted to local officials more often at this time than at any other.

In contrast to extensive agriculture, management was more important than the actual acreage under cultivation for intensive farming. In other words, the timing of farming techniques became more crucial than the mass mobilization of a labor force. With good management methods, intensive farming would require a smaller amount of acreage under cultivation, enabling a household as a unit of management to care for its own land. Social organizations evolved, with each household constituting a farming unit. Although there were probably other factors contributing to this transformation in social composition, the change in agricultural technology cannot be overlooked as an important factor. The development of the individuality of natural villages was based on enforcement of the village chief (*rijang, rijŏng*) system, which acted as one means of operating a centralized administrative system.

THE EMERGING LITERATI CLASS AND ITS INTEREST IN FARMING TECHNIQUES

Lastly, let us examine changes in the ruling class and its interest in farming techniques as one aspect of the social changes taking place

21. Yi Usŏng, "Yŏdae paiksŏng ko" (A study on commoners during the Koryŏ period), *Yŏksa hakpo* 14 (1961).

during Koryŏ-Chosŏn transition. It is clear that a new group of scholar-officials coming from small and medium landlords in the provinces emerged as the new ruling class toward the end of the Koryŏ period. The fact that scholar-officials from the three southern provinces formed the largest group within the new ruling class must be examined in the context of the development of agricultural technology in those provinces at that time.

One study has analyzed and traced by the ancestral origin the surnames of officials who advanced to the capital from the reign of King T'aejo (918–943) to the reign of King Ŭijong (1147–1170) during the Koryŏ period.[22] This research, utilizing data from epitaphs, biographies, and influential families appearing in the *Koryŏsa* (The History of Koryŏ), focused on surnames of officials who held the third rank or higher. These were classified into two groups, one that turned out more than three such officials and one that produced fewer than two such officials—all organized by surname. There were fifty-four surnames in the former group and fifty-three in the latter. An examination of the ancestral origins of the surnames disclosed that only twenty of the fifty-four, or slightly more than one-third, had their ancestral origins in the three southern provinces, while those remaining came from the northern districts. In the case of the latter group, twenty-five among the fifty-three surnames had their ancestral origins in the three southern provinces, barely failing to attain the majority. This situation however, underwent a great change after the fourteenth century.

No research has yet been done on the origins of the newly rising scholar-officials who entered the central government after the fourteenth century. To undertake this research, I have utilized the *Tŭnggwarok* (Records of the Civil Service Examinations),[23] which lists the names of those passing the examinations during the Koryŏ period (Table 1). After the end of the thirteenth century, the data on the ancestral origins of successful candidates are less comprehensive in comparison with records from the preceding period. Nonetheless, it is possible with existing sources to get a general sense of the situation. Until the end of the Koryŏ period, the ancestral seat of officials

---

22. Yi Sugŏn, "Koryŏ sidae 't'osŏng' yŏn'gu sang" (A study on native surnames during the Koryŏ period 1), *Asea hakpo* 12 (1976).

23. Concerning the nature of Tŭnggwarok, refer to Hŏ Hongsik, *Koryŏ kwagŏjedosa yŏn'gu* (A study on the history of the civil service examination system of Koryŏ) (Seoul: Ilchogak, 1981), pp. 241–43.

generally corresponded to their birthplace or main residence, unlike in the succeeding period.[24] For this reason, a lack of sources was not a problem in conducting my research. The scope of my examination begins from the period of the military coups.

Ancestral origins are known for only fifty-one of the 120 successful candidates—less than half of the total—before the military regime. This low figure, in striking contrast to the figure of more than eighty percent in the later period, resulted from the special conditions that existed when the *Tunggwarok* was compiled. The disparity, as pointed out at the outset of this section, may reflect differences between the two ages. An examination of the ancestral origins reveals that, among the total of fifty-one candidates with known ancestral origins, those in the southern three provinces numbered twenty-five. This signifies a slight but not significant increase compared to the reign of King Ŭijong. During the reigns of Kings Wŏnjong and Ch'ungnyŏl, however, the figure rose to sixty-two percent of the total candidates. Although the total number of successful candidates decreased considerably from the reign of King Ch'ungsŏn to the reign of King Ch'ungmok, the proportion of candidates whose ancestral origins are from the three southern provinces shot up to eighty percent. Though the total number of successful candidates increased rapidly during the period from the reign of King Kongmin to that of King Kongyang, the proportion of candidates from the three southern provinces remained high at seventy-seven percent.

It cannot be assumed that those who passed the state exams constituted a majority among government officials. However, as they were elites among officials, their trends can be regarded as a reflection of the conditions of their time. What is the significance of the clearly high proportion of officials with ancestral origins in the three southern provinces in the fourteenth century? Since the northern areas such as Kyŏnggi province provided the power base of the Koryŏ dynasty, it is logical that the proportion of officials from these areas was high from the early-Koryŏ period to the reign of King Ŭijong. However, other factors must be considered in explaining the changes in political forces that occurred over a span of two and a half centuries. One of these factors was the development of the agricultural economy.

As discussed above, the restrictions imposed by fallow farming could not be overcome during the early- and mid-Koryŏ periods. Dry

---

24. Hŏ Hongsik, *Koryŏ sahoesa yŏn'gu* (A study on the social history of Koryŏ) (Seoul: Asea munhwasa, 1981), pp. 420–21.

fields occupied more area than paddy fields under the restricted agricultural conditions of the time. Since wet fields occupied less than thirty percent of total farmland even until the reign of King Sejong in the Chosŏn period,[25] it would be safe to assume that dry-field farming was predominant during early and mid Koryŏ. More importantly, engaging in fallow farming on mountain slopes was more profitable than dry-field farming in plains regions. Because grass is richer on mountain slopes than plains, once reclaimed, they are far more profitable in terms of soil fertility.[26] As already mentioned, the grading of farms during the reign of King Munjong demonstrated the differences between farms in plains and those on mountain slopes. *Koryŏ togyŏng* also stated, "As plains are insufficient, people prefer mountain slopes for reclamation. It is extremely laborious to till farms on mountain slopes as farmers have to climb up and down. When seen from afar, it is as though they are climbing up a ladder or staircase."

The fact that farms on mountain slopes thrived with the predominance of dry-field farming during the early- and mid-Koryŏ helps to explain why people whose ancestral origins were in areas north of Kyŏnggi province occupied important official posts in the government. The farming techniques of the northern areas were superior to that of the three southern provinces; accordingly, the political power of the former group was strong. This situation would eventually change as agriculture transformed after the fourteenth century.

The inadequacies of dry fields continued into the fourteenth century until changes began to occur in agricultural technology. Dry fields came to be utilized more as the restrictions of fallow farming were overcome; complete fertilization became possible. Farms on plains now became more profitable than those on mountain slopes.

During the debate on the method of collecting land rents and taxes in King Sejong's reign, one official said, "Farms in the plains are divided into three grades, and those on the top and middle of the mountains are also divided into four grades; this is our law concerning land."[27] The method of grading farms on mountains suggests that those farms had a long history. More importantly, in evaluating farms,

25. Miyajima Hiroshi, op. cit., pp. 46–47. Here his inquiry is based on the figures of reclamation contained in the section of geography, *Sejong sillok*.
26. A geographical research on farms on mountain slopes during the Koryŏ period is Kim Sangho's "Yijo chŏn'gi ŭi sujŏn nong'ŏp yŏn'gu" (Research on wet-field farming in the early Chosŏn dynasty) (research report published with the assistance of the Ministry of Education in 1969), pp. 29–30.
27. *Sejong sillok*, Vol. 113, the section on July, the 28th year of Sejong (1445).

those on mountains were already distinguished from those in the plains. Another person from the early-Chosŏn period remarked that "because of the formerly imposed limits pertaining to classifying farms into three grades based on location—top, middle, and bottom—a [farm on a] mountain is counted as two ordinary farms."[28] This remark also demonstrates that farms in mountain areas were beginning to be treated differently from ordinary farms. This situation stands in stark contrast to the early- and mid-Koryŏ periods, when farms on mountain slopes were prevalent. It seems likely that when mountain farms were prevalent, farms in the plains were utilized for rice cultivation or as paddy fields. After overcoming the problems of fallow farming, farms in plains regions with irrigation available continued to develop as paddy fields. It can also be assumed, however, that the proportion of dry fields among farms in the plains was high. After the development of dry fields in the plains, the proportion of such dry fields stayed constant after the fourteenth century. It is possible to conclude that people in the three southern provinces, which had far more plains than areas north of Kyŏnggi province, could increase their economic power through dry-field farming. The noticeable rise in the number of officials from the south in the government after the fourteenth century was probably a result of such newly found economic influence.

The newly rising scholar-officials, who began to assume posts in the central government in the fourteenth century, had considerable interest in the development of agricultural techniques. Their interest became evident with the publication of a Chinese book on farming and sericulture by a group of scholar-officials.[29] It was printed as a smaller, square-sized text called the *Nongsang chipyo* (C. *Nung Sang Chi Yao*; Fundamentals of Agriculture and Sericulture), which Yi Am brought back from Beijing when he accompanied King Ch'ungjŏng, who was enthroned as the new ruler in 1349. Even though the *Nongsang chipyo*, dealing mainly with traditional dry-field farming in northern China, did not cover the most advanced Chinese technology, the scholar-officials of Koryŏ published a popular edition of the text in order to facilitate its propagation, in an effort to contribute to the development of the country's agricultural technology.

---

28. *Sejong sillok*, Vol. 109, the section on July, the 27th year of Sejong (1444).
29. Yi Tae-jin, op. cit., "Sipsa-o segi nong'ŏp kisul ŭi paldal kwa sinhŭng sajok," p. 345.

In the 11th year of King Kongmin (1362), Paek Munbo proposed that knowledge of farming methods south of the Yangzi River become compulsory, as the methods used in this region were the most advanced in China at the time. He also suggested that the utilization of the water wheel be spread throughout Koryŏ. Advanced farming techniques and the use of the water wheel had contributed to the development of paddy farming in China.[30] The newly rising group of scholar-officials in Koryŏ was quite interested in developments taking place in China and hoped to improve and transform their country's agricultural environment. In the academic and philosophical fields, they adopted Neo-Confucianism, whose core was Zhu Xi's philosophy from the Song period.

In one of his texts supporting agriculture, Zhu Xi (Chu Hsi), who developed Neo-Confucianism into a system of philosophy, wrote, "As a tenant feeds his family members by the grace of his landlords, he should not encroach upon his lord; as the landlord enriches his domestic economy thanks to his tenant, he should not mistreat his tenant." Zhu's recognition of the mutually complimentary relations between landlord and tenant cannot be found in any other system of thought in Chinese history and so can be regarded as one of the historical achievements of Neo-Confucianism. Zhu Xi's insights owed much to the achievements brought about by the agricultural methods employed south of the Yangzi River which, centered on paddy farming, overcame the limits of fallow farming during the Song period. As productivity was greatly increased through new technical improvements in agriculture and as the economic power of society as a whole expanded, the idea that the landlord was not independent but in fact was bound in a mutual relationship to his tenant became prevalent.

It is apparent that the newly emerging ruling class of Koryŏ began to adopt the new philosophy of Neo-Confucianism because of the new technological developments in agriculture in the fourteenth century. But they did not obtain the high productivity of paddy farming that the Chinese enjoyed south of the Yangzi River. Compared to the Koryŏ period, the land tax was lowered greatly by the newly emerging scholar-officials. They wanted to undertake a reform of the land system in an effort to utilize the developments in agricultural methods to expand the economic power of the country; their ideas were based in the Confucian notion of *minbon* (literally, "the people are the

30. *Koryŏsa*, Vol. 79, *Sikhwa* 2, the section on agriculture and sericulture.

foundation of the country"). In an epilogue to the popular edition of *Nongsang chipyo*, Yi Saek wrote that one of the book's merits was in suggesting the "right method for the improvement of living."[31] One of the most important tasks facing the new ruling class was how to contribute to efforts such as improving the standard of living.

There were two important issues in the fourteenth-century agricultural economy: how to eliminate contradictions in relations of land ownership and how to adjust to changes caused by the development of agricultural techniques. As is well known, the former problem was resolved with the promulgation of the Rank-Land Law. The latter problem was resolved through the revision of the Tribute Tax Law during the reign of King Sejong; thus, the problems of the fourteenth century were resolved by the mid-fifteenth century.

translated by Edward Park

---

31. *Mok'ŭn mun'go*, Vol. 9, "*Nongsang chipyo* husŏ" (An epilogue to *Nongsang chipyo*).

Social Change during the Koryŏ-Chosŏn Transition

Table 1

AN EXAMINATION OF THE ANCESTRAL ORIGINS OF SUCCESSFUL CANDIDATES OF THE CIVIL SERVICE EXAMINATIONS FROM KING MYÖNGJONG (1171–1197) TO KING KONGYANG (1389–1392)

| Years | Total Number of Successful Candidates | Number with Ancestral Origins on Record | Number with Ancestral Origins in Three Southern Provinces |
|---|---|---|---|
| Myŏngjong (1171–1197) | 38 | 15 | 7 |
| Sinjong (1197–1204) | 8 | 3 | 0 |
| Hŭijong (1204–1211) | 9 | 5 | 4 |
| Kangjong (1212–1213) | 4 | 1 | 0 |
| Kojong (1213–1259) | 51 | 22 | 14 |
| subtotal | 120 | 51 | 25 |
| Wŏnjong (1259–1274) | 25 | 19 | 11 |
| Ch'ungnyŏl (1274–1308) | 83 | 58 | 39 |
| subtotal | 108 | 77 | 50 |
| Ch'ungsŏn (1306–1313) | 4 | 3 | 3 |
| Ch'ungsuk (1313–1329) | 19 | 17 | 15 |
| Ch'unghae (1330–1332) | 10 | 7 | 6 |
| Ch'ungsuk (1332–1339) | 5 | 4 | 3 |
| Ch'unghae (1339–1344) | 9 | 6 | 5 |
| Ch'ungmok (1344–1348) | 7 | 7 | 5 |
| Ch'ungjŏng (1349–1351) | 0 | 0 | 0 |
| subtotal | 54 | 44 | 37 |
| Kongmin (1351–1374) | 210 | 118 | 87 |
| U (1374–1388) | 203 | 141 | 112 |
| Ch'ang (1389) | 65 | 30 | 27 |
| Kongyang (1389–1392) | 33 | 10 | 8 |
| subtotal | 511 | 299 | 234 |
| TOTAL | 793 | 471 | 346 |

CHAPTER 2

# The Socioeconomic Background of Neo-Confucianism in Fifteenth- and Sixteenth-Century Korea

NEO-CONFUCIANISM EMERGED IN CHINA at the end of the tenth century, came to maturity there in the twelfth century, and was introduced to Korea in the thirteenth century. The time lag in cultural exchange between these two adjacent countries was unusual, but once introduced and adopted, Neo-Confucianism became more deeply rooted in Korea than in China and maintained its dominant position for about five hundred years.

These aspects of the adoption and development of Neo-Confucianism in Korea have generally been viewed negatively. There has been a tendency to regard its late adoption as a cultural failing on the part of Koreans and its long survival as a symptom of cultural inertia or stagnation. However, these developments can also be seen in a positive light. The late adoption of Neo-Confucianism can be explained on the grounds that, superior though it may be, a foreign culture can only gain influence in response to some internal necessity, while its longevity in Korea can be seen as reflecting the unprecedented success of its transplantation.

Neo-Confucianism in Korea can be regarded positively, as no ideology or system of thought can survive unless it contains major features that elicit a positive response in the society that adopts it. Based on this assumption, I will examine the positive contribution that Neo-Confucianism has made to the development of Korean history from a socioeconomic viewpoint. This study will help to offset the strong tendency to view Korean Neo-Confucianism as mainly an academic and theoretical phenomenon.

This chapter will focus on two socioeconomic issues: first, the influence of Neo-Confucianism upon the development of Korean agricultural technology; and second, the significance of the social system prescribed by Neo-Confucianism in Korea's historical development, particularly the village granary system (*sach'ang*) and the community compact (*hyangyak*). Although this examination could cover the entire Chosŏn period, this chapter will focus on the fifteenth and sixteenth centuries, the period of Neo-Confucianism's adoption. In fact, Korean Neo-Confucianism's tendency to engage in speculative philosophy, a development of the latter half of the sixteenth century, may be seen as a flowering in the realm of scholarship and thought build on the foundation of the socioeconomic advances in the fifteenth and sixteenth centuries.

## NEO-CONFUCIANISM AND THE DEVELOPMENT OF KOREAN AGRICULTURAL TECHNIQUES IN THE FIFTEENTH AND SIXTEENTH CENTURIES

Neo-Confucianism began to be introduced from the Yuan dynasty into Korea at the very end of the thirteenth century. What was introduced into Korea at that time was the cumulative product of developments throughout the Song and Yuan periods. The early Song dynasty saw the development of so-called classified or encyclopedic learning (*lei-shu-xue*), which was concerned with the practical art of governing. Then, from the mid-Song period, especially during the Southern Song period, the study of human nature and principle (*xing-li-xue*) flourished and came to be regarded as the core of Neo-Confucian scholarship. These two forms of inquiry formed the main trends of Neo-Confucianism and continued to develop until the Yuan period, while the new historical studies that emerged in the early Song period are known to have played a role in mediating between these two tendencies.[1]

These different branches of Neo-Confucianism were introduced to Korea simultaneously, leaving it free to choose, admittedly on the basis of superficial knowledge, whatever it found useful at any given time. In fact, in the fifteenth century, in consonance with the estab-

---

1. See Naito Torairo, *Shina shigakushi* (The history of Chinese historiography) (Tokyo: Shimizu kobundo shogo, 1967), pp. 241–300.

lishment of the new system of governance of the Chosŏn dynasty, Korean literati concentrated their attention on the encyclopedic-learning aspects of the new doctrine. Only in the sixteenth century did the philosophy of human nature and principle begin to develop in earnest.

Neo-Confucianism in fifteenth-century Korea has been called the study of "literary style" (sajanghak), but the term is imprecise since it was just a subfield of encyclopedic learning. Scholarship in this period was concerned not only with literary style but also with the study of encyclopedic works such as the Tong-zhi (T'ung-chih; General Treatise), Wen-xian-tong-gao (Wen-hsien-t'ung-kao; Comprehensive Inquiry into Recorded Institutions), and the Yu-hai (Jewel Sea) because of their relevance to a Confucian reorganization of all institutions. This mode of scholarly inquiry, which reached its zenith during King Sejong's reign (1418–1450), constituted a major school of thought for about a century.[2] The discovery of the importance of the philosophy of human nature in the sixteenth century arose from an effort to overcome the increasingly apparent limitations of the centralized system of government of the fifteenth century that rested upon doctrines found in encyclopedic learning.

While the development of Neo-Confucianism in Korea in the fifteenth and sixteenth centuries can be understood in terms of these two stages, it must be emphasized that in all stages, there was always an understanding of the socioeconomic advantages on which this philosophy was based. It is believed that An Hyang first introduced Neo-Confucianism to Korea in 1289 (15th year of King Ch'ungryŏl's reign). However, the year more deserving of being remembered in the transmission and adoption of Neo-Confucianism is 1314 (1st year of King Ch'ungsuk's reign). This was the year when King Ch'ungsŏn, who had failed to reform his fading dynasty, handed the throne to his son. He went to Peking to found the Library of Ten Thousand Volumes (Man'gwŏndang) in order to facilitate exchanges between

2. The Koryŏsa (The history of Koryŏ) indicates that the Tong-zhi (Tung-chih) and Yu-hai were introduced from China in 1364. Koryŏsa (Seoul: Asea Munhwasa, 1972), 40:38a. There appear to be strong resemblances to early-Song encyclopedic learning in such works as the Kyŏngguk taejŏn and the Tongmunsŏn compiled under government aegis in the late 15th century. It has also become clear that the Liu-she-lue (Liu-she-lüeh; Brief account of six principles) of Chinese characters in the Tong-zhi helped provide the theoretical background for devising the han'gul script. See Kang Sinhang, "Sejongdae ŭi ŏnŏ gwan ŭi sŏngnip" (The establishment of views on language in the Sejong period), Tongyanghak 10 (1980), pp. 380–82.

scholars from Koryŏ and Yuan.³ In the same year, Koryŏ's Royal Confucian Academy (*Sŏnggyun'gwan*) sent some of its members to the Jiangnan area of central China to purchase ten thousand new books.⁴ It was not until King Kongmin's reign, some fifty years later, that Neo-Confucianism began to gain political ascendancy. It is worth noting, however, that the first contact had been made in the Jiangnan area. People went to Jiangnan to purchase books about Neo-Confucianism, probably because the region was widely known as a place where, from the Southern Song period, bibliophiles had published and sold many books. But the Jiangnan region was important not just as a place to purchase books.

The Jiangnan region was not only the center of the development of Cheng-Zhu Neo-Confucianism in the latter half of the Song period but also the origin of the new Jiangnan agricultural techniques that made Neo-Confucianism's emergence and development economically possible. The connection between Neo-Confucianism and the Jiangnan area provides a clue to understanding not just Confucian scholarship but also its relationship to agricultural development. In this context, the fact that the former King Ch'ungsŏn traveled with Yi Chehyŏn (1287–1367) and Kwŏn Han'gong (?–1349) in the Jiangnan area in 1319 does not seem to have been happenstance.⁵ Similarly, Koryŏ's contacts with rival leaders in South China, including Zhang Shi-cheng during King Kongmin's reign, were significant not simply as diplomatic maneuvers but also as a strong indication that a cultural reorientation was under way in Koryŏ.

Interest in Jiangnan agricultural techniques became apparent during the first stage of the adoption of Neo-Confucianism, when Paek Munbo (?–1374), a leading Neo-Confucian scholar of the time, proposed the manufacture and diffusion of the waterwheel (*shui-che* in Chinese and *such'aek* in Korean; a kind of water pump).⁶ Noting that it was only through the use of the waterwheel that the people in the regions of Jiangnan and Hui-shui were freed from concerns over flood or drought, Paek Munbo maintained that drought could be overcome through the manufacture and diffusion of this device and

---

3. The year 1314 is significant for the adoption of Zhu Xi's commentaries on the Confucian classics and the revival of government service examinations by the Yuan government as well.
4. *Koryŏsa*, 34:20a-b.
5. Kim Sanggi, *Tongbangsa nonch'ong* (Studies on East Asian history), (Seoul: Seoul National University Press, 1974), pp. 240–42.
6. *Koryŏsa*, Sikhwaji 2 Nongsang, 79:9b-10a.

that rice-transplanting would also become possible. Waterwheel usage and rice transplantation techniques were the cornerstones of Jiangnan agricultural technology.

In 1349, thirteen years before Paek's proposal, Koryŏ scholars had obtained a copy of *Nung-sang chi-yao* (Collection of Agricultural and Sericultural Practices) and compiled a popular abridged edition.[7] As is well known, *Nung-sang chi-yao* was published before the Yuan conquered the Southern Song, and its contents cover agricultural techniques in territory occupied by Yuan—for example, the traditional dry-farming regions in Northern China, excluding the Jiangnan area with its new agricultural technology.[8] The fact that Koryŏ scholars published the popular edition, despite such omissions, was a clear indication of their zeal for improving their country's agriculture. Since most of the new ruling elite came from the class of small- or medium-scale landlords, they were naturally more interested in agricultural economy than aristocrats of the previous period, who were mainly absentee landlords.

In Korean agriculture, dry-farming was prevalent until the late Koryŏ period, and its techniques are known to have been similar to those of northern China. The dissemination of a Korean edition of *Nung-sang chi-yao* was part of an effort to improve traditional methods. Once the advantages of Jiangnan agricultural technology had become known through direct observation, it was soon put into practice in Korea. The first Chinese text containing the new agricultural techniques was Chen Fu's *Nongxu* (Book of Farming), but with currently available sources, it is not possible to determine whether this text had been brought into Korea at the end of the Koryŏ period.[9] However, in the Chosŏn period, direct references to the text can be found in *Nongsa chiksŏl* (Straight Talk on Farming) published in 1429 (11th year of King Sejong's reign).[10]

Since agricultural techniques are often subject to the restrictions of natural conditions, it was necessary to resolve some problems in the adoption and application caused by differences in natural conditions,

---

7. See Yi Saek, "Nongsang chipyo husŏ" *Mogŭn mun'go* (Writings of Yi Saek) (Seoul: Taedong Munwha Yŏn'guso, 1973), in *Koryŏ myŏnghyŏnjip* (Writings of famous scholars of the Koryŏ dynasty), Vol. 3, 9:2b-4a.
8. See Amano Gennosuke, *Chūgoku nogyoshi kenkyu* (Studies on the history of Chinese agriculture) (Tokyo: Ochanomizu shobo, 1962), pp. 481–82.
9. See Nishiyama Takeeichi, *Ajia-teki nogyo to nogyo shakai* (Asian Agriculture and Agricultural Society) (Tokyo: Tokyo University Press, 1969), pp. 154–55.
10. Yi Kwangnin, "Yangjam kyŏnghŏm ch'walyo e taehayŏ" (On a Book on Sericulture titled *Yangjam kyŏnghŏm ch'walyo*), *Yŏksa hakpo* (1965). pp. 28–32.

and improvements could not be achieved quickly. Although the advantages of Jiangnan agricultural technology were known at the end of the Koryŏ dynasty, it took at least a century to apply them to Korean agriculture because of differences in local conditions. The *Nongsa chiksŏl* demonstrated noticeable achievements in improving traditional farming methods, but the application of the new principles of the Jiangnan techniques was only about half completed by this time. The remainder took another half-century to complete.

Jiangnan agricultural techniques enabled wet-field cultivation to make great progress.[11] Their introduction improved the methods and facilities for irrigation and fertilization techniques, making it possible to overcome the limitations of fallow farming in the dry season. They also led to the adoption of rice transplantation. Since Jiangnan, as is well known, had much rainfall and many rivers, its natural conditions were favorable to wet-rice cultivation. In Jiangnan, rice transplantation was made possible by using rivers and streams as direct sources of irrigation water. Rice transplantation is the practice of transferring young rice plants to a paddy field after they have been grown in a separate seedbed. This technique raises productivity by speeding up root growth and simplifies considerably the task of weeding after transplantation, since the young rice plants are grown in a separate seedbed. Despite these advantages, this method could not be used without a secure water supply. Even in China, it became widely diffused only after the Song period, when river water came to be pumped by waterwheels and "water fences" (*shuiche* in Chinese, *such'aek* in Korean; embankments built of earth and often bamboo), which channeled water to the fields.

Another characteristic of Jiangnan agricultural techniques was the development of fertilization techniques making use of human excrement and ashes. Until this time, the recovery or maintenance of soil fertility when employing wet-field cultivation had relied on the method of using mud from irrigation water (northern China) or the method of burning rice straw after the harvest (southern China).[12] Both of these methods, however, depended on the land lying fallow

---

11. This discussion is largely based on Amano, *Chūgoku nogyoshi,* Nishiyama, *Ajateki nogyo,* Okazaki Fumio and Ikeda Shizuo, *Konan bunka haihatsushi* (History of the development of the Jiangnan culture) (Tokyo: Kobundo shobo, 1941), Sudo Yoshiyuki, *Sodai Keizaishi Kenkyū* (Studies in economic history of the Song period) (Tokyo: Tokyo University Press, 1962), and Nishijima Sado, *Chūgoku keizaishi kenkyū* (Studies in Chinese economic history) (Tokyo: Tokyo University Press, 1966).

12. Nishijima, *Chūgoku keizaishi,* pp. 184–94.

for one year. In dry farming, the method of using the green manure of leguminous plants also required the land to lay fallow for one year.[13] A text on agriculture from the Tang period (618–907) introduced the method of using livestock excrement as fertilizer to enable double-cropping of millet and wheat, but it also mentioned that the method had significant quantitative limitations. The use of human excrement and ash in the Jiangnan techniques was similar in efficacy but overcame all quantitative limitations. The new fertilization techniques were initially developed for use in paddy-field cultivation but were soon applied to dry farming as well. They played a large role in enabling Chinese agriculture to escape completely from the limitations of fallow farming.

The *Nongsa chiksŏl* was compiled approximately a half-century after interest arose in the Jiangnan agricultural techniques in the late fourteenth century. For fertilization methods, the text recommended the use of human excrement and ash, just like the Jiangnan techniques, for both paddy-field and dry farming.[14] However, it also noted the danger of crop failure when transplanting seedlings in wet-field cultivation[15] and suggested the continued use of "direct dry seeding" (*chikp'a*) as a general practice. The seeding of dry fields was one way to supplement wet-field cultivation since, during the rainy season, rice seeds were sowed directly in the rice field, not in the seedbed. Nevertheless, the crop yield from direct dry seeding utilized land that otherwise would have been left fallow through the development of fertilizing techniques. This pattern of Korean rice-cultivation in the fifteenth century resulted from natural conditions in the area. The climate of Korea provides less rainfall than that of the Jiangnan area. Since droughts are especially common in spring, conditions are relatively unfavorable for wet-field cultivation. Adopting dry-field farming techniques such as direct dry seeding was a special adaptation meant to overcome spring droughts. The climate of Korea, however, is more humid than that of northern China and thus more favorable to dry-field farming. It was owing to this favorable natural condition in Korea that the *Nongsa chiksŏl* recommended the technique of triple-

13. Nishiyama, *Aja-teki nogyo*, p. 62.

14. Yi Tae-jin (Yi T'aejin), "Sipsa-o segi nong'ŏp kisul paldal kwa sinhŭng sajok" (Development of agricultural technology and the newly emerging scholar-officials during the fourteenth and fifteenth centuries), *Tongyanghak* 9 (1979), pp. 337–39.

15. The *Nongsa chiksŏl* argued that this method was vulnerable to drought, and in fact its use had already been barred, in the 14th year of King T'aejong (*T'aejong sillok*, 27:43a).

cropping in two years, which is not mentioned in *Nung-sang chi-yao* of the Yuan period.[16] Until the fifteenth century, dry-field farming constituted seventy percent of Korean agriculture.[17] Significant improvements in farming are attributable more to the efforts of Koreans themselves than to the influence of China. Even the fertilizing techniques described in the *Nongsa chiksŏl*, despite basic similarities to those of Jiangnan, differ considerably in detail.[18] Nevertheless, as there was interest in Chinese farming manuals and techniques, the influence of Jiangnan agricultural technology cannot be denied. In the case of fertilization techniques, knowledge of Jiangnan methods is believed to have been helpful in adjusting to these changes in farming. From the late fourteenth century, much of the interest in Jiangnan agricultural techniques focused on the irrigation technology of wet-field cultivation, as indicated by the proposal by Paek Munbo. In the fifteenth century, the most important issue in agricultural policy was, in fact, the introduction of the superior irrigation technology of the Jiangnan techniques and the overcoming of the technological limitations to paddy-field cultivation in order to facilitate its expansion.[19]

Until the fifteenth century, the only form of irrigation in Korea was the so-called *cheŏn* method in which mountain streams would be dammed up to collect water for use in farming. The contribution of this type of irrigation to the development of rice production in Korea cannot be denied. However, according to an official gazetteer from the mid-fifteenth century, only one-sixth of paddy fields were irrigated by this method, even in the three southern provinces where conditions were favorable for paddy-field cultivation.[20] With the low state of irrigation, the diffusion of rice transplantation was naturally regarded as risky, as it might endanger the rice supply. Apparently, direct dry seeding continued to be widely used as a more dependable alternative.

16. Miyajima Hiroshi, "Chosen nogyoshi-jo ni okeru jyugo seiki" (The fifteenth century in the history of Chosŏn agriculture), *Chosen shiso* 3 (1980), pp. 47–53.
17. Ibid., p. 23.
18. Yi Tae-jin (1979), p. 337.
19. The following discussion of irrigation methods is largely drawn from Yi Tae-jin, "Simnyuk segi ch'ŏnbang (po) kwangae ŭi paldal" (The development of "water fence" irrigation techniques in sixteenth-century Korea), *Han Ugŭn paksa chŏngnyŏn kinyŏm sahak nonch'ong* (Festschrift on history in commemoration of the retirement of Dr. Han Ugŭn) (Seoul: Chisik san'ŏpsa, 1981), pp. 345–48.
20. Yi Kwangnin, *Yijo surisa yŏn'gu* (The history of irrigation in the Chosŏn dynasty) (Seoul: Han'guk yŏn'guwŏn, 1961), p. 28.

The use of waterwheels and water fences in the Jiangnan agricultural techniques was seen as a way of overcoming the limitations of the traditional Korean *cheŏn* method. With the existing construction techniques, *cheŏn* could not be built everywhere. Of the two innovations introduced by Jiangnan agricultural technology, the waterwheel was implemented first, as the simpler of the two. After the beginning of the new dynasty, the government attempted to promote the use of this invention, once during King T'aejong's reign (1400–1418) and later by King Sejong during a seven-year period starting in 1429, the year that compilation of *Nongsa chiksŏl* began. However, both of these attempts ended in failure. The problem was how to lift the water since most Korean creeks and rivers were rambling streams. Even after solving this problem, it was found that the soil in riverbeds and creeks was too coarse or sandy to hold water and let it accumulate.[21]

After the failure of the waterwheel, the use of the water fence was encouraged. This structure, called *ch'ŏnbang* in Korea during the fifteenth century, had been partially tried earlier but had failed. After King Munjong (r. 1450–1452) ascended the throne, the government planned for a more systematic implementation.[22] The water fence, later most often called *po* ("banked river"), was constructed by first building a structure of earth and wood in the middle of a river to collect water and then directing it down through channels to irrigate the fields below. This enabled water to be transported over long distances and facilitated its use in larger quantities, thus overcoming some of the earlier problems with waterwheels. Though the water fence was more difficult to build than the waterwheel, it was successful. Initially, the dissemination of waterwheels was promoted by government policies, but from the end of the fifteenth century, local intellectuals took the lead in its promotion, and its use became widespread particularly in the three southern provinces as its advantages became increasingly known.

The progressive spread of *ch'ŏnbang* can be traced in primary sources from this period such as chronicles. In surviving local gazettes (*ŭpji*) compiled in the late sixteenth and early seventeenth centuries from various regions (e.g., Andong, Chinju, Hamyang, Sunch'ŏn), there are separate entries for *cheŏn* and *kwan'gae*. In the most

---

21. Yi Tae-jin (1981), pp. 349–55.
22. Ibid., pp. 352–58.

numerous of cases, one gazette introduced twenty to thirty *ch'ŏnbang*.²³

Achievements such as the development of the *ch'ŏnbang* and *po*, as described above, represented a turning point in the history of rice cultivation in Korea. Because of the increasing reliability of irrigation through the development of new technology, conditions for the spread of rice transplantation became more favorable. The diffusion of rice transplantation progressed through the search for new methods of irrigation in the sixteenth century, and this process can be traced through changes in the content of agricultural texts at the time. In contrast to the *Nongsa chiksŏl*, the *Nongga chipsŏng* (Compilation for Farmers), which was published in 1655, contained detailed descriptions of the technique of rice transplantation.²⁴ Thus, the general scholarly view that rice transplantation became widespread only in the eighteenth century must be revised; its diffusion must be regarded as the further expansion of developments initiated in the sixteenth and seventeenth centuries.

In addition to the development of *ch'ŏnbang* in inland areas, Korean agriculture was also transformed through the reclamation of land in western coastal regions in the sixteenth century. A new type of farmland called *ŏnjŏn* (dammed fields) was created by constructing dikes to keep out seawater.²⁵ The *ŏnjŏn* were similar to the *hai-tang*, which had been developed in Song China as part of the Jiangnan agricultural techniques. Considering the fact that this development, like the utilization of river water for irrigation, began at the end of the fourteenth century, it was also probably stimulated by the development of the Jiangnan techniques. Originally, because of technological limitations, *ŏnjŏn* were developed only to create *tunjŏn* (garrison lands) for the state in a limited number of regions, but in the sixteenth century, they were actively established along the entire coast from Chŏlla to P'yŏngan province. In *ŏnjŏn*, farmers generally engaged in paddy-field cultivation because of its location (normally located at lower elevations, which facilitated the flow of water).²⁶

23. Ibid., pp. 359–64. These include gazetteers of Andong, Chinju, Hamyang, Sŏnsan, and Sunch'ŏn.
24. Ibid., p. 369, *Nongga chipsŏng* added nine items on rice transplantation not found in *Nongsa chiksŏl*.
25. Ibid., pp. 365–66 *Chungjong sillok* (The veritable records of King Chungjong) (Seoul: Kuksa P'yŏnch'an Wiwŏnhoe, 1955–1963), 96:6a; *Myŏngjong sillok*, 16:37b–38a.
26. Sŏ Yugu, *Imwŏn simnyukchi* (Sixteen treatises for rural life) (Seoul: Seoul taehakgyo kojŏn kanhaenghoe, 1966), *ponriji* 1, *chŏnje*, *ŏnjŏn cho*, p. 56.

In sum, from the end of the fourteenth century, Korean agriculture underwent a transition from extensive to intensive cultivation. Stimulated by the Jiangnan agricultural techniques from China, technological improvements were achieved in rice cultivation, whose importance thereby increased. Considering the importance of agriculture in the economy at the time, it is easy to surmise what an impact these technical improvements had on society. With the growth of the agricultural economy, Korea's understanding of Neo-Confucianism grew more sophisticated. As is well known, it was in the sixteenth century that the learning of "human nature and principle," the core of Neo-Confucian philosophy, laid down roots in Korean society, and as examined above, it was in the same century that Jiangnan agricultural techniques resolved the largest problems facing the Korean economy since the late fourteenth century. In China, the Jiangnan agricultural techniques functioned as the economic basis for the development of Neo-Confucianism and, more specifically, of the study of "human nature and principle."[27] The fact that the widespread adoption of the Jiangnan techniques in Korea and the Neo-Confucian transformation of Korean society both occurred in the sixteenth century also provides a clue to understanding not just forms of cultural transmission in Korea but also the nature of the historical development of Neo-Confucianism and, in particular, the study of "human nature and principle."

CHANGES IN SOCIAL STRUCTURE AND THE MOVEMENT TO PROMOTE NEO-CONFUCIAN INSTITUTIONS

During the transition from extensive to intensive agriculture at the end of the Koryŏ period, other changes were also occurring in Korean society. As all natural villages (*chayŏnch'on*) came to be named in units of *ri*, one trend in rural society was the formation of belief communities called *hyangdo* that handled the sacrificial rites for the guardian deity of the natural village or *ri*.[28] The emergence of social trends centered on the natural village was a major change from the previous situation.

27. Morimoto Jun'ichiro has stressed the socioeconomic aspects of Neo-Confucianism in China. *Toyo seiji shisoshi kenkyu* (A study on the history of political thought in the Orient) (Tokyo: Miraisha, 1967).
28. Yi Tae-jin, "Sarimp'a ŭi yuhyangso pongnip undong (I)" (The *sarim* faction's movement to reestablish the *yuhyangso* (I)), *Chindan hakpo* 34 (1972a), pp. 9–10.

In early and mid Koryŏ, the most common unit of social organization was the communal village (*chiyŏkch'on*), which was composed of several natural villages. Communal villages had their own distinct names, and the local functionaries (*hyangni*) who held positions in the county and district offices and constituted the rural ruling elite acted as representatives of the communal villages. What is striking in this social structure is the fact that *hyangdo* served as the principal unit of social organization. Though the *hyangdo* of the late Koryŏ were simply a variation on those of the early- to mid-Koryŏ period, among those that had been strongly Buddhist in nature in the earlier periods, there were cases of large-scale *hyangdo* that grew beyond the bounds of the communal village and operated on a *kun* (county) or *hyŏn* (district) level.[29]

The primary cause of the differences in social structure between the early-, mid- and the late-Koryŏ periods must be sought from changes in the agricultural economy. In the stage of extensive agriculture in early and mid Koryŏ, the productivity per area of land was so low that in order to harvest the same amount, it was necessary to use more farmland compared to the stage of intensive agriculture. Since cultivation of a larger amount of land required a greater utilization of labor, it was natural for society to be organized in units that would facilitate the mobilization and utilization of labor. In this sense, the change to a social structure centered on the natural village in the late Koryŏ can be seen as arising from the collapse of the social relations based on extensive agriculture as a result of the transition to intensive agriculture during this period.

The socioeconomic changes experienced by Korea in the late fourteenth century signified the development of society as a whole. However, these historic changes created a new problem as it became necessary to develop a new political order based on the changed social conditions.

The founding of the Chosŏn dynasty was the most important historical consequence brought about by the social changes at the end of the fourteenth century. In order to establish its rule, one of the top priorities of the new kingdom was to devise a new social order based on the changes in the basic unit of society. Ultimately, the solution

---

29. Yi Tae-jin, "Yech'ŏn Kaesimsa sŏkt'apki ŭi punsŏk-Koryŏ ch'ogi hyangdo ŭi illye" (An analysis of the inscription on the stone pagoda of Kaesim Temple: a case study of the *hyangdo* in the early Koryŏ period), *Yŏksa hakpo* 53–54 (combined issue, 1972b), pp. 42–44.

was found in the social institutions promoted by Neo-Confucianism, such as the village granary system (*sach'ang*) and the community compact (*hyangyak*). Interest in these institutions did not come from a simple desire to emulate China; rather, it stemmed from an understanding of the advanced level of these ideas and a realization of their applicability to Korea's social conditions.

Both the village granary system and the community compact were ideas that emerged in Chinese society during the Song period. The first was devised by Zhu Xi (Chu Hsi; 1130–1200), the great architect of Neo-Confucianism, and the second was the idea of Lu Dai-fang (1027–1098), later revised by Zhu Xi. The progressive nature of these institutions can be understood as the result of the development of the agricultural economy in the same period. The fact that both were implemented at the level of the natural village was a reflection of the basic conditions of society created by the development of the Jiangnan agricultural techniques and intensive agriculture. In addition, the emphasis on moral harmony among members of the *hyangyak*, regardless of social status, can also be seen as a reflection of the improvement in relations of domination brought about by the development of agricultural technology.[30] These aspects appear clearly in Zhu Xi's texts on promoting agriculture, in which he expressed his views on social relationships.

The best examples of the social concern of Zhu Xi's scholarship are the three texts on promoting agriculture written during his years as a local official. Believing that it was necessary first to resolve food shortages in order to promote morality, he gave detailed discussions in these texts of techniques that would enable more effective cultivation, and he also presented his ideas on the ideal relationship between landlords and tenants and between officials and the people in the management of agriculture and the collection of taxes. What were particularly interesting were the sections on the relations between landlords and tenants. He wrote that tenant farmers should respect landlords, because landlords gave them the means to support their families; likewise, landlords should not exploit tenant farmers, because their households benefited from the labor of the tenants.[31] In Zhu Xi's conception, landlords and tenants would both be members of a community contract. Harmony among the members of this

---

30. Norimoto Jun'ichirō, *Tōyō seiji shisōshi*, pp. 145–72.
31. *Chuja taejōn* (Collected works of Zhu Xi) (Seoul: reprinted by Cho Yŏngsŏng, 1978) Vol 3, pp. 386–88.

community could only be realized through mutual cooperation between the two. Even in China, there had been no precedent for such a conception of social relations; it was a change brought about by the development of agricultural technology in this period that enabled a change in landlords' basic attitude toward tenants. This is a clear example of the historic changes brought about by Neo-Confucianism.

Although Korean rulers in the fifteenth century were not completely inattentive to these Neo-Confucian institutions, it was only in the sixteenth century that they began to show a deep interest in them. As noted previously, it was during the sixteenth century that the advanced Jiangnan agricultural techniques were utilized fully in wet-rice cultivation. During the same century, the first systemic efforts at Neo-Confucian social engineering emerged. These facts are noteworthy because they confirm the relationship between Neo-Confucianism and the development of agricultural technology, especially wet-rice cultivation, in Korea.

During the search for a new social order after the founding of Chosŏn, there was some interest in Neo-Confucian institutions even in the fifteenth century, but such interest became truly serious in the sixteenth century. In the history of Korean agriculture, the sixteenth century was, as examined above, the period when adoption of the advanced Jiangnan agricultural techniques from China in paddy-field cultivation were completed. The fact that interest in Neo-Confucian social institutions increased in the same period is further evidence of the mutual relationship between Neo-Confucianism and the development of paddy-field cultivation in Korean history.

Before efforts to promote Neo-Confucian institutions began in the sixteenth century, attempts to create a new social order had almost completely depended on material assistance from the central government.[32] The government dispatched officials to the provinces and gave them complete authority over local society in order to put all the forces of provincial society under its rule.

For instance, in natural villages, the government tried to implement the *ijang* (or *ijŏng*; "village chief") system to function as the lowest level of the administrative structure. In an effort to standardize the religious practices of the *hyangdo* in natural villages, the government also attempted to institute the *isa* (village shrine) system, which dated back to the natural villages from the Han period in China.[33]

32. See Yi Tae-jin (1972a), pp. 16–28.
33. *T'aejong sillok*, 12:4a-b.

Though the original plan was not realized in the latter case, the government was able to establish its authority over matters of belief by establishing in each county and district an altar for the guardian deities of the state (*sajikdan*) and appointing the local magistrate as its head.

From the beginning of the new dynasty, local elites tried to strengthen local autonomy by founding *yuhyangso* (local self-governing organs) at the district and county levels, thus enhancing their role in community affairs. However, the central government wanted complete authority over the *yuhyangso* and ultimately was able to place them under the authority of the local magistrate. The establishment of the *kyŏngjaeso* (capital liaison offices) system as supervisory organs created a structure in which central government officials with ties to local elites were able to exercise direct control over the regional *yuhyangso*.

The clearest sign of the central government's paramount authority over the new social order in the early Chosŏn period was the adoption, among the various regulations proposed by Zhu Xi, of the prohibition of petitions against local officials by the populace.[34] In the early years of the dynasty, the central government actually had little interest in the social institutions conceived by Zhu Xi. But it did adopt this regulation, which was based on the notion of moral duty as a way of suppressing criticism of local officials by commoners and village clerks (*sŏri*), as well as by local elites of the *yuhyangso*.

The dominant role of the central government in the creation of a new social order in the fifteenth century cannot be understood easily through economic factors or the level of agricultural technology. Though agriculture in this period clearly entered the stage of intensive agriculture in terms of its technological level, it seems that farmers were still dependent on the government for seed grain in many cases.[35] More concrete findings will have to await further research. However, what is clear is that during the fifteenth century, there was no social force strong enough to counteract the central government's dominance of social policy, despite the many problems that it caused.

The policy of establishing the dominance of government authority made it possible to establish a strong centralized political structure in the early years of the dynasty, but it also brought about many

---

34. *Sejong sillok*, 9:16a.
35. *Munjong sillok*, 4:22a, Yi Chingsŏk's memorial to the king.

problems in official circles. The legal immunity afforded county magistrates from complaints of maladministration not only made it easy for individual officials to exploit the people but also led even the officials of the *yuhyangso*, who were the elites in the provinces, to work with the central government in order to preserve their standing. This situation in itself indicated the existence of a structural relationship, but it became more evident with the involvement of high-ranking officials of the central government in the *kyŏngjaeso* system. The merit subjects (*hunsin*) and royal relatives (*ch'ŏksin*), who were the dominant groups among officials at the end of the fifteenth century, attempted to expand their economic bases by utilizing the *kyŏngjaeso* system and by seizing control of *yuhyangso* in certain regions through the development of personal contacts with local officials.

The consequence of the social policies pursued by the central government was that society was unable to achieve fundamental stability internally, despite outward success in establishing a ruling structure. Even in the process of implementing these policies, many difficulties emerged. For instance, the government reconsidered the appropriateness of the regulation prohibiting petitions against local officials, and organizations such as the *yuhyangso* were repeatedly abolished.

However, since the basic structure of the central government did not change, social contradictions became even more severe by the end of the fifteenth century. The social institutions of Neo-Confucianism began to gain attention as a concrete method to achieve fundamental social stability as criticism of existing policies emerged.

In Neo-Confucianism, a social order was to be created by granting autonomy to the lowest units of society in each region. The fundamental method of achieving social stability was the cultivation of Confucian morality and ethics in order to eliminate corruption, which was viewed as the prime cause of disruption of the social order. Concrete efforts to achieve these goals included the movement to promote the *hyangsarye* (community archery ritual) and *hyangŭmjurye* (community wine-drinking ritual) at the end of the fifteenth century and the *hyangyak* movement of the early sixteenth century, all of which were led by the *sarim* faction. However, it is necessary to examine the trial implementation of the *sach'ang* (village granary) system in the mid-fifteenth century, which preceded these other movements.[36]

---

36. For a discussion of this experiment with the village granary system, see Yi Taejin (1972a), pp. 28–34.

In 1448 (the 30th year of King Sejong's reign), the *sach'ang* system was implemented on a trial basis in one region of Taegu County in an effort to overcome problems in the operation of the existing government granaries (*ŭich'ang*), which were run by local officials. As Zhu Xi had proposed, the grain stocks of the government-run *ŭich'ang* were distributed to thirteen sites within the county, and "impartial and upright" men were selected as officials to run the *sach'ang*. The trial was so successful that three years later (the 1st year of King Munjong's reign), ten other regions in Kyŏngsang province volunteered to adopt the *sach'ang* system. The *sach'ang* system with its low interest rates was more attractive to farmers than the *ŭich'ang* system, which charged de facto high interest rates as a result of the frequently corrupted local officials and the shady practices of local office clerks. In addition, the *sach'ang* system reduced the burden of making long journeys from farmers' homes to the county and district offices, leading to a clear reduction in the need to take out informal long-term loans at high interest.

The trial of the *sach'ang* system not only achieved positive results in aiding the disadvantaged with loans of grain but also seems to have been intended to establish a more stable order in the natural villages. Some advocates of the *sach'ang* system even proposed expanding its functions to include the collection and management of seed grain so that it could help to overcome the undesirable practice in natural villages of the *hyangdo* using seed grain to provide food and liquor for their monthly gatherings (*hyangdoyŏn*).[37] While the *sach'ang* system was, as mentioned above, intended for the natural villages, this proposal indicates that, from the beginning, its advocates were concerned with the establishment of a new social order—the historical task of this period.

Though expectations were great for the trial of the *sach'ang* system, the results fell short because of the dominant influence of the central government in social policy during this period. Most of its advocates were purged because of their opposition to the usurpation of the throne by King Sejo (r. 1455–1468).[38] Ironically, the implementation of the *sach'ang* system throughout the country in 1462 (7th year of King Sejo's reign) ultimately led to its total abolition eight years later (1st year of King Sŏngjong's reign) for reasons of misman-

---

37. *Munjong sillok*, 4:22a, Yi Chingsŏk's memorial to the king.
38. See Yi Tae-jin (1972a), pp. 28–43.

agement.[39] It seems clear that the culture of exploitation among officials, including powerful families in the capital, played a role, but in actuality problems arose in the early period of the trial from the fact that the care needed to carry out the system was completely lacking.

One of the main characteristics of the *sach'ang* system was that it could not be run successfully unless there existed a group from which officials could be appointed who had an understanding of its principles. In this context, Kyŏngsang province, where the first trials were carried out, seems to have had certain advantages. There were many young scholars in the province influenced by Chŏng Mongju (1337–1392) and Kil Chae (1353–1419), Neo-Confucianists from the late Koryŏ, who had opposed the dynastic change out of a sense of righteousness and honor. As a result, Neo-Confucianism became rooted there earlier than in other regions of the country. In the mid-fifteenth century, in contrast to later eras, Kyŏngsang province was known to have the most advanced irrigation systems in the entire country and was also the only region where the technique of rice transplantation was in use.[40] In short, the superior economic conditions in the province produced the conditions under which a desire to restore local autonomy emerged earlier than in other regions.

The progressive nature of Neo-Confucianism in Kyŏngsang province, as shown in the trial implementation of the *sach'ang* system, was also apparent in the movement to promote the *hyangsarye* and the *hyangŭmjurye*.[41] The movement lasted fifteen years, from 1483 (the 14th year of King Sŏngjong's reign) to 1498 (the year of the Muo literati purge), and its leaders mainly came from Kyŏngsang province; namely, Kim Chongjik (1431–1492) and his disciples. This new group, who held orthodox Neo-Confucian views on scholarship and politics, has generally been called the *sarim* faction; however, at the time, its influence still did not extend beyond Kyŏngsang province. It was around twenty years later, during the *hyangyak* movement, that the *sarim* faction expanded to the capital and Honam regions. It seems to be no coincidence that the period of the emergence of the *sarim*, the late fifteenth and early sixteenth centuries, was also the period in

---

39. *Sejo sillok*, 24:29a. *Sŏngjong sillok*, 3:20b, 105:29a-b.
40. See Kim Yongsŏp, *Chosŏn hugi nongŏpsa yŏn'gu* (Studies in the agricultural history of the late Chosŏn period) (Seoul: Ilchogak, 1974), Vol. 2, pp. 11–18.
41. For an account of the movement to promote the *hyangsarye* and *hyangŭmjurye*, see Yi Tae-jin, "Sarimp'a ŭi yuhyangso pongnip undong" (II) (The *sarim* faction's movement to reestablish the *yuhyangso* II), *Chindan hakpo* 35 (1973), pp. 7–29.

agriculture when, as examined above, the new irrigation method of the *ch'ŏnbang* was developed and came into use, particularly in the three southern provinces.

In a sense, the movement to promote the *hyangsarye* and the *hyangŭmjurye* led by Kim Chongjik and his followers took the form of a movement to reestablish the *yuhyangso*. Since the *yuhyangso* system had been officially abolished in 1468 (13th year of King Sejo's reign), owing to the rampant corruption of the officials and county magistrates concerned,[42] their interest in it was initially to create an organ to supervise the performance of the two rituals. In other words, the revival of the abolished *yuhyangso* was not a simple revival but was meant to be the center of an effort to create a new social order in the provinces by endowing them with the duty of supervising the *hyangsarye* and the *hyangŭmjurye* as prescribed in the *Rites of the Zhou (Zhou-li)*. These two rituals differed somewhat from those of the *hyangyak* in terms of the unit of society that was targeted, but their fundamental principles were similar. Both pursued the common goal of eliminating factors that could disrupt the social order by promoting "men of righteous deeds and morality" (*hyangsarye*) and elderly men (*hyangŭmjurye*) and entrusting them with the maintenance of an order based on Confucian values.

These proposals could not be easily passed because of the strong opposition of the "meritorious subjects" who held a dominant position in the central government. The senior ministers felt that the performance of these new rituals could threaten the privileges that they enjoyed through their connection with provincial officials. After five years of stormy debate, Kim Chongjik's proposal was finally adopted. Its passage was made possible by the increased numbers of senior ministers who came to realize that even if the institution of the *yuhyangso* was revived, they would face no obstacles to seizing control. By utilizing the *kyŏngjaeso* system while maintaining individual connections with provincial officials as before, they could maintain their advantage regardless of whether the two rituals were performed or not.

The proposal to revive the *yuhyangso* was adopted in 1488 (19th year of King Sŏngjong's reign). Most of *yuhyangso* in each region did in fact come under the control of the "meritorious subjects," as they

---

42. Ibid. pp. 29–30. The discussion that follows here is essentially drawn from this study. See also *Sŏngjong sillok*, 137: Yi Kŭkpae's memorial.

had planned. Only in a few regions in Kyŏngsang province, where its *sarim* proponents were strongest, were the *yuhyangso* able to conduct the two rituals according to their original purpose. Two to three years later, the situation had deteriorated to the point where former advocates of the system now argued for its abolition. During the ten years from the decision to revive the *yuhyangso* system to the Literati Purge of 1498, its problems were an important divisive issue between the "meritorious elite" and the *sarim* faction. In some areas, *sarim* literati in the provinces even formed a separate organization called the Samaso (Association of Licentiates) in order to oppose the *yuhyangso* under the control of powerful elites with ties to high-ranking officials in the capital. When the meritorious elite launched a literati purge to exact political revenge on the *sarim* faction, they took immediate steps to abolish anything with the name *samaso*.[43] This fact is quite significant in showing that the Literati Purge of 1498 was more than a political phenomenon that ensued from a mere power struggle.

The *sarim* faction's movement for the *hyangsarye* and the *hyangŭmjurye* had the unintended result of strengthening the meritorious subjects' ability to expand their economic bases. After the Literati Purge of 1498, powerful officials aggressively sought to gain control over the *yuhyangso* through their connections with local officials and utilization of the *kyŏngjaeso* system. The conspicuously luxurious lifestyle of those officials was rooted in the exploitation of the common people that was, in turn, made possible through their control of local communities.

Cho Kwang-jo's (1482–1519) first appointment at court in 1515 (10th year of King Chungjong's reign) enabled the *sarim* faction to emerge as a political force again in the capital. After the *sarim* assumed official posts, they proposed the implementation of the *hyangyak* throughout the country and attempted to reinstitute the reforms they had been unable to carry out in the past.[44] This proposal, which was made in 1517 (12th year of King Chungjong's reign), was premised on the abolition of the *yuhyangso* system as the main factor undermining the stability of rural society.[45]

In contrast to the long struggle to win approval of the *hyangsarye* and the *hyangŭmjurye*, the proposal on the *hyangyak* easily gained the

---

43. Ibid., 26. See also *Yŏnsan'gun ilgi*, 31:2a-b.
44. For the discussion of the movement to institute the community compact, see Yi Tae-jin, "Chosŏn chŏn'gi hyangch'on chilsŏ" (Social order in rural villages in the early-Chosŏn period), *Tonga munhwa* 13 (1976), pp. 164–68.
45. *Chungjong sillok*, 31; 12a-b; 14/6 ŭrhae, 36:22a.

support of the king and was immediately implemented. Positive results were quickly achieved not only in Kyŏngsang province but also in the Honam region and the central provinces, and it was even implemented in the capital.[46] This success resulted from the expansion of the *sarim* faction's power base. As social contradictions and corruption intensified, mainly because of Yŏnsan'gun's (r. 1494-1506) tyrannical rule, the number of officials who agreed with the *sarim* faction's critiques increased. In spite of its initial success, however, the *hyangyak* movement met the same fate as the movement to promote the *hyangsarye* and the *hyangŭmjurye*. It aroused the same opposition among powerful officials in the capital, and when they conducted the Literati Purge of 1519 (Kimyo sahwa), all the achievements of the past few years were immediately reversed.[47]

Both in its aims and its implementation, the *hyangyak* movement was clearly a successor to the movement to promote the *hyangsarye* and the *hyangŭmjurye* during King Sŏngjong's reign. The fact that the concrete method of the movement was changed to the *hyangyak* was a change of great significance for the development of Neo-Confucianism in this period. During the years between the literati purges of 1498 and 1519, a new trend emerged among the *sarim* faction—as expressed by Kim Koengp'il's (1454-1504) calling himself "a schoolboy studying the *Elementary Learning* (*Xiaoxue*)" —of emphasizing the importance of this text, which Zhu Xi had regarded as the foundation for all learning. Since the *hyangyak* appeared in this text, the *hyangyak* movement was an effort to put the teachings of the *Elementary Learning* into practice.[48]

The increased importance of the *Elementary Learning* and the *hyangyak* movement suggests that a consensus was developing to adopt Neo-Confucian self-cultivation as the remedy for the chronic social ills emerging primarily in the centralized bureaucratic system of the time. The fact that this concrete social critique was, for the first time, elaborated systematically through a single ideology was of great significance. After the reappraisal of the *Elementary Learning* in the early sixteenth century, Neo-Confucianism in Korea came to maturity in mid-century through the scholarship of Yi Hwang (1501-1570) and other thinkers. In this process, the emphasis placed on the *Heart Classic* (*Xin Jing*) of Zhen Dexiu (1178-1235) and the popularity of

46. *Chungjong sillok*, 36;2a 36;18b-19a; 36;46b-47a, 51b.
47. Ibid., 38; 2a-b, 8a-b.
48. Uno Seichi, ed., *Shogaku* (Tokyo: Meiji Shoin, 1965), p. 361.

the study of ritual (*yehak*) emerged as the unique features of Korean Neo-Confucianism. The *hyangyak* movement can be seen as the culmination of a continuing effort from the mid-fifteenth century to establish a new social order; though it ended in failure, it was significant for providing the foundation for the intellectual development of Neo-Confucianism in Korea.

The above analysis has made it clear that the development of Neo-Confucianism in Korea had a strong social component. To conclude this section, I will examine problems in the agricultural economy and social relations during the stage of the *hyangyak* movement, which was a turning point in Korean Neo-Confucianism.[49]

The early sixteenth century, when the *Elementary Learning* rose in importance, was also the period when the adoption of the Jiangnan agricultural techniques brought about epochal changes in Korean rice cultivation, as examined above. The *hyangyak* movement and the opposing effort to maintain the *yuhyangso* both seem to have been closely connected with problems in the agricultural economy. High-ranking government officials supported the *yuhyangso* because they were an important means for officials to further their interests through the reclamation of land and the creation of *ŏnjŏn* (dammed fields) in western coastal areas, a government project of which they were virtually in charge. On the other hand, the *hyangyak* was related to the development of *ch'ŏnbang* (water fence), which was mainly led by the small to medium landlord class in inland areas.

Because the construction of *ŏnjŏn* required the mobilization of a large labor force to build embankments to keep seawater out, it was not easy for private individuals to undertake such projects. In this period, powerful officials were behind the construction of most of the *ŏnjŏn*. They utilized the *yuhyangso* and provincial officials in a region and forcibly mobilized its residents as labor.[50] The land reclaimed was so vast that the forced mobilization of labor continued to cultivate these fields. This illegal exploitation by powerful families in the capital sometimes met with direct resistance by the oppressed, such as the rebellion led by Im Kkŏkjŏng (?–1562) from 1559–1562 in Hwanghae province, where the development of *ŏnjŏn* was the most active.[51] However, land reclamation continued to be active and was part of the grim reality of life in the early sixteenth century. The fact that the

---

49. Yi Tae-jin (1981), pp. 364–68.
50. *Myŏngjong sillok*, 16:37b-39a. Yi Kwan's memorial.
51. Yazawa Yasui, "Im Kkŏkchŏng no hanran to sono shakai-teki kaikei," *Chosen rekishi ronso* (Tokyo: Hatada Takashi Kinen Kai, 1979), pp. 561–71.

acquisition and preservation of such privileges was a major concern of officials was the reason that politics in this period centered on the cultivation of relations with powerful figures, the fastest route to gaining power.

Since the *yuhyangso* played a key role in the construction of *ŏnjŏn* by high-ranking officials, it is easy to see the social significance of the *hyangyak* movement led by the *sarim* faction, which called for their abolition. But it is necessary to pay more attention to the fact that the advocates of the *hyangyak* also emphasized the importance of the development of *ch'ŏnbang*. One connection between the *hyangyak* and the *ch'ŏnbang* was that the labor necessary for the construction of the latter was provided by one or two natural villages, the basic unit of the former. According to records from the period, the construction of small *ch'ŏnbang* needed ten or so laborers; medium-sized ones, tens of laborers; and large ones, hundreds of laborers.[52] Although the primary purpose of the *hyangyak* movement was to eliminate the abuses of the *yuhyangso*, its mutual aid functions were meant to facilitate the efficient implementation of *ch'ŏnbang*, which were regarded as a method of improving the agricultural economy in each region. The *sarim* faction, who represented the interests of small and medium provincial landlords in their active interest in the development of *ch'ŏnbang*, argued that the land reclaimed must be distributed equitably in proportion to the labor and funds provided.

In short, Korean society in the sixteenth century experienced a tremendous increase in wealth, thanks to the development of new agricultural techniques. Two opposing views emerged over the proper method for the acquisition and distribution of this wealth, leading to serious strife in the political arena. Neo-Confucianism was adopted by the progressive side and laid a firm foundation for a new system of social ethics.

CONCLUSION

I believe that the above analysis has sufficiently demonstrated that the rise of Neo-Confucianism in Korean society in the fifteenth and sixteenth centuries, particularly the study of human nature and principle, was closely associated with socioeconomic changes. Instead

52. *Sejong sillok*, 52:32b-33a, Pak Sŏ-saeng's memorial.

of a conclusion, I will present some of my thoughts on the development of Neo-Confucianism in Korea after this period, based on my findings in this chapter.

After the Literati Purge of 1519 ended the *hyangyak* movement, the *sarim* faction, who were the main force in the introduction of Neo-Confucianism, were not active in social movements for a considerable period of time. While they produced significant intellectual accomplishments, very few mentioned issues dealing directly with the establishment and maintenance of social order. Even when they had brief opportunities to assume official posts, the most they did was to advocate the printing and dissemination of the *Elementary Learning* or the distribution of a vernacular commentary on it. However, despite the fact that relatives of the royal family dominated politics, the *sarim* faction was able to expand its power base gradually. Their long standing desire to become the central force in provincial society in each region found a new outlet through the *sŏwŏn* (local Confucian academy) movement. It is well known that *sŏwŏn* began to grow in the late sixteenth century. Though the *sŏwŏn* were educational institutions, it seems that they were also meant to be a way of continuing the social movements of the past, as suggested by Yi I's (Yi Yulgok, 1536–1584) proposal that *sŏwŏn* serve as the primary means of implementing the *hyangyak*.[53] Since the *sŏwŏn* were legal educational institutions, they had the advantage of being able to avoid political repression, and they could also facilitate the qualitative and quantitative growth of the Neo-Confucian faction.

Despite their political difficulties, the *sŏwŏn* movement represented an expansion of the economic base of the *sarim* faction as the movement expanded the existing small-scale *sŏjae* (village school). In this context, the development of *ch'ŏnbang*, which was discussed above, has an added significance. The *sarim* faction was able to undergo steady growth economically, intellectually, and in the field of education within continuing political opposition, because they ultimately gained political hegemony. When the position of royal relatives was undermined with the ascension of Sŏnjo to the throne in 1567, the rise of the *sarim* faction became a reality. The political opposition was significantly weakened, and the *sarim* faction gained positions in the central government. Even after the rise of the *sarim*,

---

53. Yi I, "Haeju hyangyak" (Community compact for Haeju), *Yulgok chŏnsŏ* (The complete works of Yi I) (Seoul: Sŏnggyun'gwan taehakkyo taedong munhwa ŏn'guso, 1968), 16:7a–11a.

there was much conflict between new and old forces early in King Sŏnjo's reign, but politics and society gradually moved in the direction that the *sarim* advocated. The *sŏwŏn* underwent steady development, and the *kyŏngjaeso* (capital liaison office) system was permanently abolished in 1597 (30th year of King Sŏnjo's reign). The abolition of the *kyŏngjaeso* was one of the most important reforms that eliminated the long-lasting corruption of central government officials that had penetrated deeply into provincial society.

After the abolition of the *kyŏngjaeso*, the *yuhyangso*, its subsidiary organization, declined in importance in all regions, and the *sŏwŏn* gained hegemony over rural society. A new order was established in most of the regions, undergoing these changes with the exception of the few areas where the *yuhyangso* had always operated according to Neo-Confucian principles. In rural areas in the early seventeenth century, *sŏwŏn* generally played a leading role in local society through its advocacy and dissemination of Neo-Confucianism. The trend for *yuhyangso* was to change their names to *hyangsadang* (communal archery pavilion), and natural villages attempted as much as possible to build a society along the lines of the *hyangyak*. As a result, Korea in the seventeenth century was developing into the society that had been advocated by social movements since the end of the fifteenth century.

The Neo-Confucian transformation of society in the early-seventeenth century was also related to the development of *yehak* (study of ritual) in this period. That this transformation had the support of the dominated classes is clearly shown by the fact that even though they suffered the seven-years war of the Hideyoshi invasion and two invasions by the Jurchens, there were no uprisings in this period. From the late-seventeenth century, Korea underwent new socioeconomic changes, including commercial development, and these changes revealed many limitations in Neo-Confucianism, which can be regarded as the ideology of small to medium landlord classes. The negative views of Neo-Confucianism in Korea that have been prevalent up to the present are based on the problems that it caused after this period, but it is necessary to distinguish the later from the earlier periods in order to gain an accurate understanding of the place of Neo-Confucianism in Korean history.

translated by Hong Sun'gwŏn

CHAPTER 3

# New Socioeconomic Trends in Fifteenth- and Sixteenth-Century Korea: Population Increase and Cultivation of the Lowlands

DURING THE FIFTEENTH AND SIXTEENTH centuries, Korea underwent one of the most important changes in its history. Intensive agriculture in the form of crop rotation became standard during these two centuries, leading to the emergence of local markets in rural areas. These developments in the economy not only changed domestic politics and the social structure but also contributed greatly to the growth of international trade in East Asia in the sixteenth century.[1]

The development of Korean agriculture in the fifteenth and sixteenth centuries was of great importance not only to Korean history but also to the history of East Asia. In this chapter, I will analyze the origins and nature of this agricultural development. In nearly all regions of the country, Korean agriculture was able to overcome the restrictions of fallow farming and shift to the intensive use of land through single-crop farming. Furthermore, the location of the fields moved from highland to lowland areas. The change from fallow to intensive farming has been thoroughly researched by a number of scholars since the end of the 1970s.[2]

---

1. Yi Tae-jin (Yi T'aejin), "Economic Transformation and Socio-political Trends in Sixteenth-Century East Asia," presented at the Conference on "International History of East Asia, 1400–1700" (1988).
2. Major works on this topic include the following: Miyajima Hiroshi, "Chosen nogyoshi ni okeru jugoseiki" (The fifteenth century in the history of Korean agricultural technology), *Chosen shiso* 3 (1980); Kim T'aeyŏng, *Chosŏn chŏngi t'oji chedosa yŏn'gu* (Studies on the land system of the early Chosŏn period) (Seoul: Chisik san'opsa, 1983).

The change from highland to lowland agriculture, however, has been virtually neglected by scholars. In this chapter, I will present the results of my recent research on this topic.³ Since Korean economic historians have only recently begun taking interest in the development of agricultural technology, there has been little research on the causes of technological change and its social impact. Although there is research on the fifteenth- and sixteenth-century development of crop rotation, very little work has been done on the background and origin of this historical change. To gain a greater understanding of this phenomenon, much research must be done, and I believe one of the most essential areas for research is the issue of population.

During the fifteenth and sixteenth centuries, Korea experienced new developments in agriculture and a period of continued, unusually rapid population growth. Using the considerable volume of historical sources on this topic, I will systematically explain the relationship between land cultivation and population growth.

Finally, I will analyze the impact of the aforementioned changes in the agricultural economy on the development of trade. While my study is primarily concerned with the development of local markets, which appeared mainly toward the end of the fifteenth century, I will also examine the nearly total disappearance of these markets during the century and a half prior to this period. This phenomenon seems to be similar to what Japanese scholars call the "reversal effect,"⁴ and this similarity between Korea and Japan suggests that this topic will be a fruitful avenue for comparative research.

TENDENCIES IN LOWLAND AND MARSHLAND CULTIVATION

Large-scale transformation of the agricultural economy, as exemplified by the spread of crop rotation in Korea, had already begun in more advanced countries in the fourteenth century. In Korean history,

---

Yi Tae-jin, *Han'guk sahoesa yŏn'gu* (Studies on Korean social history) (Seoul: Chisik san'ŏpsa, 1986).

3. Yi Tae-jin, "Sibosipnyuk segi ŭi chŏpyŏng chosŭpji kaegan tonghyang" (Trends in reclamation of lowlands and marshland in the fifteenth and sixteenth centuries), *Kuksagwan nonch'ong*, no. 2 (1989).

4. Saito Osamu, "Daikaikon jinko shono keizai, keizai shakai no seiritsu," (The great reclamations, population, and small-peasant economy) *Nihon keizaishi* 1, Hayami Akira and Miyamoto Matao, eds., (Tokyo: Iwanami Shoten, 1988).

the fifteenth and sixteenth centuries are significant as the period of development and maturation of Korea's agricultural economy.

Primary-source materials show that crop rotation in Korean agriculture was not generally widespread before the fourteenth century. According to an entry in the *Koryŏsa* (The History of Koryŏ) dated March 1054, land was classified according to the following criteria: "Land that does not require a period of fallowness was rated top quality; land that requires one year of lying fallow, medium quality; and land needing two years of lying fallow, low quality."[5] According to this system, fields that were rated "top quality" could not exceed in quantity those rated "medium" or "low." These criteria are sufficient evidence that the practice of letting fields lie fallow for one or two years was still common at the time.

Since letting land lie fallow was the primary method of restoring soil fertility, it is important to emphasize that there was a considerably high degree of highland cultivation. A text that provides supporting evidence is *Koryŏ togyŏng*, a description of Koryŏ agriculture by a Song envoy who visited Korea in the first half of the twelfth century.

> The borders of this country follow the coast of the East Sea, and the land consists of high mountains and deep valleys, which are steep and rugged, and there are only a few plains. For this reason, fields are mostly located in the mountains, and climbing up and down makes farming very difficult. Seen from far away, [the land] looks like ladders or stone stairs.[6]

In the above-mentioned regulations of 1054, recorded in the *Koryŏsa*, farmland along mountainous regions was referred to as "mountain fields." Although the regulations used the frequency of fallow periods as one standard for land quality, there was a different standard that classified fields according to their location as either "mountain fields" or "plain fields." Both of these classifications were used as methods of measurement; however, the fact that plain fields were used as the standard for classification demonstrates that they were predominant and preferred by farmers. Nonetheless, the existence of such regulations, along with the above comments of the Chinese envoy, supports the conclusion that mountain fields com-

---

5. *Koryŏsa* (The History of Koryŏ) Vol. 78, Sikhwaji 1, Kyongnijo.
6. *Sŏnhwa pongsa Koryŏ togyŏng*, Vol. 23, Chapsok 2, Chongyejo.

prised a significant proportion of total farmland. The evidence seems to be convincing that wet-field agriculture was restricted to lowlands within mountain valleys and that cultivation of the hills was far more important until the fifteenth and sixteenth centuries.

Other scholars have put forth an alternative interpretation of these two sources. According to their interpretation, fallow farming had already been abolished in ancient times, and during the Koryŏ period, its practice was restricted to a negligible number of poor farmers. However, recent studies have challenged this interpretation. Research on the medieval period in Japan has focused on phenomena such as *kata-arashi* (lying fallow in part) and *nenko* (lying fallow yearly). In addition, recent research has examined the prevalence of dry-field farming[7] and the issue of why fire-field farming (*hwajŏn*) in the highlands was prevalent until the fifteenth century in Southeast Asia, where the natural conditions for rice cultivation were optimal. Such research has produced important findings that have greatly contributed to an understanding of pre-fourteenth century Korean agriculture.[8]

A completely different picture of Korean agriculture emerges in *Nongsa chiksŏl* (Straight Talk on Farming). Compiled in 1430, this book is the oldest publication on agriculture in Korea. It described cultivation methods used in the three southern provinces, which were the most technologically advanced, and aimed to promote these methods in the northern part of the country. There is no mention of fallow farming anywhere in this compilation.

The agricultural techniques described in *Nongsa chiksŏl* focused on topics such as artificial fertilization, the proper time for plowing, sowing, and weeding; and how to achieve three harvests in two years or even two harvests in one year. Another notable aspect of the book is its promotion of intermediate sowing (*kanjong*) as a method of intensive cultivation for farmers with small landholdings. The introduction of new artificial fertilization methods through the use of human manure and ash contributed greatly to an improvement in agricultural productivity.

I want to emphasize that these developments in agricultural technology were accompanied by a large-scale change in the location of arable land. The cultivation of highlands, which was prevalent under

---

7. Saito Osamu, "Daikaikon", p. 177; "Inasaku to hatten no hikakushi" (The paddy farm and the comparative history of the development), *Tonan Ajia kara no chiteki boken*, Hara Yonosuke, ed. (Tokyo: Riburopoto, 1986).

8. Watabe Tadayo, *Ine no michi* (The way of rice) (Tokyo: NHK Books, 1977).

the practice of fallow farming, decreased as cultivation moved to lower areas. More research is needed on the technical mechanisms that made this change possible; however, there are enough historical sources to enable an examination of the overall process. The movement from highlands to lowlands can roughly be described as follows.[9] One of the main phenomena associated with the development of lowland cultivation was the relocation of training grounds, horse pastures, and other places for military use. In the second half of the fourteenth century, proposals were made for the first time to relocate pastures from coastal plains to islands. Existing sources demonstrate that approximately fifty-three pastures in the mid-fifteenth century and eighty-four at the end of the century were moved to islands. There was also a tendency either to reduce the number of military-training grounds located on coastal plains and in the Seoul area or to move them into the hinterland.

While lowland cultivation was prevalent during the fifteenth century, the development of marshland cultivation became more active in the sixteenth century. The most significant change was the cultivation of reclaimed land. In order to expand the acreage of arable land, land was reclaimed by building dikes on the western and southern coasts, and such land was referred to as *haet'aek* (coastal marsh) or *ŏnjŏn* (dammed field).[10] Large-scale reclamation was carried out under the guidance of the court and ruling class elites and required the mobilization of hundreds or thousands of workers and corresponds to a "technical adjustment" (*konghakjŏk chŏg'ŭng*).[11] This project was carried out along the entire coastline of Korea, from the southern coasts of the Chŏlla and Kyŏngsang provinces to the northern coast of P'yŏng'an province. Most state-owned (military) pastures, which had been relocated to islands in the fifteenth century, were abolished and transformed into cultivated land in the sixteenth century.

The cultivation of plains and marshland brought about an expansion of wet-field acreage. According to the first geographical survey of the Chosŏn dynasty, compiled in 1430, wet fields were clearly prevalent in coastal districts that had a high proportion of plains. While wet fields only amounted to twenty-seven percent of arable land

---

9. The following section comes from Yi Tae-jin, "Sibosipnyuk" (1989).

10. Yi Tae-jin, "Sipnyuksegi yŏnhae chiyok ŭi ŏnjŏn kaebal" (The development of diked fields in coastal regions in the sixteenth century), *Kim Ch'ŏljun paksa hwagap kinyŏm nonch'ong* (Seoul: Chisik san'ŏpsa, 1983); reprinted in Yi Tae-jin, *Han'guk sahoesa yŏn'gu*.

11. Saito Osamu, "Inasaku", (1986), p. 215.

in the 336 rural districts of the country, the percentage was substantially higher in the sixty-eight coastal districts of the four provinces of Kyŏngsang, Chŏlla, Ch'ungch'ŏng, and Kyŏnggi, ranging from fifty to sixty percent.

During the initial period of reclamation in the fifteenth century, direct sowing of seeds (*chikp'a*) was preferred to the transplantation of rice seedlings because of the low degree of irrigation. The practice of direct sowing was an adaptation to severe natural conditions such as the spring drought. There were two varieties of direct sowing: "wet-direct sowing" (*sugyŏng chikp'a*) which required at least a minimal water supply, and "dry-direct sowing" (*kŏn'gyŏng chikp'a*) which required no water at all. The latter was mainly a feature of earlier farming methods used in hill fields, and it gradually disappeared as cultivation moved down into the valleys and as the quality of irrigation improved. *Cheŏn* (dams) using mountain streams used to be the common form of irrigation, but they were mostly replaced in the sixteenth century by *po* (reservoirs) using river water, resulting in an increase in wet-direct sowing.[12] After going through several stages of development, rice transplantation came into more general use in Korea in the latter half of the seventeenth century.

POPULATION INCREASE AND SOCIAL CHANGE

The fifteenth and sixteenth centuries were a period of rapid population growth, a rare phenomenon in Korean history. Although historical demography is still a relatively new field in Korea, Kwŏn T'aehwan and Shin Yong-ha (Sin Yongha) have produced reliable data on general population trends from the sixteenth to the nineteenth centuries.[13] Figure 1 is a summary of their findings.

According to their research, the population of Korea in 1392—the first year of the Chosŏn dynasty—was 5,549,000, and in 1511, it

12. Yi Tae-jin, "Simnyuk segi ch'ŏnbang (po) kwangae ŭi paldal" (The development of irrigation in river areas in the sixteenth century" in *Han Ugun paksa chŏngnyŏn kinyŏm sahak nonchong*, (Seoul: Chisik san'ŏpsa, 1981); reprinted in Yi Tae-jin, *Han'guk sahoesa yŏn'gu*.
13. Kwŏn T'aehwan and Sin Yongha, "Chosŏn wangjo sidae ingu ch'ujŏng e kwanhan ilsilon" (An attempt at population estimates for the Chosŏn dynasty period), *Tonga munhwa* 14 (1977). See also Yi Hoch'ŏl and Yi Yonggu, "Chosŏn sidae ŭi ingu kyumo ch'ugye" (Population estimates for the Chosŏn period) (I) and (II), *Kyŏngyŏng sahak* Vol. 2, no. 3 and Vol. 3, no. 1 (1988). There are several other studies in this field, but these two contain findings the most relevant to my argument in this chapter.

passed the ten million mark. When Hideyoshi invaded Korea in 1592, the population had increased to 13,737,000. During these two centuries, the rate of population growth was extremely high, increasing annually by 0.40–0.56 percent.

Because of a lack of sources for the preceding centuries, my analysis will cover only the Chosŏn period. The only extant population statistic for the Koryŏ period is a section devoted to Korea in the historical records of Sung China (960–1279), where the total population is cited as 2,100,000 in the first half of the twelfth century. Of course, this figure represents only the official record, not the actual number of inhabitants. Even if the actual population in the twelfth century were double the official count, the figure of 5,500,000 at the end of the fourteenth century is still extraordinarily high, considering such population-reducing factors as wars, peasant and slave revolts, and invasions by the Mongols and by Japanese pirates (*wako*). In this context, it seems that the rapid population growth of the fifteenth and sixteenth centuries was not the result of the political events that led to the formation of the Chosŏn dynasty but had more to do with socioeconomic changes that had begun much earlier.

In 1988, I published the results of an analysis of birth and death data recorded on 256 grave epitaphs for children in the Koryŏ period. Although the individuals mentioned in these sources were all from the ruling class, I felt that such research would be helpful in understanding the population trends of society as a whole.[14] The most significant finding was the tremendous difference in child-mortality rates before and after the mid-thirteenth century. In the first period, the mortality rate for boys was ten percent and for girls thirteen percent, whereas the rate declined to three percent and two percent, respectively, in the second period. The average number of surviving children per family increased from 3.08 to 3.55.

Advances in medical techniques were the main reason for the significant decline in child-mortality rates between the first and second halves of the thirteenth century. From its founding, Koryŏ society was greatly influenced by the technically advanced Sung medicine and made efforts to implement Sung techniques. As a result of these efforts, "local medicine" began to make use of domestically produced herbs and became completely reconceptualized, leading to the compilation

---

14. Yi Tae-jin, "Koryŏ hugi ŭi ingu chŭngga yoin saengsŏng kwa hyangyak ŭisul paldal" (The formation of primary factors for the population increase in the late Koryŏ and the development of indigenous medical techniques), *Han'guk saron* 19 (1988).

of several new medical books in the fourteenth century. The state also pursued a policy of improving access to this medicine in an effort to increase the size of the rural work force. As demonstrated in the analysis of the epitaphs from the Koryŏ period, the reduction of child mortality indicates that members of the ruling class were the first to reap the benefits of the new advances in medicine.

During the Chosŏn period, there were tremendous advances in local medicine in the fifteenth century. The *Hyangyak chipsŏngbang* (Compilation of Native Korean Prescriptions), which brought together all the medical knowledge of the time, was compiled in 1433 and contained descriptions of 959 symptoms and 10,706 different prescriptions. A few years later, in 1445, the *Ŭibang yuch'wi* (Classified Collection of Medical Prescriptions) was published, a 365-volume medical dictionary that included prescriptions from Chinese medical texts.

Even common people were able to benefit from the advances in local medicine. Not only were medicinal herbs locally produced and easily available, but medical texts that were as comprehensive as the *Hyangyak chipsŏngbang* were also later published and distributed in provincial regions. Many concise editions and booklets for medical emergencies were available, so that anyone who read Chinese characters could easily access medical information. Local districts employed their own physicians, and common people could obtain medicine. A report by the governor of Hamgyŏng Province, the northernmost province in Korea, provides important evidence that the people of this era believed medicine could prevent premature death. The governor requested that the central government send medicine and medical books since there were many premature deaths due to a lack of physicians and medical literature in this region of reclaimed land.

The new social class of "newly rising literati" (*sinhŭng sadaebu*) played an important role in the development of local medicine since the fourteenth century. The new ruling class mainly came from small and medium land-owning families and regarded agriculture and medicine as two interrelated factors in the improvement of living standards. The fact that population increase and results of land reclamation were the criteria for judging the performance of provincial officials from 1375 demonstrates that new ways of thinking had been systematically incorporated into official policy.[15] This system remained virtually unchanged from the end of the fourteenth century to the end of the nineteenth century. At the end of the fourteenth century, it was already commonly thought that agricultural development was dependent on the number of inhabitants, demonstrating that this period was a time when agricultural techniques were changing. In view of such facts, it seems that the rapid increase in population of the fifteenth and sixteenth centuries had already begun during the fourteenth century.

Primary sources on land reclamation in the fifteenth century frequently mentioned that the population was increasing, especially in maritime regions. Statements such as "all the plains were cultivated because of flourishing population growth" appeared frequently in these documents. Reclamation was carried out mainly in the three southern provinces of Kyŏngsang, Ch'ungch'ŏng, and Chŏlla. Because of the population increase in the early fifteenth century, living conditions had worsened in these provinces to the point where requests were made to change the items that had been used to pay the tribute tax. These requests were an important sign of economic changes occurring in this period. One example is the reports made by governors of the three provinces in the years 1417, 1426, and 1427. They noted that in former times, there had been much land and few people, so deer and roe had been abundant and their hides and dried meat could be used for special tax payments. But they complained that in the present, the population had increased and so much of the land was cultivated that even soldiers found it difficult to hunt.[16]

Population growth and advances in agricultural techniques brought about many changes in the social structure and the administrative system of the country.[17] Here I will only discuss changes that are directly related to this chapter's topic. First, one important development was the establishment of the custom of equal division of inheritance. In Koryŏ society, only slaves were divided equally among

15. Pak Chin'u, "Chosŏn ch'ogi myŏllijewa ch'ollak chibae ŭi kanghwa" (The local village administrative system in the early Chosŏn period and the strengthening of control over rural villages), *Han'guk saron* 21 (1989).
16. Yi Tae-jin, "Sibosipnyuk segi ŭi chŏp'yŏng. chosŭbji kaegan tonghyang" (Trends in reclamation of lowlands and marshlands in the fifteenth and sixteenth centuries) (1989).
17. I have examined this topic in "Koryŏmal-Chosŏnch'o ŭi sahoe pyŏnhwa" (Social change in the late Koryŏ and early Chosŏn periods), *Chindan hakbo* 55 (1983); reprinted in Yi Tae-jin, *Han'guk sahoesa yŏn'gu*, but more detailed studies must be done on this subject.

children, while the eldest son inherited all the land. However, in the mid-fifteenth century, the *Kyŏngguk taejŏn* (the code of laws of the country) clearly noted that the principle of equal inheritance was being applied to land as well.[18] These changes in the customs of inheritance would have been impossible without changes in the economy and society. Osamu Saito has argued that the custom of equal inheritance, introduced after the emergence of branch families, becomes predominant in times when there is much land reclamation.[19] This interpretation also seems to be the most plausible one for explaining the changes in Korea in the fifteenth and sixteenth centuries.

Another important development was the change in community solidarity through labor mobilization. Until the seventeenth century, the central organization in rural community life in Korea was the *hyangdo*. At the beginning of the tenth century, powerful families in every province began to organize the people within their territory into *hyangdo*, and they were characterized by their large size, having several thousand members. In the mid-twelfth century, however, large-scale *hyangdo* began to disappear, and from the fourteenth century, they changed into small communities of 30 to 100 households. Although the name of the organization remained the same, *hyangdo* changed into smaller organizations at the village level.[20]

Currently, no adequate explanation exists of the relationship between the development of agricultural technology and changes in the organization of the *hyangdo*. However, there is evidence that from the fourteenth century, small-scale *hyangdo* functioned as communal labor organizations for agricultural cultivation.[21] It seems probable that advances in agricultural technology were an important cause of such changes. The new cultivation methods were much more labor-intensive, relying less on temporary mobilization of a large work force and more on long-term employment of small labor groups. Accordingly, there was no need for regional communities that went beyond

---

18. *Kyŏngguk taejŏn*, Vol. 5, hyongjon sach'on.
19. Saito Osamu, "Daikaikon" (1988), pp. 197-200.
20. Yi Haejun, "Maehyang sinang kwa kŭ chudo chibdan ŭi sŏnggyŏk" (Belief in *maehyang* and the nature of its leading organization), *Kim Ch'ŏljun paksa hwagap kinyŏm sahak nonch'ong* (1983). Yi Tae-jin, "Koryŏmal-Chosŏnch'o ŭi sahoe pyŏnhwa," *Han'guk sahoesa yŏn'gu*, p. 115.
21. Yi Tae-jin, "Sipch'il sippal segi hyangdo ŭi kinung punhwa wa ture palsaeng" (The appearance of *ture* and the differentiation of the functions of the *hyangdo* in the seventeenth and eighteenth centuries), *Chindan hakpo* 69 (1989).

the level of the village since such communities were crucial to the supply of agricultural labor.

From the late fourteenth century, the central government's usual practice was to send officials to all rural districts to govern directly the natural villages, which consisted of *hyangdo* organizations. This provincial administration policy was different from the previous system, under which *hyangni* groups from local elite families conducted administrative matters, with the central government restricting itself to regular inspections and supervision. The attempt to directly control *hyangdo* organizations in rural villages had the natural effect of centralizing the political system. As *hyangdo* came to be directly ruled by provincial officials, small- and medium-sized landlord classes challenged these officials' leadership through the introduction of Neo-Confucian practices such as the *hyangyak* (village contract), but they did not fundamentally reject the centralized ruling structure itself.

In the fifteenth century, the main objectives of central government policy were to reform the tax system in order to increase tax revenue while reducing the tax burden on farmers[22] and to increase the number of men for military service on the basis of the peasant-soldier system (*pyŏngnong ilch'i*).[23] It was the epochal changes in the economy and population that made these developments possible. As long as the rate of settlement within the agricultural society increased, these policies could be realized only through the pursuit of intensive land cultivation. It was no coincidence that the "neighborhood protection" system (*inbŏbŏp*) and the "five-family supervision" system (*ogat'ongbŏp*) were actively promoted as a response to the rural settlement that occurred as a result of state policies in the fifteenth century.

22. A new tax system was initiated in 1427 and fully implemented in 1444. It abolished the existing system which had three different levels of taxation and replaced it with one with five levels. It was also characterized by a nine-level system for determining the yearly tax burden according to the quality of the harvest. Kim T'aeyŏng, *Chosŏn chŏn'gi t'oji chedosa yŏn'gu*, pp. 265–343.
23. This term refers to a military system that was similar to the *fu-ping* system of T'ang China in which peasants rotated on and off duty as soldiers. In 1477, the standing military force of the Chosŏn dynasty was as follows: 134,973 regular soldiers and 332,746 reserve forces. While regular troops continued to receive military training for fixed periods of time, reserve forces were responsible for supporting the military and were mobilized only in times of emergency. Min Hyŏn'gu, *Chosŏn ch'ogi ŭi kunsa chedo wa chŏngch'i* (Politics and the military system in the early Chosŏn period) (Seoul: Han'guk yŏn'guwŏn, 1983), p. 89.

## INFLUENCE ON COMMERCIAL DEVELOPMENT

The development of the agricultural economy in the fourteenth and fifteenth centuries had an effect on commerce in Korea in both quantitative and qualitative terms. Changes in commerce were notable in the three southern provinces that were the most advanced agriculturally at the end of the fifteenth century. Markets appeared in various locations within a *kun* or *hyŏn* where people gathered to buy and sell merchandise. Markets started to spread to other provinces and became established throughout most of the country by the first half of the sixteenth century. To prevent an outflow of rural labor because of these developments, markets operated according to a fixed schedule. The traditional form of the rural market in Korea —the "five-day market"—began appearing at this time, a development rooted in agricultural advances at the end of the fifteenth century.[24]

It should be emphasized that while agriculture was making tremendous advances in the fourteenth and fifteenth centuries, commerce was actually in a period of decline. Although there has been no explanation of this fact until now, the concept of the "reversal effect," as mentioned above, seems to provide the most plausible explanation for the pattern of economic development in this period.

Before the period of population growth and reclamation of the lowlands, local markets had existed on the provincial and district levels. In the twelfth century, Hsu Ching, an envoy from Song China, reported the following about the Koryŏ dynasty's domestic trade: "The local products of every district are brought to the district office; the merchants, however, do not go far away, but on the scheduled day, they go to the market in the main town of the district and exchange their merchandise for other goods they need."[25] Since provincial administration during the Koryŏ dynasty was, as mentioned above, the communal responsibility of *hyangni* officials, markets were established around areas where district offices were located. As a result, there was only one market in each district in that period; by contrast, several markets could be found in each district in Korea after the late fifteenth century.

During the fourteenth and fifteenth centuries, however, there were no traces of local markets, not even one market per district. In the

---

24. Yi Tae-jin, *Han'guk sahoesa yŏn'gu*, p. 277, and Yi Kyŏngsik, "Sipnyuk segi changsi ŭi sŏngnip kwa kŭ kiban" (The establishment of markets in the sixteenth century and their foundation), *Han'guksa yŏn'gu* 57 (1987).

25. *Koryŏ togyŏng*, Vol. 19, minsŏ.

thirteenth century, Koryŏ was thrown into chaos because of civil war and foreign invasion. The disappearance of local markets can naturally be seen as a result of this turmoil. But even in the fifteenth century, when the country had nearly recovered from these problems, the market system did not reemerge. Until the reappearance of markets in southern regions at the end of the fifteenth century, markets had only existed in a few cities such as Kyŏngju, Chŏnju, and Naju or in a few counties in each province.[26] Commerce in other areas was conducted by traveling merchants known as "land traders," "inland water traders," and "maritime traders."[27] The transactions of these merchants, who were similar to caravan traders, were subject to taxation by the central government, but they do not seem to have formed a statistically important class.

The local markets that had existed during the twelfth and thirteenth centuries clearly disappeared during the fourteenth and fifteenth centuries. Merchants who traveled between regions along land and water routes came to handle the exchange of necessary goods. These developments are difficult to explain without assuming a large-scale qualitative transformation of the economic foundation of Korean society. Since it has been confirmed that such a transformation did take place in the agricultural economy of this period, it is logical to search for the causes of commercial change in the transformation of agriculture.

The continued existence of local markets at the county level during the twelfth and thirteenth centuries shows that agriculture in that period had not entirely abandoned the practice of fallow farming. Therefore, the nature of commerce in this period must be understood in the context of fallow farming. A new interpretation of medieval history recently put forth by Japanese scholars is significant for the contribution it has made to the understanding of such phenomena. To borrow from the succinct overview of Saito Osamu, the new interpretation may be summarized as follows.[28] Land already under cultivation was located in valleys between the mountains, small basins, or alluvial fans. There were many areas where cultivation would be abandoned once every few years because of the unstable conditions of the land. Also, rice farming on wet fields was so unstable that the proportion of dry fields was high. As a result, migrancy was high

26. Yi Kyŏngsik, ibid., p. 46.
27. Yi Tae-jin, "Koryŏ hugi" (1988).
28. Saito Osamu, "Daikaikon" (1988), p. 177.

among the rural population, leading to an unprecedented expansion of activities beyond agriculture, such as participating in markets. Accordingly, the percentage of people engaged in non-agricultural activities such as crafts, distribution, and transportation was extremely high, and the use of money expanded to a great degree.

According to this interpretation, Japanese agriculture in the medieval period was fundamentally very similar to Korean agriculture during the Koryŏ period. Since both societies were based on the same type of agriculture, it would not be an unreasonable distortion of history to utilize recent findings on Japanese commerce to analyze commerce in Korea during the Koryŏ dynasty. In the history of money in Korea, metal currency was issued several times between the tenth and twelfth centuries. In the fourteenth and fifteenth centuries, however, the use of metal currency declined, and there was a preference for rice and cloth as means of exchange. In order to provide a more plausible explanation of such changes, I have elsewhere examined them within the context of the international economy of the time, when silver from China was continuously exported to eastern Islamic regions.[29] However, I believe that a more basic explanation can be made by examining these phenomena as part of the "reversal effect" which was produced by the qualitative transformation of the agricultural economy.

Although historical data is insufficient to determine what percentage of the population artisans and merchants constituted in Koryŏ society, we do know that artisans lived in places called *so*, special administrative areas, which were separate from farmers' residences. Significantly, these areas decreased sharply in number during the fifteenth century. The distinction between artisans and farmers disappeared as many artisans turned to farming due to the epochal developments in agriculture.

A typical example of this phenomenon was the effort of the central government in the fifteenth century to convert "migrants," such as *chaein* and *hwach'ŏk*, into settled farmers. The *chaein* were a class of people who made their living by slaughtering animals or selling products made from animal skins; they were thought to have descended from Tartars who came to Korea during the Koryŏ period. The *hwach'ŏk* were a group of people who made a living by selling products made of dried willow twigs. Both of these groups lived in

---

29. Yi Tae-jin, Han'guk Sahoesa yŏn'gu (1986).

separate communities until the beginning of the fifteenth century and did not easily assimilate into agrarian society. As part of its policy to promote agriculture, the central government did not permit plow oxen to be sold to these people and called them *paekjong* because they were exempted from military service, although their social status was the same as that of farmers. The government attempted to integrate *paekjong* into farming communities by offering them land and allowing intermarriage with farmers. Although these groups did not easily assimilate despite such measures, it was evident that the government's intention was to transform the migrants into settled farmers.[30]

Local markets disappeared in the fourteenth and fifteenth centuries because of the tremendous development in agricultural technology, which resulted in the absorption of all available labor in agriculture. Of course, merchants and artisan groups did not entirely disappear. But markets did disappear because of the relative decline in their numbers, while itinerant merchants came to handle the exchange of necessary products. Such changes were part of the temporary "reversal effect" that arose in the context of large-scale social change and provided the internal foundation for future development.

The improvement of agricultural techniques in the fifteenth century brought about both a change in rural economic conditions and a higher rate of settlement in rural society. Through an increase in productivity, even common farmers were able to produce a surplus that they could sell on the market. As rural society changed, a new form of local market emerged in the most agriculturally developed regions of the country at the end of the fifteenth century. The emergence of these markets was based on changes in the condition of the small-farmer class. Leaving aside the issue of the production of handicraft products, it seems clear that the increase of wet fields through the development of the lowlands enabled increased production of rice, the most marketable commodity. This one fact in itself demonstrates that market conditions improved tremendously in comparison to the previous era.

With the development of new markets beginning around the end of the fifteenth century, cotton emerged as a new product that was widely cultivated by farmers. Introduced to Korea in the fourteenth

---

30. Han Ugŭn, et al., *Yŏgju Kyŏngguk taejŏn chusokp'yŏn* (Han'guk chŏngsin munhwa yŏn'guwŏn, 1986), pp. 694–95. See also Kang Man-gil, "Sŏnch'o paekjong ko," *Sahak yŏn'gu* 18 (1964).

century, the cotton plant was successfully cultivated in southern regions during the early fifteenth century and then spread to other regions later in the same century. The increase of cotton production was an important factor in the development of markets. Cotton was a revolutionary product due to its many uses, and demand was tremendous not only in the domestic market but also in international trade, especially in trade with Japan. Cotton cloth was such a marketable product that it even replaced money as currency in the sixteenth century.[31] Cotton cultivation spread to dry highland areas because highland areas were available for new uses after rice-cultivation moved to the lowlands. Even after the successive invasions of the Japanese and the Jurchen at the end of the sixteenth century and beginning of the seventeenth century, Korean agriculture was able to recover almost fully within half a century. It was also able to achieve more development through the increase of cotton acreage in the highlands and the spread of rice transplantation methods.

CONCLUSION

Most agrarian societies in the world have gone through a stage of history when farmland moved from the highlands to the lowlands; only the timing differed according to the country and natural and social conditions in each region. I have argued that this process occurred in Korea during the fifteenth and sixteenth centuries.

The movement to the lowlands occurred as follows: seashore and flatland areas along rivers were the initial targets of settlement; then, in the sixteenth century, marshland areas began to be developed. The development of marshlands, which continues to this day, largely depended upon the technological progress of society. Generally, farmland reclaimed from lowlands and marshlands were used for wet-field rice cultivation. It was from this time that rice cultivation began to be established as the basis of Korean agriculture.

In order to understand the development of Korean culture, it is necessary to examine the relation between these economic changes and Neo-Confucianism. Although I am not able to treat this phenomenon in detail here, the fact that the introduction of Neo-Confucianism coincided with the period of agricultural change is clear

31. Yi Tae-jin, "Koryŏ hugi" (1988).

evidence of their connection. Neo-Confucianism was first introduced in the fourteenth century when cultivation began to move to the lowlands, and both experienced tremendous growth in the fifteenth and sixteenth centuries.

Writing this chapter has made me realize that it is absolutely necessary to conduct comparative research on rice-cultivating societies to understand the causes of the movement of rice cultivation to the lowlands and its social and economic impact. Because of time constraints, I was only able to examine recent studies on Japanese history. I believe that broadening the range of comparison will provide a more comprehensive understanding of this phenomenon. Such research would help not only to determine the general characteristics of rice-producing societies but also to understand the unique aspects of each society.

Developments in Korean agriculture in the fifteenth and sixteenth centuries provide evidence for the close relationship between population growth and the development of rice-paddy cultivation. There were also changes in the social structure as agriculture came to be more reliant on the intensive use of labor. These socioeconomic changes stimulated the later development of commerce through the establishment of local markets, and this commerce eventually developed into an active trade with countries such as China and Japan. Existing within the same trading sphere, both countries underwent similar economic changes, though in different time periods. Therefore, it can be said that it was the epochal developments in rice-paddy cultivation that made possible the economic prosperity that East Asia enjoyed from the sixteenth to eighteenth centuries.

*translated by Edward Park*

## Figure 1

ESTIMATED POPULATION DURING THE CHOSŎN PERIOD AND TRENDS IN THE YEARLY RATE OF POPULATION GROWTH

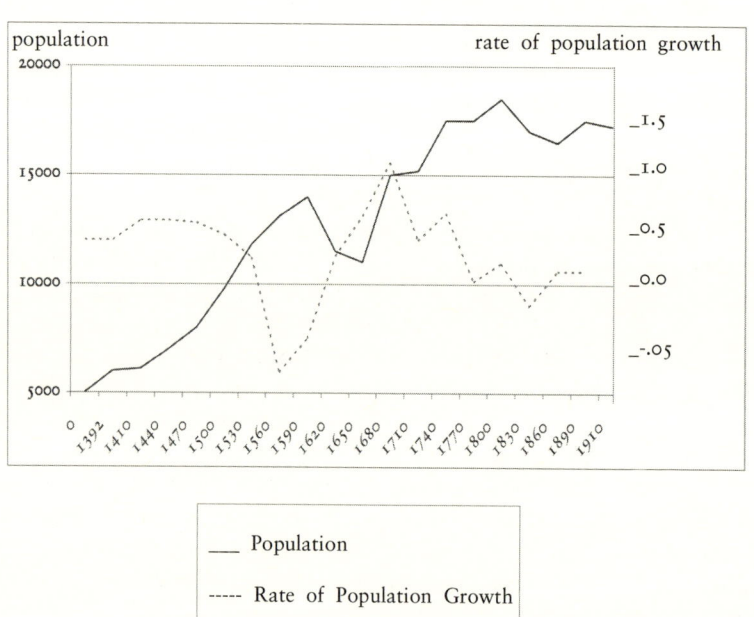

NOTES: The line for population simply connects the points for years in which the population is known.

The rate of population growth is calculated based on the difference between two adjacent points on the graph (usually an interval of thirty years).

SOURCE: Kwŏn T'aehwan and Sin Yongha, "Chosŏn wangjo sidae ingu ch'ujŏng e kwanhan ilsilon" (An attempt at population estimates for the Chosŏn Dynasty period), *Tonga munhwa* 14 (1997).

CHAPTER 4

# The Influence of Neo-Confucianism on Population Growth in Fourteenth- to Sixteenth-Century Korea

HISTORICAL DEMOGRAPHY IS AN underdeveloped field of East Asian historiography. Compared to work being done with European population records, population research in Korea and in East Asia in general still remains at an elementary level in terms of methodology or results. Population studies on Europe have made contributions to the fields of social, economic, and even cultural history. East Asian historians need to acquire more skills in order to fully utilize the methods of historical demography. Researchers should be trained in diverse methods such as statistics and must revise their selection of research topics and materials.

If population studies on East Asia are to reach the level of those on Europe, one of the first tasks of research should be to examine the relationship between population and wet-field farming—an important foundation of the rural economy. I believe the spread of wet-field farming was largely responsible for the population increase in East Asian societies. Wet-field cultivation in Korea, China, and Japan was characterized by its high intensity. The highly intensive nature of Northeast Asian farming is especially apparent when compared to that of Southeast Asia, even if differences in climate and geographical makeup are taken into account. Long-term intensive cultivation was possible in the temperate climate of Northeast Asia due to a large labor force. Indeed, a sizable population increase was a prerequisite for the extensive development of wet-field cultivation.

Westerners who visited these countries in the nineteenth century were struck by the preference for wet-field cultivation and the high population density. However, scholars have not examined the factors creating these socioeconomic conditions and their historical development deeply enough. In my view, the peculiar socioeconomic conditions of East Asia originated not in ancient times but relatively recently, during the Middle Ages. Even though the timing of the development of these conditions differed in each of the three countries, it has been confirmed that in all three, this development coincided with a high interest among the people in Neo-Confucianism. The period of these socioeconomic changes corresponds to the time after the establishment of the Song dynasty (960–1279) in China; in Korea, to that of Chosŏn dynasty (1392–1910); and in Japan, to the reign of the Tokugawa shogunate (1603–1868). Neo-Confucianism emphasized the precept that "Food is the heaven of the People." Thus, it was also emphasized that the most important goal of Neo-Confucianism, the realization of a benevolent administration, should come first of all from solid agrarian rule. In the context of these aspects of Neo-Confucian ideology, the simultaneous rise of Neo-Confucianism and wet-field cultivation cannot be viewed as a mere coincidence. The objective of this chapter is to demonstrate the relationship of these twin developments by examining known facts and details of Korean history.

KOREAN POPULATION GROWTH TRENDS FROM THE FOURTEENTH TO SIXTEENTH CENTURIES

Among extant Korean population records, there are fairly detailed accounts dating from 1392. The *Sillok* (Veritable Records) were the official annals of each successive king of the Chosŏn dynasty. The records taken as a whole represent a treasure of statistical records and other descriptive materials. Although annals predating the Chosŏn dynasty existed, they are incomplete or lost. The only surviving records are those that were republished in a later historical period in a *chŏngsa* (official history) format. There are almost no records relevant to population in these republished abridged historical records. The only record of Korea's population before 1392 comes from a Chinese document; specifically, an entry from the *Songshi* (History of the Song Dynasty) on the Koryŏ dynasty which states that "the population of 2,100,000 men and women is composed of the military, civil, and religious people." However, relations between the Song and Koryŏ dynasties began to deteriorate as the Khitan moved southward and eventually were severed in 1130. The population record in the *Songshi* is based on material acquired before the two nations severed relations and is generally presumed to date from before the early twelfth century.

During pre-modern times, each East Asian country already had a tradition of conducting a nationwide census to count households, but these records did not necessarily reflect actual population figures. In general, such records were used to determine the available labor force that could be utilized to carry out the monarch's policies. Accordingly, following the precedent of those who were excluded from the registers for old age and infirmity and designated as surplus population, there were many who would purposely omit themselves from the records. The figure of 2.1 million taken from the *Songshi* should be adjusted after taking into account such omissions. However, if the overall recorded population is small, the number of omissions would also be small. If the official population size is put at around 2.1 million, then Korea was still at middle-age levels with a population-rate increase of less than 0.1 percent.[1]

Professors Kwŏn T'aehwan and Shin Yong-ha (Sin Yongha) have done an important study on Korean population after 1392 that fully utilizes two sources to estimate the actual population. One source was a national survey of households at the district level, which was conducted regularly with results reported to the king. A Chosŏn dynasty mandate in effect from 1392 to 1896 decreed that these surveys were to be updated every three years. Although this mandate was not faithfully followed, the household census was frequently taken. These records are limited since the figures for households and individuals did not account for groups of people who were omitted for

---

1. Karl Sax, *The Population Explosion*, Headline Series, no. 120 (New York: Foreign Policy Association, 1956), pp. 12–13. Average worldwide population growth rate before the beginning of the period was less than 0.1 percent; during 1650-1850, 0.4 percent; during 1850-1900, 0.7 percent; during 1900-1950, 0.90 percent; and in 1953, 1.33 percent—a steady increase. Since 1650, Europe's population has increased six-fold and that of Asia five-fold. England, only slightly larger geographically than Korea, had a population of 3,000,000 in 1541. For a long time, the population in England remained at these levels following a steady increase of 0.1 percent, until this steady rate was disrupted. Using these figures, it is plausible that the population of Korea at the beginning of the twelfth century came as close as 2,100,000. Although the percentage of omissions once figured at 30 percent during the Chosŏn dynasty, it is unlikely that the recorded percentages strayed much above 10 percent during this era.

various reasons; thus, they did not reflect the actual number of households and population.

The second source that Kwŏn and Shin used was local census data taken by provincial officials and reported to the central government during times of economic depression to determine how much aid their subjects would require. Kwŏn and Shin examined these local records and extracted what they determined were the rare, accurate portions of the household registers. They then utilized both these records and the household census data to reconstruct a model of the entire population and achieved significant results. After observing that the figures derived from the local census were much higher than those recorded in the national household census, they correlated the data from the national census with the local census records using demographic methods. In this way, they found a way to estimate the actual number of households in a given time period. The conclusions of their research are given in Figure 1. One of the important conclusions is that the rate of population increase from 1392 to 1440 is calculated to be 0.40 percent (assuming that the population in 1392 was 5.5 million), while the rate of increase in the period from 1441 to 1519 is 0.56 percent. If estimates are extrapolated from these rates, the population of Korea stood at 10 million in 1511 and rose to 14 million by 1591.[2]

Although Kwŏn and Shin's estimates may not be exactly precise, I consider their research to be the most credible calculations on Korean population changes after the fifteenth century, and there are many points of agreement between their work and the arguments I will develop in this chapter. Therefore, I have utilized their findings in this chapter.

Earlier, I mentioned that the figure of 2.1 million underestimated the population of Korea before the beginning of the twelfth century. According to Kwŏn and Shin, since the population reached 5.5 million in 1392, it achieved this rapid increase in less than two centuries. These figures confirm that the large rise in the population growth rate from 0.10% to 0.40% was already occurring between the twelfth and fourteenth centuries. If this is true, then research on Korea's "population explosion" done by Karl Sax should begin with population trends of the thirteenth and fourteenth centuries.

2. According to this research, the "population explosion" phenomenon in Korea (based on the 0.4 percent or above derived from Karl Sax's statistical calculations) had already begun in the fifteenth century, fully one and a half centuries before 1650, the date Karl Sax cites as a standard date.

The fourteenth century was a period of significant change in Korean history. During this century, the existing political system of the Koryŏ dynasty became thoroughly destabilized, and the new scholar-officials (*sinhŭng sadaebu*) became the leading political force as Neo-Confucianism gained more acceptance as the new political ideology. These momentous changes were the historical backdrop to the establishment of the Chosŏn dynasty in 1392. It is difficult, though, to determine the population trends for that time period because of the lack of direct sources with population figures. Searching for a means to overcome this difficulty, I have utilized rather unorthodox materials, namely tomb inscriptions. During the four centuries of the Koryŏ dynasty, population-related dates were recorded on tombs, and by organizing this information with statistical methods, I have obtained the following results.[3]

Koryŏ tomb inscriptions recorded information about high government officials, their wives, and monks who reached high social positions. At present, scholars have found 266 surviving inscriptions. However, there were ten instances in which the people appearing on different tomb inscriptions were husband and wife so that in actuality, the total is only 256 subjects. The following general points have been observed from an analysis of these 256:

(1) The principle of monogamy was strictly followed and the death of one spouse and later remarriage by the survivor was duly noted on the inscriptions. There were fifty confirmed remarriages.

(2) Not only were the tomb inhabitants in high government positions, but many of them were long-lived as well. Two hundred and twenty-three cases had accurate birth and death data; among these, the average life span was 64.7 years, and 65.3 percent of these people lived past the age of sixty. It could be said that, for most of those born into aristocratic families, long life span was a factor that helped them secure and maintain their high government positions. While these statistics may be of little value in discussing the average life span of people of the time, they are still very useful in understanding the births and deaths of the subjects' children.

(3) The earliest recorded birth year among the subjects was 944, and the latest recorded death was 1382. When these data were

---

3. See Yi Tae-jin (Yi T'aejin), "Koryŏ hugi ŭi ingu chŭngga yoin saengsŏng kwa hyang- yak ŭisul paldal" (The formation of primary factors for the population increase in the late Koryŏ and the development of indigenous medical techniques), *Han'guk saron* 19 (1988).

arranged chronologically, there was an imbalance in its distribution. Looking at the various birth years, there were 174 births that were fairly evenly distributed in the period from 944 to 1179; however, after 1179, there was a nearly thirty-year gap until the next recorded birth in 1208. This lacuna in the data was the consequence of an uprising of military officers in 1170. These officers, who revolted against the tyranny of the civil ministry, expelled most of the civil officials and held control of the government for nearly eighty years, wreaking havoc on the government bureaucracy and political affairs. Many of the subjects who were born after 1208 reached high positions either after the military officers had stabilized their political power or after royal power was reestablished in 1270.

What caught my attention in the Koryŏ tomb inscriptions was the information detailing the birth and death years of children. In the Chosŏn period, after the dynastic change of 1392, there are many more surviving tombs. However, while the epitaphs on these later tombs still contain information on children, the ones mentioned are usually those who were still alive at the time of the subject's death, and, as general rule, this information is only briefly stated at the end of the epitaphs. In contrast, not only did the Koryŏ tombs include this information in the beginning or the middle of the epitaphs, they also listed those children who had died according to birth order and recorded the circumstances concerning their deaths. While we can conjecture that such inscription methods, different from that of later generations, were closely related to other social and cultural factors, I am unable to address such points in this chapter. Here, my focus is on using these inscriptions as materials that enable an examination of children's birth-death relationships. The following describes the principles of my analysis and the general patterns in the data on children's births and deaths.

(4) Among the 256 subjects, there were 575 male and 445 female births. Out of the 1,020 total births, forty-four males and thirty-six females died in early childhood. Whenever there was any doubt as to whether a recorded death had been *soa samang* (an early-childhood death), I omitted the figure. *Soa samang* is distinguished from *sinsaenga samang* (death within one month of birth) and *yŏnga samang* (death within one year of birth). I arrived at the total of eighty deaths by excluding children who died within one year of their birth. This figure represents only the deaths of children who were at least two years old and who are usually classified as *soa samang*.

(5) If the eighty early-childhood deaths are looked at chronologically, the far majority occur before the Military Coup of 1170. Seventy deaths (thirty-seven males, thirty-three females) are confirmed to have occurred before the coup, and only ten after. The seventy deaths in the earlier period were from thirty-eight different families out of a total of 158 parents (husbands and wives). The ten deaths in the later period were in three families out of a total of eighty-two registered families.

(6) Judging by the data in (5), it seems that the degree of record-keeping regarding child mortality differed from household to household. In particular, the number of children's deaths recorded in the later period decreased to such a degree as to raise doubt regarding the reality of the decrease. However, even if the records did not fully reflect reality, they can be interpreted as evidence showing that people no longer lived in fear of child mortality and therefore felt less necessity to record the deaths that did occur.

(7) The information analyzed in this section has similar problems to that in (6), because it contains unexplained disparities. However, there is a reason for the significant difference in the number of children's deaths between the earlier and the later periods, as will be explained. Therefore, it would be appropriate to use the given information. However, since the Military Coup of 1170 is the point at which the differences began to emerge, it is useful to designate it as the dividing line between the two periods. Table 1 notes the ratio of early-childhood deaths and the average number of children in both the early and late Koryŏ periods. Of the 256 cases, those considered "father-centered families" do not include Buddhist monks, and those considered "mother-centered families" also exclude Buddhist monks, but do include mothers who had remarried.

In Table 1, the figures in row seven are the most significant. According to my calculations, the average number of children born to a family that survived to infancy was 3.08 (male: 1.81, female: 1.27) in the early-Koryŏ period and 3.50 (male: 1.86, female: 1.64) in the late-Koryŏ period. While no studies have been done on the natural fertility of women in the Koryŏ period, a very general estimate of the female fertility rate can be made by looking at the number of children in mother-centered households (row 5). Taking the mean of the averages from the two periods (3.46 and 3.59), we arrive at a figure of 3.53 births per couple. As mentioned before, these figures do not include children under the age of two. In other words, none of the "young baby" (*yŏng'a*, infants under one year of age) deaths are taken into

74  Chapter Four

account in this average of 3.53 children. Studies of European population history generally estimate that the rate of "young baby" deaths before the eighteenth century was about twenty-five percent.[4] If one assumes that the rate was similar in Korea during the Koryŏ period, then the natural birth rate of women in Korea for this period can be estimated to be 4.41 children (3.53x 125/100). This estimate is similar to the average birth rate of four to five children found for French married women from the fifteenth to seventeenth centuries.[5] While the figures from the present study are several decades earlier than those of the French study, the estimate seems reasonable since the Korean data were gathered from families with aristocratic backgrounds. If this estimate is accepted as valid, then the child mortality rate can be calculated to be 1.33 for the early Koryŏ period and 0.91 for the late-Koryŏ period.

According to the data, there was a high percentage of infants among families' offspring in the early-Koryŏ period. In the late-Koryŏ period, there were only three infants among the recorded living offspring, while in the early period there were eighty-two infants (47 male; 35 female) among living children, which would suggest a higher rate of infant mortality. Analyses of the data indicate that the population during the early period increased annually on average by less than 0.1 percent, still in the "ancient or middle ages mode."[6] But the situation changed in the late period. Even though the average number of children increased by only 0.42 children (male: 0.05, female: 0.37), infant mortality was decreasing.

The disparity in population trends between the early- and late-Koryŏ periods can also be demonstrated in the average life span of the kings. From 918 to 1392, the average life span of the thirty-two Koryŏ kings was 43.93 years.[7] Considering that the quality of food and medical benefits enjoyed by the kings was the best in the country, their average life span is surprisingly low. However, if the Koryŏ period is again divided at the year 1170 into early and late periods, one will find a trend similar to that of the infant-child mortality ratio. The average life span of the eighteen kings during the early-Koryŏ period was 39.39 years, while that of the fourteen kings during the late-Koryŏ period jumped to 47.79 years. The trends in longevity

4. Jean Carpentier et al., *P'ŭrangsŏin ŭi yŏksa* (History of France), trans. by Chu Myŏngch'ŏl (Seoul: Sonamu, 1991), p. 166.
5. Ibid.
6. See note 1.
7. Yi Tae-jin, "Koryŏ hugi" (1988), p. 219.

continued even after the dynastic change in 1392, and the six Chosŏn kings of the early fifteenth century lived for an average of 55.3 years (excluding one who was assassinated). Even if one takes into account the fact that population data for the late-Koryŏ period is available only for royalty and the aristocracy, it is still apparent that changes were taking place. Infant and early-childhood mortality rates were decreasing, and the average life span increasing. These changes are indeed the most important conditions for population increase.

There is other evidence for a change in population in the late Koryŏ period. The estimated population at 5.5 million people at the founding of the Chosŏn dynasty in 1392 is in itself strong indication of change. Additional evidence is provided by the fact that the average number of children per family around that time more closely approximates the average number of children recorded during the late-Koryŏ period than the early period. Because of the continuing influence of Confucianism, there are many surviving *chokpo* (clan genealogies). The earliest known genealogy is that of the Andong Kwŏn clan. The compilation of this genealogy began during the mid-fifteenth century and was completed in 1476.[8] Using the information on the families recorded in this genealogy, it is possible to obtain the average number of children per family during this period. This early genealogy was not yet influenced by Confucian concepts of clan genealogy; instead, it was unique in following the traditional bilineal procedure and recorded relatives from the maternal as well as the paternal side. The genealogy begins with records of those still living during the tenth century and continues to the late-Koryŏ period. However, the names of only a small number of people from one side in each generation were recorded. From the original ancestor to the twelfth generation, the number of recorded descendants increases with every generation. My research focuses on the thirteenth-to-seventeenth generation descendants, who are assumed to have lived in the fourteenth and fifteenth centuries. While this type of genealogy extends to twentieth-generation descendants—since at the time of its compilation many descendants of the eighteenth and later generations were still alive and young enough to bear children—they have been excluded

---

8. The preface of the clan genealogy states that although Kwŏn Che (1387–1445) started collecting materials for the genealogy, it was Kwŏn Ram (1416–1465) who began the compilation, and maternal descendants such as Sŏ Kŏchŏng added materials regarding the maternal lineage. His work was continued and finished in 1476. See Professor Noh Myŏngho's commentary on the Andong Kwŏn's central-clan association's reissued genealogy (Andong Kwŏn ssi chungang chongch'inhoe, 1992).

from this analysis. The clan genealogy recorded a descendant's lineage and government post but did not state his or her years of birth or death. Only the number of descendants for each generation can be known for this period. Table 2 displays the distribution of those with the surname of Kwŏn.

Of the seventeen descendants of the thirteenth generation, there are two, Kwŏn Pu (1262–1346) and Kwŏn Han'gong (?–1349), whose year of death are given. Judging from their years of death, we can assume that descendants of both the thirteenth and fourteenth generations lived during the fourteenth century. It is even possible that some of the fifteenth-generation descendants lived during the fourteenth century. Though there is no information on dates of birth and death, the average number of children of thirteenth-, fourteenth-, and fifteenth-generation descendants was 3.11, 2.75, 3.41, respectively. Of course, these averages do not include those children who died in infancy. Compared to the Koryŏ-period tomb inscription data, these averages are generally higher than the early-Koryŏ period average of 3.08 and lower than the average of 3.50 for the late-Koryŏ period. However, the average of 2.75 children in the fourteenth generation is lower than the average of the early-Koryŏ period and does not follow the general trend of this period. However, it is possible that the number of children born to this particular generation was exceptionally low for this clan. The incidence of premature deaths (2.75) does not seem to be very low compared to the average for the early-Koryŏ period (3.08) as the probability of premature death was higher in the earlier period since many of the dead were infants. In my opinion, it is a matter of great significance that the fifteenth-, sixteenth-, and seventeenth-generation descendants—those who lived in the fifteenth century—had averages of 3.41, 3.73, and 3.64 children per family, respectively. These numbers strongly indicate that during the fifteenth century, at the beginning of the Chosŏn dynasty, the average number of children per family was gradually increasing, surpassing the average of the late-Koryŏ period.

As mentioned earlier, the Andong Kwŏn genealogy followed a bilineal approach and recorded both paternal and maternal descendants. The average number of recorded descendants with different surnames, which was determined according to the criteria used above, is given in Table 3.

In general, the averages of the number of children that appear in this table are somewhat lower than the averages of those bearing the Kwŏn surname. However, it is important to keep in mind that the data in this Table are less accurate than that concerning the Kwŏns. The reason for the discrepancy is that it was much more difficult to collect information on the more numerous maternal descendants than on descendants bearing the Kwŏn surname. Therefore, the compilation was less thorough and less complete from the beginning. In fact, the compilation of information on these descendants began later than that of descendants with the Kwŏn surname. This difference in the timing of compilation is apparent in the Table, which only gives information concerning six couples in the thirteenth generation. Information on maternal descendants became relatively more thorough and complete in the generations closest to those actually compiling the genealogy. Since it was compiled by descendants of the eighteenth and nineteenth generations such as Sŏ Kŏjŏng, Pak Wŏnch'ang, Ch'oe Yongwŏn, and Yun Ho, it is not a coincidence that the average number of children for the seventeenth generation (3.65) is the highest and most accurate. Since the averages for the sixteenth and seventeenth generations are similar to those of the Kwŏn-surname descendants, we can reasonably assume that these averages also reflect general tendencies of the aristocracy in the fifteenth century.

An analysis of Koryŏ tomb inscriptions and the Andong Kwŏn genealogy shows that the average number of children per family in the fourteenth and fifteenth centuries, which had always been below 3.05 children, increased to an average of over 3.50 children. Even though these data pertain only to the ruling class, they provide supporting evidence of a population increase from just over 2.1 million at the beginning of the twelfth century to 5.5 million near the end of the fourteenth century.

ADVANCES IN MEDICINE AND POPULATION GROWTH FACTORS

The latter half of the twelfth century was a turbulent period in Korean society both internally and externally. Internally, the military established its own apparatus after it overthrew the civil government, leading to a radical political change. Externally, the Mongols invaded, forcing the government to move the capital to a remote island where it fought the invaders for several decades. After the fighting ceased in 1259, the Mongols imposed their own government and economic systems on Korea, which made it difficult for Koryŏ society to regain peace. Until 1350, Koryŏ was powerless to resist Mongol interference. However, at this time, Koryŏ began to suffer repeated incursions by wako (Japanese pirates) from the south and two attacks by Red Turbans (*Honggŏnjok*) from the north. In these trying circumstances, it would be difficult to expect social developments in Koryŏ such as population increase. And yet, in spite of these difficulties, there was progress.

While the late-Koryŏ period witnessed great political turmoil both internally and externally, it was also a time of significant development in medical techniques. Korean medicine began to rely less upon Chinese medical practices and began to develop its own native cures by utilizing locally available ingredients—the so-called *hyangyak ŭisul* (native Korean prescriptions).[9] The decisive turning point for this development was the compilation of *Hyangyak kugŭpbang* (First-aid Prescriptions Using Native Ingredients) in 1243. In the following century, there was little change due to internal and external turmoil until the latter half of the fourteenth century. Other new texts began to appear, culminating in the compilation of the eighty-five volumes of the *Hyangyak chipsŏngbang* (Compilation of Native Korean Prescriptions). It is no coincidence that these medical developments occurred during the same period when the average number of children and the average life span for adults was increasing.

As with the increase in the average number of children and adults, sources on medical developments focus on noble families. Therefore, it cannot be automatically assumed that the factors behind the population increase applied throughout the entire country. However, since natural herbs were readily available to all and if medical remedies and techniques were widespread, it is more likely that the situation of commoners was similar to that of the nobility. Since these medical practices were not complicated, many commoners would have been able to benefit directly from such developments.

The first Korean medical text, *Hyangyak kugŭpbang*, devoted separate chapters to obstetrics and pediatrics and showed great interest in the diseases of newborn infants and young children. The chapter on obstetrics described twenty-one symptoms and cures; the one on pediatrics, sixteen. Because this book was meant to teach first-aid, it did not describe many symptoms or cures. However, the fact that it treated obstetrics and pediatrics separately is very important in the context of the history of population. Newer and varied texts in the same vein began to appear later, and the number of treatable symptoms and cures increased. In the latter half of the fourteenth century,

9. Yi Tae-jin, "Koryŏ hugi" (1988), p. 219.

the text *Hyangyak kugŭpbang*, which represents the greatest achievement among medical encyclopedias, included 957 symptoms, 17,706 remedies, and 1,476 acupuncture methods. In addition, there were 184 symptoms for obstetrics and 114 for pediatrics. While the eight-five volumes of this compilation included some medical theory and symptoms derived from Chinese texts, the publishers generally attached great importance to treatment by indigenous natural herbs.

The proliferation of Korean medicine texts during the late-Koryŏ period was not accidental but was the result of continual efforts to cure illnesses. The rulers and the literati of the early-Koryŏ period were profoundly aware that by comparison, their medical skills lagged behind those of the Chinese. They knew that during the Taiping period (976–983) of the Song dynasty, the Chinese emperor ordered the compilation of a book entitled *Taiping shenghuifang* (Remedies Given by the Grace of Heaven), which clearly revealed the superiority of Chinese medical skills. This compilation, spanning one hundred volumes, summarized all known medical knowledge into a new organizational system, an epoch-making event in Chinese medical history. This text combined earlier works relating to pediatric illness such as *Bingyuan houlun* (Discussions on Examinatoin of the Nature of Disease), *Xiaopinfang* (Small Book of Prescriptions), and *Qianjinfang* (Thousand Gold Prescriptions), which contributed to the development of pediatrics as a separate medical discipline. Though Koryŏ intellectuals showed great interest in this medical text, they could not utilize this knowledge fully because they were unable to obtain most of the materials described in it. If they wished to practice the described techniques, they would have had to import Chinese materials. However, not only was it difficult to obtain all of the necessary materials, it was also prohibitively expensive to do so, and thus their usefulness was limited. The development of medical techniques utilizing local herbs was the result of efforts to overcome these limitations.

While Koryŏ medical scholars were greatly interested in the Chinese medical text *Taiping shenghuifang*, they also had their own medical techniques, which they fully utilized. In addition to traditional folk cures, they were able to utilize Buddhist medical skills, as well as Chinese medical techniques from before the Song dynasty. However, these techniques were greatly inferior to the new medical skills described in the *Taiping shenghuifang*. Though overcoming this inferiority was a primary concern at the time, this objective was not easily realized for the above-mentioned reasons. Yet it is worth noting that during this time, while such limitations were yet to be solved, Koryŏ's medical scholars were recompiling and republishing medical texts on obstetrics and pediatrics to make them easily accessible. In 1058, government officials of Ch'ungju county districts submitted to the king seven medical compilations, two of which focused on pediatrics. These two texts were compiled from one or two Chinese medical texts.[10]

There is another example of such an effort: around 1240, those who compiled the Buddhist scriptures also collected materials from the Chinese texts. In order to gain Buddha's favor in the struggle against the Mongols, they undertook the great work of compiling eighty thousand volumes of scriptures, which included fifteen volumes of medical texts, four of which specialized in obstetrics and pediatrics.[11] These facts suggest that Koryŏ society suffered from a high rate of infant mortality and that great efforts were made to solve this problem.

The compilation of Buddhist medical texts around 1240 also marked the dividing point between old and new medical science. War inevitably resulted in famine and disease; these medical texts were chosen for compilation as a way of lessening the suffering. Of the four compiled books, two had been first translated from Song Chinese texts in 998 and 1002, so they were not new to Koryŏ. In addition to previously known texts, there were entirely new ones as well. This compilation also included the *Hyangyak kugŭpbang*, the first Korean medical text. Although it is difficult to say that the new text, *Hyangyak kugŭpbang*, had an immediate effect, it was of great significance as it represents a new beginning in Korean medical history. Based on the situation at the time of its publication, it seems that the main focus of this medical text was not on infant diseases. However, since as mentioned earlier, it contained separate sections on obstetrics and pediatrics, we might safely infer that Koryŏ society had its share of childbirth and infant diseases. Specialized medical knowledge was necessary to understand much of the writing in these texts; however,

---

10. The titles of these two books are *Xiaoya chaoshi bingyuan* and *Xiaoya yaozheng bingyuan yishi balun*, the first being comprised of the pediatric-related materials compiled from *Bingyuan houlun* by Chao Yuanfan and the second pediatric-related materials obtained from the first book and *Xiaoya yaozheng* by Liu Jingyu.

11. These four books were *P'ot'aegyo* (Prenatal care, Volume I), *Pulsŏlju soa kyŏng* (Buddhist scripture on incantation of infants), *Kuryo soabyŏng kyŏng* (Buddhist scripture on curing infant diseases, Volume I), and *Kasŏp sŏninsŏl ŭiyŏin kyŏng* (Volume I).

this would not have been true for many fever-related illnesses and diseases common in infancy and early childhood. These illnesses had symptoms of fever that were relatively easy to diagnose[12] and could be described simply. The spread of these new medical techniques had the social consequence of reducing the infant mortality rate in Koryŏ society by providing proper cures for fever-related illnesses, the most prevalent of infant maladies.

## THE NEO-CONFUCIAN VIEW OF AGRICULTURAL ADMINISTRATION AND THE NEW POPULATION POLICY

If the advent of native Korean prescriptions and medical techniques was a contributing factor in the amelioration of infant diseases in this period, then such developments were historically significant. However, in order to assess these factors accurately, it is necessary to understand the political and ideological trends of the time. No matter how advanced these techniques may have been, they would not have had a social impact without political and ideological support.

The late-Koryŏ period, especially the fourteenth century, was a time of significant political and ideological change. A new political power group, the so-called newly rising scholar-officials (*sinhŭng sadaebu*), emerged and pushed for government reforms that incorporated Neo-Confucianism into its political doctrine. The Neo-Confucian movement gained momentum especially in the middle of the fourteenth century, when anti-Yuan reformist political sentiment grew increasingly strong, ultimately leading to the founding of the Chosŏn dynasty. It is precisely these ideological and political trends that were closely linked with the development of native Korean treatments and medical techniques.

Neo-Confucianism had a completely different worldview and conception of the universe from that of Buddhism. As is well known, the Buddhist doctrine of *kong* (emptiness) stresses that the future life is more important than the present life; naturally, it adopted a passive

---

12. All the pediatric illness described in *Hyangyak Kugŭbpang* are enumerated by a Japanese scholar and doctor, Sakae Miki, in his massive book: *Chosen shippeishi* (History of diseases in Korea), part 2 of *Chosen igakushi oyobi shippeishi* (History of Korean medicine and diseases) (Sakai: Miki Sakae, 1955; reprint, 1962), pp. 8–9. He listed all the pediatric diseases and summarized them in terms of modern names. He also wrote, "In consultation with a practicing doctor about these pediatric illnesses, this writer learned that they are mostly fever-related illnesses."

attitude toward problems of everyday life. By contrast, Neo-Confucians believed that one should accept and understand the natural order of the universe as it is. This was the principle upon which they established their philosophy of government; therefore, they were naturally much more active in dealing with the problems of everyday life. The Neo-Confucian view on the natural order of the universe held that all creatures exist and reproduce according to heaven's will, which is "to give life to living things." The essential tenet of Neo-Confucianism was the concept that the goal of all living things was to embody heaven's will by extending their individual lives. Thus, it strongly stressed that the foremost concern of a monarch, the receiver of Heaven's decree, was to see that his subjects were able to live out their natural life spans under his rule. In order to accomplish this, a ruler was required to do many tasks, but the most important was to guarantee the provision of food and clothing for his people. Neo-Confucian discourses on kingly rule frequently discussed the notion that "Food is the heaven of the people." Hence, agricultural administration was of the greatest importance in Neo-Confucian conceptions of kingly rule. Native Korean medical knowledge, which was first systematized in the mid-thirteenth century, combined with the pragmatically reform-minded and activist political ideology of Neo-Confucian scholars in the fourteenth century, leading to many important developments.

After the fourteenth century, the Neo-Confucian emphasis on agricultural management brought about many important changes in bureaucratic administration. One interesting change was the introduction of items on agricultural management and population in regulations governing the duties of the officials appointed to each village in the provinces. During the Koryŏ period, there were two kinds of regulations governing the duties of provincial officials. The first concerned general regulations for government officials, patterned after those of the eleventh century Tang dynasty (*Che chubuwŏn ponghaeng yuk cho*). The second was modeled after the fourteenth- century Song dynasty (*Suryŏng o sa*). The latter soon replaced the former. The crucial difference between the two is that regulations pertaining to agriculture and population are found only in the latter. Among the five items in the fourteenth-century regulations, the first two items were "to improve agriculture and sericulture" and "to increase population." This suggests that radical changes occurred in views on agricultural administration.

The fact that the two issues of agriculture and population were of equal importance in the implementation of agricultural policies after the introduction of Neo-Confucianism reflects the close relationship between the two. It is obvious that an increase in population would be a matter of concern to agricultural administration since it would affect the ability to secure the labor force for agriculture. However, from a historical perspective, it is no coincidence that these issues were all raised at the same time. In China, the Song period marked the beginning of Neo-Confucianism. During this period, intensive farming techniques for wet-field cultivation developed in the vicinity of the Yangzi River and regions southward. Not only did these new farming methods, commonly called "Jiangnan farming techniques," make continuous cultivation possible in the same field, but the yield per unit area greatly increased. The wet-field farming technique was a development of epoch-making significance. It was not by chance that local government regulations emphasized issues related to agriculture and population during the period these changes were occurring. Since an increase in the labor force, together with increased yield per unit area, would guarantee higher profits, it is natural that active measures would be emphasized. Thus, it is also no coincidence that the same period saw epochal developments in medicine with the publication of *Taiping shenghuifang*. Compared to the southern river areas in China, the land in Korea was not as conducive to the development of wet-field agriculture. Despite many relative disadvantages, the preference for wet-field farming increased after the middle of the fourteenth century, and the two countries were similar in terms of agricultural administration. Since it was realized that an increase in population was necessary in order to develop agriculture, there was an enhanced effort to discover and develop medical techniques utilizing indigenous herbs.

The three trends that emerged in the mid-fourteenth century—agricultural improvements, population increase, and the development of medicine—continued to be closely related after the founding of the Chosŏn dynasty in 1392. In fact, medicine became more systematized and practiced more widely as time passed. To promote the development of medicine, many previously published medical books were reissued, and diverse kinds of medical texts were published, either through the efforts of the government or through the initiative of private individuals. During the two centuries from the founding of the Chosŏn dynasty to the Japanese invasion of Korea in 1592, we can confirm that a total of forty-five books were published through both public and private efforts.[13] This is not a small number of books, but the more significant development during the fifteenth and the sixteenth centuries lies in their content.

During the fifteenth and sixteenth centuries, the two most authoritative medical texts were the *Hyangyak chipsŏngbang* (Compilation of Native Korean Prescriptions), which was completed in 1433, and the *Ŭibang yuch'wi* (Classified Collection of Medical Prescriptions), which was published in 1445. As mentioned above, the former compiled native medicinal techniques, describing more than 900 symptoms and 1,700 varieties of prescriptions. It also included a supplement, *Hyangyak ponch'o* (Native Herbal Medicines), which recorded the characteristics of more than 630 medicinal substances.[14] Thus, it clearly established itself yet again as a major collection of native medicinal arts. The *Hyangyak chipsŏngbang*, which summarized the most important areas of knowledge in native medicine, and the *Ŭibang yuch'wi*, which included organized excerpts of Chinese medical methods, together constituted the two most valuable treasures. The latter work, consisting of approximately 365 volumes, attests to Korea's high degree of interest in the medicine of other countries as a means of further developing its own medicinal techniques. Many medical texts written and published during the following century and a half were selections from the contents of these two important texts.

The enormous amount of material in these two books often made them inaccessible and awkward for everyday use. Therefore, excerpts of the essential contents from the two texts were later published as first-aid medical texts to make them more accessible. The most important texts were the following: *T'aesan yorok* (Summary of Obstetrical Medicine), *Kugŭpbang* (First-Aid Medicine), and *Ch'on'ga kugŭpbang* (First-Aid Medicine for Villagers). I will briefly discuss their main characteristics:

The authors of *Hyangyak chipsŏngbang* published the *T'aesan yorok* in the year immediately following the former's publication. The two volumes of *T'aesan yorok* compiled information only on obstet-

---

13. This number comes from Sakae Miki, *Chosen shippeshi*.
14. Medical materials described in this book are plant-, animal-, and mineral-based. Compared to European medicine during the same period, which was only plant-based, it was pointed out that medicine in East Asia was more advanced in utilizing more diverse cures than European medicine. See Chŏn Sang'un, *Han'guk kwahak kisulsa* (History of Korean science and technology) (Seoul: Chŏngŭmsa, 1976).

rics and remedies for childhood disease.[15] The arrangement of these specialized texts immediately after the compilation of as many as eighty-five medical texts enables us to deduce what the most critical problems were that medical science tried to solve. The second text, Kugŭpbang, was compiled thirty-three years later in 1466 and was also organized into two volumes so as to facilitate ready distribution. Its contents were not limited to newborn and early-childhood diseases but rather combined the most practical and commonly used native medicinal techniques with Chinese medicinal techniques.[16] In other words, it was meant to realize the goal of the publication of the Hyangyak chipsŏngbang and the Ŭibang yuch'wi. The third text, the Ch'on'ga kugŭpbang, was created by the efforts of an individual, Kim Chŏngguk, in 1538. The title itself, which may also be translated as "Treatments for Medical Emergencies of Rural Villagers," is very interesting. Its contents consist of an introduction listing the names of more than 200 native Korean medicinal herbs, and a body divided into three sections: common adult diseases, gynecology, and pediatrics.[17] This text is further evidence of the great interest at the time in the treatment of newborn and infant diseases.

According to Kwŏn T'aehwan and Shin Yong-ha's research, as mentioned above, the fifteenth and sixteenth centuries witnessed a rapid increase in population from 5.5 million to 14 million. It is not a coincidence that the above-mentioned medical advances occurred during this period. The influence of Neo-Confucian conceptions of agricultural administration on these leaps in the development of medicine can be demonstrated just by the fact that important medical texts were generally compiled according to a royal decree which was based on the notion that the primary goal of kingly rule was the embodiment of Heaven's will. In addition to compiling medical texts, the government devoted much effort to cultivating and gathering medicinal herbs and plants, training of medical doctors, and the construction and maintenance of medical facilities. There are many instances in which the compilation of medical and agricultural texts was directly related, and this connection supports the notion that the development of medicine was linked to agricultural administration. For example, the compilation of the largest Korean medical text, Hyangyak chipsŏngbang, began at about the same time that the

---

15. Sakae Miki, "Chosen igakushi," part 1 of Chosen igakushi oyobi shippeishi, p. 132.
16. Ibid., pp. 151–52.
17. Ibid., p. 173.

earliest known agricultural text, *Nongsa chiksŏl* (Straight talk on agriculture), was being compiled. In 1518, a local district official, Kim An'guk, annotated two medical texts along with *Nongsŏ* (Book on agriculture) and *Chamsŏ* (Book on silkworm farming). The fact that these medical and farming texts were frequently annotated for use by both commoners and farmers is yet more evidence of the close relationship between the two fields.

The most important evidence for the close connection between Korean medical advances and agricultural administration in the fifteenth and sixteenth centuries is the fact that during this period, the area of arable land increased simultaneously with the increase in population due to medical advances. While the only records pertaining to the amount of arable land are the national land-tax records, these indicate that at the beginning of the fifteenth century, the amount of arable land totaled about 930,000 *kyŏl* (the traditional unit of land measurement in Korea), but by the middle of the sixteenth century, there was more than 1.7 million *kyŏl* of arable land.

CONCLUSION

In the pre-modern era, China, Korea and Japan had the following characteristics in common: (1) all three had a high population density, (2) their economies had a strong preference for wet-field farming, and (3) each culture witnessed the development of Neo-Confucianism. This chapter has demonstrated that these characteristics were simply three aspects of a single phenomenon. While the focus of this chapter was limited to the case of Korea, it is likely that the same relations among these factors can be found in the other two countries as well. In the case of China, based only on my research for this chapter, I expect that similar conclusions can be made about Chinese history after the Song dynasty. In the case of Japan, during the dramatic population increase of the seventeenth and eighteenth centuries, Neo-Confucian medical scholars such as Motoōri Norinaga were very active. At the very least, it has been clearly shown that in Korea's case, the period of the fifteenth and sixteenth centuries was one of significant advances in medicine and population growth. Because of these new developments, the Neo-Confucian emphasis on agriculture was able to create the social conditions for wet-field farming. While it is impossible to determine precisely the causal relations among the three factors of medical advances and population increase, the strong preference for wet-field farming, and the Neo-Confucian emphasis on agricultural policy, it seems clear that these three elements were closely interrelated.

My research on this topic is still in its early stages and must be supplemented by further research. For example, similar studies on Japan and China are absolutely necessary to supplement this study. If high population density and the strong tendency to prefer wet-field farming are an undeniably important characteristic of pre-modern East Asian culture, this issue cannot be overlooked in Japanese and Chinese historiography. I am very eager to see studies from the same perspective on the history of these two countries in the near future.

In order for this field of study to develop in the future, detailed empirical research is necessary on medicine and medical techniques. It is very likely that historians will need the help of medical scholars to confirm the efficacy of indigenous medical treatments for each region. If developments in medical techniques influenced the population increase, a detailed investigation of the effectiveness of the treatments will also be necessary. My understanding is that many European scholars are skeptical about claims that pre-modern medical developments contributed significantly to increases in population. However, the results of European historiography cannot be directly extrapolated to Eastern medicine, because European medicine and Eastern medicine in the pre-modern era have different systems. Even though modern Western medicine is superior to that of the East, we cannot conclude that this was the case in pre-modern times. For example, it has been pointed out that in the period of Neo-Confucianism, Northeast Asia utilized three kinds of medicine: plant-based, animal-based, and mineral-based, while European medicine was only plant-based. The question of how medical advances influenced societies in pre-modern East Asia requires careful examination of each country's history. The abundant labor force in pre-modern East Asian societies did not develop by accident but rather was the result of tireless political and philosophical efforts for the development of society.

This chapter has focused on the period from the fourteenth to the sixteenth century. Though it is true that this period underwent an "explosive" population increase, this trend did not continue until the nineteenth century. Korea underwent a "crisis" in the seventeenth century which historians refer to as the "Little Ice Age" caused by severe climatic changes: continuous natural disasters such as droughts, floods, and extreme cold spells. These extreme and unusual natural disasters left disease, famine, and war in their wake, leading to a dramatic decrease in population. The crisis finally began to abate beginning in the late seventeenth century. I believe this unexpectedly rapid recovery was due to the agricultural and medical developments of the fourteenth and sixteenth centuries.

translated by Edward Park

Table 1

THE RATIO OF THE EARLY DEATHS OF CHILDREN AND THE AVERAGE NUMBER OF
CHILDREN BORN DURING EARLY AND LATE PERIODS KORYŎ PERIODS

| No. | Category | Early Period | Late Period |
|---|---|---|---|
| 1. | Frequency of families with deaths of children | 38/176 (21.6 percent) | 3/90 (3.4 percent) |
| 2. | Ratio of children's deaths/ Total number of children (Male) | 37/367 (10 percent) | 7/208 (3 percent) |
| 3. | Ratio of children's death/ Total number of children (Female) | 33/264 (13 percent) | 3/181 (2 percent) |
| 4. | Average number of children (Male-headed household) | 3.99 children (M-2.32, F-1.67) | 4.75 children (M-2.54, F-2.20) |
| 5. | Average number of children (Female-headed household including those who remarried) | 3.46 children (M-2.01, F-1.45) | 3.59 children (M-1.92, F-1.67) |
| 6. | 4, excluding dead children | 3.54 children (M-2.08, F-1.46) | 4.62 children (M-2.45, F-2.17) |
| 7. | 5, excluding dead children | 3.08 children (M-1.81, F-1.27) | 3.50 children (M1.86, F-1.64) |

Source: "Kukchŏng kamsa charyo" requested by Representative Yi Yong-gwŏn, 1988.

Table 2

AN EXAMINATION OF THE AVERAGE NUMBER OF CHILDREN OF 13TH-17TH GENERATIONS' DESCENDANTS WITH THE SURNAME KWŎN

| Generation | Number of Couples | Number of Children (M,F) | Average Number of Children |
|---|---|---|---|
| 13th | 17 | 53 (31, 22) |  |
| 14th | 29 | 80 (46, 34) | 3.11 |
| 15th | 34 | 117 (62, 55) | 2.75 |
| 16th | 52 | 194 (106, 88) | 3.41 |
| 17th | 73 | 266 (140, 126) | 3.73 |

Source: Andong Kwŏn-ssi sŏnghwabo (Genealogy of the Andong Kwŏn Clan).

Table 3

AVERAGE NUMBER OF DESCENDANTS WITH DIFFERENT SURNAMES

| Generation | Number of Couples | Number of Children (M,F) | Average Number of Children |
|---|---|---|---|
| 13th | 6 | 8 (6,2) | 1.33 |
| 14th | 24 | 73 (38,35) | 3.04 |
| 15th | 53 | 164 (87, 77) | 3.09 |
| 16th | 231 | 761 (407, 354) | 3.29 |
| 17th | 478 | 1,745 (952, 793) | 3.65 |

Source: Andong Kwŏn-ssi sŏnghwabo.

PART II

# International Relations in a Period of Historical Transition

CHAPTER 5

# Economic Transformation and Sociopolitical Trends in Sixteenth-Century East Asia

RESEARCH ON CHINA AND JAPAN during the past two decades has paid much attention to the sixteenth century, deeming it an important era of transformation. For scholars of China this period is fascinating in that it represents a critical juncture in history: massive social changes are clearly revealed for the first time. Similarly, students of Japanese history view this century with considerable interest, for they consider it the period when the transition from medieval to modern society was achieved.[1]

In contrast to the active state of research on the sixteenth century in China and Japan, scholarly inquiry into this era in Korea lags badly behind that on other periods. Conventional wisdom presumes this period to have been a declining one, a "dark age."

There are reasons why sixteenth-century Korea has been viewed in such negative terms. As is well known, numerous distortions were introduced into Korean historiography during the Japanese colonial

---

1. A turning point in research on the Ming and early-Qing periods of Chinese history was the publication of Suzuki Shun and Nishijima Sadao, eds., *Chugokushi no jidai kubun* (The periodization of Chinese history) (Tokyo: Tokyo daigaku shuppankai, 1957). These scholars have continued their studies down to the present using a variety of perspectives, including debate over the nature of the local gentry as a ruling class. In the past there were misguided conceptions of the Japanese *Sengoku* period, which viewed it as a dark age. However, in the 1920s and 1930s, research had already started heading in a more progressive direction. Especially since the 1960s, there has been active and systematic research viewing this era as one of preparation for the "modern" age.

era; these have bequeathed an unnecessarily negative understanding of the Korean past that has lasted until the present day. As one example—one of the most tenacious—we may cite the belief that the Chosŏn monarchy was ruined by literati purges, factional feuding, and reliance upon Neo-Confucianism. The sixteenth century is precisely the period in Korean history when the literati purges were most frequent and when Neo-Confucianism had reached its apex. Since negative preconceptions of these phenomena held sway, it is not surprising that scholars have lost interest in this period as an object of research. Very recently, there have been efforts to shatter such stereotypes in some areas of Korean history. However, even now, scholars generally avoid this period due to the power of such preconceptions.[2]

In Chinese and Japanese historiography, the sixteenth century is treated as a period of fundamental transformation, when the large-scale circulation of commodities was realized. Internally, markets in farm villages formed and developed into a unified market system; externally, foreign trade volume expanded greatly. One must realize that political conditions accompanying such economic transformation were by no means tranquil. Late-Ming China saw incessant conflict between court eunuchs and literati, in addition to suffering a series of popular uprisings. Similarly, Japan experienced peasant rebellions (*ikki*) and the internecine struggles of the *sengoku* period for a century. In this context, the literati purges of the sixteenth century should be viewed in a more positive light by tracing their relationship to the social and economic changes of that era.

Recent scholarship attempting to take a fresh perspective on sixteenth-century Korea may seem extremely meager compared to similar research on China and Japan. However, the existing scholarship provides a good basis for comparing and contrasting, from an economic point of view, the crucial transformations already confirmed in China and Japan with those known to have occurred in Korea. Such a comparative project is not only interesting in its own right but

---

2. For studies on sixteenth-century Korea urging a fresh understanding of the era, see Kang Man-gil, "Simnyuksegi sahoe ŭi pyŏnhwa" (Changes in society in the sixteenth century), *Pundan sidae ŭi yŏksa insik* (Seoul: Ch'angjak kwa pip'yŏngsa, 1980); Yi Tae-jin (Yi T'aejin), "Juroku seiki no Kankokushi ni taisuru rikai no hoko," *Chosen gakuho*, no. 110 (January 1984); and Yi Tae-jin, *Han'guk sahoesa yŏn'gu* (Studies on the social history of Korea) (Seoul: Chisik san'ŏpsa, 1986). The authors are in basic agreement on economic history but show major differences in their views of political and intellectual history.

is, I believe, fundamental to the larger goal of coherently and systematically understanding the transformation in sixteenth-century East Asia.

## DEVELOPMENT OF RURAL MARKETS AND THE MATURATION OF A MONETARY ECONOMY

The most important factor responsible for the growth in the circulation of goods in sixteenth-century China and Japan was the rise and growth of rural markets. Commercial transactions had been common in administrative centers and other cities linked to political power, but it is, by and large, from this period that the marketplace began to establish a firm base in rural society.

In China, we find the first signs of village markets as far back as the Song dynasty. However, it is generally believed that markets having fixed schedules of operation and organized into larger regional units did not mature until the late-Ming and early-Qing periods.³ These markets had various forms and were known by a variety of names, including *xiaoshi* (*hsiao-shih*), *cunshi* (*ts'un-shih*), *xushi* (*hsu-shih*), *caoshi* (*ts'ao-shih*), and *shiji* (*shih-chi*).

The growth of the market in Japan followed a similar pattern. While one school of thought dates the advent of the regularized market—conducted three times a month—to the mid-fourteenth century, the prototypical form of Japanese rural market, the *rokusai-shi*—meeting six times a month—is thought not to have undergone full-scale development until the Sengoku Period, which followed the Onin Rebellion in 1467.⁴

Coincidence or not, it has been established that a rural-market system was gathering strength during roughly the same period in Korea. During the Koryŏ dynasty, there was a market known as the *hyŏnshi*.⁵

---

3. There are numerous studies on rural Chinese markets; the main source I have used for this section is the work of Shiba Yoshinobu, "Chugoku chusei no shogyo," in *Chuseishi koza 3, chusei no toshi* (Tokyo: Gakuseisha, 1982) is the principal source I have used for this section.
4. Toyoda Takeshi, "Chusei shogyo no shujyuso," in *Taikei Nihonshi sosho, ryutsu-shi* 1 (Tokyo: Yamakawa shuppansha, 1969). pp. 68–69.
5. Yi Kyŏngsik, "Simnyuk segi changshi ŭi sŏngnip kwa kŭ kiban" (The establishment of markets in the sixteenth century and their foundation), *Han'guksa yŏn'gu* 57 (1969), pp. 76–79.

However, like markets in China before the Song dynasty, these markets did not extend beyond administrative centers, and even they disappeared in the series of domestic and foreign disorders of the thirteenth and fourteenth centuries. In the mid-fifteenth century, it was noted that provincial markets had not yet formed: "At present in our nation there are markets in the capital, but there are no markets in the towns and counties of the various provinces."[6] Documents from this period contain references to several types of merchants (e.g., *haengsang, yuksang, susang,* and *haesang*),[7] but the existence of long-distance commercial activities provides no basis for classifying such merchants as agents of a regularized market. Later in the century, early-Chosŏn commerce underwent great change. From around 1470, markets began to appear across the entire Chŏlla province. The earliest appearances involved various localities where people would open *sip'o* (market stalls) on the streets several times a month on fixed days; collectively, these were known as *changmun.*[8] Such activity began to show up in two additional provinces, Kyŏngsang and Ch'ungch'ŏng, and spread to other areas to such an extent that by the early-sixteenth century "markets (*changmun*) have been established in all the provinces."[9]

The emergence of rural markets at the end of the fifteenth century in the Chosŏn dynasty has not been glossed over by scholars of this period, but there has been a general reluctance to relate this phenomenon to the development of commerce and the growth of a monetary economy. Rather, standard interpretations of these markets, no doubt strongly influenced by negative preconceptions of this period, merely judge them to be the result of famine brought about by natural disasters or by heavy military and tax burdens imposed by the government. They are seen as nothing more than efforts by the peasantry to succor the needy.[10] I am convinced that an investigation of the general conditions surrounding the advent and development of rural markets in East Asia provides a welcome opportunity to sweep away such a negative treatment of this topic, one which has been specifically inflicted upon Korean historiography.

---

6. *Sejong sillok*, Vol. 59, Sejong 15, 1, *imsin.*
7. *Kyŏngguk taejŏn, hojŏn, chapsejo. Sŏngjong sillok*, Vol. 20, Sŏngjong 3, 7, *imsul.*
8. *Sŏngjong sillok*, Vol. 20, Sŏngjong 3, 7, *imsul.*
9. *Chungjong sillok*, Vol. 38, Chungjong 15, 3, *kiyul.*
10. A prime example is Miyabara Toichi, "Jugoroku seiki Chosen ni okeru chiho ichi," *Chosen gakuho*, no. 9 (1955).

The simultaneous appearance and growth of rural markets in the three East Asian nations during the fifteenth and sixteenth centuries seems far from coincidental. All three nations had greatly expanded their agricultural economic power through innovations in agricultural technology. It was this base of enhanced economic might that supported the rise of village markets.

While there were slight differences in the specific timing among the three nations, peasants switched to continuous cultivation, an advance that represents one of the most important transitions in the history of agriculture. In general, this change occurred some time during the twelfth to the fourteenth centuries. In China, the common practice through the Tang dynasty was to allow the land to lie fallow during alternate years, using legumes to supply nitrogen necessary for the restoration of soil fertility.[11] Fallow farming and the practice of crop rotation were technically the most superior systems available.[12] In Japan, where the *shoen* system was widespread, common practice was to cultivate only part of the farmland, as signified by terms such as *kata*, *arashi*, and *nenko*. In the Muromachi period, the use of continuous cultivation (*mansaku*) became prevalent for the first time.[13] In Korea as well, through the mid-Koryŏ period, regular periods of letting the land lie fallow were widely employed, as evidenced by the terms *ilyŏk-chŏn chaeyŏk-chŏn*. Yet another result of the development of agricultural technology in Korea was the reformation of the land-tax system around the mid-fifteenth century, whereby in principle all good agricultural land was considered taxable and under constant cultivation; no official allowance was made for land to lie fallow.[14]

A complex of factors, both social and technical, was responsible for overcoming limitations posed by fallow-field techniques. Among social factors, we may surmise that population increase was one of the

---

11. Nishijima Takeichi, "Seiminyojutsu no nogaku," *Ajiateki noho to nogyo shakai* (Tokyo: Tokyo daigaku shuppankai, 1969), pp. 62–63.
12. Nishijima Sadao, "Daidenho no shin-kaishaku," *Chugoku keizaishi kenkyu* (Tokyo: Tokyo daigaku shuppankai, 1966).
13. Toda Yoshimi, "Chusei shoki nogyo no ichi tokushitsu" (One characteristic of agriculture in the early medieval period) in Kyoto daigaku bungaku tokushikai, ed., *Kokushi ronshu*, Vol. 1 (1959).
14. Yi Tae-jin, "Sipsa-sibo segi nong'ŏp kisul ŭi paldal kwa sinhŭng sajok" (The development of agricultural technology and newly rising aristocratic families in the fourteenth and fifteenth centuries), *Tongyanghak* 9 (1979); Yi Tae-jin, *Han'guk sahoesa yŏn'gu* (1986); and Yi Tae-jin, "Koryŏ mal-Chosŏn ch'o ŭi sahoe pyŏnhwa" (Social change in the late Koryŏ and early Chosŏn periods), *Chindan hakpo* 55 (1983); see also Miyajima Hiroshi, "Chosen nogyoshi jo ni okeru jugo seiki" (The fifteenth century in Chosŏn agricultural history), *Chosen shiso* 3 (1980).

most important. Daubing seeds in fertilizer prior to planting was an early form of fertilizer application that had been practiced since ancient times, but there were many technical difficulties involved in full-scale application of fertilizer for the restoration of soil fecundity. These included the need to develop superior cultivation tools for weed removal and the production of fertilizer in the large quantities needed for full-scale cultivation. Such tasks were by no means simple.[15]

The solution to these technical problems would come with the use of Jiangnan-farming methods, which were first developed during the Southern Song dynasty and appeared elsewhere throughout East Asia from the twelfth to the fourteenth centuries.[16] The resolution of the difficulties in securing sufficient quantities of fertilizer through the use of human waste and ashes of vegetable matter was a feature common to the entire region.[17]

In terms of agricultural technology, the historical significance of the use of new fertilizer technology on a large scale was considerable. It brought in its wake the continuous cultivation of land and greatly increased the productivity of a given acreage. Furthermore, the formation of rural markets may also be understood as resting upon the foundation of this achievement. Following the improvements in the agricultural economy and in society as a whole, even small-scale peasants were able to gain access to commercial products. Markets in rural villages became more rooted and began to become visible in some localities, leading to a wide distribution of goods. In sum, the simultaneous growth of rural markets in sixteenth-century East Asia stemmed from a prior history of improvement in agricultural technol-

15. The discussion of fertilizer technology is based upon Nishiyama Takeichi's "Jukufun ko" in *Ajia-teki noho to nogyo shakai*.
16. There are a number of outstanding studies in Japan on the Southern Song *Chiangnan* farming technique, especially those of Amano Gennosuke, Nishijima Sadao, and Nishiyama Takeichi. In Korea, there is evidence that from the late-fourteenth century, the *Chiangnan* technique came into use, and at last overcame the limitations of fallow-field agriculture (see Yi Taejin, "Koryŏ mal-Chosŏn ch'o ŭi sahoe pyŏnhwa"). There exists the possibility that the change in farming technology might be dated somewhat earlier. In Japan, it is generally understood that a distinct change in agricultural practices occurred around the late-thirteenth century, with evidence showing this was a switch to more intensive agriculture. See Nagahara Keiji, "Chusei keizaishi soron" (An introduction to medieval economic history) in *Nihon keizaishi taikei*, Vol. 2, *Chugokuhen* (Tokyo: Tokyo daigaku shuppankai, 1966).
17. Nishiyama Takeichi, "Jukufun ko"; Yi Taejin, "Sipsa-sibo segi nong'ŏp kisul ŭi paldal kwa sinhŭng sajok"; Hogetsu Keigo, "Chusei no sangyo to kijitsu" (Industry and technology in the medieval era) in *Iwanami koza Nihon rekishi* 4 (Tokyo: Iwanami shoten, 1976).

ogy. Additionally, as will be seen below, the growth of commerce also helped provide the stimulus, in the form of international trade, for the mutual development of the three East Asian nations.

Another aspect of the growth in the circulation of commercial goods in sixteenth-century East Asia is the maturation of a monetary economy. While the history of money dates back to ancient times, the establishment of a unified economic system based upon the common use of a standardized currency is entirely different in nature from the mere production of currency and is a much more recent phenomenon.[18] For example, in China, low-denomination currency already existed in ancient times but had no connection with the rural economy and was not suitable for settling major transactions; high-denomination currency was needed for this. In ancient times, low-denomination currency was issued as part of the policy on tax and tribute payments. In other words, ancient currency was characterized by its limited sphere of use; it was a low-denomination measure of value needed and used only for a specific set of purposes.

A true monetary economy in China originated in the late Tang dynasty with the increased use of gold, silver, and silk and during the Five Dynasties period as various states minted and circulated silver and copper coinage in their territories. The new stage of monetary development thereby attained was extended and became systematized in the unified Sung state. Copper coinage and silver currency were put into general circulation and used for transactions everywhere, whether large or small, foreign or domestic.[19] However, great as they were, the developments of this period were still a far cry from those of the flourishing economic state of the sixteenth century.

For about three centuries beginning in the mid-tenth century, China suffered a huge outflow of silver resulting from the great demand among Islamic traders. This brought economic dislocations so severe that even maintaining a metallic-currency system became problematic.[20] The issuance of paper currencies such as the *jiaochao* (chiao-ch'ao) and *baochao* (pao-ch'ao) by the Southern Song and its contemporaries, the Jin and Yuan states, was an inevitable policy

---

18. The following discussion of Chinese currency follows Shiba Yoshinobu, "Chugoku chusei no shogyo."
19. Miyazaki Ichisada, *Godai shosho no tsuka mondai* (Kyoto: Hoshino shoten, 1943).
20. Otagi Matsuo, "Ortaq-sen to sono haikei—jyusan seiki" (Altal money and its background—the thirteenth century), *Toyoshi kenkyu* 32, no. 2 (1973), pp. 23–61.

whose implementation resulted directly from this shortage of silver.[21] This fiscal bind in China was not ameliorated in the slightest until after the founding of the Ming dynasty when the Yongle (Yung-lo) Emperor (reign 1402–1424) instituted an active policy of silver mine expansion.[22] This subsequently proved to be a major factor in the economic growth of the sixteenth century, and the reign of the Yung-lo Emperor constitutes a pivotal period in Chinese economic history.[23]

The primary importance of the expansion of silver mines in China lay in its contribution to the restoration of silver as the basic currency. Later, building upon this achievement, a land- and head-tax system was instituted using silver for payment, thereby establishing a bimetallic system based on a silver and copper standard. The result was a revitalization of the domestic economy. Accompanying this change was the popularity of Chinese goods such as textiles and porcelain on the international market, which resulted in silver from all over the world flowing into the Middle Kingdom and leading to prosperity in the sixteenth century.[24]

In Japan, in the eighth and ninth centuries, the Nara and early-Heian periods, respectively, the model of Tang China was followed, and there were instances where copper coinage was minted and circulated. However, this was an ancient form of currency, and the territorial extent of its circulation is said to have been limited to the capital and the surrounding *kinai* areas.[25] Additionally, in succeeding periods, from the Kamakura Period until the late sixteenth century, there was no unified political force, and no coinage was minted. Instead, copper cash from China was brought in as part of a tributary arrangement and widely used as the standard currency.[26] Minting resumed from the end of the sixteenth century under Toyotomi Hideyoshi, during a time of fresh economic and political development following the Warring States Period. In the beginning, only gold and copper currencies were minted, but with the establishment of the

---

21. Ibid. pp. 56–57.
22. William S. Atwell, "International Bullion Flows and the Chinese Economy Circa 1530-1650," *Past and Present* 95 (1983), p. 78.
23. Ibid., pp. 78–79.
24. Ibid., pp. 80–86.
25. Kobata Atsushi, *Nihon no kahei* (The currency of Japan) (Tokyo: Shibundo, 1958), p. 14.
26. Ibid., Chapter 5, "Chugoku senka no ryutsu."

Tokugawa Shogunate, the system became more complex, and silver was added as well.[27]

In Korea, the Koryŏ dynasty minted iron and copper cash and silver vessels as currency at various points during the tenth to the thirteenth centuries.[28] Although the scarcity of documents makes it difficult to know the motivation behind this minting, examination of the varieties of currency allows us to hypothesize that the Koryŏ government was attempting to keep in step with developments in China. However, this proved difficult since conditions in the two countries differed. Iron and copper coins proved to be unsuccessful, as the general populace strongly preferred using grain and cloth as mediums of exchange. Only the system of silver vessels, inaugurated at the beginning of the twelfth century, found any great frequency of use, most likely due to its convenience in transactions involving international trade. But this system, too, faded in the fourteenth century—a victim of the Chinese shortage of silver—as the vessels were made smaller or melted down.[29] During the period of Mongol interference in Koryŏ domestic affairs, the use of Yuan currency such as the *baochao* was forced on Korea; this system also proved unpopular and was later discarded.[30]

After extricating itself from Mongol influence, Koryŏ in the late-fourteenth century launched a new currency system by issuing paper currency known as *chŏhwa* (mulberry currency).[31] In summary, the Koryŏ government, like other states in East Asia, was unable to avoid currency problems in the wake of the general shortage of silver in East Asia beginning in the thirteenth century.

The development of the mulberry-currency system was temporarily delayed because of the political problems attendant upon the change from the Koryŏ to the Chosŏn dynasty, but once stability had been attained, the new regime set its hand to the task.[32] The imple-

---

27. Toyoda Takeshi, *Chusei shogyo no shujyuso*, p. 74, and "Shohin ryutsu no yakushin" (The progress of commodity circulation), *Taikei Nihonshi sosho*, Vol. 13, *Ryutsushi 1* (History of circulation), p. 120.
28. *Koryŏsa*, Vol. 79, sikhwaji hwap'yejŏn.
29. In 1287, because the practice of melting down silver vessels and blending them with copper to mint coinage had become alarmingly prevalent, the Koryŏ government issued an edict banning such activity; in 1331, small silver vessels were produced, thereby ending the use old of silver vessels, loc. cit.
30. Loc. cit.
31. *Koryŏsa*, 79, Kongyang-wang 3 nyŏn 7 wol kon.
32. Yi Chong'yŏng, "Chosŏn ch'ogi hwap'yeje ŭi pyŏnch'ŏn" (Changes in the currency system in the early Chosŏn period), *Inmun kwahak* 7 (1962).

mentation of this system was far from smooth in that conversion was not guaranteed. The strong preference of the populace for cloth currency led the government to tinker with the system on several occasions. Around the time when the Yung-lo Emperor of Ming China was actively pursuing his policy of expanding silver mines, the mulberry currency system was replaced with a copper one. It seems that the Ming policy gave fresh hope to prospects for a metallic-currency system in Chosŏn.

In 1429, only four years after the enactment of a copper-currency system, the Ming authorities granted the Chosŏn court their long-standing request that gold and silver be excluded from Korean tributary goods (on the grounds that they were not domestically produced). This clearly indicates a relaxation in the diplomatic tension around this time between the two countries over the issue of precious metals.[33] However, this diplomatic success meant that the Chosŏn court could not enact a policy of active mine development, since they feared that the active excavation of copper, gold, and silver would only lead to the eventual reinstatement of these precious metals as tribute items. The copper-currency system was in line with this cautious policy as well, for it was inaugurated with the purchase of copper from Japan.[34] In short, the implementation of this system came at a time when prospects for the development of a metallic-currency system were virtually ensured because of the Ming mining policy. However, at the same time, it was impossible to have confidence in its long-term diplomatic implications. As a result, the system ended up being terminated after only twenty years. In the end, the copper-coinage system was thwarted by the difficulties in formulating policy on how to obtain raw materials for its maintenance.

After the abandonment of the copper-coinage system, the government settled on cloth currency that was highly popular even during periods when mulberry and copper currencies were in circulation. The selection of this dual system signified official recognition of this reality. In the *Kyŏngguk taejŏn*, the new legal code of the Chosŏn state

33. At present no concrete evidence exists demonstrating a relation between the Ming-Chinese policy of silver-mine development and the operation of the copper-coin system in Chosŏn. However, in view of the temporal congruity between the two and the exclusion of gold and silver from Chosŏn tribute goods, it is possible to infer the existence of such a relation as detailed this section. I intend to examine this issue in greater detail in the future. For the operation of the copper-coin system in Chosŏn, see Yi Chong'yŏng, "Chosŏn ch'ogi hwap'yeje ŭi pyŏnch'ŏn."

34. Yi Chong'yŏng, "Chosŏn ch'ogi hwap'yeje ŭi pyŏnch'ŏn."

promulgated in the late-fifteenth century, both cloth and mulberry were designated as official currencies.[35] During the sixteenth century, cloth currency came to enjoy greater popularity. From the latter half of the fifteenth century, cotton cloth production expanded due to a shift from ramie and hemp cloth to cotton as the principal variety of cloth currency. Cloth currency became so widespread that it almost completely eclipsed mulberry currency.

The dominance of cloth currency in Korea during the fifteenth and sixteenth centuries is a phenomenon that has not escaped notice in prior studies on this period, but it has, if anything, been commonly used as evidence demonstrating the "backwardness" of the Korean economy during this time. Those who hold this naive view believe that a metallic currency was unable to take root and that the use of cloth currency was indicative of a primitive barter economy.[36] Yet, in view of the close economic ties between China and Korea up to this period, this judgment can only be termed hasty, based as it is on external evidence. Since the copper-coin system was suspended in the early-fifteenth century and resumed only in 1625, it is impossible to deny that Korea lagged in the development of a metallic-currency system. However, the sophistication of the cloth-currency economy should not be underestimated. From the latter half of the fifteenth century, cotton was the main material used as cloth currency. As I will relate later in this chapter, not only did cotton become a major commercial item both at home and abroad, but the circulation system based upon it underwent tremendous development.

The cloth-currency system in Korea during the fifteenth and sixteenth centuries[37] used *osŭngp'o* (five-ply cloth) as the standard cloth currency (*chŏngp'o*). *Osŭngp'o* consisted of five *sŭng*, or 400 *ol* (1 *sŭng* = 80 *ol*, "strands").[38] In addition, the cloth was woven of 160 *ol* and 240 *ol*, with one *p'il* being 30 *ch'ok* in length. These were so crudely woven that, in popular parlance, they became known as *ch'up'o* or *akp'o* and could not be used to make clothing. The only purpose of such cloth was for use as currency. In fact, the reason that *sangp'o* was created in the first place—by cutting short

35. *Kyŏngguk taejŏn, hojŏn, kukp'ye.*
36. Miyabara Toichi, "Jugoroku seiki Chosen ni okeru chiho ichi."
37. The discussion of cloth currency below follows Song Chaesŏn, "Simnyuk segi myŏnp'o ŭi hwap'ye kinŭng" (The function of cotton cloth as currency in the sixteenth century) in *Pyon T'aesŏp paksa hwagap kinyŏm sahak nonch'ong* (Seoul: Samyongsa, 1986).
38. One *p'il* (bolt) was 35 *ch'ŏk* in length.

*osŭngp'o*—was to create a cloth currency suitable for use in minor transactions. Table 1 shows the relative values of the standard *osŭngp'o* (also *chŏngpo*) and *sangp'o*.[39]

As the chart shows, there was a regular variation in the relative value of the *chŏngp'o* and *sangp'o* tantamount to a currency system with three levels of value. In light of various developments in agrarian society such as the rise of provincial markets, it seems clear that two- and three-*sŭng* cloths became established as low-denomination currency because they were essential to peasants for use in their daily lives. In addition to these two denominations of cloth currency, more valuable silver was still in wide use. Taken as a whole, it seems difficult not to view the economy of the time as a developed monetary economy with the systematic use of currency.

As will be discussed later, Korea entered a new phase of silver mine development in the sixteenth century. Private merchants increased their trade with China greatly, intensifying the demand for silver as a means of settling purchases of textiles and stimulating the active development of silver mines.[40] The monetary economy of sixteenth-century Korea only lacked the minting of copper coins; in essence, Korea's metallic currency systems were the same as those of China and Japan.

The improvement in economic conditions was the underlying factor behind increasingly forceful proposals urging the minting of copper coinage.[41] However, these suggestions were not followed not because of their economic infeasibility but rather because of the corrupt practices of the official class. In the politics of this era, real power was in the hands of royal in-laws and their allies among the officials. With the sharp decline in public morality, officials manipulated the military-procurement and tax systems and thereby accumulated cotton cloth, which was regarded as being equivalent to currency.[42] Such unjust practices were ultimately reformed thanks to

---

39. Taken from Song Chaesŏn, "Simnyuk segi myŏnp'o ŭi hwap'ye kinŭng," p. 421.
40. See chapter three.
41. Song Chaesŏn, "Simnyuk segi myŏnp'o ŭi hwap'ye kinŭng" demonstrates that in the tenth year of Chungjong there was division in court over the issue of currency: some called for the exclusive use of "mulberry currency" while others advocated minting coinage.
42. Yi Tae-jin. "Kunyŏk ŭi pyŏnjil kwa napp'oje silsi," *Han'guk kunjesa: kŭnse Chosŏn chŏn'gi p'yŏn* (Seoul: Yukkun sagwan hakkyo, Han'guk kunsa yŏn'gusil, 1968).

criticism by a new political force so that, though late, the copper-coin system was officially adopted by 1625.[43]

This overview of the changes in the monetary systems in East Asia allows us to identify a new character in the development of the monetary economy in all three countries in the sixteenth century. As a result of improvements in agricultural technology, the economic might of the agricultural economy greatly improved as a whole. As markets developed in response to changes in farm-village society, the commercial-monetary system, whose most important role had been in trade with distant lands, now took on different roles.

Another sign of commercial development in East Asia during the sixteenth century was the trend toward payment of taxes in money rather than in kind. A prime example of this trend was the adoption in China of the "single whip" tax system, whereby payment was tendered in silver. In Chosŏn, aspects of the tax-collection system such as the substitution of tax farming (*pangnap*) for local tribute goods and the payment of cloth instead of military service may be best understood in the same light.[44] In the case of China, there has been considerable research on this topic; however, there is no space to address these issues here.

In the next section, I will examine international trade and examine the degree to which circulation of commercial goods in East Asia developed.

EXPANSION OF INTERNATIONAL TRADE AND WARFARE

In the late-Tang and early–Northern Song dynasties, trading relations in East Asia already augured change as Chinese merchants ventured as far abroad as Southeast Asia. However, a major international transformation began with China's pursuit of a new international order toward the end of the fourteenth century, based upon the tributary system. The Ming tributary system was a form of diplomacy stemming from traditional Chinese conceptions of the civilized and the barbar-

---

43. See Song Ch'ansik, "Yijo ŭi hwap'ye" (The currency of the Yi dynasty), *Ch'unch'u mungo* 9 (1975), pp. 12–13, for a discussion of the first minting of coinage and its relation to cloth currency in the sixteenth century.
44. Ko Sŏkgyu, "Simnyuk-sipch'il segi kongnapje kaehyŏk ŭi panghyang" (The direction of reform of the tribute tax system in the sixteenth and seventeenth centuries), *Han'guk saron* 12 (1985); Yi Tae-jin, "Juroku seiki no Kankokushi ni taisuru rikai no hoko."

ian (*hua-i*), which demanded ritual submission from the governments of neighboring nations. Since the system required tribute as a concrete expression of this subservience, the significant practical gains to be obtained from the tribute trade came to have at least equal importance as issues of prestige. As the significance of the tributary system lay in its establishment of a variety of "trade frameworks," one of its important goals was to secure the creation of an international order in the form of an expanded trading region extending over all of East Asia.[45]

As trade in East Asia exhibited lively development within a new unitary "trade framework" and the volume of trade greatly expanded, the region became one of the centers of world trade by the mid-sixteenth century, with even European traders participating. The geographical core of the trade was, of course, the three East Asian nations, but the importance of traders from other areas, such as the Ryukyu Islands and Europe, as intermediaries was considerable, though to an extent such trade was an artifact of the operation of the system itself.

The Ming tribute system operated in conjunction with the Chinese policy of marine exclusion. Marine exclusion did not signify a total blockade of trading activities but rather was a domestic policy measure aimed solely at the Chinese themselves. Its main intent was the preservation of the Ming government's right to monopolize trade. Accordingly, the Ryukyu islanders, acting in place of inhabitants of Chinese coastal areas, came to serve as trading intermediaries. Acquiring spices and medicinal herbs from the South Seas, they appeared frequently not only in Ming China but also in Chosŏn and Japan, as well as other areas. However, with the acceleration of domestic commercial development in the sixteenth century, Chinese living in coastal areas were no longer hindered by the marine-exclusion policy and were able to disguise themselves as Japanese *wako* and conduct trade. As a result, the role of the Ryukyu islanders began to decline. In the mid-sixteenth century, the entry of European traders led by the Portuguese made it impossible for the Ryukyu traders to reverse this trend.[46]

---

45. Tanaka Takeo, "Higashi Ajia tsuko kiko no seiritsu to tenkai," in *Iwanami koza seikai rekishi*, 16, *kindai*, 8, *seiyohen* (Tokyo: Iwanami shoten, 1970).

46. The above discussion is based upon Tanaka Takeo, "Higashi Ajia tsuko kiko no seiritsu to tenkai"; Yamaguchi keiji, "Nihon no sakoku," in *Iwanami koza seikai rekishi. chusei* 3 (1976); Sasaki Ginya, "Higashi Ajia boeikiken no keisei to kokusai ninshiki," in *Iwanami koza seikai rekishi, chusei* 3 (Tokyo: Iwanami shoten, 1976).

In its early years, the Chosŏn dynasty devoted its greatest effort to the goal of reducing the burden mandated under the tributary system. Hence, trade between Chosŏn and China was, if anything, stagnant. However, from the end of the fifteenth century, Chosŏn began importing large quantities of high-quality silk cloth and raw silk thread from China, creating an entirely new situation.[47] The great demand for silk fabric at this time originated in the growth of agricultural economic power due to improved agricultural technology. While this high demand for silk cloth was, for a considerable time, a topic of major political discussion denouncing the drift toward luxury in society, the social range of those demanding silk cloth expanded to the extent that even among commoners, it had become necessary for use in wedding ceremonies.[48]

Because China demanded silver in exchange for silk cloth and thread, this era provided new opportunities for the development of domestic silver mines.[49] Following the success of Chosŏn in 1429 (11th year of Sejong's reign) in obtaining the exclusion of gold and silver from its tributary offerings, almost no domestic production was permitted out of a concern that these precious metals might be reinstated as tribute items. Purchase of some gold and silver was unavoidable, but when necessary, it was purchased from Japan in the smallest possible quantities. However, from the end of the fifteenth century, as the transformation detailed above began to take hold, the persistent demands on the part of large-scale, wealthy merchants made a change of policy inevitable. The tax-remittance system adopted in 1515 (10th year of Chungjong's reign) formally permitted the private operation of mines in return for payment of military tax. A further revision of the law in 1551 (6th year of Myŏngjong's reign) provided for an expansion in the openness of the system by integrating taxes assessed on such mining operations into the general tax system.

The development of a new technology contributed to the development of silver mining. In 1503 (the ninth year of Yŏnsan'gun's reign), a commoner, Kim Kam-bul, and a slave, Kim Kom-dong,

---

47. Han Sanggwŏn, "Simnyuk segi tae-Chungguk samuyŏk ŭi chŏn'gae" (The development of private trade with China in the sixteenth century), in *Kim Ch'ŏljun paksa hwagap kinyŏm sahak nonch'ong* (Seoul: Chisik san'ŏpsa, 1983).
48. Yi Tae-jin, "Juroku seiki no Kankokushi ni taisuru rikai no hoko," pp. 24–25.
49. The following discussion is based upon Han Sanggwŏn, "Simnyuk segi tae-Chungguk samuyŏk ŭi chŏn'gae"; Yu Sŭngju, "Chosŏn chŏn'gi huban ŭi ŭn'gwangŏp yŏn'gu" (A study of silver mining in the latter half of the early Chosŏn period), *Chindan hakpo* 55 (1983).

invented a new technique for the extraction and refinement of silver from lead ore.[50] Nuggets of lead ore contain a high proportion of silver, but until this time, there had been no way to extract it. The ore had been useless until these two discovered, for the first time, the technology to solve the problem. Tanch'on in Hamgyŏng province, renowned as the location of the premier silver mine in Chosŏn, was originally a lead-producing region and only switched to silver mining at this time.[51] This technology was soon transmitted to Japan, where it was to make a decisive contribution to expansion in the volume of silver production in the late sixteenth century.[52] Keeping these facts in mind, it is clear that the invention of this process cannot be omitted from the history of commercial and industrial development of the sixteenth century.

In its trade with Japan at the time, Chosŏn purchased copper, gold, and silver, while exporting grain (rice and beans), unpatterned silk (*myŏnju*), and cotton cloth.[53] As mentioned above, the import of precious metals stemmed from Chosŏn's tributary obligations to China in the fifteenth century. In addition, silver continued to be imported in considerable quantities, even after the private operation of mines became permissible. This was due to the necessity of ensuring a silver supply greater than the quantity needed for the increased import of silk from Ming China.[54]

According to Japanese historical sources, the culture of the commoner class in Japan was more influenced by trade with Chosŏn than with China. Relations between Japan and China were carried out in the form of tributary offerings under the "tally-trade system." This trade, which began in the early fifteenth century, was at first conducted by the *bakufu* and scheduled on the basis of only one tribute mission every ten years. After the mid-fifteenth century, the participa-

50. Sin Sŏkho, "Chosen Chushyutai no kingin mondai" in *Inaba hakushi kanreki kinen Man-Senshi ronso* (Keijo: Inaba hakushi kanreki kinenkai, 1938), pp. 410–11.
51. Ibid., p. 421.
52. Ibid., pp. 421–22; Here I introduce a source dealing with Japanese acquisition of new technology, *P'aegwan chapki* by ŏ Suk-kwon; concerning the expansion of Japanese silver production in the late-sixteenth century, see Kobata Atsushi, *Kingin boeikishi no kenkyu* (Tokyo: Hosei daigaku shuppankyoku, 1976), and Tashiro Kazui, *Kinsei Nitcho tsuko boekishi no kenkyu* (Tokyo: Sobunsha, 1981).
53. Sasaki Ginya, "Higashi Ajia boeikiken no keisei to kokysai ninshiki;" Nakamura Hidetaka, *Nissen kankeishi no kenkyu* (Tokyo: Yoshikawa kobunkan, 1965–1969); Tanaka Takeo, "Chusei ni okeru Min-Chosen-Ryukyu to no kankei," *Taigai kankei to bunka koyru* (Kyoto: Shibunkaku shuppan, 1982).
54. Sin Sŏkho, "Chosen Chushyueai no kingin mondai;" Han Sanggwŏn, "Simnyuk segi tae-Chungguk samuyŏk ŭi chŏn'gae," pp. 474–78.

tion of large monasteries, powerful *daimyo* and merchants from Sakai, Hakata, and other areas vitalized the trade somewhat, but at this time as well, the goods imported (in theory, "bestowed") were far removed from commoner society.[55] The major imports were silk fabric, silk thread, and copper coins. Silk cloth and thread were carried back mainly in response to demand from upper-class society, while the copper coinage was mostly exchanged on the return trip to Japan for silk goods.

Japan's trade with Chosŏn, on the other hand, differed from this pattern of trade with China. Chosŏn did impose restrictions on the trade, limiting it to three Korean ports (the so-called *samp'o*) that dealt with Japanese merchants from Tsushima. However, the trade not only involved a wide range of Japanese society, from the shogunate to peasants and fishermen, but also had a large impact on commoner society, since the items of trade were more oriented toward daily necessities.[56]

The largest gains for Japan from trade with Chosŏn were those stemming from the import of cotton products and training in the techniques of cotton cultivation. According to pioneering research on the Japanese cotton industry,[57] the indigenization of cotton production in Japan in the early sixteenth century was wholly the result of importation of seeds and weaving technology from Chosŏn. From the early fifteenth century, the import of cotton products from Chosŏn by Japan increasingly emphasized unprocessed cotton (*myŏnju*), while in the latter half of the century, particularly following the large rebellions in the Onin and Bunmei periods, the transfer of technology took place in the midst of a sudden increase in demand for cotton cloth, with imports reaching 100,000 *p'il* per year. The Japanese rebellion at the three Korean ports in 1510 may be seen as having arisen due to resistance on the part of Tsushima islanders to new restrictions enacted by the Koreans on the outflow of cotton cloth, trade of which brought large profits to the Japanese.

Cotton cloth imported from Chosŏn was widely used in a number of areas of Japanese life and brought about great innovations to both the people's livelihood and technology, to the degree that such change

---

55. Tanaka Takeo, "Chusei kaigai boeiki no seikaku" in *Nihon keizai taikei* 2, *Chuseihen*.
56. Sasaki Ginya, "Higashi Ajia boeikiken no keisei to kokusai ninshiki."
57. Ono Koshi, "Honpo mokumen kigyo seirtsu no katei," in *Nihon keizai taikei* 2, *Chuseihen*.

may be termed a "cotton revolution."[58] In addition, it may be said that cotton made a decisive contribution to the development of transportation in Japan. Previously, ships had used sails constructed of woven reeds. When the Japanese switched to cotton-fiber sails, the carrying capacity of their ships was enhanced and techniques of sail rigging were greatly streamlined, resulting in an increase in sailing speed. In Gifu Prefecture, there is said to be a ritual, transmitted down to modern times, in which the people construct an effigy of a Korean king, dressing him in traditional Korean clothes and ceremonially placing cotton shoes on his feet.[59] In these cotton shoes, we find traces of the impact left upon Japan by the "cotton revolution."

International trade in sixteenth-century East Asia developed generally along the lines detailed above, demonstrating a clear relation with developments in each of the individual economies. This complex web of relationships among the three major trading partners was rudely shattered, however, at the end of the century by Toyotomi Hideyoshi's so-called entry into China (*tonyu*). On a political level, Hideyoshi's continental adventure may be explained as an attempt to reduce conflict among the *sengoku daimyo*. However, on an economic level, it may be understood as a revolution against the system: it represented an attempt to destroy a system that had been unfavorable to Japan and placed it in an inferior position.[60] In Chosŏn, Japan's unfavorable trading position may be traced back to the aftermath of the riots in the three Korean ports when the volume of trade authorized by Korea was reduced by half. In China, the decision in 1547 to end tribute missions from Japan on the pretext of rampant *wako* activity was decisive. Subsequently, virtually all trade between China and Japan fell into the hands of the *wako*, but the Portuguese later proved "superior" at playing this role, while relations between Chosŏn and Japan showed no signs of improvement.[61] It was precisely this system, so disadvantageous to Japan, which Hideyoshi intended to dismantle, using the military might assembled in the wars of unification.

---

58. The discussion below on the uses of cotton in Japan is based upon Sugiyama Hiroshi, "Chugoku-Chosen-Nanban no kijutsu to junjiryoku," in *Iwanami koza Nihon rekishi, chusei*, 4 (1976).
59. Yi Chinhŭi, "Karako odori to Chosensan," in Eizo bunka kyokai, *Edo jidai no Chosen tsushinshi*, (Tokyo: Mainichi shinbunsha, 1979), p. 59.
60. Nakamura Eiko, *Nissen kankeishi on kenkyu*, Vol. 2, p. 55.
61. Yamaguchi Keiji, "Nihon no sakoku," pp. 447–49.

Commerce and industry in Japan first developed within the confines of domains managed by the *sengoku daimyo*. The encouragement of commerce and industry stemmed from the need of the individual domains to provide the financial resources necessary for maintaining a large-scale military during the struggles of the Sengoku Period. While there were efforts in the field of agriculture such as land reclamation and other water-management projects, the focus of the domains' policies during this period was the promotion of commerce and the handicraft industry (e.g., the *rakushi rakuza* systems) and the development of mines to supply needed gold and silver.[62] As these policies were integral to the management of domains, the Nobunaga and Hideyoshi regimes—composed as they were of the domains—also had no choice but to attach political importance to domestic commercial and international trading rights. The Nobunaga regime hastened to seize control of Sakai, the bastion of domestic commerce, and the succeeding Hideyoshi regime captured, in the final push of the unification drive, Hakata and adjoining areas which were Japan's window of communication with the continent.[63] Since commercial and trading rights were so highly valued during the establishment of the unified government after unification was complete, the "entry into China" became the object of the search for a new focus of action.

Hideyoshi's ambitions may have represented an irresistible trend in Japanese history, but they were impossible to achieve considering the conditions of sixteenth-century East Asia. While it is true that preunification Japan underwent tremendous economic development, this development by no means surpassed that of Ming China or Chosŏn. Not only was Japan educated in the techniques of cotton cultivation and silver refining in the early sixteenth century, it also acquired firearms from the Portuguese after 1543 and, for a time, purchased the gunpowder necessary for these new weapons from the Chinese. In sum, even until the first half of the sixteenth century, Japan was in the position of having to import crucial technology. The indigenization of this technology during the latter half of the century was extremely important for Japan. But in the East Asian context, these develop-

62. Kozo Yamanura, "Returns on Unification: Economic Growth in Japan, 1550–1650," *Japan before Tokugawa* (Princeton: Princeton University Press, 1981); Nagahara Keiji, "Daimyo ryokokusei no kozo," in *Iwanami koza Nihon rekishi, chusei* 4; Fujuki Hisashi, "Daimyo ryokoku-sei no keisai kozo," in *Nihon keizaishi taikei* 2 (Tokyo: Tokyo daigaku shuppankai, 1965).

63. Wakita Osamu, "Shokuho seiken no shogyo-tohsi seisaku," in Nagahara Keiji, ed., *Sengoku jidai* (Tokyo: Yoshikawa kobunkan, 1978).

ments represented nothing more than a recovery from backwardness and could hardly be called an advance to regional preeminence.[64]

It is true that the muskets employed by the Japanese military in their invasion of Chosŏn possessed considerable power. However, Japan had only this one variety of firearm, a fact that suggests a point of cultural weakness. During naval battles, Japanese muskets were no match for Chosŏn's large cannons.

At first, the Chosŏn army was unable to counter the Japanese muskets and fought desperate, losing battles. Subsequently, drawing upon a long tradition of firearm technology, it manufactured various weapons and recovered from a position of overwhelming inferiority.[65] Both the Chosŏn forces and the Ming Southern Army were able to crush the Japanese army by skillfully employing *Chekiang* military tactics, which had been developed earlier for the purpose of dealing with the *wako*.

Hideyoshi's construction of the magnificently luxurious Jurakutei (Palace), with the prospect of unification before him, is a celebrated fact. But as Sugiyama Hiroshi expresses so well in describing the destruction of the palace following the suicide of Hideyoshi's son Hidetsugu in 1595, "It was similar to the sight of the military might of Hideyoshi's invasion forces being totally routed by the martial strength of the Chinese and Korean armies."[66] Unlike the expansionism practiced by the Hideyoshi regime, the Tokugawa bakufu hastened to restore relations with Chosŏn through a policy of national seclusion and simplified and restricted foreign trade. This foreign policy may have been the very best option at this time.

SOCIAL AND POLITICAL UNREST AND THE IDEOLOGICAL RESPONSE

Since the three countries of East Asia underwent important economic transformations during this time, it is not surprising that substantial political and social upheavals followed. As briefly mentioned in the introduction, the political conditions in each of the three countries were far from tranquil. In China, there was a violent collision of court eunuchs and literati amid a series of popular uprisings. In Japan, the

64. Sugiyama Hiroshi, "Chugoku-Chosen-Nanban no kijutsu to kunjiryoku."
65. For an account of the development of firearms in Korea up to the Imjin invasion, see Hŏ Sŏndo, "Chosŏn chunggi hwagi ŭi paldal" (The development of firearms in the mid-Chosŏn period), *Yŏksa hakpo*, Vols. 30–31 (1966).
66. Sugiyama Hiroshi, "Chugoku-Chosen-Nanban no kijutsu to kunjiryoku."

continuing peasant rebellions (*ikki*) formed the backdrop for the outbreak of fighting known as the *sengoku*. In Chosŏn, tax rebellions (*chŏngnan*), most notably that of Im Kkŏk-chŏng (?–1562), broke out all over the country.[67] The fact that all three countries suffered unrest among different groups in society, regardless of social class, points to the enormity of the economic transformation.

Historiography on China and Japan has already examined the relation of the factors behind these disturbances to economic changes. These instances of political unrest have been treated as events caused by conflicts within the ruling class over newly created wealth and by the dislocations brought about by the dissolution of the peasant class. In the case of China, the explanation runs as follows: After the mid-Ming period, growth in commerce and handicraft industries accelerated, and small-scale merchants and hired workers drawn from the peasant class appeared in sizable numbers. Popular rebellions arose to protest abuses in direct management or the taxation of mining, salt production, textiles, and porcelain by officials and eunuchs, both of whom enjoyed a great deal of actual power derived from the absolute authority of the emperor. The local gentry and literati, who also belonged to the ruling class, resisted abuses through the formation of elite groups composed of members of their own class, such as the Tung-lin Academy faction, but also directly participated in uprisings instigated by merchants, peasants, and wage laborers.[68]

In the case of Japan, a similar line of economic argument has been advanced. During the Muromachi Period, the surplus in production increased in various economic sectors, including agriculture, commerce, and handicrafts, thus triggering a struggle between the class of high feudal lords such as the *shugo daimyo* and the class of low feudal lords who were residing on domain property. As the tension between these two groups peaked, peasants at the village level formed community organizations and fomented rebellion as an expression of their

---

67. Yazawa Yasasuke, "'Im Kkŏkjŏng' no hanran to sono shakai-teki haikei" (The Im Kkŏkjŏng rebellion and its social background) in Hatada Takahashi sensei koki kinenkai, ed., *Chosen rekishi ronshu* (Tokyo: Ryukei shosha, 1979).

68. Fu I-ling, Ming-tai, *Chiang-nan shih-min ching-chi shi-t'an* (Shanghai: Jenmin ch'u-p'an-she, 1957); Liu Yen, "Ming-mo ch'eng-shih ching-chi fa-chan-hsia ti ch'u-chi shih-min yun-tung," in *Ming-tai she-hui ching-chi shih lun-chi* (Hong Kong: Tsun tsui hsueh she, 1979); Sakai Tadao, "Minmatsu no shakai to shijin" in *Chugoku zensho no kenkyu* (Tokyo: Kobundo, 1960); since research in this field is voluminous, this list is far from exhaustive.

concerns. Thus, according to this argument, Japan was simultaneously pressured by both the *ikki* and the *sengoku* rebellions.[69]

The disturbances in Chosŏn were, at root, not at odds with the conditions of the two other East Asian nations. In Chosŏn, the dissolution of the peasant class had reached severe levels due to the development of commerce. Although this statement was undoubtedly an exaggeration, one contemporary observer asserted that, "At present, of peasants everywhere, nine out of ten have deserted farming for some other occupation, and only one holds to his original profession."[70] The statement shows that the number of peasants switching from agriculture to small-scale commerce had reached extreme proportions. In the process of such change, "the wandering dispossessed" (*yusuja*), who had lost their means of subsistence, had no choice but to become members of "tax rebellion" mobs.

While these disruptions were occurring at the local level, the ruling class split into two groups. The first was the meritorious elite with their royal in-law allies (*hun'gu ch'ŏksin*); they were established officials who showed a strong propensity for special privilege. The second group was the *sarim*, who were newly rising officials (*sinhŭng sadaebu*).[71] Of the two, the meritorious elite was comparable in social position to the eunuchs of the Ming or the great feudal lords of Japan. There was fundamentally no difference between them and the Ming eunuchs since they attempted to maintain their status through a special relationship with royal authority or the royal household establishment.

The meritorious elite also showed quite a few similarities with their Japanese and Chinese counterparts in their deliberate acquisition of wealth. They regularly granted to specific groups the rights to collect taxes on parcels of farmland in return for a fixed share of the proceeds. In addition, the coalition of meritorious elite and royal in-laws would order local officials in coastal areas in the southwest to mobilize local citizens forcibly to develop low-lying tidal land. They then used the profits reaped from this newly developed land as capital

---

69. These are many excellent works by Japanese historians on the Sengoku Period. Here I will only cite Nagahara Keiji (ed.), whose work on this period has received much attention.

70. *Chungjong sillok*, 29, Chungjong 12, 8, *musin*.

71. Yi Tae-jin, "Sarimp'a ŭi yuhangso pongnip undong," (I)+(II) *Chindan* hakpo, Vols. 33–34 (1972+1973); and "Sarimp'a ŭi hyangyak pogŭp undong" (The movement of the *sarim* faction to spread the *hyangyak*), *Han'guk munhwa* 4 (1984). These studies look in detail at the confrontation between the two groups against the background of the *muo* and *kimyo* literati purges.

for the grain trade or as investment in mine development.[72] In the midst of economic change, the meritorious elite was the group able to attain the most wealth, using the power of their office in collaboration with rich merchants. The relationship between these two groups was precisely the same as it was in China and Japan, where collusion between officials and merchants became a major problem. In Chosŏn, the *sarim* criticized and attacked the meritorious elite for the impropriety of their methods of acquiring wealth. Driven into a corner, the entrenched conservatives took revenge, and the result was repeated literati purges. The social position of the *sarim* literati, who came from the small- and medium-scale landlord classes, was akin to that of the lesser feudal lords in Japan and the local gentry and literati who formed the Tung-lin Academy faction in China.

Although this may be a sweeping generalization, the numerous similarities in the political and social conditions of the three East Asian countries must be seen as a consequence of the historical similarity of the economic changes in the region.

Lastly, it would be very interesting to examine the various responses of the three countries to these social and political disturbances. However, since this would require investigating trends across the entire spectrum of philosophy during the sixteenth and seventeenth centuries, there is not enough space in this chapter to provide specific details on the many issues involved. In general, it could be said that small- and medium-scale landlord classes—or their equivalent—tended to search for a new social order using Zhu Xi's Neo-Confucianism (*Sŏngnihak*) or a combination of Zhu Xi's Neo-Confucianism and Wang Yang-ming's school of Neo-Confucianism. Next, I will briefly discuss how Chosŏn's landlord class only took up *Sŏngnihak* (i.e., Neo-Confucianism).

It is not exactly clear why Chosŏn, unlike China and Japan, rejected the Wang Yang-ming (1472–1529) school. *Sŏngnihak* is often understood as an ideology of rule mainly based on agriculture. However, as I have already made clear, it would be unreasonable to conclude that Chosŏn took up *Sŏngnihak* due to an inherent preference for agriculture and, hence, that commercial development was either nonexistent or backward at best. In fact, *Sŏngnihak* established roots in Chosŏn society amid the great change ushered in by the circulation of goods in markets.

---

72. Yi Tae-jin, "Simnyuk segi yŏnhae chiyŏk-ŭi ŏnjŏn kaebal," in *Kim Chŏljun paksa hwagap kinyŏm sahak nonch'ong*.

The most important political initiatives involved in the process of establishing *Sŏngnihak* in Chosŏn were the *hyangŭmjurye*,[73] the movements in the 1480s to propagate *hyangsarye*, and the movements in the 1510s to encourage adoption of the *hyangyak*.[74] The objective of the *sarim*'s reform-oriented politics was nothing other than to calm the disturbances caused by the growth in the circulation of commodities. In other words, the goal was the restoration of stability through the use of Confucian methods applied to a rural society in the throes of severe social agitation stemming from the dissolution of the peasant class. It is clear that *Sŏngnihak* put high priority on the stability of rural society. The initiative taken by the *sarim* in disseminating new techniques of irrigation and making use of waterways can be seen as one instance of the *Sŏngnihak* program of rural stabilization, since water conservation was vital to the development of wet-field agriculture.[75]

However, the importance placed on agriculture did not mean the *sarim* were opposed to commercial development. When the *sarim* debated over whether to abolish rural markets (*changmun*), Yi Hwang (T'oegye, 1501–1570), one of the most prominent literati, favored their continuance along with a majority of the members of this group, as long as the markets proved beneficial to the livelihood of the people.[76] In addition, during the movement to propagate the *hyangyak*, an effort was made to promote the production of silk cloth by making sericulture a secondary occupation of rural households.[77] The *sarim* also gave substantial support to the proposal to mint metallic currency, whose aim was to make it the center of the monetary system.[78]

The degree to which Korean *Sŏngnihak* was an ideological response to commercialism is clearly visible in the importance it placed on respect for frugality. As mentioned above, one of the social consequences of economic change in Chosŏn—evident from the latter part of the reign of Sŏngjong (r. 1469–1494) through the reign of Myŏngjong (r. 1545–1567)—was the drift toward luxury, centered on

---

73. Yi Tae-jin, "Sarimp'a ŭi yuhyangso pongnip undong."
74. Yi Tae-jin, "Sarimp'a ŭi hyangyak pogŭp undong."
75. Yi Tae-jin, "Simnyuk segi ŭi ch'ŏnbang(po) kwangae ŭi paldal" (The development of *ch'ŏnbang* irrigation in the sixteenth century), *Han Ugŭn paksa chongnyŏn kinyŏm sahak nonch'ong* (Seoul: Chisik san'ŏpsa, 1981).
76. Yi Tae-jin, "Juroku seiki no Kankokushi ni taisuru Rikai no hoko," pp. 20–22.
77. Yi Tae-jin, "Sarimp'a ŭi hyangyak pogŭp undong," pp. 332–33.
78. Song Chaesŏn, "Simnyuk segi myŏnp'o ŭi hwap'ye kinŭng," pp. 20–22.

clothing and jewelry, wedding accessories, and housing. This trend to luxury became the object of denunciation in political circles. In this atmosphere, the original Confucian attitudes of diligence, frugality, and thrift received special attention. To sum up, the *sarim* adherents, while not blindly rejecting commerce itself on the ideological basis of *munbon ŏngmal* (literally, "striving for agriculture, suppressing commerce"), took a position arising from their class base in small- and medium-scale landlord classes and pursued a commercial policy whose goal was the stabilization of rural society.

As implied by the repeated literati purges, the political position of the *sarim* through the sixteenth century was one of opposition and lack of access to power. They had few opportunities to implement the reform agenda they advocated. Toward the end of the century, the end of rule by the meritorious elite and royal in-laws brought about a favorable political change for the *sarim*, and their long-cherished plans could finally be implemented. The best examples are the first-ever minting of metallic currency in 1625 and the enactment of the *Taedongbŏp* in 1650—after a considerable period of discussion—that aimed at reforming the structural irrationalities of the local tribute tax system.[79]

*Sŏngnihak* was by no means a system of thought which actively advocated commercialism or industrialization. Yet, in response to the conditions of the time, it strove to stabilize the rural economy and society. One of the main reasons that Chosŏn did not collapse in the seventeenth century, despite suffering the Japanese and two Manchu invasions, was the secure and solid foundation of *Sŏngnihak* thought.

CONCLUSION

I have examined the development of the circulation of commodities in the three East Asian countries during the sixteenth century and the political disturbances caused by such change. The historiographical literature on China and Japan is full of studies on these issues; the material presented here on these two countries contains nothing new. However, there has been a critical lack of studies that attempt to illuminate this period from the perspective of East Asia as a whole. Without an examination of the same transformation in Korean history,

79. Ko Sŏkgyu, "Simnyuk-sipch'il segi kongnapje kaehyŏk ŭi panghyang," *Han'guk saron* 12 (1985).

a truly balanced and complete understanding of the total East Asian region during this period remains impossible. The objective of this chapter has been to attempt to remedy this situation. In this chapter, there are a number of specific issues concerning sixteenth-century Chosŏn that need to be supplemented by further research. I think it has been highly valuable to reconsider a number of issues from a comparative historical perspective; this is one area in which Korean historiography has lagged behind.

As has been pointed out in research on China and Japan, the development of the East Asian economy involved the wide circulation of commercial goods, which began in the sixteenth century and peaked in the eighteenth century. This is highly significant in light of the influence that the East Asian economy exerted on world history during this period.

The importance of these three hundred years of economic growth to East Asian history was amply demonstrated by the fact that when the world economic center began to move toward the West in the nineteenth century due to the industrial revolution, the three East Asian nations were all undergoing major rebellions: the Taiping rebellion in China, the Yonaoshi rebellion in Japan, and popular rebellions in Korea. The root causes of these major upheavals must, to a certain extent, be sought in the specific domestic conditions of each nation. But in view of the timing of these outbreaks, I believe that the primary factor had to be a change in international economic conditions.[80] The world preeminence of the East Asian economy began to decline, as indicated by the outflow of silver from China following the rise of industrial capitalism in the West. As a result, both China and other countries within the Sinitic economic sphere, such as Korea and Japan, were unable to avoid internal rebellion.[81]

translated by Milan Hejtmanek

---

80. Terada Takanobu, "Shinan shonin to Sanshi shonin," *Chuseishi koza* 3 (Tokyo: Gakuseisha, 1982). This work details the economic conditions of the time and their changing nature based upon an examination of the merchants of Shinan.

81. Among the studies of the East Asian trading region in the seventeenth and eighteenth centuries is Tashiro Kazui's *Kinsei Nitcho tsuko boeikishi no kenkyu*, which focuses on the bilateral trading relations between Japan and Korea. This study has also received a great deal of attention for its attempt to perceive the structure of the Chinese, Korean, and Japanese trading regions from a fresh perspective.

Table 1
COMPARATIVE VALUES OF CHŎNGP'O AND SANGP'O, WITH RICE VALUES

| Year | Chŏng : Sang Ratio | Ply and Length | Value in Rice | Rice Value Index |
|---|---|---|---|---|
| 1469 | 1:1 | 5 ply, 35 ch'ŏk | 4 tu | 1.00 |
| 1501 | 2:1 | 3 ply, 30 ch'ŏk | 4 tu | .50 |
| 1415 | 3:1 | 1 ply, 30 ch'ŏk | 4 tu 3 sŭng | .33 |

*1 tu = 10 sŭng

CHAPTER 6

# Separating Fact from Fiction about Pre-Modern Sino-Korean Trade

AS NEIGHBORING COUNTRIES, KOREA and China have shared a long history of interaction. Based largely on an awareness of close cultural affinity, most of their history has been marked by friendly cooperation and interchange. Although there have been military confrontations, they were primarily limited to ancient history. Aside from Emperor Han Wu-di's invasion of Old Chosŏn, Koguryŏ's clashes with the Sui and Tang, and the struggle between the Silla forces and their Tang allies immediately after the Silla Unification, there have been no other conflicts of similar scale. Through close interaction, a cultural affinity developed that transcended any military discord and even extended to the shared use of Chinese written characters.

The cultural relationship between the two countries was somewhat one-sided, as Korea adopted many more aspects of Chinese culture than China did of Korean culture. The influx of Chinese culture was a boon to Korea's cultural advancement—in many cases Korea used new religions and ideologies from China to advance its own development. Needless to say, China also benefited from its ties with Korea. In several instances when China faced aggression from a third country, Korea provided both diplomatic and military cooperation in the belief that the two countries should jointly defend their superior culture. Although this strong cultural bond occasionally led to humiliating defeat, it was the primary driving force behind East Asian civilization for centuries, until the arrival of the West in the nineteenth century.

The close historical relation between Korea and China not only was cultural and political, but also involved economic interactions as well. In light of the overwhelming influence of Western capitalism following its expansion into Asia, some scholars have tended to underestimate the economic aspects of Sino-Korean relations when examining the history of East Asian international trade, which also included Japan. In reality, they played a crucial role, and it could be argued that the close political and cultural relationship between the two countries was made possible through their economic interactions.

Especially after the sixteenth century, the thriving international trade in the region contributed greatly to economic development. This growth had its limits, however, as East Asia was not able to develop beyond the stage of commercial capitalism. Its development stands in stark contrast with the European economy, where international trade contributed to the transformation from commercial to industrial capitalism. This lack of an industrial base led to the subjugation of East Asian countries as colonies and semi-colonies to both the Western capitalist nations and eventually Japan in the early twentieth century. What, then, were the reasons that international trade in East Asia was not able to overcome these limitations to its growth?

Many explanations have been proposed but are unsatisfactory because most studies have downplayed the achievements of East Asian economic development. The prevalent tendency has been to view the past history of East Asia's interactions with the West as a historical error that should not be repeated. I will examine the causes of these historical changes as part of an effort to reflect on Korea's past. However, it is also necessary to be careful of underestimating the level the East Asian economy achieved before the invasions of the West. Any attempt to study the situation with the preconceived notion and bias that the East Asian economy was relatively under-developed and only began to grow following Western inroads into Asia will not do justice to historical reality. East Asia's current search for the best path to future development can only benefit from deeper reflection upon its past.

## THE HISTORICAL NATURE OF EAST ASIA'S TRIBUTARY-TRADE SYSTEM

The history of East Asian trade can be roughly separated into two periods, divided by the Ming dynasty's decision to restrict seaborne trade in the second half of the fourteenth century. Through this policy, the Ming tried to strengthen China's traditional tributary-trade system, but in doing so, it changed the nature of international trade in East Asia.

Connected by the Yellow Sea, Korea and China have participated in active trade since early times. The interaction and trade through the Gulf of Bohai of the Yellow Sea was of considerable importance in the development of Old Chosŏn on the Liaodong Peninsula. It served as an impetus to the growth of ancient Korean society, and it is said that the evolution of ancient Korean civilization originated from this geographic spot. Furthermore, the advent of Yellow Sea trade was made possible only through the Gulf of Bohai. Needless to say, the Yellow Sea played a crucial role in the development of trade between Korea and China, even though the nature of trade on the Yellow Sea began to change with the implementation of Ming's sea-trade restrictions.

The Ming dynasty's restrictive sea-trade policy did not, however, prohibit all sea trade. The original intent of the maritime trade restrictions was to block all unauthorized private trade routes. Despite these regulations, private trade flourished in the early decades of the fifteenth century. The trade restrictions were also meant to maintain the central government's jurisdiction over all overseas trade. The expeditions of Ming official Zheng He (1371–1435?) were part of the central government's efforts to establish an international trade system. The Ming dynasty utilized the sea-trade restrictions in its foreign policy by granting investiture to states and levying tribute. By restricting its trade only to those countries that had accepted investiture status, the Ming dynasty adopted a trade policy based on formal tribute trade. To maintain and manage this system, the Chinese allowed open and friendly maritime relations.

China has traditionally pursued diplomatic and economic relations based on a conception of an international order centered on itself. Not surprisingly, the restrictive sea-trade policy of the Ming dynasty was founded upon this concept. As the importance of sea commerce among East Asian nations continued to rise, negative reactions from states affected by this policy began to increase as well.

During the Yuan dynasty, the bulk of China's international trade was conducted over land routes, as illustrated by the prosperity of the Silk Road. The rise of the Yuan dynasty as a vast empire in both the East and West attested to the importance of overland trade. The Silk Road trade route reached its pinnacle during this period; as a result of its tremendous success and generous profits, the emperor extended the realm of the Silk Road as far west as Europe.[1]

While the Chin and Yuan dynasties pursued profits generated by the Silk Road, the Southern Song dynasty, centered on the southern region of the Yangzi River, focused on seaborne trade with countries in Southeast Asia. The Southern Song's emphasis on sea commerce had a considerable impact not only on China but also on the economies of all Southeast Asian countries. Beginning in the thirteenth century, commerce in Southeast Asian countries showed greater vitality, and the expansion of trade routes to East Asia clearly opened a new chapter in the history of East-West trade relationships. Not surprisingly, Chinese resistance to Yuan control over sea routes emerged toward the end of the dynasty in Canton, Chekiang, and other coastal regions. Leaders like Fang Guozhen (?–?) from Canton and Zhang Shichen (1321–1367) from Zhejiang, who rose to power as a result of friendly maritime relations, initially held greater influence than Zhu Yuanzhang (1328–1398) from An-shih province.[2] After a fierce struggle for supremacy, Zhu Yuanzhang emerged victorious. Among his motives for sea-trade restrictions was the establishment of control over his rivals. The Ming dynasty's restrictive sea-trade policy, which initially stemmed from similar domestic power network relationships, was linked to the tribute system with the purpose of establishing a new world order. The tribute system became the basis of the Ming's new diplomatic policy, and it was no coincidence that large-scale expeditionary commerce emerged upon the implementation of the tribute system.

The tribute system, the sea-trade restrictions, and other Ming policies were applied to Koryŏ and Chosŏn. In fact, they were implemented in Korea before being applied to Southeast Asia. Since China had more direct interests in Korea, China placed higher priority on applying these policies to the tense situation in Korea. When Fang Guozhen and Zhang Shicheng in the south ascended to power, they had already established friendly relations with Koryŏ. The rival leaders of southern China adopted an open diplomatic stance, and Koryŏ accommodated their requests for friendly relations. However, after these leaders were defeated by Zhu Yuanzhang, Koryŏ found

---

1. Otagi Matsuo, "Ortaq-sen to sono haikei" (Altai money and its background), *Toyoshi kenkyu* 32, nos. 1-2 (1973).
2. Otagi Matsuo, "Cho Gokoku to Shu Gokoku—shoki Min ocho no seikaku ni kansuru ichi kosatsu" (Zhang Shicheng and Zhu Yuanzhang—an examination of the nature of the early Ming dynasty), *Bunka* 17, no. 6 (Nov. 1953).

Separating Fact from Fiction   125

itself in a difficult situation. Although Koryŏ quickly responded to the change in circumstances by sending an emissary to Zhu upon his victory, Zhu still remained wary of Koryŏ due to its past friendly relations with his enemies.

Zhu's feelings of distrust toward Koryŏ evolved into paranoia as he took control of Liaodong. During the Yuan dynasty, Koryŏ exerted influence on the Liaodong region, where many Koryŏ people resided. Since Koryŏ held sway over Liaodong and had ties to the rival leaders of southern China, Zhu feared a possible rebellion against his control over the region. Therefore, he prohibited all traffic by sea to Koryŏ and, with the intention of lowering the status of Koryŏ to that of a tributary nation, required that Koryŏ pay tribute once every three years. While the number of tribute missions to be sent to China was raised and then officially set at three per year at Koryŏ's request, Zhu still remained anxious. This lingering suspicion led him to apply the same policy to Chosŏn, which succeeded Koryŏ in 1392. Chosŏn denounced this policy and planned an attack on the Liaodong region in retaliation, though actual military conflict was averted at the last minute.[3]

The restrictive sea-trade policy of the Ming dynasty was adopted as a means for maintaining a centralized government structure in a changing age in which maritime commerce was of increased importance. Although its new international policy faced temporary opposition from the Muromachi Bakufu in Japan, the Ming dynasty established a "unitary trade system" throughout all of East Asia. In Korea, the Chosŏn dynasty established its position within the tributary system by establishing semi-tributary relations with Japan, the Ryukyu Islands, the Jurchens, and other countries while avoiding friction with the Ming. The Ming dynasty's sea-trade restrictions and tributary policy were significant in creating a system for the new conditions of Asian international trade in the thirteenth and fourteenth centuries.

THE SINO-KOREAN TRIBUTARY TRADE SYSTEM: FACT AND FICTION

The Ming dynasty established the investiture-tribute system in pursuit of a Sinocentric world order, and it was maintained by the succeeding

3. This section on the policy of Zhu Yuanzhang, the first emperor of the Ming dynasty (Hongwu Emperor), toward Chosŏn is taken from the volume on the early Chosŏn period of *Chosŏnsa kanghwa*, which I am currently preparing. This volume will be published in 1995 by the publisher Hongmundang.

Qing dynasty in the sixteenth century as the foundation for the East Asian world order. However, this did not mean that the restrictions on sea trade that supported this structure remained unchanged. As international commerce expanded because of economic development in each country, it became difficult to sustain the original intent of the restrictive policy. From the sixteenth century onward, flourishing private trade exceeded the restrictions on trade established under the tributary system and rendered the sea trade restrictions ineffectual. In this section, I will examine the fact and fiction of the tributary-trade system.

In the sixteenth century, international trade in East Asia began to undergo tremendous changes in terms of quantity, products traded, and countries involved.[4] The major East Asian countries—China, Korea, and Japan—participated in this trade, along with merchants from other parts of the globe such as Portugal and Ryukyu that were now playing a greater role in East Asian trade. The latter enjoyed profits from dealing in Southeast Asian goods or selling Chinese silk to Japan. Each country produced a fixed list of products in large quantities. While China continued to sell goods such as pottery and silk—its traditional export item—the quantity had greatly increased. While the volume of silk carried by Portuguese merchants to Europe was no small amount, the quantity of silk fabric and thread exported to Chosŏn and Japan was also significant. Chosŏn merchants reaped substantial profits by serving as intermediaries in the silk trade with Japan and, in addition, exported large quantities of domestically produced cotton cloth and grain to Japan. In return, Japan exported copper, herbal medicine, and other products to Chosŏn.

By the sixteenth century, silver prevailed as the main currency in East Asia's international trade. In the mid-fifteenth century, China streamlined its tax system and began to assess all taxes in silver. Eventually used in most business transactions, silver naturally became the common currency as it facilitated international trade. As a result, silver from many other nations began to flow into China. A significant amount of Mexican silver found its way into China via European merchants. Recent research also shows that a large quantity of silver flowed into China from Chosŏn and Japan. The development of a technique that separated silver from lead led to a boom in silver

4. This section on the sixteenth century is taken from Yi Tae-jin (Yi T'aejin), *Chosŏn yugyo sahoe saron*, chapter 5, "16segi Tong Asia kyŏngje pyŏndong kwa chŏngch'i-sahoejŏk tonghyang" (Seoul: Chisik san'ŏpsa, 1989). The English translation can be found in chapter 5 of this book.

mining. Famous even today for its silver mines, Tanch'ŏn (Hamgyŏng province) was originally an insignificant lead-rich mountainous region that developed silver mines after the discovery of this technique. The smuggling of this technique into Japan was the direct impetus for the development of silver mining also emerged in northern Kyushu in the mid-sixteenth century.

To understand fully the vitality of East Asian trade in the sixteenth century, it is necessary to look at the development of the agricultural economy. From the twelfth century, East Asian agriculture showed remarkable progress thanks to the dissemination of advanced wet-field farming techniques from southern China. New agricultural methods overcame the limitations of farming fallow land through improvements in fertilization and weeding techniques. They led to increased productivity and contributed greatly to the growth of the East Asian economy. Due to differences in local conditions, however, the development of wet-field farming in China, Korea, and Japan occurred at different speeds and with different outcomes. By the fifteenth century, each country had overcome the inadequacies of fallow-land farming, and all were able to reap the benefits of increased productivity. The growth in the agricultural economy increased purchasing power and enormously energized both domestic markets and international trade.

Sino-Korean trade was limited to overland trade during the expansion of international commerce in the sixteenth century. Despite this limitation, Chosŏn merchants were able to profit substantially by collaborating with tributary envoys to procure large quantities of raw silk and in turn exchange this silk with Japanese merchants who were given special privileges to trade at three Chosŏn ports. In the Chinese coastal regions, there was brisk trade as merchants from Japan, Ryukyu, Portugal, and other countries came to sell various articles and to buy Chinese pottery and silk. The widespread activity of private merchants essentially rendered the restrictions on sea trade ineffective.

The thriving international trade of this period also brought about trade disputes and caused friction among the three East Asian countries. In 1510, Japanese merchants at the three Chosŏn trading ports rioted in objection to export limitations on grains and cotton material imposed by the Chosŏn government. In 1547, the Japanese started a similar insurrection at the Ningpo port in China. In retaliation, the Ming dynasty ended tributary trade with Japan. Consequently, Japanese pirates preyed on the Chinese coast, smuggling or pillaging the goods they needed. However, the Japanese were not the only ones involved in piracy. While many Portuguese were involved, natives of Chinese coastal regions who disguised themselves as Japanese pirates accounted for seventy to eighty percent of these activities. Piracy often involved landowners, nobility, and wealthy merchants from the coast of southeastern China, and these unauthorized activities were seen as inevitable as long as the Chinese government adhered to its sea-trade restrictions. The Ming government thus finally adopted a measure in 1567 to end the restrictive sea-trade policy, allowing the Chinese people to participate in overseas private commerce.

The measure ending the restrictive sea-trade policy is significant in the history of East Asia's international trade for its impact on the economic development of the East Asian countries. Since the Ming state did not abandon the tributary-trade system, however, restrictions on sea trade were not completely lifted. Even after the promulgation of the new measure, Chosŏn merchants uninterested in maritime trade continued to travel between China and Chosŏn using only land routes. As neighboring countries were still bound by the tribute system, the new policy provided more freedom only for Chinese merchants. Hideyoshi's attempted invasion of the Ming dynasty in 1592 was also strongly motivated by the desire to break free of the constraints of the tributary-trade system.

Toyotomi Hideyoshi, after succeeding in the monumental task of unifying Japan, wanted to achieve a complete change in Japan's trade with countries on the Asian continent. He felt it was necessary to push for a repeal of the punitary exclusion of Japan from the tributary-trade system after the *Ningpo* rebellion. Around 1589, he considered a plan to regain tributary-trade status by offering to put an end to piracy.[5] Though his proposal was rejected, it demonstrates that as the new ruler of a unified Japan, Hideyoshi viewed the tributary-trade system as being of paramount importance and saw it as the mainstay of East Asian international order. Three years later, he gave up the pursuit of participating in the tributary trade and ordered his army to land in Chosŏn with the intention of invading Ming China. Mobilizing the massive military force he had used to unify the Japanese islands, he wanted to break free of the constraints that exclusion from the tributary trade had placed on Japan's international trade.

5. Fujiki Hisashi, *Toyotomi heiwarei to sengoku shakai* (Tokyo: Tokyo daigaku shuppankai, 1985), pp. 218–38.

Although Hideyoshi's war ended in defeat, the impact of the war on East Asia was tremendous. Ming China was hit hard by burdensome war expenditures at a time when its finances were already weakened because of an interruption in the inflow of Mexican silver.[6] Exacerbating the situation, the southward movement of the Jurchens created a sense of vulnerability within the Ming state. The subsequent dynastic transition from the Ming to Qing had huge repercussions on the East Asian international order. The Qing maintained the Ming's tribute system but also revived the restrictive sea-trade policy, in effect negating much of the progress that East Asian trade had made in recent decades.

In the seventeenth century, East Asia suffered a crisis more severe than any intra-Asian conflict—the onset of the natural disaster known as the "Little Ice Age."[7] The "Little Ice Age," a result of global meteorite collisions, was marked by a severe drop in temperature and inflicted heavy damage, particularly on the northern hemisphere. Frequent hailstorms, unseasonal heavy snowfall, wind damage, drought, flood, and other natural disasters dealt a fatal blow to agricultural output for a period of seventy to eighty years. This natural disaster, which caused a series of continual poor harvests, dramatically reduced the size of the population in the countries of the northern hemisphere. Population studies on China and Chosŏn reveal that famine and widespread epidemics led to a drop in population by about a third from the end of the sixteenth century to 1670.[8] The southward migration of the Jurchen tribe was one consequence of this natural disaster.

The Jurchens, who lived in the northernmost region of East Asia, were severely affected by the "Little Ice Age." Originally a nomadic tribe, by the sixteenth century they had shifted toward an agriculture-based society through the influence of China and Chosŏn. Their dependence on the quality of harvests for their very existence left them highly vulnerable to the climactic whims of nature. Changes in

6. William S. Atwell, "International Bullion Flows and the Chinese Economy Circa 1530–1650," *Past and Present* 95 (1983).
7. On the crisis of the seventeenth century, see Yi Tae-jin, "Kukje muyŏk ŭi sŏnghaeng," *Han'guksa simin kangjwa* 9 (1991), pp. 74–75 and Yi Tae-jin, "Chosŏn hugi yangban sahoe ŭi pyŏnhwa," *Han'guk sahoe paljŏn saron* (Seoul: Ilchogak, 1993), p. 184. However, it is necessary to undertake a more thorough investigation of relevant materials on this topic.
8. Kwŏn T'aehwan and Sin Yongha, "Chosŏn wangjo sidae ingu ch'ujŏng e kwanhan il siron" (An attempt at population estimates for the Chosŏn dynasty period), *Tonga munhwa* 14 (1977).

weather patterns caused by this quasi "ice-age" reduced the agricultural harvest such that their last hope for survival lay in migrating southward. It was no coincidence that their ensuing conflicts with the Ming dynasty stemmed from the struggle for control over the fertile agricultural land of the Liaodong region.[9]

The revival of the restrictive sea-trade policy after the founding of the Qing China was aimed at isolating and controlling the remnants of the former Ming government, as many Ming loyalists had fled to Taiwan. This objective is apparent from the fact that the government passed a measure allowing Chinese people to travel abroad again a year after Taiwan's remaining insurgents were completely suppressed in 1683. However, as will be discussed later, this measure was narrower in scope than the similar measure adopted by the Ming government in the late sixteenth century. Since the victorious Qing dynasty was still trying to achieve many goals through the tribute system, they were not as open to abolishing sea-trade restrictions as the Ming dynasty had been.

As East Asia began to emerge from the crisis caused by the "Little Ice Age" toward the end of the seventeenth century, the economies of China, Japan, and Korea also began to revive. The various emergency measures adopted in response to this long-lasting natural disaster were the main factors behind the economic revitalization; as a result, each country's economy showed greater vitality than ever before. Research on the East Asian economic history has shown that there was greater economic activity in the eighteenth century than in the sixteenth. This economic revival obviously had a great impact on international trade as well.

The revision of the Qing's restrictive sea-trade policy at the end of the seventeenth century brought about significant changes in East Asian trade in the eighteenth century. Chinese merchants were now able to trade in places such as Nagasaki and Southeast Asia, and Japanese merchants began to engage in direct trade with Southeast Asia. There was also a change in overland commerce between Chosŏn and China.[10] At several points along the Sino-Korean border, private trade was officially permitted, designated by the term *husi*. Due to its agricultural development from the sixteenth century, Manchuria

---

9. Records on the Later Jin dynasty's conflicts with Ming China are filled with anger at the fact that Ming soldiers plundered their agricultural goods. See *Manbun roto* (in Chinese, Man wen lao dang), translated and annotated by Kanda Nobuo, et al. (Tokyo: Toyo bunko, 1960).

10. This section is based on Yi Tae-jin, "Kukje muyŏk ŭi sŏnghaeng."

played an increased economic role in the region, leading to the growth of private trade in the border region. The increased importance of this region as a supplier of agricultural produce was already apparent at the time of Hideyoshi's invasion. When Chinese troops were dispatched to Chosŏn to repel the Japanese invasion, they carried with them only silver and very little in the way of food provisions, assuming that food supplies could be obtained in Manchuria or Chosŏn. The region's agricultural development increased international trade as well. Although forcing tribute envoys to take the Manchurian route was done in part because it was the original homeland of the Qing dynasty, another reason was to incorporate this area into the eastern trading region. The widespread appearance of Chinese merchants traveling north to south through the Yellow Sea was further evidence of Manchuria's increased economic importance. However, east-to-west trade between China and Korea through the Yellow Sea, still bound by the sea-trade restrictions, was limited to the illegal smuggling of trading products.

After escaping the crisis of the seventeenth century, the East Asian economy surpassed by far the level that it had reached in the late sixteenth century. However, the Qing dynasty's lifting of sea-trade restrictions was not as liberal as the measure taken by the Ming dynasty. As mentioned earlier, after the suppression of Taiwan, the Qing permitted the overseas travel of Chinese; control over private trade was soon reinstituted, and several restrictions were tightened. The Qing court also instituted the *Cohong* system, which created a guild of licensed monopoly merchants. In the second half of the eighteenth century, this arrangement was limited to one port, Canton. The Qing dynasty, as a foreign dynasty which had conquered China, clearly faced many problems in maintaining its domestic rule. It had no choice but to pursue an isolationist foreign policy.

Following its suppression of Taiwan, the Qing dynasty spent the next seventy years subduing other ethnic minorities in the northwest regions.[11] The emperor believed in the concept of a "grand unity" of

11. In writing this section, I was greatly aided by the following papers presented at a conference sponsored by the Asia munhwa yŏn'guso of Hallym University on November 26–27, 1993, on "17segi Tong Asia kakguk ŭi sinkukje chilsŏ mosaek—Han-Chung-Il-Wŏl kan ŭi pigyo." Yi Tae-jin, "Chosŏn hugi tae Myŏng uiriron ŭi pyŏnch'ŏn" (Changes in the discussion of loyalty to Ming China in the late Chosŏn period); Cho Pyŏnghan, "Ch'ŏngdae Chungguk ŭi 'taeilt'ongjŏk chunghwa ch'egye wa taewoe insik ŭi pyŏndong" (Qing China's sinocentric system of "grand unification" and changes in views on foreign affairs); Min Tŏkgi, "Tŏkch'ŏn makbu ŭi taewoe ch'eje wa Myŏng-Ch'ŏngjo ŭi

his country, seeking a peaceful and unified China proper. Given that peace and unity in China proper could not be achieved without control over the northern tribes, the subjugation of these peoples was the Qing's first priority in creating its empire. Chinese rulers, beginning with Emperor Kangxi (r. 1662–1722), had believed that in order to establish the Middle Kingdom—a unified China—the monarch had to be both learned and skilled in military maneuvers. Accordingly, the Qing attached the greatest importance to its policy of subjugating the northwest region and concentrated its energies on this task. In the process, its foreign relations were stunted. While retaining its investiture-tribute policy, the Qing dynasty soon rescinded its policy of opening sea trade. As foreign conquerors, the Qing were so obsessed with the domestic tasks of building the Middle Kingdom that their external policy become far more rigid than that of the Ming.

By the eighteenth century, the traditional China-centered trade framework was no longer compatible with the new world order. During this period, East Asia enjoyed unprecedented prosperity as the economic growth of its individual countries contributed significantly to the expansion of international trade. However, these gains were more or less negated by the obligations of the China-centered international order. Despite the progress made in lifting the sea-trade regulations in the sixteenth century, the reversion to the original restrictive trade policy by the victorious Qing in the seventeenth century marked a regression in the development of East Asian trade.

The Qing also made changes to the tribute system. As the campaign to subdue the northwest region dragged on, the Qing conceded to the wishes of surrounding tributary nations to reduce the required tribute in both variety and quantity. The goal was to ease unnecessary diplomatic friction that might impede Qing's unification of China. In the eighteenth century, items such as gold, silver, other precious metals, and animal furs and skins were for the most part not required as tribute articles, leaving only paper goods and woven fabrics as tributary goods. Except for an increase in paper goods, the Qing substantially reduced the quantity required for all other goods.[12]

---

kyoch'e" (The foreign relations of the Tokugawa bakufu and the dynastic change from Ming to Qing); Yu Insŏn, "Wŏlnam Wŏnjo ŭi sŏngnip kwa 'taenam' cheguk chilsŏ" (The establishment of the Nguyen dynasty and the imperial order of the "great south"). These papers will be published in an issue of *Asia munhwa* in 1994.

12. See table 6 in Chŏn Haejong, *Han-Chung kwan'gyesa yŏn'gu* (Seoul: Ilchogak, 1970), p. 18.

The underlying conception of the Middle Kingdom, which served as the basis of the tribute system, also changed. Since the leadership of the Qing dynasty did not descend from the Han-Chinese ethnic majority, the previous standards for Chinese-ness and foreignness in ethnicity and geography could no longer apply. Stressing that Confucian culture should be the criterion for determining what was Chinese, Emperor Yong Cheng declared that not just the Han people but also neighboring peoples such as the Manchus, Mongols, and Tibetans should be considered native Chinese. Under this declaration, emperors of ethnic minority descent attempted to realize their vision of China as the Middle Kingdom through their own learning and military achievements.[13] They worked toward achieving domestic and political stability. China's new vision caused large-scale repercussions in the surrounding tributary states as many proclaimed themselves the "true" Middle Kingdom.

In the early eighteenth century (1714), Chosŏn declared itself to be the true successor of Ming dynasty culture.[14] At almost the same time, Confucian scholars in Japan declared the same thing, saying that Japan was a sacred land whose emperor was descended from an unbroken imperial line.[15] The redefinition of the term "Middle Kingdom" by these two countries weakened the traditional Chinese tribute system. The Qing dynasty did not even retaliate against the declarations by its neighbors, and at the beginning of the nineteenth century, even Vietnam declared itself the "true" Middle Kingdom.[16] At the end of the eighteenth and the early nineteenth centuries, changes in the East Asian world order produced internal conditions that would enable the countries to conduct trade in new areas of the globe. However, the Qing court had no intention of abandoning its tribute policy. The more aware China was that its status as the Middle Kingdom was weakening, the more it closed its doors to the outside world.

As the East Asian economy continued to develop in the eighteenth century, the only way the region could further develop was to stimulate private trade through the complete lifting of restrictions on seaborne trade and the abolition of the tribute system. Although there were some modifications in those policies, no fundamental changes occurred in the nineteenth century. It could be argued that as the

13. Cho Pyŏnghan, ibid.
14. Yi Tae-jin, "Chosŏn hugi tae Myŏng ŭiriron ŭi pyŏnch'ŏn."
15. Min Tŏkgi, ibid.
16. Yu Insŏn, ibid.

dominant nation in East Asia whose influence could not be ignored by its neighbors, China should bear responsibility for the economic stagnation of the region. One of the major differences between East Asia and Europe was the fact that one country, China, was so much larger in scale than its neighbors. As long as China would not unilaterally change the tribute system that was the foundation of the international order, there was no hope of change or improvement. It was thus significant that the surrounding states succeeded in annulling the restrictive sea-trade policy by developing a flourishing private trade on their own.

Although China's continued support of the tribute system hindered overall East Asian economic development, neighboring countries were equally at fault in failing to mobilize active resistance to the system. During the eighteenth century, all of East Asia, including the three major kingdoms of China, Korea, and Japan, developed commerce by linking their ports to its interior regions. As the volume of trade increased, the importance of overseas and inland water routes increased as well. These developments created the potential for the further growth of overseas trade in the region, but surrounding countries needed to be more demanding in pursuing their trading interests with China. In the latter half of the eighteenth century, some Korean intellectuals began to advocate sea trade with China instead of overland trade. The Korean king even proposed a plan to levy taxes on merchants participating in international trade. At the time, there were many instances of members of tribute delegations and merchants engaged in private trade (*husi*), borrowing silver from the government. When they had problems repaying it, there were proposals to eliminate the lending system and to levy taxes on merchants when they returned from abroad. It could be argued that these proposals were a proper response to the trends of the time as an attempt to achieve the ideal of a "rich country and powerful army" (*puguk kangbyŏng*) through international trade.

However, at the beginning of the nineteenth century, as a young monarch ascended the throne and powerful clans gained control over the government, commercial profits became monopolized by powerful families, rather than accruing to the nation as a whole. A few influential persons were able to monopolize the right to manage ports and the commerce conducted at these ports. Some monopolized even official trade; some members of government tribute delegations began to engage in trade directly, pushing aside state interests. The amount of ginseng these delegation members were allowed to carry to China was originally limited to 10 gŭn (about 0.6 kg), but by the latter half of the nineteenth century, the amount increased to 40,000 gŭn.[17] The same trend emerged in China's monopolistic *Cohong* system of overseas trade, similar to Chosŏn in the nineteenth century. Though flourishing, private trade was illegal, and its monopolization by a limited number of powerful individuals cast a dark shadow on East Asian development. The circumstances in Japan at the time are not well known, and the limitations and weaknesses of the East Asian international trade in the nineteenth century and its underlying internal structure and relationships deserve further study.

CONCLUSION

From the second half of the fourteenth century, the relationship between the East Asian international order and international trade had been strongly tied to China's tribute policy, its restrictive sea-trade policy, and other policies. Having examined the formation, changes, and historical significance of this order, I present the following summary of my main points.

The tribute system was instituted to maintain a Sinocentric world order. However, the consequences of this system were not limited to the area of diplomatic relations. The tribute policy, coupled with the restrictive sea-trade policy, was intended to have a similar effect on international trade. However, because this single framework covered two distinct realms, time restrictions compromised the singular effectiveness of each area. This two-in-one structure rising out of a specific historic condition had inherent limitations, which surfaced amid later historical changes. These limitations were already apparent by the sixteenth century, and authorities had to separate the restrictive sea-trade policy from the tribute policy and make subsequent modifications. As international trade flourished due to each individual country's economic development, it eventually became necessary to remove the shackles that restricted seaborne trade.

With the establishment of the Qing dynasty in the seventeenth century, the unity of the tribute policy and the restrictive sea-trade policy was restored. These policies clearly represented a historical regression in the development of East Asian international relations. Once the crisis of the seventeenth century passed, the East Asian

17. Yi Tae-jin, "Kukje muyŏk ŭi sŏnghaeng."

economy as a whole enjoyed prosperity until the eighteenth century, when restrictions on sea trade were reimposed and the economy began to regress. The restoration of these restrictions was related to the Qing government's efforts to promote domestic stability. In pursuit of a "grand unity" centered on China, the Qing proceeded with its campaign to subdue the ethnic minorities of the northwest region of China. In the process, restrictions on sea traffic were restored, and they remained in place until China's doors were later forced open by the Western powers.

Until the eighteenth century, the East Asian economies underwent continual development. The maturation of the agricultural sector vitalized both commerce and handicraft industries, leading to a high level of commercial development within each country. However, the East Asian economy, faced with a situation in which further development was not possible, collided directly with Western industrial capitalism in the middle of the nineteenth century. Though countries continued individual development, East Asia's inability to free itself fully of the restraints of international trade was one of the reasons it was unable to go beyond a certain level of commercial development. Europe's industrial capitalism, on the other hand, grew largely on account of the accumulation of capital through the expansion of free and open international trade. Since East Asia was unable to remove the restraints of the tribute system, it could not achieve such development. While the surrounding countries share part of the responsibility for this inability, the bulk of the blame lies with China.

China's traditional approach of linking its internal and external policies appears again in contemporary Chinese history. After World War II, China adopted communism as the basis of its domestic administration. Ideologically, there are many parallels between this doctrine and the Qing dynasty's conception of China as the Middle Kingdom. The only notable change was the replacement of the emperor by the common people as the object of highest honor. The adoption of an isolationist policy to promote domestic stability also resembles China's past. During the process of communization, foreign vessels were not permitted to pass through the Yellow Sea. Although this can be viewed a consequence of the Cold War, it is difficult to avoid calling it another incarnation of China's traditional approach when viewed in the context of Chinese history. Interaction with other countries through the Yellow Sea was more limited at this time than in any other period in its history. While concentrating on its agrarian economy during the process of communization, China placed tighter restrictions on overseas trade.

As China pursues industrial development today, the government has adopted a more open diplomatic policy. Such changes are fundamentally similar to moments in the past when the economic development of each country led to a growth in international trade that, in turn, led China to revise its policy of restricting overseas trade. A historical examination of modern China's path needs to address the issues of how far these changes will go, which direction openness will take, and what the basic circumstances will be. From an international perspective, it is clear that there will be changes at least as broad in scale as the amendment of the restrictive sea-trade policy. However, the mere breadth of change is insufficient. Because of changes in the international situation, the focus of debate must be on the standards of market liberalization, not just the degree of openness.

In the past, China's moves toward openness were mainly based on China-centered considerations. Perhaps present moves toward openness are of the same mold. The degree of openness pursued correlates strongly with the degree of China's own economic development. These moves toward openness are undeniably necessary to bring the Chinese economy to a higher level. However, if this trend continues, it will be difficult to ignore criticisms that this is a reappearance of the Chinese egocentrism inherent in the traditional world order it once maintained. A country of enormous size, China's economic stability and development in and of itself are issues of considerable importance; it will be difficult to ignore criticism of China's reversion to the traditional world order. Since China's interest in the development of international relations has historically been somewhat weak, it is important to be vigilant against the recurrence of this attitude for the smooth development of East Asian international and economic relations.

In the 1880s, confronted by difficulties caused by Western imperialism, China began to treat Chosŏn as a vassal state. As its western and southern regions were falling to Western powers, China attempted to use Chosŏn as a shield to block danger coming from the east.[18] Although these actions are commonly believed to have

---

18. Kim Chŏnggi, "1876-1894nyŏn Ch'ŏng ŭi Chosŏn taech'aek yŏn'gu" (A study of Qing China's policies toward Chosŏn in 1876–1894) (Ph.D. diss., Seoul National University, 1994).

stemmed from the traditional tributary relationship, this in reality was not the case. The use of military force to convert Chosŏn into a vassal state was fundamentally different in nature, as the traditional tributary relationship refrained from interference in domestic affairs. The dire situation that China, as well as the rest of East Asia, faced was fundamentally the result of China's adherence to the tribute system. Under this traditional system, in trying to escape from difficult situations, China's first step should not have been to use other countries as sacrifices. Rather, its first step should have been to gain strength from its relations with other countries. China's movement in the opposite direction was a product of its traditionally egocentric worldview. Using the history of past failures as an example, China must completely rid itself of its historical egocentric attitude toward international relations if it expects to play a significant role in the development of East Asian international relations.

translated by Edward Park

CHAPTER 7

# Chosŏn's Adoption of International Law and Its Conflicts with China in the 1880s

IN THE MIDDLE OF THE nineteenth century, Chosŏn Korea began to adopt international law. To enter a new world order based on international law, it was important for Korea to end its traditional relations with Qing China. Korea had already become aware of this problem at the time of signing the Treaty of Amity with Japan in 1876, and a concrete step was taken with the signing the Treaty of Amity and Commerce with the United States in 1882. The objective of this chapter is to examine this process and resulting conflicts with China. Conflicts with China were of such importance that they nearly dominated Korean history during the 1880s. It can be said that Korea's struggle to end its traditional relations with Qing China was an issue of greater import than Meiji (1868–1912) Japan's efforts to revise the unequal treaties signed with the Western powers. China took strong steps to block the Chosŏn government's efforts to break away, and Chosŏn's struggle against China was fierce. Such conflicts were unavoidable for a country that had maintained close relations within the Sinocentric world order.

Up to now, some scholars have examined these conflicts with China through the concept of the "*yangjŏl* [dual] system." However, this concept misrepresented many aspects of the situation. The term *yangjŏl* was an expression appearing in Yu Kiljun's *Sŏyu kyŏnmun* (Observations while Traveling in the West). He noted that at a time when each East Asian country was entering a new international order through Western-style treaties concluded among independent states, if China continued to demand that Chosŏn maintain its subordinate status as in the past, the two countries' relations with other countries would lose their coherence like a piece of wood split into two.[1] When scholars first began to use this expression, they erred in believing that Yu Kiljun (1856–1914) used this term to describe the current system.[2] Although it is true that China had applied this kind of pressure, the Chosŏn government did not accede to it, displaying instead strong resistance. Yu Kiljun's text simply seems to have described these efforts of the Chosŏn government.

In writing this chapter, I was greatly aided by the following three studies: Kim Jongwŏn's research on Korean relations with China (1966), Kim Kyŏngt'ae's studies on Korea's treaties with Japan and the United States (1972, 1975), and Im Kyesun's work on Korean-Russian relations (1984).[3] Their work displayed a high level of empirical rigor through their use of primary sources from all of the countries involved. Through this empirical work, these studies clearly revealed the efforts of the Chŏson ruler and government to establish a new form of international relations. However, twenty to thirty years ago, when these studies were written, negative views of Korea's modern history were very strong. Unable to break free of these negative views, these studies are flawed by their occasional use of

1. Yu Kiljun, *Sŏyu kyŏnmun* (Observations while Traveling in the West), volume 3, Rights of Sovereign States, translated by Ch'ae Hun, in *Hanguk sasang taejŏnjip* (Collected Works of Korean Thought), 29 (Yang'udang, 1988), p. 90; p. 97 in the original.
2. This expression was first introduced by Harada Tamaki in his "Pak Kyusu no tainichi kaikokuron" (Pak Kyusu's thoughts on the opening of Japan), *Jinbun gakuho* 46 (Kyoto University, Research Institute in the Humanities, 1979). Later, in an article entitled "Cho-chu 'ryosetsu' taisei seiritsu zenshi" (The prehistory of the establishment of the "duality" system between Chosŏn and China) *Kindai Chosen no shakai to shiso* (Tokyo: Miraisha, 1981), he contributed to an understanding of the existence of the *yangjŏl* system as a form of bi-national relations. Both articles are collected in Harada Tamaki's *Chosen no kaikoku to kindaika* (The opening of Korea and modernization) (Hiroshima: Keisuisha, 1997).
3. Kim Chongwŏn, "Cho-Chung sangmin suryuk muyŏk changjŏng e daehayŏ" (On the agreement of overlands and maritime trade between Chosŏn and Chinese merchants), *Yŏksa hakbo* 32 (1966); Kim Kyŏngt'ae, "Kaehang jikhu ŭi kwansegwŏn hwoebok munje—Pusan haegwan suse sagŏn ŭl chungsim ŭro" (The problem of recovering custom autonomy after the opening of Korean ports—with a special focus on the tax collection incident at the Pusan maritime customs office), *Han'guksa yŏngu* 8, (1972) and "pulp'yŏngdŭng choyak kaejŏng kyosŏp ŭi chŏn'gae" (The negotiations to revise the unequal treaties), *Han'guksa yŏngu* 11, (1975); Im Kyesun, "Han-Ro milyak kwa kŭ hu ŭi Han-Ro kwangye" (The Russo-Korean secret treaties and subsequent Russo-Korean relations), *Han-Ro kwan'gye 100-nyŏnsa* (A 100-year history of Korean-Russian relations) (Seoul: Han'guksa yŏn'gu hyŏpŭihoe, 1984).

Chosŏn's Adpotion of International Law    141

negative terms regarding the Chŏson king and government. But this flaw is not sufficient to discredit their work. The problem is that their valuable findings have not received much attention despite the passage of time because of the negative view of early modern Korean history. The objective of this chapter is to give a more accurate picture of modern Korean history in the 1880s by putting together the findings of these neglected studies. If this chapter produces a new view of Korean history that is meaningful, the credit should go entirely to the empirical research of these three scholars.

CHOSŎN'S CONCLUSION OF TREATIES WITH JAPAN AND THE UNITED STATES AND THE ATTEMPT TO TERMINATE TRADITIONAL RELATIONS WITH QING CHINA

There has been a strong tendency to regard Korea's modern period as a history of failure. Modern Korean history has been characterized as the history of the loss of national sovereignty due to Chosŏn's refusal to adopt superior Western technology and its adherence to a policy of "seclusion" in the new encounter between East and West in the nineteenth century. Such views have usually been reinforced through a comparison with Japan. Two of the dominant themes in the discourse on modern East Asian history have been Japan's success and Korea's failure in westernization. However, such negative views are simply a version of history deliberately made with the intention of justifying Japan's forced annexation and its rule over Korea.[4]

From the time of Japan's annexation of Korea in 1910, modern Korean history began to be portrayed in following way. The Chosŏn dynasty "insolently" rejected the demands made by the government of Meiji Japan to enter into new international relations and showed "stupidity" and "ignorance" in firing upon the Unyo (K. Unyang), a ship flying the Japanese flag, in 1875. Seeking to awaken this benighted country, Japan demanded that Korea take responsibility for its illegal attack and demanded that it sign a treaty of amity. Through Japanese force, Chosŏn was at last able to become a member of the international community. The basic aspects of this explanatory framework have remained the same to this day with only minor

4. Yi Tae-jin (Yi T'aejin), *Kojong sidae ŭi chaejomyŏng* (A reexamination of the Kojong era) (Seoul: T'aehaksa, 2000).

changes in expression. Only very recently have scholars begun to raise questions about this view of history.

According to the above interpretation, Chosŏn's entry into the new international society was due to Japanese "benevolence." However, it is clear that in reality, Chosŏn's opening was undertaken of its own accord. The fact that Kojong ended the ten-year regency of his father, the Taewŏngun, and assumed direct rule in December 1873 was the result of such initiative. Believing that his father's policy of "seclusion" would jeopardize the country's future, Kojong announced his desire to assume direct rule. He realized that it was unavoidable to establish diplomatic relations with Japan, a measure that his father had opposed. Kojong had a startling interpretation of Japan's use of the words "emperor" (K. *hwang*) and "imperial" (K. *ch'ik*) in its diplomatic correspondence that the Chosŏn side had strongly opposed. Namely, he stated that a neighboring country had no say over the terms the Japanese used for their monarch. His statement represented a rejection of the Sinocentric world order and, more specifically, of the tributary system. With their new worldview, Kojong and his ministers willingly accepted Japanese demands to sign a commercial treaty three years later.

Recently, new light has been shed on the details of the Unyo Incident of September 20, 1875.[5] According to the first report written by the captain of the Unyo, Inoue Ryŏkei, on September 29, a boat carrying soldiers of the Unyo approached the garrisons on Kanghwa Island without flying a flag. The report did not mention that their purpose was to obtain fresh water; their purpose was to instigate an attack from the Chosŏn garrison. The battle between the two sides was intense and lasted for three days. After the Unyo failed to reach the onshore garrison on the first day, it launched an all-out attack on the second day. However, it failed again to land because of rapid current, silt, and the strong defense of the Chosŏn forces. On the third day, the Japanese changed their focus to an adjacent island (Yŏngjongjin) where it would be easier to land and launched a surprise attack in the morning, killing a number of people and plundering some goods.

---

5. Yi T'ae-jin, "Unyangho sagŏn ŭi jinsang—sakŏn kyŏngwŭi wa ilbon kukki keyang ŭi jinwŭi" (The reality of the Unyo incident—details on the incident and the truth about the hoisting of Japanese national flag), *Chosŏn ŭi chŏngch'i wa sahoe* (Korean politics and society) (Seoul: Chipmundang, 2002), p. 12.

Chosŏn's Adpotion of International Law    143

After the leaders of the Japanese government received this report, they had the captain submit a new report on October 8. The new report changed the length of the battle to one day and hid the difficulties that the Unyo faced; it also now claimed that several Japanese flags were always flying on the ship and that their purpose was to obtain fresh water. From the very next day, the new report was used to respond to inquiries from the British and French legations in Tokyo. Several days later, overseas Japanese legations were directed to use the report to inform the host governments about the details of the incident. Because of this information campaign, the Western powers came to regard Chosŏn as an uncivilized country ignorant of international law. In December 1875, when Japan was putting together a mission to conclude a treaty with Chosŏn, ministers of Western powers stationed in Tokyo expressed enthusiastic support for its opening of Korea.[6] Japan instigated the Unyo Incident because it was necessary to have the firm support of the international community to move into Chosŏn, an "ignorant country" under the influence of China. If Japan used force to overcome Chosŏn's reluctance to its demands to open their country, Japan calculated that the international community would be willing to support their actions as justifiable.

When the Japanese mission arrived on Kanghwa Island and met with representatives of Chosŏn in January 1876, the Japanese Minister Plenipotentiary mentioned the attack on the Unyo at the beginning of the negotiations and reproached his counterpart for Chosŏn's disrespectful treatment of the Japanese flag. The Chosŏn representative countered by asking whose ship it was. He also replied that Chosŏn forces only saw a yellow-colored flag and not the Japanese flag and that they still did not know the identity of the ship. The Japanese representative made no further reference to this matter, probably fearing that Japan would just be put in a difficult situation.

Japan prepared a thirteen-article treaty draft, and after reviewing it for a few days, the Chosŏn side requested the following revisions.[7] They demanded the removal of the most favored nation provision (article thirteen), and they also presented an alternative draft, claiming that the wording of article nine needed to be revised in order to ensure

6. *Nihon gaikō bunsho* (Japanese official records of diplomacy), no. 8 (1956), pp. 152–57. Yamada Shoji, "TaiChōsen seisaku to jyōyaku kaisei mondai" (Japan's foreign policy toward Chosŏn and problems over treaty revision) in *Nihon rekishi* 2, no. 15 (Tokyo: Iwanami shoten, 1976), p. 61.
7. Yi (2002), p. 436; see also footnote 2.

the equality of the two countries. The Japanese side accepted virtually all of the alternative draft. Just before it departed, the Japanese mission received an additional directive from the prime minister (Dajokan) to regard the signing of a treaty as an accomplishment even if things proved to be difficult; thus, Japan accepted the treaty and regarded their efforts as a success. Since the 1876 Treaty of Amity between Chosŏn and Japan (aka Kanghwa Treaty) was quickly concluded entirely due to the active efforts of Chosŏn, the Unyo Incident did not exert influence on the process. There was no need for Japan to use the incident as a pretext to threaten Chosŏn.

Following the conclusion of the Treaty of Amity between Chosŏn and Japan, the Chosŏn government made additional efforts to enter the new international order during the next five years. Concerning trade by Chosŏn and Japanese merchants, the treaty stipulated that "as both countries have experience in friendly commerce, the peoples of both nations shall trade according to their own free will and without interference from government officials" (clause nine). In short, trade was to be conducted on the principle of free trade without tariffs. Chosŏn accepted this provision for the following reasons. First, trade between the two countries had traditionally been conducted without tariffs, as emphasized in the preamble ("both countries have maintained friendly relations in the past"). This was not an unequal relationship resulting from Japanese manipulation or from a Chosŏn's ignorance of tariff autonomy. Chosŏn had no choice but to follow traditional customs in trade because it lacked a banking system to handle the collection of tariffs.

In reality, however, tariff-free trade quickly put Chosŏn in an unfavorable situation. Within a few years, imports of cotton goods from Japan increased, and exports of cowhide, rice and other goods from Korea also increased. In September 1879, Chosŏn opened a maritime customs office in Pusan and instituted a heavy tariff (15 percent on exports, 24 percent on imports) on Korean merchants who traded with Japanese merchants. This tariff did not conflict with the 1876 Treaty since it was a domestic tax levied intermittently on merchants active in international trade.[8] When the treaty was concluded, the principle of tariff-free trade took into account such emergency measures. When this policy was instituted, trade between the two countries dropped off immediately. Taken by surprise, Japan re-

---

8. Kim Kyŏngt'ae (1972), pp. 99–102.

sponded by making a show of force and strongly protesting to the Chosŏn government. Within a few weeks, Chosŏn was forced to repeal this measure.

After the incident at the Pusan Maritime Customs Office, the Chosŏn government sought to use diplomatic channels to resolve the tariff issue. From 1880 to 1882, the Chosŏn government attempted several times to negotiate with Japan on the issues of tariff rates, tariff autonomy, and the authority to ban the export of rice in order to secure its tariff income. However, the Japanese representatives avoided these issues every time, asserting that the Chosŏn representatives did not carry plenipotentiary credentials. The Chosŏn diplomatic mission visiting Tokyo even received assistance from the Chinese legation in Japan. Li Hongzhang (1823-1901) in Tianjin, who was in charge of China's diplomacy in Northeast Asia, even encouraged Chosŏn to develop friendly relations with the United States as part of his policy of countering Russia and Japan (K. *pia-hangil ch'aek*).

In January 1881, the Chosŏn government established the Tongni kimu amun (Office for Extraordinary State Affairs) as the central state organ and reorganized the state into a more Western system. Also in January, the government sent a mission to Japan (*Chosa kyŏnmundan*) to gather information about Japan's adoption of Western institutions, and in July (by the lunar calendar), it sent students to Tianjin to learn about the production of the new machines. In the same year, Chosŏn attempted a new round of negotiations in Seoul and in Tokyo on tariff regulations and commerce. However, in both cases, Japan refused to negotiate for the reason that the Chosŏn representatives did not carry plenipotentiary credentials. As a result, the Chosŏn government changed its strategy; it would first sign a treaty with the United States that secured tariff autonomy and then use it as the basis to open negotiations with the Japanese. It is for this reason that Chosŏn hurried to sign a treaty of amity and commerce with the United States in April 1882. Although Li Hongzhang's good offices were of considerable help in opening diplomatic relations with the United States, Chosŏn's independent efforts were more important. Chosŏn felt that if it could conclude a treaty with a major Western power guaranteeing its tariff autonomy, then it could simultaneously resolve the tariff issues that Japan had been avoiding.[9]

9. That Korean officials from this period had a high consciousness of the importance of tariff autonomy is manifested in the preface to Min Ch'ungmok's "'Ilbon kakguk choyak" (Japan's treaties with foreign countries), a report based on his visits to the

Based on the principle of tariff autonomy, the Treaty of Amity and Commerce between Chosŏn and the United States set tariffs at 30 percent for imports and 10 percent for exports. No other country in East Asia had achieved such a treaty. In June 1882, Chosŏn also concluded nearly identical treaties with England and Germany. However, the two countries did not take measures for ratification and, in November 1883, asked the Chosŏn government to lower the tariff on British cotton goods, the biggest import item, to 7.5 percent. Tariff rates on imports and exports were adjusted to a minimum of 5 percent and a maximum of 10 percent. As will be discussed below, this adjustment was a concession made in order to contain pressure coming from China. Because of the most favored nation clause, this tariff rate was also applied to the United States and Japan. Japan had gained most favored nation status in the "Regulations on Commerce between Korea and Japan" (Han-Il t'ongsang changjŏng), which was signed on June 22, 1883. This agreement was concluded when Chosŏn was put in a difficult position because of the outbreak of the Imo Soldiers' Riot in June 1882. Although these changes represented a loss of some of the initial gains from the treaty with the United States, their terms were still relatively favorable, especially considering the fact that import and export duties in Japan were a specific tariff (*chongnyangse*) set at 5 percent.[10] In contrast to the relative successes in diplomacy with the Western powers, relations with Qing China became very tense; in particular, the decisive factor was the Imo Soldiers' Riot.

In January 1881 (18th year of Kojong's reign), the Chosŏn government asked the Qing government to allow Chinese merchants to trade in Chosŏn treaty ports opened to Japanese trade. The stated purpose for its request was that Chinese merchants would be able to block the high-handed behavior of Japanese merchants since Chosŏn was ill-informed about commercial regulations.[11] However, this was not its true intention. In order for Chosŏn government to act as a truly independent state in the new world of international law, it was

---

Japanese Customs House and the Ministry of Foreign Affairs as part of the Gentleman's Mission. See Yun Chŏng, "'Yŏn'gu not'ŭ: 'Chosŏn Kojongdae Ilbon kakguk choyak' ŭi p'yŏnch'an mokjŏk kwa sŏnggyŏk e taehan koch'al" (Research notes: an examination of the purpose and nature of the compilation of "Japan's Treaties with foreign countries during the Kojong era in Chosŏn"), *Sŏul kukjebŏp yŏn'gu* 8, no. 1 (2001).

10. Kim Kyŏngt'ae (1975).
11. Kim Chongwŏn (1966), p. 128.

necessary to establish new relations with China just as had been done with Japan. The fundamental purpose behind the proposal to invite Chinese merchants to Chosŏn was to create an occasion to begin this process.

The effort to establish new relations with China began in earnest in October 1881. In that month, King Kojong ordered Ŏ Yunjung (1848–1896), who had remained in Japan after the mission, to travel from Nagasaki to Tianjin to discuss this matter. He was accompanied by Yi Dongin (?–?), who was given the responsibility of consulting with the Chinese about a treaty with the United States. Ŏ Yunjung's proposal included the following issues:

(1) ending Qing China's traditional policy of prohibiting maritime trade with Chosŏn and engaging in trade;
(2) abolishing Chosŏn's traditional system of providing funds used to receive Chinese envoys;
(3) abolishing the traditional system of sending envoys and stationing a permanent Chosŏn envoy in Beijing.[12]

QING CHINA'S RESISTANCE AND THE STRENGTHENING OF ITS SUZERAIN RELATIONS WITH KOREA

Because of the momentousness of its proposal, the Chosŏn government sent another envoy to China in April 1882. After further negotiations,[13] the following provisions were approved by Emperor Guangxu on April 29:

(1) matters relating to trade are to be handled by the Office for Foreign Affairs (Zongli Yamen) rather than the Board of Rites;
(2) the system of sending envoys to present tribute to the Emperor is to remain the same;
(3) due to various problems, the system of stationing a permanent Korean envoy in Beijing is not to be implemented.[14]

---

12. Kim Chongwŏn (1966), p. 131.
13. On the details of Qing China's debate over Ŏ Yunjung's proposal, see Ibid., pp. 134–45.
14. Ibid., pp. 146–47.

Chosŏn's only gain was that commerce was no longer to be conducted as tribute trade under the supervision of the Board of Rites but was to be handled by the Zongli Yamen, just as it was with other countries (item 1). The Chosŏn side delicately broached the issues related to items 2 and 3. However, the Chinese completely rejected their proposals, reacting strongly since they regarded them as bold demands that belittled the Qing court. In particular, the prevalent opinion on the proposal to station a permanent envoy was to see it as a sign that Chosŏn was betraying the Qing court since it was similar to the minister system of the Western powers.[15]

However, the Qing court was also concerned that complete rejection would cause Korea to leave China's sphere of influence and be divided up among the Western powers in their search for profits, ultimately leading to Chosŏn's subordination to Japan. Thus, some at the Qing court felt that it was also necessary to exercise caution; in fact, item 1 was the result of this concern. According to this decision, Chosŏn's trade affairs officer would conduct diplomatic protocol on an equal footing (p'yŏngdŭngnye) with the Chinese Minister for Foreign Affairs (Prime Minister), just like the ministers of Western countries.[16] For Qing China, it was difficult to allow this change in view of the traditional protocols of sadae (serving the great). In terms of traditional protocol, the Chinese Prime Minister was the equal of the Chosŏn king; it was unacceptable for him to conduct affairs with Chosŏn's trade officials on the basis of equality. However, since countries that had concluded treaties with Chosŏn would protest if China did not allow this change, China agreed to make a minimal compromise.[17]

Because of the problems raised by item 1, the Qing court delayed preparing the relevant documents.[18] China sought to buy time by requesting that Ŏ Yunjung bring an official document from Chosŏn granting him plenipotentiary powers. Meanwhile, the Imo Soldiers' Riot (Imo Kullan) broke out on July 23 (9th day of the sixth lunar month). The Qing court saw this incident as a golden opportunity to block Chosŏn's efforts to move away from China's sphere of influence. China asked Kim Yunsik, a high-ranking official stationed in Tianjin, whether the Chosŏn monarch welcomed this mutiny. If not, China

15. Ibid., p. 139.
16. Ibid., p. 147.
17. Ibid., p. 148.
18. Ibid., p. 150.

would send four thousand troops to Chosŏn under the pretext that the Chinese emperor, the suzerain of Chosŏn, could not ignore this situation. Ŏ Yunjung and Kim Yunsik (1835–1922), who were stationed in Tianjin as Chosŏn's *hyŏpsanggwan* (negotiation officer) and *yŏngsŏnsa*, respectively, returned to Chosŏn on June 27 as guides (K. *hyangdogwan*) for the Qing troops.[19]

As the soldiers' mutiny was put down, relations between Chosŏn and Qing China developed exactly as China wished. On August 23, China drafted an eight-article "Regulations for maritime and overland trade between Chosŏn and China" (Cho-Chung sangmin suryuk changjŏng), which lowered Chosŏn's status by one rank.[20] Even the preface to this document made a point of emphasizing that "since these regulations pertain to Chosŏn as a subordinate state of China, they are not an example of the most favored nation provision." This document did not take the form of a treaty between countries in accordance with the new international law. The "Regulations" addressed the dispatch of a trade commissioner and the treatment of officials from both countries, and it established the status of the Chosŏn monarch as equal to that of the Chinese Minister of the Northern Ocean (Li Hongzhang, the viceroy of Zhili province). The Chosŏn king had been the equal of the Prime Minister; the "Regulations" lowered the king's status one more level. There had been no discussion on article two of the "Regulations," which recognized extraterritoriality for the Chinese trade commissioner stationed in Chosŏn. The document also contained one-sided and unreasonable articles concerning the activities of Chinese merchants in Chosŏn. The document was not a treaty but rather a unilateral declaration.

Chosŏn objected to the draft of the "Regulations" for being so different in content from treaties signed with other countries.[21] Since trade issues had never been subject to the rituals of *sadae* relations, Chosŏn protested that China was not observing the principle of equality and reciprocity and was forcing the one-sided submission of *sadae* on Chosŏn. However, China countered that the principle of equality and reciprocity could be applied to relations between a suzerain country and its tributary. China even noted that there were regulations on trade between suzerain and tributary countries in

19. Ibid.
20. For an analysis of the contents of this agreement, see Kim Chongwŏn (1966), pp. 51–58.
21. Ibid.

international law. Since the "Regulations" differed from treaties that were conducted among countries on the basis of equality, it was not possible to take issues with "deviations" from international law. China also rejected the request to revise extraterritorial rights, citing what was written in *Da Qing huidian* (Collected Statutes of the Great Qing). For Chosŏn, the result was a great diplomatic defeat caused by the domestic troubles of the Imo Soldiers' Riot. On August 8, 1882, Li Hongzhang reported the conclusion of negotiations to Emperor Guangxu, and the "Regulations" obtained imperial sanction and came into effect on September 12.[22] This was the critical moment that inaugurated the situation that Yu Kiljun called *yangjŏl*.

When China established relations with Chosŏn on the basis of its subordinate status, the reaction of the Western countries was generally negative. The United States and most of the other countries maintaining diplomatic relations with Chosŏn frowned upon this agreement. According to the standards of Western international law, the "Regulations" appeared to be a vague and ambiguous agreement whose legal validity was suspect. Other countries recognized the agreement only to the extent that it did not interfere with the activities of their own merchants. They accepted the official notice sent by Chosŏn, which stated that although Chosŏn had traditionally been under Chinese suzerainty, its internal affairs and diplomatic relations were carried out autonomously by the sovereign of Chosŏn. They viewed Qing China's assertion of its suzerainty as something existing in name only.[23]

Alarmed at Qing's dominance in Chosŏn, Japan forced Chosŏn to grant it a number of concessions. In January 1883, Japan obtained an agreement on the boundaries of its settlement in Inch'ŏn, and on June 22 of that year, it concluded the "Commercial Agreement between Chosŏn and Japan." Article forty-two of the trade agreement granted most favored nation status to Japan; consequently, its terms were extended to the other treaty powers.[24] During the Imo Soldiers' Riot of 1882, the Japanese legation in Seoul was set on fire. Japan used this as the pretext to apply the maximum diplomatic pressure on Chosŏn and succeeded in establishing unequal relations. Six years earlier, most favored nation status had not been granted in the Treaty of Amity between Chosŏn and Japan. In response to these moves by Japan, the

22. Ibid., p. 156.
23. Ibid., pp. 159–61.
24. Ibid., p. 159.

United States rushed to send a minister to reside in Seoul, a move that had been delayed after the conclusion of its treaty with Chosŏn. China also hurriedly sent a commercial attaché to Seoul, and Chosŏn followed by dispatching its trade representative to Tianjin.[25]

CHOSŎN'S TURN TOWARD RUSSIA

(1) The Background to the First Secret Agreement between Korea and Russia

Using the Imo Soldiers' Riot as a pretext, Qing China sent its forces to Chosŏn to implement its policy of maintaining suzerainty over its tributary state. Disconcerted by these developments, Chosŏn saw Russia as the power that would be able to serve as a counterbalance to China. Both China and Japan were concerned about Russia, and the measures that they recommended to Chosŏn were all focused on defending against Russia. When China emerged as the greatest threat to Chosŏn, it was forced to change its thinking. Chosŏn came to see Russia not as a threat but as a potential ally.

Before approaching Russia, Chosŏn established relations with England and Germany. In April 1883, England asked for an extension of the deadline to ratify the treaty it signed with Chosŏn (April 1882), which was concluded a year after the Treaty of Amity and Commerce between Chosŏn and the United States. The British Parliament had delayed ratifying the treaty because it had many objections to the tariff regulations set in the treaty. As mentioned above, Chosŏn concluded treaties with the Western powers (the United States, England, and Germany) on much more favorable terms than those Japan had signed with the Western powers. The British parliament was not willing to approve of such a treaty with Chosŏn and postponed ratification in order to buy time to revise the tariff provisions.

In September 1883, before leaving for Korea, the British minister to China, Harry Smith Parkes (1828–1885), told Li Hongzhang that if Chosŏn did not agree to revise the tariff provisions, his country would renounce the treaty. Parkes also expressed England's opposition to China's policy of turning Chosŏn into a subordinate state. His words hinted that in return for England's opposition to China's high-handed attitude toward Chosŏn, England wanted Chosŏn to agree to the tariff

25. Kim Chongwŏn (1966), p. 160.

revisions.²⁶ When England, together with Germany, communicated their position to the Chosŏn government, Chosŏn accepted their request, hoping that the result would be to eliminate Chinese pressure. The Treaty of Amity and Commerce between Chosŏn and the United States had recognized Chosŏn's tariff autonomy and established fair tariff rates, but these accomplishments were revised as a result of these events. Chosŏn's departure from the Sinocentric world order was a perilous undertaking that exacted a high price.

In the revision of the tariff provisions with England and Germany (October 27, 1883), Chosŏn permitted merchants of both countries to conduct business within Chosŏn territory beyond the treaty ports. Since China had forced Chosŏn to allow Qing merchants complete freedom to conduct business within Chosŏn through the "Regulations," Chosŏn hoped that giving the same rights to Western merchants would undermine the monopoly of Qing merchants.²⁷ Shortly before this, Li Hongzhang asked the Chosŏn king to send an official document to both England and Germany on Chosŏn's status as a "Chinese tributary," but the king refused. At a time when such resistance to Qing China was emerging, the measure permitting English and German merchants to conduct business beyond the treaty ports can be seen as the product of a desire to contain China.²⁸

Chosŏn's contacts with Russia began when the *susin taesa* delegation (Kim Okgyun, Pak Yŏnghyo, and Min Yŏngik) went to Tokyo in September 1882 for negotiations to settle issues related to the Imo Soldiers' Riot.²⁹ While in Tokyo, the delegation visited Baron Roman Romanovitch Rosen (1847–1922), the Russian chargé d'affaires in Japan. They asked Rosen to convey to the Russian government Chosŏn's indignation over Chinese intervention and hopes to conclude a treaty with Russia.³⁰ At the beginning of 1884, Kojong sent an

26. Ibid., pp. 160–61.
27. Ibid., p. 161.
28. Ibid.
29. The *susin taesa* delegation was a plenipotentiary and goodwill envoy. *Kojong sillok* (Veritable Records of King Kojong), volume 19, August 4, 1882 (19th year of Kojong's reign).
30. Im Kyesun, p. 83. In regards to the secret agreements between Korea and Russia, I relied heavily on the Prof. Im's research, the empirical reliability of which is high. From the Russian side, B.G. Weber and S.R. Diamond (eds.), "Russian Documents Relating to Sino-Japanese War, 1894-95" in *Kransy Archives*, vol. L-LI, pp. 3–63; *The Chinese Social Political Science Review* 17, no. 3 (Oct. 1933), pp. 480–515 and (Jan. 1934), pp. 632–70; from the Chinese side, *Qiaoxiaodang* (Archives on Korea), *Qinji*

envoy to Novekievskoe and conveyed to the administrative officer of this remote district (N.G. Matiunin) Chosŏn's hopes for amicable relations with Russia in order to terminate Chinese suzerainty.[31] In May 1884, Russia agreed to conclude a treaty with Chosŏn, anticipating the outbreak of a war between China and France (August 1884). It sent Carl Waeber, the resident minister in Tianjin, to Chosŏn as a plenipotentiary minister. Chosŏn appointed the German advisor Paul G. von Möllendorff (1847–1901) as its representative, and the Treaty of Amity and Commerce between Chosŏn and Russia was concluded on July 7, 1884. Although von Möllendorff had been recommended by Li Hongzhang, the former was on such friendly terms with the Chosŏn King that he even advised the monarch that only Russia could protect his country.[32] Kojong expected much assistance from the United States, which was the first country to send a warship and demonstrated its goodwill during the Imo Soldiers' Riot. However, Lucius H. Foote, the first American minister to Chosŏn, made it clear that the United States would not interfere in Chosŏn-Chinese relations.[33]

As these events were taking place, radical members of the Kaehwap'a (Enlightenment Faction) such as Kim Okgyun and Pak Yŏnghyo instigated a coup d'état in October 1884 with the help of Takezoe Shinichiro, the Japanese minister in Seoul, in order to drive out Chinese forces. Since the coup, which ended in three days was anti-Qing in nature, it caused a great deal of trouble for the Chosŏn government. China put increasingly greater pressure on the Chosŏn monarch. In order to overcome this difficult situation, King Kojong had to devote more effort to gaining Russian assistance, focusing on two initiatives.

The first initiative was to approach the Russian Governor-General in Vladivostok. In early November 1884 (lunar calendar), Kojong sent four subordinates of Han Kyujik (?–1884; Right Garrison Officer; *uyŏngsa*), who had advocated ties with Russia, to Vladivostok. They

---

*zhongrihan guanxi shiliao* (Documents on the historical relations among China, Japan and Korea during the late Qing period), *Li Wenzhonggong quanji* (The complete works of Li Wenzhonggong), *Qing Guanxu chao zhongri jiaoshe shiliao* (Documents on the negotiations among Korea, China, and Japan during the reign of the Qing dynasty Emperor, Guanxu), Zhongyang Yanjiusuo Jindaishi Yanjiusuo (Academia Sinica), Qingdai zonggeguoshiwuyumen (Institute of Modern History).

31. Im Kye-sun, p. 83.
32. Ibid., pp. 86–87.
33. Ibid., p. 86.

reached an agreement with the Governor-General on the following six items:

(1) if Kim Okgyun were to enter Russian territory, he would be sent back to Chosŏn
(2) Russia will intervene to block Japan's demand for a large indemnity
(3) Russia will try to mitigate other country's (i.e., Qing China's) contempt for Chosŏn
(4) a treaty should be signed quickly and ministers exchanged
(5) Russian warships will also patrol Chosŏn's three seas
(6) the two countries will engage in overland trade

The Russian emperor received a report of this agreement and sent a telegram ordering that item six be carried out from early April 1885.[34]

The Chosŏn delegation returned in May and conveyed the Governor-General's reply to Kojong. When this matter became known, Qing China strongly objected and applied pressure on Chosŏn. In response, the Chosŏn court had to explain that the visit to Vladivostok was a personal one and that the agreement in question was also private in nature.[35]

The second initiative was pursued through von Möllendorff. Having received a royal order, von Möllendorff sent a telegram to the Russian minister in Tokyo requesting that a warship and a Russian naval force of two hundred strong be sent to Inch'ŏn to protect the royal family.[36] After receiving the telegram, the Russian minister sent Secretary Alexis de Speyer to Chosŏn to verify the truth of its contents. De Speyer arrived in Seoul at the end of 1884 and had an audience with Kojong. He also met with von Möllendorff and Cho Pyŏngho, the Korean minister in charge of commercial and diplomatic affairs, to discuss the issue of Russian assistance in protecting Chosŏn in case hostilities broke out between China and Japan. de Speyer returned to Japan on January 7, 1885, but contact between von Möllendorff and the Russian minister in Japan continued.

At the time, Qing troops were still stationed in Seoul, and Japan was negotiating with Chosŏn over the indemnity for the damage

---

34. Ibid., p. 87.
35. Ibid., p. 88.
36. Im, pp. 88–89.

Chosŏn's Adpotion of International Law    155

caused by the fire on the Japanese legation.[37] Under these circumstances, pursuing ties with Russia was significant as a form of active diplomatic struggle by Chosŏn, regardless of its outcome. In order to follow the procedures following the conclusion of the Hansŏng Treaty, von Möllendorff went to Japan in February 1885 with Sŏ Sang'u, the Vice-Minister of the Board of Rites, and during their two-week stay, they continued to make overtures to the Russians.[38] They met with Russian Minister Davidov, Secretary de Speyer, and others and discussed Chosŏn-Russian relations.

After von Möllendorff returned to Chosŏn, he had an audience with Kojong. He reported the details of the negotiations and received the king's approval of the results. However, von Möllendorff deliberately did not report this to Kim Yunsik, the minister in charge of diplomacy, because he was pro-Qing. It is known that the key items of the agreement were the dispatch of a military training team (four officers and sixteen petty officers) and Russian assistance in protecting Chosŏn's coastal areas.[39]

When the Chosŏn government sought close relations with Russia in order to overcome pressure exerted by Qing China following the Imo Soldiers' Riot, China, Japan, and England each responded to this development. China's Li Hongzhang and Japan's Ito Hirobumi met at Tianjin on March 14, 1885, and began discussions. After nearly a month of negotiations, they agreed on the following items on April 18 (Treaty of Tianjin). Both China and Japan agreed to withdraw the troops that had entered Chosŏn during the Imo Soldiers' Riot and the Kapsin Coup, respectively. The condition was that if a situation arose in the future where one of the two countries had to send troops to Chosŏn, it would notify the other, and they would then dispatch troops together. They also agreed to help form a militia for the Korean monarch in order to strengthen national defenses. The former measure aimed to eliminate the grounds for a Russian intervention, while the latter sought to block the request for Russian military advisors by the Chosŏn government.

While China and Japan were engaged in negotiations at Tianjin, England made its own moves. On April 15, three days before the Treaty of Tianjin was signed, a British naval battleship occupied

37. Korean officials reported that the fire was committed by Japanese as they abandoned their legation.
38. Im, p. 89.
39. Ibid.

Kŏmun Island (aka Port Hamilton) in Chosŏn's South Sea. Its justification was that their actions were a response to Russia's attempt to occupy a Korean port.[40] In response to this provocative act by England, some in China suggested that Qing temporarily overlook England's occupation of Port Hamilton in exchange for recognition of China's suzerain authority in Chosŏn; however, Li Hongzhang did not approve of this proposal. Instead, he wanted to strengthen China's status as the suzerain power in the process of resolving this issue.[41]

With the outbreak of the Kŏmun Island incident, diplomatic channels between London, Beijing, and Seoul surged with activity. However, the incident was not officially communicated to the Chosŏn government until a month later on May 19, 1885. During this time, England negotiated primarily with Qing China; notification was belatedly sent to the Chosŏn government when Li Hongzhang insisted that Chosŏn be informed.[42] England was trying to resolve this issue with the backing of China. The Chosŏn government had no choice but to take a hard-line stance toward these British actions.

The day after receiving the British documents (May 20), the minister in charge of diplomatic affairs in the Chosŏn government sent a strong letter of protest to Nicholas R. O'Connor, the English chargé d'affaires in China. The letter was full of reproach for England, wondering how a country knowledgeable about international law could do something so incomprehensible. Almost identical letters requesting assistance were also sent to all the foreign legations in Seoul.[43] The Chosŏn government already knew about the British actions by mid-May even before receiving official notification from the British government. Chosŏn sent officials to Kŏmun Island and was conducting negotiations with the commander of the English squadron.[44]

Arriving in Kŏmun Island on May 16, the delegation first observed the actions of the British navy. They then visited the commander-in-chief of the British squadron, Vice-Admiral William Dowell, in Nagasaki and lodged a protest. They declared that having six British warships anchored in Kŏmun Island flying the British flag was a clear violation of Korean sovereignty. It was no surprise that the

40. Ibid., p. 90.
41. Kim Yongku, p. 241.
42. Im, p. 92.
43. Kim Yongku, p. 242.
44. Ibid., p. 241.

Chosŏn government protested the forcible occupation of its territory by a foreign country. This incident demonstrated that the Chosŏn government was pursuing an independent foreign policy as the interest of the Western powers became focused on Chosŏn. It is a good example of what the Chosŏn government sought to gain from joining a world order based on international law.

From the beginning, China's Li Hongzhang was not very involved in this issue. Even though China saw itself as the suzerain of Chosŏn, he did not make any protest to England because the two countries had maintained friendly relations up to this time. Li's involvement was limited to sending naval admiral Ding Ruchang (1836–1895) to Kŏmun Island and requesting that Korean officials handle all negotiations.[45] Chosŏn's measured yet forceful protest took the British government by surprise, making China's position necessarily appear weak. Seizing this opportunity, Chosŏn made clear moves to approach the Russians and attempted a counter-attack against the Chinese.

Arriving in Nagasaki on May 19, 1885, the Korean delegation, Ŏm Seyŏng and von Möllendorff, sent a telegram to Davidov, the Russian minister in Tokyo. They informed him that the king approved the agreement concluded three months earlier that included a provision on the sending of military advisers. The Russian minister responded that preparations were complete to send the military advisors.[46] On June 10, de Speyer went to Seoul again. The purpose of his visit was to stop negotiations on the lease of Kŏmun Island being conducted by the British minister in Seoul, William George Aston (1841–1911), and to obtain the right to send Russian troops to the peninsula in order to "protect" Chosŏn on an equal basis with China and Japan. After having an audience with Kojong, de Speyer even drew up a draft of an agreement. However, the draft of this agreement was leaked to Minister Kim Yunsik, and when the Chinese learned of its contents, Chosŏn was put in a difficult position.[47]

On June 20, de Speyer met with Kim Yunsik. However, Kim strongly represented the Chinese position and had no intention whatsoever of accepting the agreement made by von Möllendorff with the Russians. Chosŏn's long standing diplomatic efforts thus came to naught. After de Speyer left on July 7, the Chosŏn court hurried to address the aftermath of this failure. Chosŏn sent a delegation to

45. Im, p. 91.
46. Ibid.
47. Ibid., p. 92.

China in order to overcome any misunderstandings arising from Chosŏn's contacts with Russia. King Kojong also sent a letter to Li Hongzhang requesting the dismissal and recall of von Möllendorff, who had played an important role in the negotiations.[48] The outcome was humiliating for the Chosŏn monarch.[49] These are the details of the incident that later came to be known as the First Secret Agreement between Korea and Russia.

(2) The Second Secret Agreement Between Korea and Russia
After the incident caused by the First Secret Agreement between Korea and Russia, Chinese pressure on Chosŏn became even more intense. In June 1885, the Chinese government allowed the Taewŏngun, who had been captive in Tianjin for his role in instigating the Imo Soldiers' Riot, to return to Chosŏn. China's decision was based on the belief that the Taewŏngun was the only figure capable of containing the king, who was the main figure behind the effort to build closer relations with Russia. In October, Yuan Shikai (1859–1916) was appointed Commissioner and Imperial Resident in Chosŏn, and he strengthened Chinese intervention in Chosŏn's internal affairs.

Russia did not remain idle toward these moves by Qing China. Carl Waeber was appointed chargé d'affaires in Chosŏn in June and left for Seoul in November. He was of mild temperament and skilled at diplomacy, and Kojong and Queen Min were especially fond of him. After von Möllendorff's dismissal, Li Hongzhang recommended Owen N. Denny, an American, to serve as an advisor to the government, and since Denny's thinking agreed with that of Waeber, they worked together to contain China.[50]

Even after Yuan Shikai's appointment as Imperial Resident began, Kojong did not abandon his efforts to pursue an independent foreign policy. Even in late 1885, Kojong discussed state affairs with officials who supported his policies, including Min Yŏngik (1860–1914), Right Garrison Officer (*uyŏngsa*); Min Yŏnghwan (1861–1905), an official in the Ministry of Internal Affairs (*hyŏpp'an naemubusa*); Min Ŭngsik, Left Garrison Officer (*chwayŏngsa*); Min Chongmok (1835–1916); and Min Kŭngsik.[51] In January 1886, Yuan sent a report to Li

48. Ibid., p. 95.
49. Ibid., p. 96.
50. Im, pp. 99–100.
51. Although many of these figures had the surname of Min, it is inaccurate to lump them together into a category that is often referred to as "Min family in-law-politics."

Hongzhang that the power of anti-Qing officials was increasing.[52] In June, the king dismissed Kim Yunsik, who had been a supporter of China within the court and maintained friendly relations with Yuan Shikai.[53] Infuriated, Yuan suggested to Li Hongzhang that Kojong be dethroned and that the Taewŏngun be allowed to rule.[54]

In mid-August 1886, Yuan Shikai intercepted a telegram that Minister Waeber was going to send to his home government and sent it to Li Hongzhang.[55] The telegram requested that Russia block Chinese intervention in order to support Chosŏn independence and that Russia should support Chosŏn's efforts to become equal to other countries and should send warships if Qing China did not support this. A few days later, Yuan sent another document affixed with the government's seal and that of Sim Sunt'aek, Chief State Councillor (Ch'ongni naemubusa), as evidence verifying the contents of the telegram. Yuan also noted that Kojong and Queen Min were resentful over the repatriation of the Taewŏngun's repatriation and that they were seeking Russian support.[56] At the same time, Yuan threatened the Chosŏn court by presenting a fake telegram stating that a large Chinese force had boarded a steamboat and was heading to Seoul in order to demand an explanation about the Chosŏn government's recent actions.[57]

Yuan's coercive strategy was effective. Because it was true that the Chosŏn king had sent a letter of verification to the Russian minister, it was difficult to deflect Yuan's accusations. On the evening of August 14, Yuan entered the royal palace and demanded to know who had sent the letter of verification, threatening, "What will Chosŏn do if the country of the Son of Heaven is enraged and sends a large military

Japan assigned this name to describe court politics as it became increasingly involved in Korean affairs in the late 19th century. In reality, figures with the Min surname were divided into three groups: the king's maternal cousins, the queen's brothers, and people totally unrelated. Yi Sangch'an, "1896nyŏn ŭibyŏng ŭi chŏngch'ijŏk sŏnggyŏk (On the political character of the righteous army in 1896) (Ph.D. diss., Seoul National University, 1996).
52. Im.
53. Ibid., p. 101.
54. Ibid., p. 101.
55. On the following incident regarding the contents of the telegram, I have relied on Ibid., pp. 102–3.
56. According to Jerome Ch'en, the original document that Min Yŏngik sent to Yuan Shikai was forged. When this became a matter of concern, Min fled to Hong Kong. Ibid., pp. 102–3, 107.
57. Ibid., p. 104.

force to punish it?" He even tried to intimidate Kojong himself, saying "How are you going to explain away this matter?"[58] In the end, the Chosŏn court acknowledged the fact that it had made contact with the Russian legation but claimed that it was the work of low-ranking officials (Cho chondu, Kim Kajin, Kim Hwak'u, Kim Yangmok) who had acted without the knowledge of the king or the government. The Chosŏn government sent a secret message to Chargé d'Affaires Waeber requesting that related documents be returned, citing the same reason. The message also asked him to handle matters by acting as if there never had been an agreement. After receiving the message, Waeber announced that he had never received a letter of verification from Kojong, thereby helping the Chosŏn position. These were the circumstances behind the incident of the Second Secret Agreement between Chosŏn and Russia.

The Chosŏn king's effort to conduct an independent diplomacy was thus an arduous struggle against Qing China. On August 26, 1886, Yuan Shikai reinstated Kim Yunsik as the Minister of Foreign and Commercial Affairs. Yuan then notified all the foreign legations that even government documents stamped with the royal seal were not official without the seal of this ministry. Yuan's intention was, of course, to gain control over Chosŏn's diplomacy through Kim Yunsik.[59] Since Kojong led a struggle against China by establishing a Ministry of the Interior (Naemubu) separate from the T'ongni amun (Office of Foreign Affairs; C. Zongli Yamen) system, Yuan felt it was necessary to block these efforts. Only the German consulate replied to this announcement while Japanese, American and English officials took no notice of it, seeing it as improper according to diplomatic protocol.[60]

Although all of Chosŏn's attempts at concluding an agreement with Russia ended in failure, they did bring about a change in China's attitude. After the incident caused by the Second Secret Agreement between Chosŏn and Russia, Li Hongzhang changed his position. He felt that an international agreement recognizing Qing China's pre-

---

58. The queen was present on this occasion and responded to Yuan Shikai, "Even if the letter of verification is brought back, it will still be as if the Agreement was never carried out; we can thus do nothing about thousands of Chinese troops coming to Chosŏn in reponse." Tabohashi Kiyoshi, *Kindai Nissen kankei no kenkyu* (Research on Japan–Korea Relations), vol. 2 (Keijo: Chosen Sotokufu Chusuin, 1940), pp. 39–40, and Im Kyesun, p. 104.

59. Im, p. 105.

60. Ibid., p. 106.

## Chosŏn's Adpotion of International Law    161

dominance over Chosŏn would no longer be necessary if Russia promised that it had no intention of invading Chosŏn.[61] In late June 1886, Denny, Kojong's American advisor, sent a letter to Li Hongzhang stating that, according to a Russian official in Seoul, even if England were to withdraw from Kŏmun Island, Russia had no intention of occupying this port; however, if England did not withdraw, Russia would then be forced to occupy Yŏnghŭng Bay in Hamgyŏng province. Li used this opportunity to begin considering agreements between China and Russia on Chosŏn's territorial integrity. He calculated that if these agreements were concluded, England would withdraw, and Japanese power could be checked together by Russia and China. In his view, Chinese predominance over Chosŏn would be able to continue in such an international situation. The incident of the Second Secret Agreement between Chosŏn and Russia thus led China to rethink its strategy since Chosŏn would ultimately seek protection from other countries if China continued to acknowledge tacitly England's occupation of Kŏmun Island.[62]

In September 1886, Denny went to Tianjin to meet with Li Hongzhang. Li requested that Denny meet with the Russian chargé d'affaires stationed in China (Ladygensky) to sound him out on the possibility of concluding an agreement establishing the neutrality of the Korean peninsula. The Russian chargé d'affaires responded that his home government had already granted him the authority to announce that Russia had no intention of occupying any territory. Li then requested that Russia issue an official statement proclaiming this. After four rounds of negotiations, the Russian legation presented a draft of such a statement in French on October 1.[63] However, Li was not satisfied with the draft because it acknowledged Chosŏn's autonomy, effectively denying Chinese suzerain status. On October 24, another verbal promise was made ensuring Chosŏn's territorial integrity. The Russian government named this the Tientsin Agreement of 1886 and sought to recognize the status quo. As a result of this agreement, the English ended its twenty-month occupation of Kŏmun

61. Ibid., p. 112.
62. Ibid., pp. 112–13.
63. Ibid, p. 113. This contents of this document included: (1) that relations between Chosŏn and Qing China and between Chosŏn and other countries be maintained in the present state and not be changed; (2) that Chosŏn's territory be safeguarded, (3) that the Korean king's autonomy be recognized, and that Russia and China agree to mutually handle the occurrence of an unexpected situation in the future by allowing Chosŏn to act autonomously; etc.

Island and withdrew on February 27, 1887.[64] Denny's activities thus represented the wishes of the Chosŏn monarch.

CONCLUSION

With the signing of the Treaty of Amity between Chosŏn and Japan in 1876, the Chosŏn dynasty began to enter the Western world order of international law. The conclusion of treaties of amity and commerce with the United States, England, and Germany in 1882 demonstrated Chosŏn's strong desire to enter this new system. This desire was so strong that concluding treaties with the Western powers presented few worries for Chosŏn. Because the Chosŏn government actively undertook the preparations for signing these treaties, it was able to achieve tariff autonomy through these agreements. Japan's situation stands in contrast with that of Chosŏn. After the shock of the sudden appearance of the "black ships," Japan concluded treaties in the midst of a divided public opinion and was forced to endure unequal tariff rates. What posed a burden to Chosŏn was not its relations with the Western powers but the necessity to adjust its traditional relations with China.

When the Treaty of Amity and Commerce with the United States was concluded, the Chosŏn monarch and his court had already been looking for a way to solve this problem. They quickly sent an official to negotiate with the Chinese to put an end to the long-standing system of sending temporary envoys to China, and they cautiously proposed implementing a system of permanent diplomatic envoys. Although Qing China did recommend that Chosŏn establish friendly relations with the United States, China had no intention of modifying its traditional relations with Chosŏn. China naturally responded negatively toward Chosŏn's proposal. The Qing court regarded this proposal as an attempt to break away from its sphere of influence and countered by enforcing its tributary policy toward Chosŏn.

The Chinese tributary system posed the greatest obstacle to Chosŏn's modernization, and the struggle by the Chosŏn government with China was more arduous than Japan's efforts to revise its unequal treaties with the Western powers. In order to overcome the stronger than expected resistance from China, the Chosŏn government

64. Ibid., p. 114.

attempted several times to open negotiations with the Russians. All of the secret contacts with Russia ended in failure, and each time, the Chinese applied even more pressure on Chosŏn. The 1880s were the most crucial period for Chosŏn to implement modernization policies (*kaehwa chŏngch'aek*). But it was forced to waste that valuable time because of China's strong efforts to block its attempts at joining the new international order.

Chinese pressure on Chosŏn ended with China's defeat by Japan in the Sino-Japanese War of 1894–1895. Nevertheless, Chosŏn's troubles continued because of Japan's efforts to establish a protectorate over the country. The Chosŏn government tried to block Japan's protectorate policy by requesting American intervention. However, Japanese efforts continued with the isolation of the Chosŏn king in Kyŏngbok Palace and the brutal assassination of Queen Min in October 1895. In the early hours of February 11, 1896, the king evaded Japanese military surveillance and moved his place of residence to the Russian Legation (Agwan p'ach'ŏn). During his year long residence at the legation, he adopted various measures to restore royal authority and completed preparations to elevate the dynastic state to the status of an empire. Inaugurated in October 1897, the Great Han Empire quickly promoted industrialization and efforts to build a modern state. These initiatives produced considerable results until the outbreak of the Russo-Japanese War in February 1904.

As a part of its effort to build a modern state, the Great Han Empire promulgated guidelines for a constitution in a document entitled "Kukje" (State System) in August 1899. Laws relating to accounting, the military, the penal system, and administration had been created recently, and these guidelines were an attempt to organize them within a single system. Since the Chosŏn dynasty had a long tradition of systematizing ordinances into a legal code dating back to the *Kyŏngguk taejŏn* (Grand Code for State Administration) of the fifteenth century, the establishment of modern law was carried out in a similar manner. Legal history scholars have shown that the principles of modern law adopted by the Great Han Empire were derived from the system of national laws described in Johannes C. Bluntschli's *Das Moderne Voelkerrecht der Civilisiernen Staten als Rechstbuch Dargestellt.*

What is significant is the fact that the Chosŏn government accomplished its longstanding task of terminating its traditional relations with China at this time. From February 1898, the Great Han Empire proposed signing a new treaty with China on the basis of Chosŏn's status as an independent state. After eight rounds of negotiations that ended in September 1899, the representatives of both countries agreed to a fifteen-clause treaty. In October, the Korean Foreign Ministry requested the emperor's decision through the State Council (Ŭijŏngbu) in October, and it was ratified on December 14.

The Korea–Qing Treaty (*Han-Ch'ŏng choyak*) was significant in many respects since it was carried out according to procedures governed by the domestic laws of the Great Han Empire. According to the "Regulations of Cabinet Ministers of the State Council," the Foreign Ministry was to submit matters to the State Council, and then in a cabinet meeting, the State Councilors were to authorize the Foreign Minister to conduct negotiations. The result of the negotiations was to be submitted again to the State Council, and after passing through all these steps, the matter could be presented to the emperor for his approval.[65] In the age of "classical" international law, it was customary for domestic law to take precedence over international law; therefore, these legislative measures of the Great Han Empire can be considered a significant effort to safeguard its sovereignty.

The Korea–Qing Treaty of 1899 was the first treaty signed between Korea and China as equal and independent states in accordance with the methods of Western international law. It was significant for its complete termination of Chosŏn's traditional relations with China, a process that had begun in 1882. Coincidentally, 1899 was the year when the treaty revisions that Japan had achieved in 1894 began to take effect. The Korea–Qing Treaty is of great significance for faithfully following the treaty laws of the Great Han Empire. However, from the time of the Russo-Japanese War of 1904–1905, Japan forced on the Korean government a series of treaties with the aim of wresting away Korea's national sovereignty. These treaties completely undermined the achievements of Korea's legal system during the trials and tribulations of the previous twenty years. This is the real reason for raising concerns over the illegality of the treaties that brought about the Japanese "annexation" of Korea.

translated by Todd A. Henry

65. The course of negotiations between both countries was issued as a typed edition under the name of *Han-Ch'ŏng ŭiyak kongdok* (The public record of agreements between Chosŏn and China). See p. 108 for the detailed proceedings of these negotiations.

CHAPTER 8

# Forced Treaties and Japan's Annexation of the Great Han Empire: An Argument for the Illegality of the Annexation

OVER THE YEARS, JAPAN'S political leaders have consistently maintained that Japan's rule of Korea from 1910 to 1945 was legitimate. According to an informal survey by the Korean government, there were at least twenty-six instances of "unacceptable statements" by the Japanese government that caused diplomatic problems between 1951 to 1995. Prime Minister Yoshida Shigeru's remarks at the first Republic of Korea-Japan talks in 1951 was the first such statement. Each subsequent occurrence has angered the Korean government as well as the Korean people, causing serious diplomatic problems and jeopardizing future relations between the two countries. Why has there been no change in Japan's view of its past, even though half a century has passed since Korea was liberated from Japanese rule?

When Japan's political leaders have commented on the "annexation" of Korea, their arguments generally fall into one of two types:

(1) Japan's annexation of Korea was completely legitimate, carried out for the sake of peace in Asia. There was nothing morally or legally wrong with the annexation.
(2) Japan may have moral or ethical responsibilities for its aggressions, but no legal ones.

The first argument captures the view of the Japanese people at the time of the "annexation," while the second reflects the current view based on a "change" in the Japanese understanding of history. At the time of the annexation, Japan's leaders tried to show that the annexation was conducted "amicably" between two equal countries and that there were no irregularities in the relevant documents. Public statements by the Japanese government declared that the motive for annexation was to help Korea. The Japanese portrayed Korea as a weak country that was constantly threatened by the aggressions of China and Russia and argued that the very existence of Korea was the root of trouble in East Asia. Japan claimed that the annexation of Korea, after Japan's defeat of both China and Russia in war, brought peace to East Asia and contributed to Korean development through Japan's reforms of its government. This view was expressed in *Daitoa senso sokatsu* (An Overview of Wars in Greater East Asia), which was published in August 1995 by the Historical Review Committee of the rightist faction of the Liberal Democratic Party in Japan.

In shifting from the first to the second argument, the Japanese have abandoned the claim that the annexation was for the sake of peace in Asia; however, the two arguments agree on the issue of its legality. According to the second argument, Japan's annexation of Korea was lawful, though it may have been morally wrong. The Japanese government maintains that the two diplomatic agreements that put Korea under Japanese rule—the Convention of 1905 and the Treaty of Annexation of 1910—were perfectly legal. Though unacceptable to Koreans, this view seems to be accepted by "progressive" intellectuals in Japan. One example is a 1995 speech by Japanese Prime Minister Murayama Tomiichi, who was expected to usher in a new age in Korea-Japan relations as a member of the Socialist Party. He caused a controversy in Korea when he spoke at the Japanese Diet and asserted that Japan's annexation of Korea was legal, not long after apologizing for Japanese rule. His apology was concerned only with Japan's moral wrongdoing, while his statement at the Diet concerned legal issues. There are very few intellectuals in Japan who acknowledge both Japan's moral and legal responsibilities.

How should Koreans, the victims of the annexation, respond to the reluctance of Japan's leaders and intellectuals to admit their legal culpability? Various responses should be considered, but no matter which response is chosen, Koreans must have a clear understanding of the extent of illegalities in those events and convey them to the Japanese. In order to contribute to this task, I will focus on introducing recent research that details the facts surrounding the forced transfer of Korean sovereignty to Japan and provides evidence on the coercion involved in the treaty documents.

Among the Japanese, another popular view is that Japan's "annexation" of Korea was simply a result of the imperialism of the age, refusing to view the annexation as a crime. They reason that Japan is not at fault because, in an age of survival of the fittest, the annexation of a weaker country by a stronger was perfectly acceptable at the time. This logic was demonstrated in a resolution passed by the Japanese Diet in June 1995, on the fiftieth anniversary of the end of World War II. While admitting Japan's wrongdoing in its colonial rule and aggressions, the Diet claimed that the annexation had to be seen "in the context of the numerous colonizations and acts of aggression in modern world history." While such views greatly reduce the responsibility that Japan has to bear, Japan's forceful seizure of Korea's sovereignty cannot be defended by an appeal to the general logic of imperialism.

Japanese imperialism was different from that of the Western powers, whose aggressions were a product of the external expansion of their capitalist economies. Japan, on the other hand, pursued traditional expansionism for the sake of its own capitalist development. The Japanese government had long sought to seize the Korean peninsula. When the Great Han Empire (Taehan Cheguk) belatedly achieved clear progress in establishing a foundation for modernization, Japanese leaders became uneasy and moved quickly to achieve their goals in Korea. They declared war on Russia and used it as an opportunity to take over the Great Han Empire by military force. Since the seizure of Korea's sovereignty was carried out with coercion, evidence of deceit, force, and illegality can be discovered in the process of annexation. I hope to correct the accepted wisdom about the annexation by analyzing the concrete facts surrounding the negotiations of the forced treaties.

THE DETAILS AND PROBLEMS OF THE FORCED TREATIES

Japan's expansionist designs on Korea can be traced to the rise of Kokugaku (National Studies) during the Edo period. Perhaps because Toyotomi Hideyoshi's invasion of Chosŏn in 1592 had been unsuccessful, hostility against Korea was pervasive in Japan. After returning from the war, soldiers spread many stories about the war that increased animosity toward Koreans. While the educated elite in Japan at the time admired and preferred the products of Chosŏn's culture, Kokugaku, with its strongly chauvinist tendencies, spread the historical view that Japan was superior to Chosŏn, beginning in the eighteenth century. Scholars of Kokugaku cultivated feelings of superiority by treating legends and myths as if they portrayed actual historical events. These legends and stories described how Japanese deities and emperors ruled Korea in ancient times and how Korean aristocrats and kings submitted to the authority of Japan. Transmitted as if they were historical facts, such stories pandered to the animosity toward Korea that was prevalent among commoners in Japan.

The feelings of superiority toward Chosŏn later developed into various theories of expansionism such as *Chosen koryakron* (Theory of Invading Chosŏn), *Seikanron* (Theory of Conquering Korea), *Daito gapporon* (Theory of the Annexation of Greater East Asia), and *Datsua ron* (Theory of Escaping from Asia) in the late-nineteenth century after Korea opened its ports to the West. These theories served as the ideological basis for the Sino-Japanese War in 1894 and the Russo-Japanese War in 1904.[1] The connection between these two wars and the Kokugaku of the Edo period weakens Japan's claim that its seizure of Korea was simply a result of its capitalist development and imperialism of the late nineteenth century.[2] Japan was the victor of the Sino-Japanese War, but due to the Triple Intervention in 1895 involving France, Germany, and Russia, there was no economic gain for Japan. After the war, Japan suffered a severe recession for several years. In addition, realizing its main objective of the war—the seizure of Korea—became much more difficult after the pro-Japanese cabinet fell when King Kojong of Korea, concerned about Japan's influence in Korea, moved to the Russian legation in 1896 (Agwan P'ach'ŏn).

After returning to his palace, Kojong changed the official name of the country to the "Great Han Empire" as part of an effort to emphasize Korea's status as an independent nation. At the same time, he actively implemented the Kwangmu Reforms to establish a sound economic and military basis for the state that would preserve the country's autonomy. From 1896 to 1903, the Great Han Empire steadily carried out various preparations for industrialization. For Japan, Korea's progress meant that its opportunity to seize Korea was fading; therefore, Japan obstructed every effort of the Korean government to purchase arms or obtain foreign loans. In December 1903,

---

1. See Pak Yŏngjae, "Kŭndae Ilbon ŭi ch'imnyakjuŭijŏk taeoeron kwa Han'guknon" (Modern Japan's foreign expansionism and views toward Korea), *Han'guksa simin kangjwa* 19 (1996).
2. There needs to be detailed research on the relationship between Japan's policy of aggression and its capitalist development to determine which preceded the other.

## Forced Treaties and Japan's Annexation of the Great Han Empire  169

Japan's cabinet finally resolved to declare war against Russia and thus achieve its goal of domination over Korea. Japan decided to go to war with Russia because Korea was using Russia to contain Japan and also because it wanted to ally with Russia's enemies, Great Britain and the United States, thus avoiding a repeat of past mistakes such as the Triple Intervention. Great Britain and the United States viewed Japan's aggression toward Russia as a way of achieving their own goals and therefore supported Japan's efforts.

When Japan instigated the war with Russia, it quickly dispatched the Temporary Military Contingent to Korea (*Kankoku rinji hakentai*), which had already been mobilized, to begin preparations for seizing Korea's sovereignty. As the tide of the war became favorable to Japan, the military contingent sped up its operations. The majority of Japan's military forces passed through Inch'ŏn and Seoul on their way north. Under pressure, Korea was forced to sign the first of the agreements that deprived the country of its sovereignty. The Temporary Military Contingent was soon renamed the "Resident Army in Korea" (*Kankoku chusatsugun*) and stationed in Seoul. Its function was to provide the military force needed to coerce the Korean government into accepting the successive diplomatic agreements pursued by Japan. At the time, international law permitted unequal treaties to be concluded between the victorious and defeated countries in a war—beginning with a formal declaration of war; however, it stipulated that treaties signed under military threat were not legally binding. Since Great Britain and the United States did not want Japan to declare war against Korea, Japan chose the latter method: i.e., the less aggressive path of diplomatic agreements.

After the Russo-Japanese War, Japan forced Korea to accept the following diplomatic agreements with the purpose of seizing its sovereignty:

(1) Protocol, February 23, 1904 (Ni-Kan giteisho; Japanese-Korean Protocol)
(2) Agreement, August 22, 1904 (No title; the first Japanese-Korean agreement)
(3) Convention, November 17, 1905 (No title; the second Japanese-Korean agreement)
(4) Korean-Japanese Agreement, July 24, 1907 (Ni-Kan kyoyaku; Japanese-Korean Agreement)

170  Chapter Eight

(5) Treaty of Annexation, August 22, 1910 (Kankoku heigo jyoyaku; Treaty regarding the Annexation of Korea to the Empire of Japan)[3]

These agreements involved the use of coercion and represent the steps taken to seize Korea's sovereignty, beginning with territorial use rights (1), proceeding to diplomatic rights (2 and 3) and domestic and military affairs (4), and then concluding with the annexation (5).

Korean scholars have argued for the nullification of these agreements by focusing more on Japan's use of a military threat in concluding the compacts than on their procedural illegalities. Korea's position has been based on the fact that under international law, diplomatic agreements are null if the representative of one side threatened the other. Among the five agreements, the Convention of 1905 has received the most attention because it was the most important and because coercion and the threat of force were evident in the negotiations. Although Japan has maintained that the Treaty of Annexation had no legal flaws in form or procedure, Korea has argued that it should be nullified because it was based on the Convention of 1905. Recently, detailed research has demonstrated that in addition to the use of force and coercion, there were also many problems in the forms and procedures of the agreements. I will discuss these issues for each of the agreements.[4]

(1) Protocol (February 23, 1904; Ni-Kan giteisho)
Soon after Japan declared war on Russia in February 1904, Japan forced this protocol on Korea, concluding the agreement on February 23. The Korean government had expected the outbreak of hostilities between the two countries as early as August 1903, but because it had no military-draft system, it was considering proclaiming itself a neutral country. When Japan sped up preparations for war at the end of 1903, Korea declared itself a neutral country on January 21, 1904.

---

3. The titles in parenthesis are those used by the Japanese government. "No title" means that the original document had no title.
4. The following sections are based on the following three chapters: Yi Tae-jin (Yi T'aejin), "Choyak ŭi myŏngch'ing ŭl puch'iji mothan 'Ulsa poho choyak'" (The 'Convention of 1905' had no title), "T'onggambu ui Taehan Cheguk poin t'alch'ui wa Sunjong Hwangje sŏmyŏng wijo" (The Resident-General's seizure of the royal seal and the forgery of Emperor Sunjong's signature), and "Kongp'o ch'ikyu ka naljo toen 'Il-Han pyŏnghap choyak" (The Japan-Korea Annexation Treaty and the forgery of the royal edict), in Yi Tae-jin, ed., *Ilbon ŭi Taehan Cheguk kangjŏm* (Japan's occupation of the Great Han Empire) (Seoul: Kkach'i, 1995).

Forced Treaties and Japan's Annexation of the Great Han Empire    171

On February 6, Japan severed all diplomatic relations with Russia and declared war. Ignoring Korea's declaration of neutrality, Japan occupied Korea by dispatching five battalions of the Temporary Military Contingent to Korea, which had already been mobilized. After these troops arrived in Seoul, reinforcements also passed through the city on their way north, heightening the atmosphere of threat and violence.[5] Coerced upon the Korean government under a state of military occupation, the protocol was marked by the following problems:[6]

5. The scale and organization of the Japanese forces stationed in Korea were as follows. The "Temporary Military Contingent to Korea" mainly consisted of the 1st Infantry Battalion of the 14th Regiment, the 2nd Battalion of the 47th Regiment, the 1st Battalion of the 24th Regiment, and the 2nd Battalion of the 46th Regiment, which were all from the 12th Division. These were the main forces that made up the contingent, and additional battalions were to be sent from each regiment for support if necessary (Commander: Infantry Commander of the 23rd Brigade, Major General of the Army, Kikoshi Anbou). The "Temporary Military Contingent to Korea" was renamed the "Permanent Military Force in Korea" on March 11 (*Nihon gaiko bunsho* [Diplomatic Documents of Japan, supplemental book to Vol. 36 and 37, Russo-Japanese War, pp. 83–88, chapter 1, "Severing National Ties]." *Keijo fushi* [History of Keijo (Seoul) Prefecture], volume 1, chapter 3. Japanese General Staff Office, ed., *Nichiro senekishi* [History of the Russo-Japanese War]. The contingent secretly sailed from Sasebo military port at 2:30 a.m. on February 6, with a fleet of around 60 ships under the command of Vice Admiral Togo Heihachiro. Together with the troops headed to the Russian front, the contingent arrived in Inch'ŏn late in the afternoon on February 8 and began moving ashore at 5:30 p.m., completing the operation by the morning of February 9. The landing force was divided into two separate groups. The 2nd Infantry Battalion of the 46th Regiment and the 2nd Battalion of the 47th Regiment went to Seoul under the command of Commander Kikoshi. This advance force arrived at Seoul Station at 11:30 a.m. on February 9 and began making shows of force. Following the advance force, additional Japanese troops continued to arrive at various Korean ports to supplement the "Temporary Military Contingent" and to reinforce the troops up north at the Russian front. Roads between Inch'ŏn and Seoul were filled with Japanese soldiers and military supplies, and key buildings in Seoul were used as barracks for the Japanese troops. Book five of *Maech'ŏn yarok*, written by Hwang Hyŏn (1855–1910), described the situation in Korea as follows: "The Japanese troops that landed in Inch'ŏn numbered fifty thousand and had over ten thousand horses. They set up eighteen military camps all over Seoul, including at Ch'angdŏk Palace, Munhŭijŏn Hall, Wŏngu'dan, Chŏgyŏng Palace, Kwangjewŏn Garden, and other government offices. They purchased hundreds of houses outside the West Gate and turned them into horse stables. They set up tents to sleep in by the banks of the Han River, and the smoke from their cooking fires could be seen for miles around. In the southern part of the country, Japanese forces passed through Tongnae and arrived in Taegu, passed through Namhae on the way to Namwŏn, and passed through Kunsan on the way to Chŏnju. In the western part of the country, they occupied Pyongyang and Samhwa, and in the northern part, they landed at Wŏnsan and Sŏngjin. They marched northward toward Liaodong while maintaining a constant distance from each other."

6. See Yi Tae-jin, "The 'Convention of 1905' had no title."

(1) The protocol is dated February 23, 1904; however, according to *Nihon gaiko bunsho* (Diplomatic Documents of Japan), Hayashi Gonsuke (1860–1939), the Japanese Minister to Korea, asked Komura Jutaro (1855–1911), the Japanese Foreign Minister, on the 24th to set a date for its announcement. Komura directed that an announcement be made in the *Kwanbo* (Official Gazette) of the Korean Government, and it appeared in the February 27 issue.[7] The fact that Japan unilaterally determined the day and the method of the announcement is sufficient evidence that the protocol did not follow normal procedures. The situation was similar during the negotiations for the Agreement of 1904.

(2) The protocol clearly states in Item 3, "The Imperial Government of Japan definitely guarantees the independence and territorial integrity of the Corean Empire." However, after only one year, on November 17, 1905, Japan deprived Korea of its diplomatic rights, one of the most important rights of an independent nation, by forcing Korea to sign the Convention of 1905. Because this convention expressly violated the clause in Item 3 of the Protocol of 1904, the convention should have had no legal force, as was pointed out in a 1906 paper by Francis Rey, a French scholar of international law.[8] Sources reveal that the Japanese government had no intention of protecting the independence of Korea, even though it was guaranteed in the protocol. At a cabinet meeting held in May, the Japanese government passed a resolution on "Japanese Policy toward Korea."[9] The resolution stated, "Since the survival of Korea is directly tied to the security of the Japanese Empire, [we] cannot allow another country to take over Korea. This is the reason that we have been making every effort to help Korea maintain its independence and territorial integrity."

---

7. "Memo for Immediate Circulation on the Japanese-Korean Protocol," *Nihon gaiko bunsho* (Documents on Japanese foreign policy), vol. 37, no. 1, item no. 5, document no. 379 (February 24) and no. 380 (February 24) (Tokyo: Gannando shoten). See also document no. 381 (February 25).

8. "La Situation Internationale de la Corée," *Revue Générale de Droit International Public*, Tome XIII, (Paris, 1906). Rey's paper has been translated into Korean by Ch'oe Chonggo and Nam Hyosun with the title "Taehan Cheguk ŭi kukjebŏp chiwi" (The Great Han Empire's status in international law" in Yi Tae-jin, ed., *op. cit.*

9. *Nihon gaiko bunsho*, vol. 37, no. 1, pp. 351–56.

(2) Agreement (August 22, 1904; the First Japanese-Korean Agreement)

When Japan appeared to be winning its war with Russia, it forced Korea to sign this agreement. The agreement contained the following three items:

> (a) The Korean Government shall engage a Japanese financial advisor to be recommended by the Japanese Government.
> (b) The Korean Government shall engage a foreigner recommended by the Japanese Government as diplomatic advisor.
> (c) The Korean Government shall first consult the Japanese Government representative before concluding treaties with foreign powers and dealing with other important diplomatic affairs.

Korea vehemently refused to sign the agreement because item (c) meant that Korea had to transfer its diplomatic rights to Japan. As a result, the Japanese decided to group items (a) and (b) together and to take care of them first, and handle item (c) in separate negotiations. Thus, items (a) and (b) were signed by the Korean Ministers of Finance and Foreign Affairs on August 19 while negotiations on item (c) were still going on. The Korean government offered stiff resistance because the "Japanese government representative" stipulated in item (c) would have had the same powers as the Resident-General, who was later stationed in Korea as a result of the Convention of 1905. The central figure in the resistance was the emperor himself. After lengthy negotiations, Yun Ch'iho (1865–1945), the Deputy Foreign Minister of Korea, signed the document on August 22, on the condition of deleting the word "representative" from the term "Korean government representative." Because of the coercion involved in the negotiations, the agreement contained the following problems:[10]

1. Negotiations initially strove for a "memorandum," but at the very end, the Japanese side suddenly changed it into an "agreement." Under international law, documents resulting from negotiations among nations are classified as "treaties," "agreements," or "protocols." For a treaty, the sovereign of a nation must issue a special proxy statement to the head negotiator, who then has the authority to conduct negotiations on behalf of the nation.[11] Agreements and

---

10. See Yi Tae-jin, "The 'Convention of 1905' had no title."
11. At the beginning of the Protocol of 1904 (according to the original kept by Korea), there is the following statement: "Emperor Kojong's Deputy Minister of Foreign Affairs and Chief of the General Staff Yi Chiyong, and Hayashi, the Special Proxy Representa-

protocols become official if the official proxy statements are included in the final document. By contrast, memoranda, which do not fall into the category of official diplomatic documents, do not include a proxy statement from the country's sovereign or government in the actual documents. A memorandum indicates the official titles of the negotiating parties and contains their signatures and seals (see Figure 1a). Accordingly, a memorandum has less authority than the other three types of diplomatic agreements. Items agreed upon in a memorandum apply only to those nations explicitly mentioned in the document, and when the content of a memorandum affects a nation not mentioned, another official document is required.

There was no official title on the document of this agreement; neither was there any mention of the power of proxy. The agreement simply listed the three items agreed upon and was signed by the diplomatic officials of the two countries concerned. Throughout the negotiations, official reports sent between the Japanese Foreign Ministry and the minister to Korea referred to this document as a "memorandum," not an "agreement" (see Figure 1b). On August 22, after all three items in the document were agreed upon, Japan notified the American and British governments of the result of the negotiations. When they did, however, the Japanese government suddenly changed the name of the document to an "agreement."[12] This change was made to assure the United States and Great Britain, countries Japan would need as allies in the future, that both Japan and Korea recognized the document as an official diplomatic agreement. In order to hide its flaws, the titles "Japanese-Korean Agreement" and "First Japanese-Korean Agreement" were added to the document after the conclusion of negotiations.

These maneuvers by Japan convinced Great Britain and the United States that Korea had truly turned over its diplomatic rights to the Japanese government. After the Convention of 1905 was forcibly concluded in November 1905, Min Yŏngch'an (1873–?), a Korean diplomatic minister, received a secret order from Emperor Kojong to visit Elihu Root (1845–1937), the United States Secretary of State. When Min requested assistance in dealing with Japan under the terms of the Treaty of Amity and Commerce of 1882 between Korea and the United States, Root officially denied help, saying that Korea had no

tive of the Empire of Japan, accepted their respective appointments and agreed to conclude this protocol."
12. *Nihon gaiko bunsho*, vol. 37, no. 1, item 6.

official diplomatic rights under the Agreement of 1904.[13] Having misrepresented the actual situation to Great Britain and the United States, Japan secretly requested that the two countries recognize the Japanese protectorate of Korea and so concluded the secret Taft-Katsura Agreement with the United States (July 27, 1905) and the Second Anglo-Japanese Alliance (August 12, 1905). It is well known that these two secret agreements played a decisive role in turning Korea into a Japanese protectorate. It is shocking that these important diplomatic agreements were, in the end, based on deliberately falsified documents.

2. As they had done with the Protocol of 1904, the Japanese Foreign Ministry sent a complete draft of the agreement, entitled "Ni-Kan kyoyaku" (Japanese-Korean Agreement) to their minister to Korea on September 4. However, the agreement had already been signed on August 22, some ten days earlier. The Japanese Foreign Ministry also instructed their minister to Korea to direct the Korean government to announce the news of the agreement in the September 5 issue of the *Kwanbo* (Official Gazette) and to inform other countries as well.[14] Such directives by the Foreign Ministry after the agreement was signed are clear evidence that it was concluded under coercion from Japan. In conclusion, this agreement, strictly speaking, was never actually valid; therefore, Korea should be compensated for all the damages caused by later diplomatic agreements based upon it.

(3) Convention (November 17, 1905; Second Japanese-Korean Agreement or New Japanese-Korean Agreement)

Although the idea of a protectorate of Korea had been discussed among the Japanese political leadership from the time of the Sino-Japanese War, it was first mentioned at the policy level during a cabinet meeting on the Russo-Japanese War on December 30, 1903 in a resolution on "Policy toward Korea" (Tai-Kan hosin). Under the premise that "Korea must be placed under Japanese control even by

---

13. Root to Min (December 19, 1905), "Note to the Korean Legation," National Archives (microfilm 99). Professor Tyler Dennett also believed that the Great Han Empire willingly subjected itself to the rule of Japan through the Agreement of 1904. Therefore, he believed that the person who betrayed Korea was Emperor Kojong himself, not President Roosevelt as the Korean people believed (Tyler Dennett, *Roosevelt and the Russo-Japanese War: a critical study of American policy in Eastern Asia in 1902-5*, (Gloucester, MA: P. Smith, (1925–1959). His statements were made without knowledge of the deceitful maneuvers of Japan.

14. "Note on the Announcement of the Japanese-Korean Agreement," *Nihon gaiko bunsho*, vol. 37, no. 1, item 6, document no. 418 (September 4), p. 369.

military force," the Japanese government decided to establish a mutual alliance or a different kind of protection treaty with Korea, as it had done during the Sino-Japanese War. With the Russo-Japanese War developing in its favor, Japan began to implement its plans to turn Korea into a protectorate. Japan had already received the approval of both Great Britain and the United States through its secret agreements with both countries in July and August of 1905, respectively. However, the Japanese encountered stiff resistance from the Korean government; as a result, the final agreement contains the following flaws and problems:[15]

1. It is hardly necessary to mention that this agreement was also achieved through coercion, with threats and demonstrations of military force. In a cabinet meeting on October 27, 1905, Japan decided on an eight-item guideline for reducing Korea to a protectorate and even prepared a draft of an agreement that was attached to the guidelines. Item 6 contained an order that Hasegawa Yoshimitsu (1850–1924), the commander of the "Resident Army in Korea," would provide military assistance to Hayashi, the minister plenipotentiary to Korea, and item 7 stated that reinforcements would quickly be sent from Japan if necessary. These two items show that the Japanese government planned from the beginning to use military force to achieve its goals. After these preparations were completed, Japanese troops surrounded Kyŏng'un Palace (modern-day Tŏksu Palace), where the emperor was residing, on November 17, 1905 and even entered the negotiating room to threaten Korean officials. There exists an official Japanese document that reported on the army's actions; it notes that Japan dispatched its regular and military police to Kyŏng'un Palace on the pretext of guarding the Korean ministers and did not remove them despite the protests of the Korean emperor.[16]

2. Because there was no final decision on the formalities appropriate to the agreement's importance, it contains many flaws in its form and procedures. From the very beginning, Japan anticipated that it would be difficult to get Korea's approval for the protectorate, so they planned to use more forceful methods. Their plans were demonstrated by item 8 of the guidelines established at the cabinet meeting of October 27:

---

15. See Yi Tae-jin, "The 'Convention of 1905' had no title."
16. "The sixth report on Marquis Ito's visit to Korea," *Jukan nihon koshikan kiroku* (Records of the Japanese Legation to Korea), vol. 24, document no. 69, temporary secret no. 6, p. 397.

## Forced Treaties and Japan's Annexation of the Great Han Empire 177

If there is no possibility that Korea will agree [to the protectorate], as a last resort, Japan will unilaterally notify the Korean government that the compact has been completed. At the same time, Japan will explain to the other countries of the world why it had to use force to conclude the compact. Furthermore, Japan will reassure other countries that Korea's treaties with them will remain in effect and that their financial and industrial benefits within Korea will not be affected at all.

As shown in item 8, the plan of the Japanese government was to prepare for the worst-case scenario. A draft of the document was prepared as an "agreement" rather than as a formal "treaty." In general, important matters such as the transfer of diplomatic rights should be covered by a treaty rather than an agreement. For a treaty to be official, it must have the following three documents:

(a) A special proxy statement, issued by the sovereign of a country to the head representative, that gives express authority to conduct negotiations on behalf of the country (see Figure 2a).
(b) Signatures on the treaty itself of the head representatives from both sides.
(c) Ratification statements from the sovereigns of both nations (see Figure 2b).

Since the Japanese had anticipated resistance from the Korean government, they did not expect to receive all the necessary documents. This was the reason that Japan originally prepared an "agreement" rather than a "treaty." As an agreement concluded by force, it contained fundamental flaws. The Convention of 1905 contained only a document of the agreement; it did not have a special proxy statement or the emperor's ratification statement. Therefore, it lacked the fundamental items necessary to serve as a diplomatic agreement covering important matters such as the transfer of diplomatic rights.

3. The Japanese government vacillated between pursuing a full treaty versus an agreement and at the last moment chose the form of an agreement. However, in the last-minute confusion, Japanese officials failed to give the document a proper title (see Figure 3a). Although the Japanese expected fierce resistance from the Korean government and had prepared a draft of an "agreement," they still pressured Korea to accept an official "treaty" in the early stage of

discussions. Japanese officials initially used "*Kankoku gaiko itaku joyak*" (Treaty to Transfer Korea's Diplomatic Rights) as the official title for the document, as confirmed in telegrams sent to and from Seoul and Tokyo after November 17. When Ito Hirobumi (1841–1909) paid a visit to Kojong, Ito requested that Kojong issue a proxy statement to the Korean representative, showing that Japan wanted negotiations to lead to a treaty if possible. Kojong refused to comply with this request to the end, and Korean officials also put up stiff resistance when the cabinet was forced to convene. Proceeding with their original plan, Japan presented Korea with a draft of an agreement and pressured the Foreign Minister to sign it. In all communications between Seoul and Tokyo after November 22, the document was always referred to as an "agreement" and not as a "treaty."

The Convention of 1905 was concluded on November 17 as an "agreement," giving Japan a protectorate over Korea. However, the first line of the agreement, where the title should have been, was left blank. Because the nature of the agreement was still undecided during preparations of the document, the space for the title was left blank even though the draft was completed. In the midst of all the confusion of Japan's coercion and Korea's resistance, the blank space remained unfilled. It is possible that the Japanese intentionally avoided using the term "agreement" since it was not suitable for a matter of this magnitude, even after they had agreed on making it an "agreement." For whatever reason, the Convention of 1905, the document that brought about the greatest tragedy in modern Korean history, had no title attached to it. "The Second Japanese-Korean Agreement," the "New Japanese-Korean Agreement," and the "Protectorate Treaty of 1905" were all titles added afterwards in order to gloss over its flaws.

4. When Japan notified Great Britain and the United States of the agreement's completion, it engaged in deception and changed the status of the document. The Japanese government translated it into English and then notified the two countries on November 22. In the translation, the agreement was called a "convention," a term which was not in the original (see Figure 3b). Since the original document had no title, it would have been proper to leave the space for the title blank in the translation as well. If it were necessary to add a title, "agreement" would have been the proper term. Since the term "convention" is usually used for special matters such as postal agreements, admissions to the Red Cross, and copyright protection, it has a higher status than an "agreement." By using the term "convention" instead of "agreement" in the translation, Japan was acknowl-

edging that an "agreement" was inappropriate to deal with matters of such importance. In fact, there are extremely few instances of "conventions" being used for political matters such as the transfer of diplomatic rights.

5. During the last stage of negotiations for this "agreement," the Japanese used force to obtain the seal and signature of Korea's Foreign Minister on the document. Escorted by military police, Maema Kyosaku (1868–1942), the official interpreter for Ito Hirobumi, entered Korea's Ministry of Foreign Affairs and confiscated the official seal of the Foreign Minister. After forcing the minister to sign the document, the Japanese affixed the seal themselves.[17] The signing of the agreement was a clear instance of coercion. The fact that the Foreign Minister did not bring his seal to the negotiations shows that he was not attending as the representative of his country. In fact, Kojong had never appointed a representative for the negotiations as he had not acceded to Ito Hirobumi's request to issue a proxy statement. In official letters sent to nine heads of states in June 1906, as will be discussed below, Kojong later wrote, "I never allowed the government to affix the official seal on that document." While Hayashi's title was given in the document as "minister plenipotentiary of the Japanese Empire," Pak Chesun's official title was "Foreign Minister." Unable to resist Japanese coercion, Pak Chesun (1858–1916) signed the document but did so only as a member of the Korean cabinet. As Kojong himself stated in his letters, an agreement with so many flaws that it has no proxy or ratification statements clearly has no legal force.

## (4) Korean-Japanese Agreement (July 24, 1907, Japanese-Korean Agreement)

After the conclusion of the Convention of 1905, all foreign legations in Korea returned to their respective countries at Japan's request. Kojong then turned to the sovereign leaders of countries with which Korea had earlier established treaties of friendship or commerce. On at least five occasions over the next few years, Kojong requested assistance in recovering Korea's diplomatic rights. His efforts had to be conducted in secret because the Emperor's palace was surrounded by Japanese spies and troops. When he realized that his efforts were likely to fail because of the lack of support from Britain and the

---

17. *Hwangsŏng sinmun*, November 25, 1905 (9th year of Kwangmu); "Note on the newspaper article regarding the signing of the Japanese-Korean Agreement," *Nihon gaiko bunsho*, vol. 38, no. 1, item 11, document no. 287, pp. 550-51.

United States, he planned to present Korea's case to the International Court at The Hague by sending a special delegate to the Second Hague Peace Conference in June 1907. When his plans were uncovered, Japan declared that Kojong had committed treason and that sending a delegate to The Hague was a violation of the Convention of 1905. It used this opportunity to force Kojong, who had continuously resisted Japan's efforts to colonize Korea, to abdicate on July 22.[18] Early in the morning that day, the Japanese Resident-General ordered the Fifty-first Regiment of the First Battalion of the Resident Army in Korea to enter the palace and arrest all the key supporters of the emperor under the pretext that the officers of the emperor's Royal Guards were plotting to assassinate the pro-Japanese members of the Korean cabinet, including Yi Wanyong (1858–1926). Japan felt that the crown prince would be easier to manipulate than the emperor in completing their seizure of Korea. The crown prince was still suffering both physically and emotionally from a recent attempt to poison him.

Claiming that a new emperor had ascended to the throne on July 22, the Japanese demanded a new agreement from Korea on July 24. The objective of this agreement was to transfer not only Korea's diplomatic rights but also authority over domestic affairs to the Resident-General, who would function as the regent of the emperor. Since this agreement was concluded under coercion and without Kojong's recognition of the Convention of 1905, it is even more problematic than the previous agreements discussed above (Figure 4).[19]

1. Because preparations for the new agreement involved the emperor's abdication and the dissolution of the Royal Guards, more Japanese troops were needed. On July 21, the Japanese government decided to dispatch an additional brigade to supplement the Resident Army in Korea.

2. Ito Hirobumi, Resident-General of Korea, and Yi Wanyong, Prime Minister of Korea, signed and affixed their official seals to the document. Significantly, neither one used the title of "Plenipotentiary" (see Figure 5). Since the position of Resident-General was established after the Convention of 1905, it had no meaning to Korea, which rejected the validity of the convention. To validate the convention, the Korean representative would have needed a proxy statement from the new emperor, as demanded by Japan. However, as was true for the

18. See Yi Tae-jin, "The Resident-General's seizure of the royal seal and the forgery of Emperor Sunjong's Signature" (see footnote 4).
19. Ibid.

Convention of 1905, no such documents have yet been found for this agreement. Kojong was in conflict with Japan by maintaining the position announced in the royal edict of July 18 that he had handed over only administrative duties to the crown prince. Therefore, it is unlikely that the "new emperor" had appointed a plenipotentiary representative.

3. For a matter such as the transfer of authority over domestic affairs—or the transfer of diplomatic rights—an agreement must follow the forms and procedures of a formal treaty in order for it to have legal force. However, it was handled as an informal agreement solely for the sake of Japan's convenience. Just like the Convention of 1905, this agreement contains neither a proxy nor a ratification statement.

4. After this agreement was concluded, Resident-General Ito Hirobumi had virtually complete authority over Korea's domestic affairs, having become like the regent of the emperor, and committed the following illegal acts. On July 31, Ito committed forgery by authoring a royal edict to dissolve the Korean army in the emperor's name, which he then had translated and announced in Korean. Between October 18, 1907, and January 18, 1908, he enacted sixty pieces of legislation that dealt with the reorganization of the government and deprived Korea of control of government finances. Ito overlooked or arranged matters so that officials of the Resident-General's Document Section could forge the emperor's signature.

**(5) Treaty Regarding the Annexation of Korea to the Empire of Japan (August 22, 1910)**

The most important basis for Japan's claim to the legality of the annexation of Korea is this treaty, which was signed on August 22, 1910 and proclaimed on August 29. To this day, Japan claims that there were no irregularities in the form of this treaty, believing it was prepared with all the necessary documents and signatures. However, it has been revealed that a decisive mistake was made in obtaining the Korean emperor's final approval.[20]

Perhaps out of concern for the problems with the previous agreements, Japanese officials in charge of the treaty took the utmost care to make sure that it had no flaws. They believed that if the annexation treaty were carried out properly, the problems of the previous

---

20. See Yi Tae-jin, "The Japan-Korea Annexation Treaty and the forgery of the royal edict."

agreements could all be resolved by substituting the new agreement for the earlier ones. The original documents related to the treaty are kept in the Kyujanggak Archives at Seoul National University:

(a) A proxy statement from Emperor Sunjong to Prime Minister Yi Wanyong.
(b) A treaty document signed and sealed by the plenipotentiary representative from both sides.
(c) A memorandum from both sides to proclaim the treaty with a royal edict to announce the annexation of Korea to Japan.
(d) A royal edict from Emperor Sunjong announcing the annexation of Korea to Japan.

These documents fulfill all the necessary conditions for a treaty: there is the proxy statement, the treaty itself, and a royal edict that was used as a ratification statement. There is even a document from both representatives agreeing to use the announcement of royal edicts from both emperors instead of a ratification statement. Although it seems that these documents would be enough to substantiate claims for the legality of the treaty, an examination of their contents reveals that there is a significant flaw in document (d).

Terauchi Masatake (1852–1919), the third Resident-General, was in charge of treaty negotiations, and in a top-secret document, he described the events that led to the treaty. Terauchi asked Yi Wanyong to cooperate as much as possible because he wanted the treaty to be concluded through mutual agreement although it could also be done according to the "time-honored custom" whereby the treaty would simply be read in front of the emperor. After many secret communications between the two, they were successful in obtaining the proxy statement (document a) from Emperor Sunjong on August 22. Although there are records showing that Sunjong initially resisted, he did affix the royal seal and sign his name on the proxy statement. Yi Wanyong then brought the proxy statement to Terauchi's office and signed the treaty there; therefore, there were no irregularities in the actual form of the treaty.

The next problem was obtaining a document that could serve as a ratification statement. Since Korea would no longer exist as a country once the treaty was announced, there would be no time to obtain ratification of the treaty, the final step for its approval. To solve this problem, the Japanese government prepared a memorandum in advance showing that representatives of the two sides agreed to issue a

Forced Treaties and Japan's Annexation of the Great Han Empire 183

royal edict from both emperors announcing the annexation in place of a ratification statement. In item 8 of the treaty document prepared by Japan, it was noted that the treaty had already been approved by the emperors of both countries. However, it is illogical to announce a treaty's approval beforehand since a treaty cannot be valid until its contents are ratified. The memorandum on issuing the royal edict was a belated way of handling this problem. In any event, this was how the royal edict by the two emperors came to replace the inclusion of ratification statements.

However, there is no signature over Sunjong's official seal in the original of the royal edict that is kept in the Kyujanggak archives. Citing the Agreement of 1907, Japan ordered on November 18, that all official documents in Korea must be composed according to Japanese convention and have a signature as well as an official seal (see Figure 2b). Since that date, all official documents requiring the emperor's approval followed this procedure. The proxy statement (document a) also had the emperor's signature, albeit shaky, written over the official seal (see Figure 5). All the royal edicts, orders, and statutes from Sunjong's reign that are kept in the Kyujanggak have the emperor's seal and signature, with the sole exception of the final royal edict that announced Korea's annexation. There was also no signature, only a seal, on duplicates of the edict that the Government-General of Korea later produced for propaganda purposes (see Figure 6). Similar evidence can be found in the *Chosŏ choyak kŭp pŏmnyŏng* (Royal Edicts, Treaties, and Laws) which was published by the Resident-General of Korea on September 8, 1910. All the relevant documents, including the Japanese emperor's edict, have both affixed seals and signatures, except for the Korean emperor's proclamation edict, appended at the very end of the volume, which had only a seal (see Figure 7).

Since the Agreement of July 23, 1907 stipulated that all domestic matters were subject to prior approval by the Resident-General, the Korean emperor's official seal was in his possession. The seal alone is not sufficient to demonstrate that the emperor gave his approval to the treaty. There were only two days between the drafting of the royal edict and its planned announcement (August 27–29). England and the United States had been notified in advance about the announcement of the annexation. The only possible explanation for the emperor's missing signature is that he resisted the efforts to coerce him to sign it during those two days. Unable to miss the deadline that had been announced to the international community, Japan submitted the document affixed with only the seal that was kept by the Resident-General. If this interpretation is correct, it means that the Korean emperor did not approve of the "annexation" and that, therefore, the annexation of Korea had no legal validity.[21]

A detailed analysis of the five agreements that Japan obtained through coercion to seize Korea's sovereignty leads to the conclusion that Japan's annexation of Korea need not be nullified because it never actually occurred. In the case of the Convention of 1905, nullification may have been necessary, but now that all the coercion, deceit, manipulations, and military threats have been revealed, it would be closer to the truth to argue that the annexation never was legal. Without a legal annexation, Japan's thirty-six year rule of Korea was, of course, an illegal occupation. If the illegality of the annexation is acknowledged, then there is no longer any need to continue the discussion between the two countries on when the agreements became nullified.

THE MOVEMENT TO NULLIFY THE FORCED TREATIES

Japan's seizure of Korea's sovereignty after the Russo-Japanese War was carried out with coercion and force through the five major diplomatic agreements discussed above. Although the Great Han Empire had known of Japan's intentions at least six months earlier, it was too weak militarily to prepare an effective defense. As soon as Kojong assumed power in 1872, he devoted much effort to building up Korea's armies. However, the country was in such political turmoil after the Soldiers' Riot of 1882 that even the smallest efforts were unsuccessful. When the country became an independent state and its financial situation improved after the proclamation of the Great Han Empire, efforts to reform the military began to produce long-desired results. However, even at the turn of the twentieth century, Korea's only true military force was the fourteen thousand troops of the Royal

21. Before he died in April 1926, Emperor Sunjong left a deathbed statement in which he denied approving the annexation. He said, "The annexation was approved in the past by our strong neighbor together with an evil crowd, doing as they pleased. They promulgated it on their own accord; it was no doing of mine. "His deathbed statement was published in the *Sinhan Minbo*, July 8, 1926 (a newspaper published by Korean residents in San Francisco, California). Sunjong's statement is in agreement with my findings. See Yi Tae-jin, "Ryakkusiki choyaku de kokken o icho dekiru noka" (Can state sovereignty be surrendered with a summary treaty?), *Sekai* 676 (June 2000), pp. 279–80.

Guards. The Royal Guards had sufficient strength to defend the capital, but Korea still had not begun building an army and navy for national defense. In May 1903, Kojong issued a royal edict ordering preparations to create the first-ever military-draft system with the purpose of establishing an army and a navy. By the end of the year, the situation in Japan already became worrisome. Since Korea lacked a strong military force, it had to rely heavily on diplomatic means to deal with external threats. Anticipating the outbreak of hostilities between Russia and Japan, Kojong sent a personal letter to the Russian czar on August 15, 1903, proposing that their two countries enter into an alliance. As an alternative, he also considered the possibility of declaring Korea a neutral country. When it became clear that Japan would declare war on Russia, Korea quickly proclaimed its neutrality to the foreign powers on January 1904. However, Japan sought to obstruct Korea's proclamation of neutrality and finally declared war on February 6.

When Japan began the war with Russia, it attempted to kidnap Kojong's supporters such as Yi Yong'ik (1854–1907), Hyŏn Sanggŏn (1875–1926), Yi Hakgyun (?–1909), and Kil Yŏngsu (?–1919), the officials behind the neutrality proclamation. The Japanese captured Yi Yong'ik, but the other three officials escaped. Japan then presented Korea with the diplomatic agreement that became the Protocol of 1904. The protocol contained a provision that granted Japan the use of Korean military bases, but it also clearly guaranteed Korea's independence. However, the guarantee was nothing more than a ruse to draw Korea to Japan's side since the outcome of the war was still in doubt at the time. When the tide of the war turned in Japan's favor, Japan pressured Korea in August 1904 to negotiate a new agreement, clearly revealing its aggressive intentions toward Korea. In article three of the draft of the agreement, Japan demanded that the Korean government consult in advance with a representative of the Japanese government concerning Korea's relations with other countries. Kojong vehemently opposed this demand. Japan used military threats and succeeded in obtaining the signature of the acting Foreign Minister on the condition that the term "representative" be omitted. When Japan informed the United States and England of this agreement, they changed the title of the document from "memorandum" to "agreement" and made it appear that Korea had willingly entrusted its diplomatic rights to Japan. On the basis of this agreement, Japan concluded secret agreements the following year with these two countries acknowledging Japan's right to establish a protectorate over

Korea. In November, the Japanese forced Korea to accept the Convention of 1905, which officially turned Korea into a protectorate. Kojong consistently expressed his opposition to the convention that deprived Korea of its diplomatic rights. In audiences with the emperor and in their memoirs, some Japanese officials later claimed that Kojong had agreed to the provision in the convention's preamble that the protectorate would last only until Korea could support itself and that Kojong had delegated his authority to the cabinet. However, none of these accounts is reliable. Even if they were true, they have no legal relevance because they do not appear in any official document. There is documentary evidence that clearly shows Kojong's opposition to the protectorate. Kojong's efforts to nullify the Convention of 1905 focused on the United States and other Western powers, and they were carried out in the following six stages:[22]

(1) November 26, 1905: Kojong sent a telegram to Homer B. Hulbert (1863-1949) through Chefoo (now Yantai) asking him to convey to the government of the United States a message that the convention was essentially invalid. Hulbert forwarded this letter to the Deputy Secretary of State, but his efforts were ignored.

(2) November 22-30, 1905: Through Eliot, an attorney for the Seoul office of Collbran & Bostwick Development Company, Kojong sent a confidential letter and a blank statement of proxy to Horace N. Allen (1858-1932), the United States minister to Korea, who happened to be in the United States at the time.

(3) December 11, 1905: Kojong ordered Min Yŏngch'an (1873-?), Korean minister to Paris, to go to the United States to meet Secretary of State Elihu Root. In a December 19 letter, Root refused Korea's request for assistance.

(4) January 29, 1906: In order to prevent the imminent establishment of the Resident-General of Korea, Kojong made a request to the other powers that they become co-protectors of Korea for five years. Kojong expressed his desire through Douglas Story, a reporter for the British newspaper, *The Tribune*.

(5) June 22, 1906: Through Homer Hulbert, Kojong sent personal letters to the heads of state of each of the nine countries with which Korea had signed treaties of commerce and amity and requested that they send their consuls to Korea again since the Convention of 1905

---

22. The section below is based on Kim Kisŏk's "Kwangmuje ui chugwon suho oegyo, 1905-1907: Ŭlsa choyak muhyo sŏn'ŏn ŭl chungsim ŭro" (Emperor Kojong's diplomatic efforts to defend Korea's sovereignty, 1905-1907: focusing on the declaration of the nullification of the Convention of 1905," in Yi Tae-jin, ed., op cit.

was invalid. He also expressed a desire to petition the International Court of The Hague.

(6) April 20, 1907: Kojong sent a special envoy to the Second International Peace Conference at The Hague to inform the nations of the world about the invalidity of the Convention of 1905.

Immediately after the conclusion of the Convention of 1905, Kojong actively began efforts to nullify the convention, focusing his efforts on the United States as mentioned above. America was the first country with which Kojong concluded an equal treaty of commerce and amity in order to break away from the Chinese world order and enter the new world order as an independent state. The ministers and personal advisors sent from the United States had increased Kojong's trust in the country. America had also demonstrated its willingness to keep its promise of "good offices" as indicated in the Korean-American Treaty of Amity and Commerce of 1882. When Korea tried to send Pak Chŏngyang as the first Korean minister to the United States in 1887, the United States blocked China's efforts to prevent his departure. In view of its past efforts to aid Korea, the United States should have felt a duty to help Korea in the new crisis it was facing. On the contrary, the United States government was extremely unresponsive to Korea's efforts to nullify the Convention of 1905. The United States' attitude resulted from a change in foreign policy that occurred when a Republican administration came to power.

From the 1880s, there were significant differences in the foreign policies of the Democratic and Republican administrations of the United States. In general, the Republicans pursued a much more expansionist foreign policy. For example, while Democratic president Grover Cleveland (presidential terms 1885–1889, 1893–1897) opposed a military occupation of Hawaii, Republican Theodore Roosevelt (presidential term 1901–1909) supported the claims of American plantation owners and carried out a military occupation there. After the Spanish-American War, the Republican administration pursued an aggressive policy of expansion in the Pacific, seeking to occupy the Philippines. Since a military occupation of Hawaii and the containment of Russian expansion became important to the United States, it supported Japan in the Russo-Japanese War. Kojong's diplomatic efforts toward the United States failed not because he was ignorant of international affairs and put too much trust in the United States but because of the change in U.S. foreign policy after the change of administrations.

Kojong gave explicit reasons why the Convention of 1905 was invalid in the personal letters sent to nine heads of state mentioned above. The leaders to whom he wrote were not chosen randomly, but were the rulers of countries with which Korea had signed treaties of commerce and amity.[23] The reasons he gave were:

(1) The signature of the Foreign Minister of my government was not obtained properly but through intimidation.
(2) I never authorized the Cabinet to sign the document.
(3) The cabinet meeting for the approval of the convention was not conducted according to the laws of Korea; Japan convened the meeting by force by detaining the ministers.

After pointing out these facts, Kojong stated that the convention was automatically null because it was in violation of international law. Kojong's arguments were unassailable with respect to international law; however, his letters never reached the heads of state. His efforts were unable to overcome the international status that Japan gained after its victory in the Russo-Japanese War. As a final effort, Kojong sent an envoy to the Second International Peace Conference to expose Japan's brutality, but Japan forced Kojong to abdicate, claiming that his acts were a violation of the Convention of 1905.

Emperor Kojong's resistance was ineffective in the face of Japanese military power, but his efforts were not meaningless. Even though he was forced to abdicate, he continued to be a symbol of the Korean people's resistance to Japan. Even after the annexation, the trust and loyalty of the subjects of the Great Han Empire toward their king remained unchanged. Most of the resistance movements, both domestic and overseas, had the objective of restoring the sovereignty of the Great Han Empire. When a rumor spread in January 1919 that Kojong had been poisoned to death by the Japanese, nationwide demonstrations broke out. While Kojong was alive, there was no group in the independence movement that officially renounced the Great Han Empire. The independence movement changed the name of the country from the "Great Han Empire" to "Taehan Minguk" [Republic of Korea] only after the March First Movement in 1919. Kojong occupied a central place in the history of modern Korea as it changed from a dynasty to an empire and then to a republic in its

---

23. Professor Kim Kisŏk was the first to confirm that the original letter by Kojong is kept in the Library of Rare and Manuscript Documents at Columbia University. See the article mentioned in note 22.

efforts to resist foreign threats and preserve its existence as an independent state.

Even foreigners argued that Japan's annexation of Korea was unlawful. A few months after the conclusion of the Convention of 1905, Francis Rey, a French legal scholar, published a paper entitled "The International Situation of Korea," in which he strongly denounced the convention as illegal according to international law.[24] Rey pointed out two reasons why the convention had no legal force. First, the Korean representative was coerced to sign the document, and second, Japan ignored its duty to guarantee Korean independence and territorial integrity as agreed to in the Protocol of 1904.

Rey's article was not the end of interest in Korea in the international legal community. In 1927, a United States Commission on International Law asked Harvard Law School to prepare a draft of a legislative bill on the enactment of international treaty law. The Harvard Law School report, which was submitted in 1935, followed Rey's arguments closely and cited the Convention of 1905 as one of four historical precedents of a treaty that was legally invalid because the representative of one side was subjected to coercion.[25] The judgment of the international legal community was acknowledged by the United Nations after World War II. In a 1963 report to the General Assembly on international treaties, the United Nations Commission on International Law accepted the arguments of the Harvard Law School report on the illegality of treaties concluded through force or coercion.[26]

The international legal community's view on the illegality of Japan's annexation of Korea was not unrelated to the efforts of the Great Han Empire, led by the emperor, to nullify the treaty and the

24. "La Situation Internationale de la Coree," *Revue Generale de Droit International Public*, Tome XII (1906). A translation of Rey's paper into Korean by Ch'oe Chonggo and Nam Hyosun appears in Yi Tae-jin, ed., op cit.

25. "Law of Treaties," *Supplement to the American Journal of International Law*, vol. 29, Supplement: Research in International Law (1935). See Article 32, "Duress."

26. The four historical precedents were as follows: 1) the surrounding of Poland's Diet in 1773 to coerce its members into accepting the treaty of partition; 2) the coercion used on the Great Han Empire and his ministers in 1905 to obtain their acceptance of a protectorate treaty; 3) the surrounding of the national assembly of Haiti by the United States military in 1915 to force its members into ratifying a convention; and 4) The obtainment by force of the signatures of President Hacha and the Foreign Minister of Czechoslovakia for a treaty establishing a German protectorate over Bohemia and Moravia. "Documents of the fifteenth session including the report of the Commission to the General Assembly, United Nations," *Yearbook of the International Law Commission*, vol. II (New York: United Nations, 1963).

agreements that preceded it. The Great Han Empire had employed several foreign advisors such as Laurent Cremazy, a French jurist, and their efforts were probably what enabled the research by international law scholars such as Francis Rey. In this context, the 1963 report of the United Nations Commission on International Law acknowledging the invalidity of the Convention of 1905 can be seen as the culmination of Kojong's efforts to nullify the agreements, even though the report was not presented to the General Assembly. The resistance movement originally led by Emperor Kojong had never ceased even at the international level.

CONCLUSION

In 1951, Korea and Japan began negotiations to settle past grievances, and after numerous meetings, the two countries concluded the ROK-Japan Normalization Treaty as well as several other agreements in June 1965. They "considered the historical background of the relationship between their peoples and their mutual desire for good neighborliness and for the normalization of their relations on the basis of the principle of mutual respect for sovereignty." Article 2 of the treaty explicitly stated, "It is confirmed that all treaties or agreements concluded between the Empire of Korea and the Empire of Japan on or before August 22, 1910, are already null and void." However, Korea and Japan have held completely different views on the meaning of the phrase "already null and void."

The South Korean government clearly stated its position that all agreements concluded before 1910 were invalid. It declared that "the Annexation Treaty of August 22, 1910, and all previous agreements concluded between the Great Han Empire and the Empire of Japan were null and void regardless of their titles and regardless of whether they were concluded between the two governments or the two emperors."[27] On the other hand, the Japanese government took the position that all past agreements became null and void on August 15, 1948, when the Republic of Korea was founded, claiming that the Annexation Treaty of 1910 and all preceding agreements were valid at the time of their conclusion.[28] The different views on when the

27. Government of the Republic of Korea, "Commentary on Treaties and Agreements between the Republic of Korea and Japan" (1965).
28. Response by Fujisaki Ichiro, director of the treaty office of the Japanese government, to the Special Committee of the House of Councilors (Nov. 27, 1965).

agreements became nullified led to a difference of opinion on the financial payment that Japan would make to Korea. Korea viewed it as reparations for the illegal thirty-six-year occupation of the country, while Japan saw it as a congratulatory "grant" for Korea's independence.

Considering the importance of the 1965 Treaty, there was insufficient discussion on the differences of opinion between the two sides. Rather than resolving past grievances, the agreement was concluded with the main issues left unsettled. The failure to resolve these issues is one of the main reasons that Japanese political leaders have continued to make "unacceptable statements" even half a century after Korea's liberation. The ROK-Japan Normalization Treaty of 1965 is generally seen as resulting from the combination of United States policy to create an economic bloc in Northeast Asia and the economic development policies of Park Chung Hee's military regime. With the Allied victory in World War II, the United States originally planned to hold Japan responsible for the war in order to make Japan a democratic state. However, after China became communist in the late 1940s, the United States felt it necessary to revive Japanese industry and allow capitalist development in order to use Japan as a bulwark to block the southward expansion of communism. It was generally assumed that the South Korean economy would develop through Japanese assistance. Under this policy, the United States allowed Japanese bureaucrats from the prewar period to form the Liberal Democratic Party and return to power, and it also encouraged Korea to enter into talks with Japan to settle past grievances. These events were the background to the start of talks between Korea and Japan in 1951.

At the time, the Syngman Rhee regime adopted vehemently anti-Japanese policies and refused United States requests to enter into negotiations with Japan. South Korea began to fall in line with United States policy during the Third Republic, which was formed through the military coup of May 16, 1961. The military regime's justification for the coup was its ability to promote economic development, and they needed capital to carry out these policies. Accordingly, Korea found it difficult to ignore U.S. requests to enter into talks with Japan. Korea also had little choice because the United States was extremely critical of the justification for the coup. Korea-Japan talks began to progress rapidly after the conclusion of the Kim-Ohira Memorandum in 1963, which settled the amount of the "Economic Assistance Fund" that Japan would pay to South Korea. After the treaty documents were drafted and exchanged in 1965, the Korean government maintained a bit of national pride in its interpretation of the phrase "already null and void," but it cannot avoid responsibility for the controversy and problems caused by the treaty. At the time, many Koreans criticized the treaty as unsatisfactory and opposed the government's approval of it. Above all, the Korean government made a serious mistake in abandoning the opportunity to alter Japanese views of Korea. Is it still possible to argue that everything was settled with the Normalization Treaty of 1965?

While proclaiming to resolve the past grievances between the two countries, the Normalization Treaty left many key issues unresolved. The intellectuals and political leaders of the two countries should not view these issues as part of an unalterable past but should seriously reexamine them, staking their consciences and reputations. It would be irresponsible to avoid reopening discussion on the treaty since it is clear that its failure to resolve key issues has aggravated nationalist sentiments and has not narrowed differences of opinion between the two countries on their past history. Even if the treaty is viewed only as an agreement between two governments, it should be reexamined because of its potential to cause problems affecting the future of the two countries.

The situation that led to the Normalization Treaty was not permanent. Beginning with the resistance of the emperor of the Great Han Empire and his subjects, the movement to nullify the Convention of 1905 was supported by scholars of international law and came to a close with recognition by the United Nations Commission on International Law in 1963. The United States' policy of establishing an anticommunist bloc in Northeast Asia after 1950 brought the nullification movement to an end and marked the beginning of a new period of history. However, the United States' policy on Northeast Asia changed thirty years later with the end of the cold war. American policy began to change from the mid-1980s, and the political dominance of Japan's Liberal Democratic Party, which had been established under this policy, also came to an end. Changes in international affairs brought Korea and Japan back to the "starting point" from which it is necessary for the two countries to resolve past grievances. Within the long history of relations between the two countries, the period of American influence was actually only a brief moment in time. If circumstances in the past prevented certain issues from being resolved or even discussed, then there should be renewed efforts to find a fundamental solution to these problems. It is important to keep in mind that a fundamental solution can be achieved only if there is respect for the truth. It is impossible to exaggerate the importance of investigating the actual facts of the unfortunate relations in the past between the two countries. The officials involved in the 1965 Normalization Treaty ignored the position taken by the United Nations Commission on International Law in 1963 on the Convention of 1905. Their actions clearly show how the movement to nullify previous treaties and agreements between the two countries became superseded by the exigencies of United States policy which sought to create an anti-communist bloc in Northeast Asia. While it is true that the decisions of the United Nations are not legally binding, they are important for international justice. It is necessary to keep in mind the significance of the United Nations Commission on International Law's report since both popular sentiment and relations between the two countries have worsened because of the "unacceptable statements" made by Japanese politicians. While the United Nations Commission followed international standards of justice and accepted the facts about the events surrounding the treaties, the Normalization Treaty disregarded both the standards of international justice and historical facts, rooted in temporary historical conditions. Since such facts clearly can no longer be ignored, there needs to be an effort to focus on the main issues again. Only through such an effort will it be possible to find a fundamental solution to these problems.

Up to now, debate on the legality of Japan's annexation of Korea has focused on the nullification of the agreements. Examples include Kojong's efforts to nullify the Convention of 1905 and the controversy over the phrase "already null and void" in Article 2 of the 1965 Normalization Treaty. However, recent research on the five agreements leading to the annexation suggests that the focus of the debate should be shifted from determining when the protectorate treaty became "null and void" to showing that the annexation never took place. So many instances of coercion, deceit, and illegalities in the procedures and drafting of the documents have been revealed that it is impossible to argue that the annexation ever was legal. And if the annexation never took place, then it is no longer necessary to argue about nullification because it is not necessary to nullify an event that never happened. In addition, since Japan's thirty-six year rule of Korea was based on an annexation that was never legal, then the evidence for the illegality of Japan's occupation is even stronger.

If Japan accepts the fact that its occupation was illegal, then it must pay reparations to Korea. However, in arguing that the two countries must resolve past grievances it was not my intention to obtain more reparations from Japan. Rather, once the illegality of the annexation is acknowledged, there will emerge other ways of handling the issue of reparations. For example, rather than requiring further monetary reparation to the South Korean government, the Economic Assistance Fund that Japan paid according to the Normalization Treaty should be designated as "reparations" rather than a "congratulatory grant" for independence. There could also be discussion on the issue of reparations for individual damages and for North Korea. The future of the two countries will depend on whether the Japanese government will acknowledge the coercion and deceit committed in the process of annexation, whether it accepts the illegality of its harsh thirty-six year rule of the "colony," and whether it will make proper reparations as a sign that it accepts responsibility for its past actions.

translated by *Korea Journal*

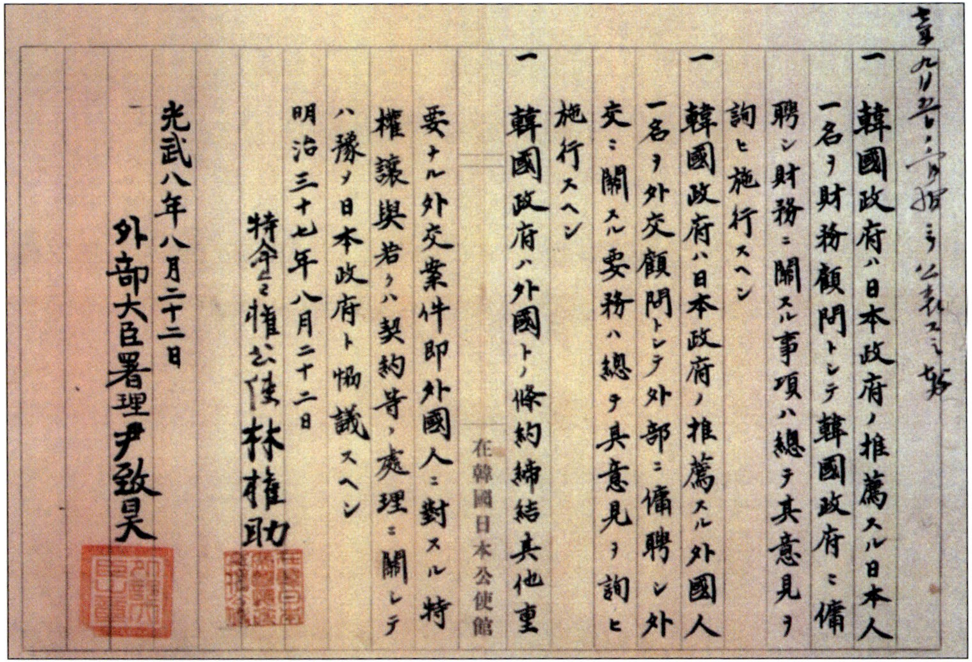

一、韓國政府ハ日本政府ノ推薦スル日本人一名ヲ財務顧問トシテ韓國政府ニ傭聘シ財務ニ關スル事項ハ總テ其意見ヲ詢ヒ施行スヘシ

一、韓國政府ハ日本政府ノ推薦スル外國人一名ヲ外交顧問トシテ外部ニ傭聘シ外交ニ關スル要務ハ總テ其意見ヲ詢ヒ施行スヘシ

一、韓國政府ハ外國トノ條約締結其他重要ナル外交案件即外國人ニ對スル特權譲與若クハ契約等ノ處理ニ關シ豫メ日本政府ト協議スヘシ

明治三十七年八月二十二日

特命全権公使 林 権助 印

在韓國日本公使館

光武八年八月二十二日
外部大臣署理 尹致昊

FIGURE 1a. The original document of the memorandum known as the "First Japanese-Korean Agreement." There is no designation of the proxy representative at either the beginning or the end of the document. The fact that only Japan (Diplomatic Record Office of the Ministry of Foreign Affairs) is in possession of this document supports the argument that the necessary steps were not taken for an official diplomatic agreement. All the documents relating to Korea's foreign affairs since the Russo-Japanese War are kept at the Kyujanggak Archives of Seoul National University. However, the documents relating to the "First Japanese-Korean Agreement" are nowhere to be found.

*Translation.*

(*Signed, August 22, 1904.*)

第 一 號
政治上ニ關スル條約

I. The Corean Government shall engage as financial adviser to the Corean Government a Japanese subject recommended by the Japanese Government, and all matters concerning finance shall be dealt with after his counsel being taken.

II. The Corean Government shall engage as diplomatic adviser to the Department of Foreign Affairs a foreigner recommended by the Japanese Government, and all important matters concerning foreign relations shall be dealt with after his counsel being taken.

III. The Corean Government shall previously consult the Japanese Government in concluding treaties and conventions with foreign powers, and in dealing with other important diplomatic affairs, such as the grant of concessions to or contracts with foreigners.

HAYASHI GONSUKE, (Seal)
*Envoy Extraordinary and Minister Plenipotentiary.*
*The 22nd day of the 8th month of the 37th year of Meiji.*

YUN CHI HO, (Seal)
*Acting Minister of State for Foreign Affairs.*
*The 22nd day of the 8th month of the 8th year of Kwang-Mu.*

FIGURE 1b. The English version of the First Japanese-Korean Agreement. Contained in the Kankoku choyaku ruisan (K. Han'guk choyak yuch'an) compiled by the Residency-General in 1908. It contains a title, "Agreement," that does not exist in the original.

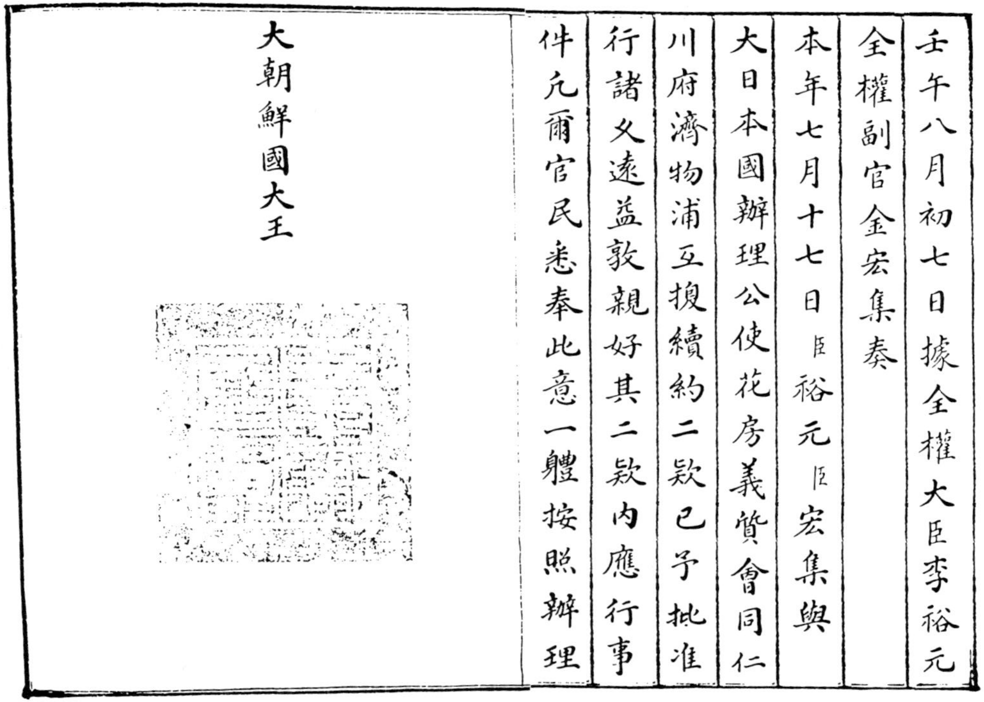

大朝鮮國大君主

全權大臣李裕元
全權副官金宏集奉
大日本國辨理公使花房義質會同仁
川府議立修好條約其二欵內應行辦理
諸文憑盖欽奉此意一體按照辦理
本年七月十七日 臣裕元 臣宏集與
壬午八月初七日據全權大臣李裕元

FIGURE 2a. A proxy statement issued by King Kojong for the representative to the Treaty of Amity between Chosŏn and Japan which was concluded together with the 1882 Treaty of Chemulp'o (stored in the Diplomatic Record Office of the Japanese Ministry of Foreign Affairs).

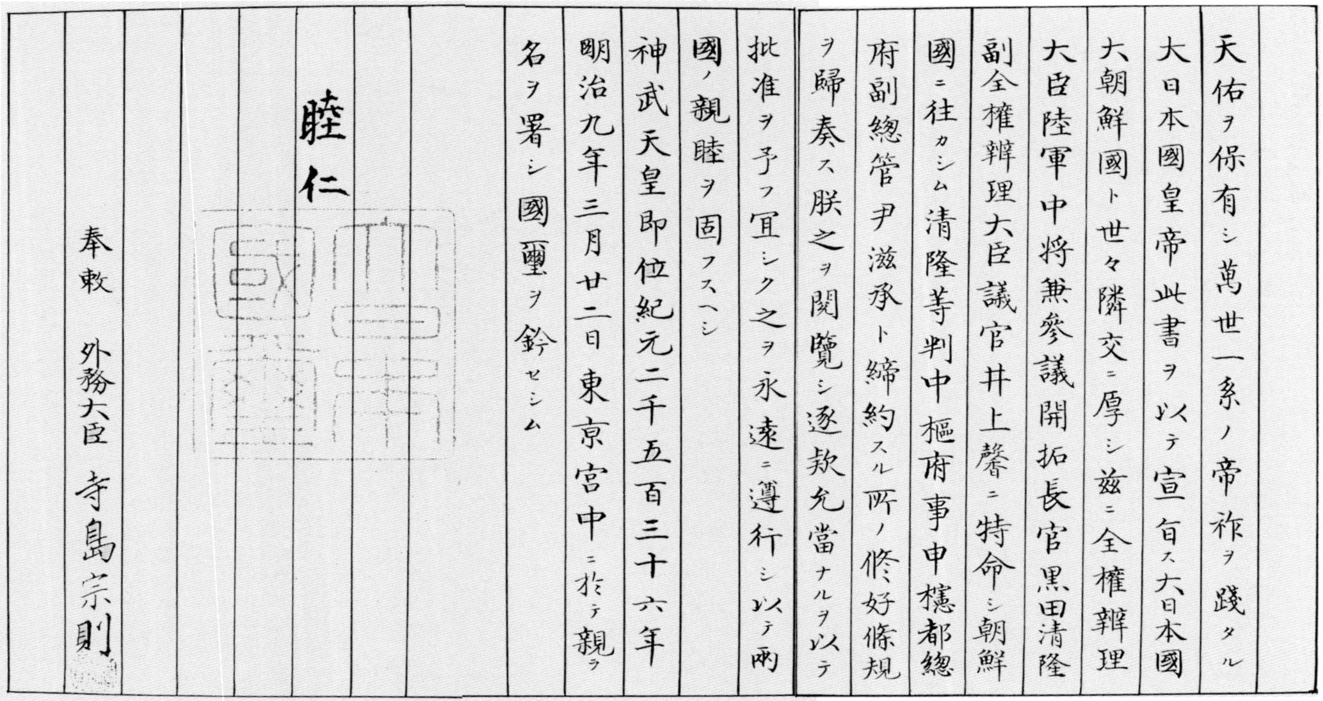

天佑ヲ保有シ萬世一系ノ帝祚ヲ踐タル
大日本國皇帝此書ヲ以テ宣旨ス大日本國
大朝鮮國ト世々隣交ニ厚シ茲ニ全權辨理
大臣陸軍中將兼參議開拓長官黑田清隆
副全權辨理大臣議官井上馨ニ特命シ朝鮮
國ニ往カシム清隆等判中樞府事申櫶都總
府副總管尹滋承ト締約スル所ノ修好條規
ヲ歸奏ス朕之ヲ閱覽シ逐款允當ナルヲ以テ
批准ヲ予フ宜シク之ヲ永遠ニ遵行シ以テ兩
國ノ親睦ヲ固フスヘシ
神武天皇即位紀元二千五百三十六年
明治九年三月廿二日東京宮中ニ於テ親ラ
名ヲ署シ國璽ヲ鈐セシム

睦仁

奉勅　外務大臣　寺島宗則

FIGURE 2b. A ratification statement by the Japanese emperor Meiji on the 1876 Treaty of Amity between Chosŏn and Japan (stored in the Diplomatic Record Office of the Japanese Ministry of Foreign Affairs). *Editor's note: The image was edited with blank spaces removed to make it fit on the page.*

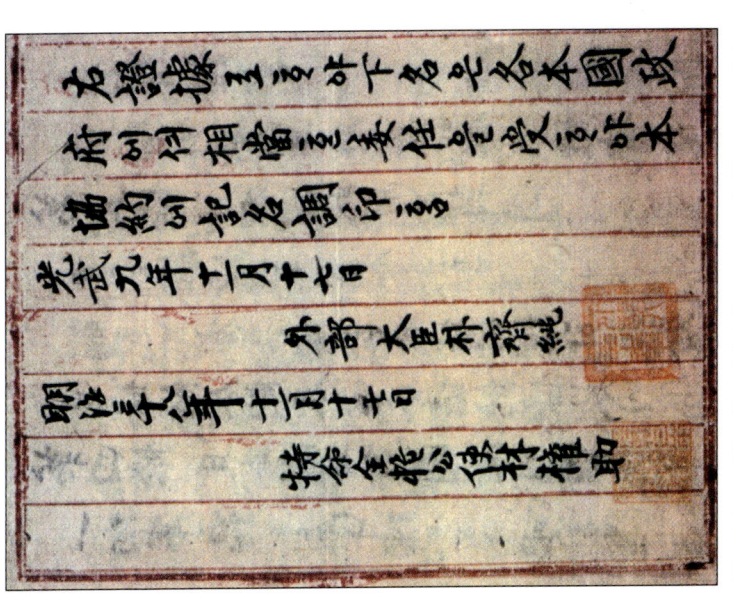

FIGURE 3A. The first (right) and last (left) pages of the "Convention of 1905" between Korea and Japan. The first line where the title should have been was blank.

*Translation.*

(*Signed, November 17, 1905.*)

The Governments of Japan and Corea, desiring to strengthen the principle of solidarity which unites the two Empires, have with that object in view agreed upon and concluded the following stipulations to serve until the moment arrives when it is recognized that Corea has attained national strength :—

ARTICLE I.

The Government of Japan, through the Department of Foreign Affairs at Tokyo, will hereafter have control and direction of the external relations and affairs of Corea, and the diplomatic and consular representatives of Japan will have the charge of the subjects and interests of Corea in foreign countries.

ARTICLE II.

The Government of Japan undertake to see to the execution of the treaties actually existing between Corea and other Powers, and the Government of Corea engage not to conclude hereafter any act or engagement having an international character except through the medium of the Government of Japan.

ARTICLE III.

The Government of Japan shall be represented at the Court of His Majesty the Emperor of Corea by a Resident General, who shall reside at Seoul, primarily for the purpose of taking charge of and directing matters relating to diplomatic affairs. He shall have the right of private and personal audience of His Majesty the Emperor of Corea. The Japanese Government shall also have the right to station Residents at the several open ports and such other places in Corea as they may deem necessary. Such Residents shall, under the direction of the Resident General, exercise the powers and functions hitherto appertaining to Japanese Consuls in Corea and shall perform such duties as may be necessary in order to carry into full effect the provisions of this Agreement.

FIGURE 3b. The English version of the Second Japanese-Korean Agreement. It contains a title, "Convention," which should not be there. Compiled in the *Kankoku choyaku ruisan* (1908).

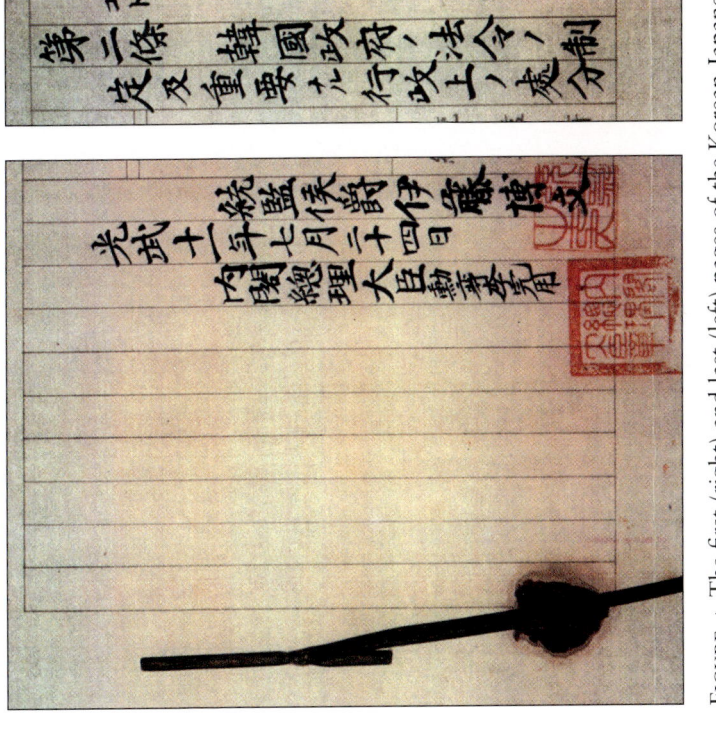

FIGURE 4. The first (right) and last (left) pages of the Korean-Japanese Agreement of 1907. Although the title of this agreement appears at the beginning of the document, unlike the Convention of 1905, neither of the representatives have the title of "Plenipotentiary Representative."

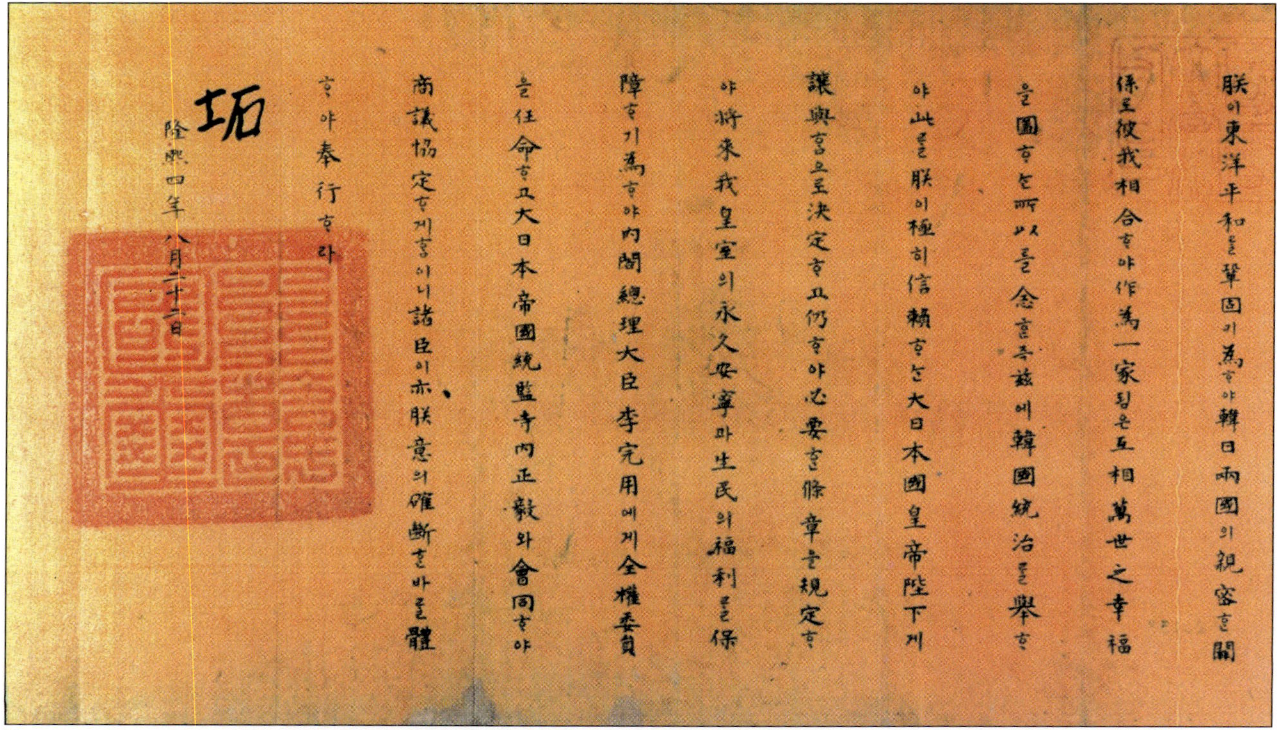
朕이東洋平和를鞏固기爲ᄒᆞ야韓日兩國의親密ᄒᆞᆫ關
係로彼我相合ᄒᆞ야作爲一家ᄒᆞᆷ은互相萬世之幸福
을圖ᄒᆞᄂᆞᆫ所以를念ᄒᆞᆷ으로玆에韓國統治를擧ᄒᆞ
야此를朕이極히信賴ᄒᆞᄂᆞᆫ大日本國皇帝陛下게
讓與ᄒᆞ기로決定ᄒᆞ고仍ᄒᆞ야必要ᄒᆞᆫ條章을規定ᄒᆞ
야將來我皇室의永久安寧과生民의福利를保
障ᄒᆞ기爲ᄒᆞ야內閣總理大臣李完用에게全權委員
을任命ᄒᆞ고大日本帝國統監寺內正毅와會同ᄒᆞ야
商議協定ᄒᆞ게ᄒᆞᆷ이니諸臣이亦朕意의確斷ᄒᆞᆫ바를體
ᄒᆞ야奉行ᄒᆞ라

坧

隆熙四年八月二十二日

FIGURE 5. A proxy statement issued by Emperor Sunjong authorizing Prime Minister Yi Wanyong to act as "Plenipotentiary Representative" for the Treaty of Annexation. Sunjong's signature is above the royal seal.

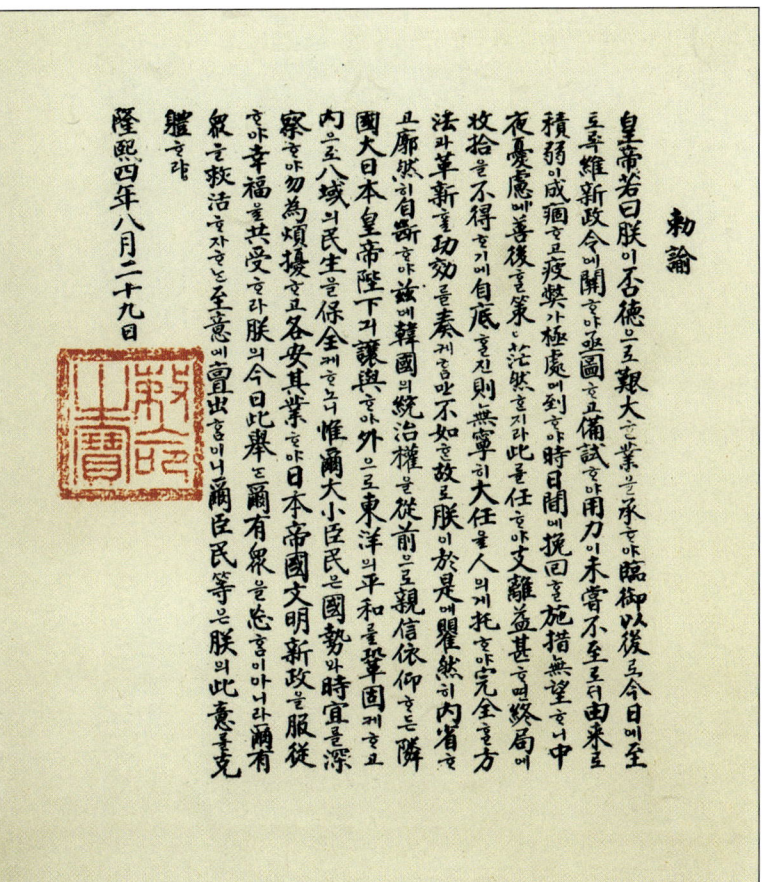

FIGURE 6. Emperor Sunjong's royal edict to announce the annexation of Korea to the Empire of Japan (for public relations purposes). Sunjong's signature, which should have been placed over the official seal, is missing. The Residency-General of Korea has kept the official seal since June 1907.

○詔書

朕東洋ノ平和ヲ永遠ニ維持シ帝國ノ安全ヲ將來ニ保障スルノ必要ナルヲ念ヒ又常ニ韓國ガ禍亂ノ淵源タルニ顧ミ曩ニ朕ノ政府ヲシテ韓國政府ト協定セシメ韓國ヲ帝國ノ保護ノ下ニ置キ以テ禍源ヲ杜絕シ平和ヲ確保セムコトヲ期セリ

爾來時ヲ經ルコト四年有餘其ノ間朕ノ政府ハ銳意韓國施政ノ改善ニ努メ其ノ成績亦見ルヘキモノアリト雖韓國ノ現制ハ尙未タ治安ノ保持ヲ完スルニ足ラス疑懼ノ念每ニ國內ニ充溢シ民其ノ堵ニ安セス公共ノ安寧ヲ維持シ民衆ノ福利ヲ增進セムカ爲ニハ革新ヲ現制ニ加フルノ避ク可ラサルコト瞭タルニ至レリ

御名御璽

明治四十三年八月二十九日

　　内閣總理大臣　侯爵　桂太郎
　　大藏大臣
　　陸軍大臣　子爵　寺內正毅
　　外務大臣　伯爵　小村壽太郎
　　海軍大臣　男爵　齋藤實
　　内務大臣　法學博士　男爵　平田東助

FIGURE 7 (this and facing page). Chosŏ choyak kŭp pŏmnyŏng (Royal Edicts, Treaties, and Laws), published by the Residency-General of Korea on September 8, 1910, included the Japanese emperor's royal edict (right) announcing the annexation of Korea to the Empire of Japan and the royal edict (left) issued by the Korean emperor. The latter document does not contain the characters for the name of the emperor.

韓國皇帝勅諭

皇帝若日朕否德ニシテ艱大ナル業ヲ承ケ臨御以後今日ニ至ルマテ維新政令ニ關シ亟圖シ備試シ用力未タ嘗テ至ラスト雖由來積弱痼ヲ成シ疲弊極處ニ到リ時日間ニ挽回ノ施措望無シ中夜憂慮善後ノ策茫然タリ此ニ任シ支離益甚シケレハ終局ニ收拾シ能ハサルニ底ランヨロ大任ヲ人ニ托シ完全ナル方法ト革新ナル功效ヲ奏セシムルニ如カス故ニ朕是ニ於テ瞿然内ニ省ミ廓然自ラ斷シ茲ニ韓國ノ統治權ヲ從前ヨリ親信依仰シタル隣國大日本皇帝陛下ニ讓與シ外東洋ノ平和ヲ鞏固ナラシメ内八域ノ民生ヲ保全ナラシメントス惟爾大小臣民ハ國勢ト時宜ヲ深察シ煩擾スルナク各其業ニ安ンシ日本帝國ノ文明ノ新政ニ服從シ幸福ヲ共受セヨ朕カ今日ノ此擧ハ爾有衆ヲ忘レタルニアラス宣ヲ爾有衆ヲ救活セントスル至意ニ出ツ爾臣民等ハ朕ノ此意ヲ克體セヨ

御璽

隆熙四年八月二十九日

PART III

# Modernization and Confucianism

CHAPTER 9

# King Chŏngjo: Confucianism, Enlightenment, and Absolute Rule

IN THE FIFTH INTERCALARY LUNAR month of 1762 (the 38th year of King Yŏngjo's reign), a tragedy was unfolding at the royal palace. Stripped of his title and rank, the young Crown Prince lay dying inside a wooden chest by the order of his own father, the King. The Crown Prince's only son was undoubtedly a witness to the affair. Designated as heir to the throne three years before, the Crown Prince's son was only eleven years old when his father was put to death. Fourteen years later, he would ascend the throne as Chŏngjo.

Nearly every Korean is familiar with the heart-wrenching tale of the death of Chŏngjo's father. The story became a legend, thanks in part to *Hanjungnok* (A Record of Sorrowful Days), a bitter account of the affair written by the Crown Prince's wife, Lady Hong of the Hyegyŏng Palace. But few are aware of Chŏngjo's accomplishments as king, obscured perhaps by the famous story of his father's tragic death. Although Chŏngjo reigned for twenty-four years, from 1776 to 1800, the founding of Kyujanggak, the royal library, is the only well-known legacy of his reign. Moreover, what people do know about the Kyujanggak is not completely accurate. It was more than a library; it was a major political institution where academic and policy research was conducted and studies were published. The Kyujanggak played a central role in the formulation and dissemination of policies, and it was the most important political institution of Chŏngjo's administration. The fact that Chŏngjo created such an important interdisciplinary body combining scientific research with politics indicates that his ruling policies were quite advanced. However, modern scholars have only recently begun to give these policies the attention they deserve. Parallels can be drawn between Chŏngjo's efforts to achieve his political agenda through scholarship and research and those of Sejong, who reigned during the early Chosŏn period. Indeed, it can be said that Sejong's purpose in establishing Chiphyŏnjŏn (Hall of Worthies) was similar to Chŏngjo's in founding the Kyujanggak. However, there is a 350-year gap between the two reigns, and their respective accomplishments and historical stature are quite different. For one thing, when Sejong took the throne, a new dynasty was trying to establish its legitimacy, and many of his policies were aimed at developing the nation's agrarian-based economy. By the time Chŏngjo became king—about 300 years after the establishment of the new dynasty—the entire administrative system needed reform, while economic policies needed to be updated to take into account the rise of commerce and industry over the previous three centuries. In other words, Chŏngjo's reign came at a crucial crossroad in Korean history. In order to meet such challenges, Chŏngjo established the Kyujanggak and went to great lengths to prepare the nation for the modern age. Chŏngjo's policies may best be understood in the context of what was happening in Western Europe at the time. It was the age of Enlightenment, the age of absolute monarchy. Though half a world apart, the East and the West not only experienced similar economic conditions, as seen in the burgeoning development of commercial capitalism, but also had similar types of monarchy. Chŏngjo's policies were thus quite significant in that they ushered in a uniquely Korean form of modernization.

THE KING REACHES OUTSIDE THE WALLS

One notable aspect of Chŏngjo's rule was his willingness to leave the royal palace and venture outside the city walls to meet with his subjects face to face. In order to become familiar with their thoughts and sentiments, Chŏngjo frequently toured the city, more so than any of his predecessors. The Chosŏn kings were certainly not kept under lock and key inside the palace, but until the reign of Sukjong, they generally remained within the palace compound except for special occasions such as hunting exercises for military training, processions, royal funerals, or visits to the royal tombs. The practice of going outside the palace to learn about the hearts and minds of the people began with Chŏngjo's grandfather, Yŏngjo. Yŏngjo (reigned from 1725–1776) frequently met with petitioners at the gates of the palace or those of the city. According to the most recent scholarship, Yŏngjo held fifty-five such sessions with commoners during his fifty-two-year reign.[1] According to one story, Yŏngjo was revising the Equalized Tax Law (Kyunyŏkpŏp), but he could not reach an agreement with his ministers. After soliciting opinions from commoners outside the Myŏngjŏngmun gate, he went back inside and implemented the law according to his original wishes. Yŏngjo would often walk through the market district to listen to the opinions and plight of licensed merchants and tradespeople, calling them the "foundation of the nation."

Since Chŏngjo, as the crown prince, observed firsthand his grandfather's frequent contact with the people, it was natural for him to continue the tradition after he became king. In fact, Chŏngjo preferred to meet with a wider variety of people than his grandfather had and to see them more often. While Yŏngjo met with his subjects at the gates of the palace or the city, Chŏngjo went outside the walls. Chŏngjo would create opportunities to leave Seoul with the objective of paying homage to the royal tombs of all previous Chosŏn kings and queens, beginning with Kŏnwŏnnŭng, the royal tomb of T'aejo, the founder of the Chosŏn dynasty. Yŏngjo also left the city proper to visit royal tombs, but only two such visits have been confirmed in extant sources so far—Ŭinŭng in his first year as king and Kwangnŭng in the twelfth year. In contrast, during his twenty-four-year reign, Chŏngjo made seventy such visits, particularly throughout Kyŏnggi province, where most of the royal tombs and graves are located.[2] There was probably no royal tomb that he did not visit.

The first place Chŏngjo visited was the grave of his father, Suŭnmyo. Shortly before Yŏngjo's death (the second month of the 52nd year of his reign), Chŏngjo was authorized to rule on Yŏngjo's behalf as crown prince. During this time, Chŏngjo made a special request to excise all mention of *imo ch'ŏbun* (the act by which the Crown Prince was stripped of his title and reduced to commoner status in the 38th

---

1. Han Sanggwŏn, "Chosŏn hugi sahoe munje wa sowŏn chedo ŭi paldal—Chŏngjo tae sangŏn-kyŏkjaeng ŭi punsŏk ŭl chungsim ŭro" (Social issues and the sowŏn system of the late Chosŏn dynasty—an analysis of Chŏngjo's sangŏn and kyŏkjaeng systems) (Ph.D. diss., Seoul National University, 1993). Most of the information in this chapter regarding the sangŏn system or petitioning of kings by commoners is taken from this dissertation.

2. This information was taken by the author from the records of the Chŏngjo's life appended to the *Chŏngjo sillok* (The veritable records of King Chŏngjo).

year of Yŏngjo's reign) from the historical records. Yŏngjo agreed to the request and even allowed Chŏngjo to visit Suŭnmyo. Chŏngjo's visit to his father's grave can be seen as a prelude to his father's reinstatement to royal status. After Chŏngjo ascended the throne, he conferred on the Crown Prince Hyojang (the half brother of Chŏngjo's father, upon whose death Chŏngjo became the next in line to the throne) the posthumous name of Chinjong and renamed Hyojang's tomb Yŏngnŭng, in accordance with his grandfather Yŏngjo's wishes. He also conferred upon his father the title "Crown Prince Changhŏn" and renamed Suŭnmyo "Yŏnguwŏn." After restoring the authority of his father and making other changes to the royal lineage, in his third year on the throne, Chŏngjo paid a visit to Wŏnnŭng, the tomb of his grandfather, Yŏngjo. This was the first of his planned visits to all of the royal tombs. According to biographer Yi Mansu's account of the life of Chŏngjo, Chŏngjo made at least seventy-five visits to the royal tombs during his twenty-four-year reign, an average of three outside the city walls each year.

Chŏngjo's visits to the royal tombs were more than expressions of filial piety toward his ancestors and predecessors. The visits had a political purpose as well. As Confucianism was the foundation of Chosŏn's ruling policies, it was important to him to observe Confucian rites and put its precepts into practice. However, it is known that Chŏngjo also regarded these visits as opportunities to meet with the people. Yi Mansu's records of Chŏngjo's life contain several anecdotes about these royal processions. One of the more notable incidents occurred in autumn of the 12th year of his reign, when he was travelling to Sŏnnŭng and Chŏngnŭng. Chŏngjo had just reached the ferry crossing at Sŏbinggo, but heavy rains from the night before had damaged the pier so badly that his subjects entreated him to return to Seoul. Chŏngjo replied that he could not turn back the entire procession over such a minor matter. He said that because so many people knew that the royal carriage had departed Seoul and were waiting for him, he could not disappoint them now. He ordered the commanding officer of the troops, the Minister of Taxation, the Minister of Public Works, and Kyŏnggi-do officials to join forces in conscripting the residents of Kwach'ŏn and Kwangju to repair the pier. The soldiers and the many onlookers answered the call with such alacrity that they almost fought each other for the chance to repair the pier. By daybreak, the royal procession was able to cross the Han River. The following day, on his way back to Seoul, Chŏngjo returned to the pier and thanked the residents of Kwach'ŏn and Kwangju. As a reward for their loyalty and assistance, he gave a special order exempting the two towns from the grain tax.

Chŏngjo's visits to the royal tombs were a means of widening the scope of contact with his subjects from inside the city walls to the whole of Kyŏnggi province. One of his reasons for doing this was to see and hear for himself the hardships suffered by ordinary people. During Chŏngjo's reign, the *sowŏn* (petition) system was a way for people to file grievances with higher authorities, and a recent study has shown that it was an epoch-making development in the history of the *sangŏn* system.[3] The *sangŏn* system originated with the implementation of the *sinmun'go* (petitioners' drum) during the reign of T'aejong, third king of the Chosŏn dynasty. If a person had a particular grievance, he could bring it to the attention of the relevant government office in Seoul or to the provincial governor. If the matter was not resolved through those offices, the petitioner could appeal to the king directly by pounding the *sinmun'go*, a large drum installed near the palace. Thus, from the early days of the Chosŏn dynasty, there was a mechanism by which people could file petitions, at least in theory. In practice, it was rarely used because commoners were not able to bring suit against government officials unless they were accusing them of treason. Furthermore, the *sinmun'go* was often situated in a location that was inaccessible to ordinary people. The petition system was revised in the sixteenth century, enabling people to file petitions with government officials for four reasons: to appeal a death sentence, to clarify paternity issues, to clarify the legality of a marriage union, and to clarify class status. In the eighteenth century, the right to file a petition was expanded so that a petitioner's grandsons, sons, husband or wife, younger brothers, and servants could do so on his or her behalf. It was not until Chŏngjo that restrictions on the class of the petitioner were eliminated.

Every time Chŏngjo visited the royal tombs, crowds flocked to the front of the royal procession seeking an audience with him. Chŏngjo saw how earnestly they sought an avenue for redress and realized that to deny their requests would not be a proper way to rule. In response, he revised the *sangŏn* system by removing all restrictions on bringing suits. Sukjong (r. 1675–1720) had faced a similar problem when commoners were allowed to strike a gong to alert him to their petitions; as a result, the gong was sounded quite frequently. However, until the time of Chŏngjo's reign, there had been no active effort to

3. Han Sanggwŏn, *op. cit.*

find a solution. Indeed, most of Chŏngjo's subjects were quite opposed to his revolutionary approach to dealing with grievances. Chŏngjo, however, did not yield to their arguments and, in fact, went to great lengths to implement systematically new *sangŏn* and *kyŏkjaeng*, direct petition systems that established bureaus specifically for processing and resolving petitions. He thereby ensured that the reforms were permanent and not piecemeal.

For ordinary people, there were two ways of filing a petition, *sangŏn* and *kyŏkjaeng*. Under the former, the petitioner would wait until the royal carriage reached a designated stop and petition the king either as an individual or as part of group by presenting an official document. Under the latter, the petitioner would strike a gong during the procession, thus creating an opportunity to file a grievance. This method was also known as *wioe kyŏkjaeng*. Petitioners were subject to minor fines or punishments in return for having their grievances heard, since they were impeding the royal procession. People from all across the country took advantage of both methods. To ensure that petitions were duly processed and resolved, Chŏngjo ordered his subjects to record all matters relating to them in the *Ilsŏngnok* (Records of Daily Reflection), the royal diary that he started when he became king. According to Han Sanggwŏn's analysis of *sangŏn* and *kyŏkjaeng*, 3,217 petitions were noted in the *Ilsŏngnok*, and 2,671 petitions were recorded in the *Chŏngjo sillok* (The Veritable Records of King Chŏngjo). They ranged from disputes over graves (*sansong*), commendations for fidelity, filial piety, and chastity (*hyŏn'yang*), to issues of birthright and inheritance (*iphu*). Apart from disputes and grievances stemming from matters related to Confucian ethics and practices, there were also complaints over taxation and conflicts among craftsmen and merchants over their economic interests. We can clearly see that there was a wide range of cases covered by the *sangŏn* and *kyŏkjaeng* systems.

## THE KYUJANGGAK AND CHANGYONGYŎNG

Chŏngjo needed new institutions to help implement and support his policies. The Kyujanggak and Changyongyŏng (Royal Guard Garrison) were two such institutions, one representing the scholar and the other the soldier.

As mentioned earlier, the Kyujanggak was one of the most important institutions in Chŏngjo's government, serving a variety of functions.⁴ However, this was not the case from the beginning. Chŏngjo was enthroned on the tenth day of the third lunar month of 1776. The very next day, he ordered the building of the library, personally selecting its location in the back garden of Ch'angdŏk Palace (widely known as Piwŏn, or the Secret Garden), on a hill north of the lotus pond. Next to the lotus pond was Yŏngwhadang, the pavilion where civil-service examinations were conducted. The library enjoyed the most spectacular views in the entire garden. Two buildings were erected on the hill. A two-story tower was built in the middle of the hill. The upper level of the tower was called Chuhamnu, and the lower level, Ŏjejon'gak, was a storehouse containing tens of thousands of books. To the west of the tower was Sŏhyanggak, a building for reading and writing. Just as construction was nearing completion in the seventh month of the year, however, Chŏngjo proposed a last-minute change in design. Originally the calligraphy and writings of previous kings were to be safeguarded in the first story of Chuhamnu, but Chŏngjo instead decided to store his own portraits and writings there. He decided to build a separate building called Pongmodang as a repository for the writings of his predecessors. As the functions of the building changed, the name Ŏjejon'gak was changed to "Kyujanggak." New buildings such as Yŏlgogwan (a library for old books), Kaeyuwa (storehouse for all books), Sŏgo (West Library) and others were built nearby for the storage of books and manuscripts. Sŏhyanggak, which was originally conceived as a study area for reading and writing, had its name changed to "Ihyanggak," and it became a center for airing the books.

The changes in the design of the new library amounted to more than just an expansion in scale. Because Chŏngjo chose the first story of the main building to house his writings and other documents and materials related to his reign, he clearly considered the library to be the foundation of the monarchy. The Kyujanggak was modeled after Tianzhangge (Tower of the Writings of Heaven) and Longtuge (Tower of the Drawings of Dragons), which were among the ten royal libraries of Song China. Since many of Korea's institutions had originated from China, Chŏngjo thought the lack of a royal library

4. The following description of Kyujanggak (Royal Library) is based largely on Yi T'ae-jin (Yi T'aejin), *Kyujanggak sosa* (A Brief History of Kyujanggak) (Seoul: Seoul National University Library, 1990), and "Chŏngjo ŭi taehak t'amgu wa saeroun kunjuron" (Chŏngjo's Study of Daxue and His New Theory of Monarchism), in Yi Hoeje, *ŭi sasang kwa kŭ segye* (Yi Hoeje's thinking and his world), vol. 11 of Taedong munhwa yŏn'gu ch'ongsŏ (Taedong Cultural Research Series) (Seoul: Sungkyunkwan University, 1992).

system needed immediate rectification. The term "kyujang" refers to the monarch's astrological sign as well as his writings, and by establishing the Kyujanggak, Chŏngjo was aiming to elevate the status of both the monarchy and the court.

The Kyujanggak was established as the royal library to house the writings of the reigning king, but it was not until the second month in the fifth year of Chŏngjo's reign that it assumed a significant role in political affairs. Until that time, Chŏngjo had entrusted the day-to-day administration and implementation of policy to Hong Kukyŏng, a retainer who had assisted Chŏngjo since his days as the crown prince. Chŏngjo spent much of his time at the Kyujanggak planning policy and his future political agenda. However, Hong, emboldened by his newfound authority, harbored other ambitions. When Chŏngjo learned of these plans in the fifth year of his reign, he expelled Hong and took over the handling of administrative affairs himself. As the Kyujanggak's functions expanded to political administration, so did its strategic importance. Chŏngjo ordered all the civil servants at the Kyujanggak to assume duties at bureaus such as the Yemun'gwan (Office of the Royal Decrees) and Hongmun'gwan (Office of the Royal Secretariat), in addition to their scholarly duties at the Kyujanggak. Chŏngjo allowed them to use the former building of the Owi Toch'ongbu (Five Military Commands Headquarters), which was near the main hall of Ch'angdŏkkung palace, as a working office and conferred on the building the new name "Imunwŏn," the building for compiling writings. Chŏngjo even referred to the Kyujanggak as his "cabinet" because of its importance in his handling of political affairs.

The Kyujanggak was more than a center for scholarship. On the day of the inauguration ceremony for Imunwŏn in the third month of the fifth year of his reign, Chŏngjo personally gave a special lecture at the Kyujanggak and the Office of the Special Advisors on the texts of the *Jinsilu* (Book of Thoughts) and the *Xinjing* (The Way of the Mind), employing all the formality and ceremony of the Song dynasty. This special lecture, called a *ch'in'gang*, marked the last time that Chŏngjo held a *kyŏngyŏn* (literally, "classics mat"; discussions between the king and his subjects regarding text on Confucian studies and historical records), a tradition that he had observed until then with Kyujanggak officials. The *kyŏngyŏn* was a sort of round table in which the king read Confucian classics and histories together with his most learned scholars while discussing politics. Previous kings had held similar forums, but Yŏngjo began holding them much more frequently. Following his example, Chŏngjo held *kyŏngyŏn* three times a day at the Kyujanggak, in the morning, afternoon, and evening. However, after this *ch'in'gang*, Chŏngjo never held a *kyŏngyŏn* again. Instead, he introduced the *ch'ogye munsin* system, under which the most promising civil servants under the age of thirty-seven working in administrative bureaus were handpicked for intensive study at the Kyujanggak for a set length of time. Previously, government officials had asked the king to study *sŏnghak* (the study of the sages), but with the new system, it was the king who chose the officials to study *sŏnghak* or provided them with the opportunity to do so. Thus, the initiative had shifted.

Since his appointment as the crown prince, Chŏngjo had studied *sŏnghak* with such devotion that he could read texts that were difficult to understand for even the most advanced scholars. Chŏngjo cultivated himself with strict discipline and upheld the highest standards. He personally deplored the tendency of many young bureaucrats to never read a book again after passing the torturous civil service examination. The *ch'ogye munsin* system was designed to reverse that trend. On another level, Chŏngjo felt that it was necessary to encourage civil servants to study *sŏnghak* as part of his efforts to have them embody his concept of an enlightened monarchy. If nothing else, the system would increase the number of civil servants and subjects who supported Chŏngjo's policies. In fact, after ten sessions of *ch'ogye munsin* over twenty years, the number of alumni reached one hundred, so that by the end of Chŏngjo's reign, virtually all of his officials had graduated from the system. Chŏngjo was able to expand his base of support gradually from the Kyujanggak subjects to the graduates of the *ch'ogye munsin* system.

Chŏngjo is often called the "scholar-king." From an early age, he showed great skill in composition. In an appended record of the *Chŏngjo sillok* (the appendix itself was an unusual addition), his mother, Lady Hong of Hyegyŏng Palace, described how clever Chŏngjo looked even as a young baby wrapped in a swaddling cloth, and she mentioned that Chŏngjo was often praised by his grandfather Yŏngjo for his extraordinary features. She relates how Yŏngjo was particularly pleased with the back of Chŏngjo's head, which was nicely rounded, and his high forehead. Chŏngjo was able to stand on his own before his one hundredth day and began walking at ten months. At his first birthday celebration, Chŏngjo walked right to the table, and from all of the symbols of future fortune from which to choose, he picked up a writing brush and opened a book to read. Onlookers were amazed by his mature demeanor and precocity. By the time he was two, he was able to form brushstrokes correctly; within a few years, he became proficient at calligraphy and painting. Chŏngjo practiced writing and painting everyday so that by the time he was five or six, examples of his penmanship were made into folding screens. Chŏngjo had mastered speaking and writing by the age of four, and his letters and compositions were comparable to those of an adult.

Chŏngjo excelled not only in writing but also in the martial arts due to his large physique. He was particularly renowned as an archer. Once, he participated in an archery contest with his subjects in which they took turns shooting rounds of five arrows each. Chŏngjo continued to hit the target through the fourth arrow of the tenth round (i.e., forty-nine out of fifty arrows), before leaving the last arrow unshot in accordance with archery traditions. His officials congratulated him on his performance and proposed sending the scoring board to former King T'aejo's palace in Hamhŭng to commemorate the event. As part of their congratulatory message on the plaque, they extolled Chŏngjo's prowess as directly descending from the legendary T'aejo himself, whose skill was said to have been superhuman.

Because of his extraordinary talents in both scholarship and martial arts, it was natural that as king, Chŏngjo would place equal emphasis on scholarship and military affairs. In restructuring the functions of the Kyujanggak in the second month of his fifth year on the throne, Chŏngjo said, "Lectures on the literary classics, lectures on military affairs, composing literary works, and the martial arts—they are like the wheels of a wagon or the wings of a bird. No one side can gain an advantage over the other." He also implemented a system similar to *ch'ogye munsin* for high-ranking military officers and guards to study military theory and practice martial arts. Chŏngjo's efforts to raise the quality of military personnel such as *sŏngŏn'gwan* (the elite royal heralds also in charge of guarding the king) had the strategic effect of bolstering support for his reformist government and laying the groundwork for building up the nation's military. Chŏngjo believed deeply in military strength as a deterrent force, so he invested great effort in building up arms and developing training for defensive purposes. To improve the skills of his soldiers in the martial arts, Chŏngjo took up the task of compiling a book that his father had started but never completed. In the fourteenth year of Chŏngjo's reign, the book was completed and entitled *Muyedobo t'ongji* (Comprehensive Illustrated Manual of Martial Arts). In addition, he edited or compiled six more volumes of military strategies and tactics, including the *Pyŏnghakt'ong* (Manual of Military Science). Chŏngjo also tried to strengthen his fighting forces by recruiting troops and officers on the basis of skill rather than family background, upholding the principle of cultivating talent as a national resource. His efforts to implement these military policies culminated with the founding and operation of Changyongyŏng.

Chŏngjo spent the early part of his reign trying to eliminate hostile factions. One night, an intruder broke into the outer hall of his sleeping chamber. The incident may or may not have been connected with his initial purges, but it spurred Chŏngjo to form a night guard, the Sugwiso, and to strengthen the Royal Guard. However, the night guard, which was under the administration of Hong Kukyŏng, was disbanded after Hong's seditious acts were discovered. Hong's treachery convinced Chŏngjo that the Royal Guard system could not depend on one specific person. Instead, he decided to raise the caliber of the entire regular military. This change in his thinking was evident in the fifth year of his reign when he embraced the principle of promoting the *sŏngŏn'gwan* based on their individual improvement and achievements. Based on his principle that even the Royal Guard should be commanded by the elite military professionals, Chŏngjo established a policy of elevating the quality of the *sŏngŏn'gwan*, from whose ranks the elite would be chosen, and also promised to expand upon this system in the future.[5]

During his seventh year on the throne, Chŏngjo officially changed the name and title of his father from Crown Prince Sado to "Crown Prince Changhŏn" and conducted a special session of the national examination (*kyŏnggwa*) to commemorate it. From the two thousand finalists who passed the martial arts test, he selected the most outstanding ones and tried to press them into the service of the Royal Guard. He believed that those who passed an exam that had been conducted in honor of his father would naturally show him greater allegiance. Even if the occasion of the examination did not necessarily guarantee a greater degree of loyalty, it remained nonetheless symbolically significant. It took two years for Chŏngjo to realize his plans. The first step was to establish a new royal guard unit called the Changyongwi. The Changyongwi slowly grew in size, but it was not

5. The descriptions of Sugwiso, Changyongwi, and Changyongyŏng that follow are from Yi T'ae-jin, "Chosŏn hugi ŭi chŏngch'i wa kunyŏngje pyŏnch'ŏn" (The system of Central Army Garrisons in the development of the political structure in the late Chosŏn Dynasty), Han'guk yŏn'guwŏn ch'ongsŏ, no. 53 (Seoul: Han'guk yŏn'guwŏn, 1985).

until the first month of Chŏngjo's seventeenth year that it developed into a full-scale army unit, when he decided to move his father's grave to Suwŏn and build the new city of Hwasŏng there. Originally, the function of the Changyongwi had been to guard the king, but the Changyongyŏng, as it was later called, evolved into the country's central army unit. It was divided into two garrisons, one to defend the capital (inner garrison) and the other to guard the castle in Suwŏn (outer garrison). Because Chŏngjo often left the city limits, he needed to strengthen his guard detail, and this necessity would explain in part why the Changyongwi developed into the two-garrison system of the Changyongyŏng (literally, "stout brave garrison"). However, another reason for its growth was more political: Chŏngjo wanted to contain the entrenched political forces that opposed his policies.

Since Sukjong's reign, the greatest impediment to the stability of the monarchy had been the influence of certain powerful clans known as *kyomok sega*. These families derived their authority from having generations of members in high-ranking offices. The driving force behind factional politics, these families not only held a vise-like grip over policy-making bodies such as the Pibyŏnsa (the Border Defense Council) but also held sway over the Ogunyŏng (Five Army Garrisons) and other military affairs. Yŏngjo introduced the *t'angp'yŏngch'aek*, or policy of impartiality (literally, "leveling factions policy"), to neutralize their influence, but he was not entirely successful. The unfortunate fact that Yŏngjo had to kill his own son was evidence of the vicious, yet ever so delicate, power play between him and the various court factions. Although Yŏngjo managed to build support for his *t'angp'yŏng* policy, he failed to wrest away control over the central army, which had connections with powerful economic interests. In creating the Changyongyŏng, Chŏngjo sought to address the limitations of his grandfather's rule. By widely expanding the functions and rules of the Kyujanggak, Chŏngjo shifted the center of political operation away from the traditional stronghold of the Pibyŏnsa. He also weakened the authority that the powerful clan families had traditionally held over the Ogunyŏng by expanding the scope of his guard detail, the Changyongwi. With its two garrisons, the Changyongyŏng expanded in size and financial strength at the expense of the rapidly downsized Ogunyŏng. It boasted twenty thousand soldiers, enough to provide support for Chŏngjo's rule.

The two-garrison structure of the Changyongyŏng also held symbolic significance for Chŏngjo. Ten years after bestowing on his father the posthumous name of Crown Prince Changhŏn in the seventh year

King Chŏngjo: Confucianism, Enlightenment, and Absolute Rule 219

of his reign, he decided to relocate his father's tomb to Suwŏn because of problems with its site and scale. He chose a site south of the Han River that was considered the most propitious place for a royal tomb; it was also where the Suwŏn military command was stationed. However, the command had to be moved before the tomb could be relocated. This was the impetus for the conception and design of the city of Hwasŏng, today known as Suwŏn. As the new city developed, the Suwŏn military command was promoted to the Hwasŏng military command. It was around this time that the tomb of the Crown Prince Changhŏn was relocated to the new auspicious site. The new tomb was named Hyŏllyungwŏn about the time that the Changyongwi was being transformed into the Changyongyŏng. The new city was completed by the eighteenth year of Chŏngjo's reign, which was the year his mother, Lady Hong of Hyekyŏng Palace, turned sixty. Since Chŏngjo's mother and father were the same age, that year held great personal significance. Chŏngjo celebrated the two birthdays with his subjects by promoting by a full rank all civil servants over the age of seventy, literati and scholars over eighty, and all long-married couples even if they had not reached eighty. It is recorded that 75,145 people benefited from this gesture. Furthermore, Chŏngjo published the Insŏrok (Records of Auspicious Events), which contains records of such events in order to highlight further the significance of the celebration. In the following year, when the Hyŏllyungwŏn was at last completed, Chŏngjo took his mother with him to pay their respects. Undoubtedly, the seventeenth, eighteenth, and nineteenth years of Chŏngjo's reign were marked by many significant changes and events, reinforcing the impression that these years were the peak of his reign.

THEORY OF THE VIRTUOUS, ABSOLUTE MONARCH

With the relocation of his father's tomb and the construction of Hwasŏng, Chŏngjo felt supremely confident in his political authority. Buoyed by this confidence, he wrote, in the twenty-second year of his reign, a treatise of political philosophy called *Manch'ŏn myŏngwŏl chuinong chasŏ* (referred to hereafter as "Chasŏ"), in which he discussed the proper relationship between a monarch and his subjects.[6] The title refers to the nature of the politics being pursued by Chŏngjo, describing the people as countless streams of water and the monarch

6. See Yi T'ae-jin (1992).

as a bright moon reflected in each stream. The text is also significant as an account of how Chosŏn had evolved by the late eighteenth century. Chŏngjo's philosophy of the relationship between monarch and subject represents the highest level attainable according to Confucian political thought. To appreciate Chŏngjo's theory of the monarchy fully, it is necessary to understand what Chŏngjo studied as he was being groomed for the throne. His theory is derived from the concept of *myŏngmyŏngdŏk* (*mingmingde* in Chinese; literally, "brightening man's inherent virtuous nature") as described in the first part of the *Daxue* (The Great Learning), a text that he studied devoutly, spurred by the influence of his grandfather Yŏngjo.

The essence of Neo-Confucianism is widely considered to be the study of *sugi ch'iin*. The premise of this concept is that a ruler is not fit to rule unless he makes the effort to attain *sugi* (self-edification). This applied not only to high-ranking officials but also to the king himself, as seen in the aforementioned tradition of *kyŏngyŏn* ("classics mat" or royal lectures). *Sugi ch'iin* was the rationale that Yŏngjo had used to promote his *t'angp'yŏngch'aek* policy, which called on the monarch to be absolutely impartial and to show no favoritism to any faction or party. Such an ideal of impartial politics in the Yao-Shun period was recognized as a level that could not be attained by a king without thorough efforts at *sugi*. Indeed, before his officials had a chance to urge him to engage in self-cultivation, he himself zealously studied *sŏnghak* (the study of the Chinese sages). As a measure of his zeal, Yŏngjo held 3,458 royal lectures during the fifty-two years of his reign. That number amounts to an average of sixty-six lectures per year or roughly five per month—far more often than any of his predecessors.[7] If he had not temporarily suspended the lectures when he had his son, the Crown Prince, rule as regent (from the 25th to the 34th years of his reign), the number would have been higher still.

For the *kyŏngyŏn*, Yŏngjo read the Confucian classics and histories extensively. After resuming the *kyŏngyŏn* in his 34th year, he began to focus on two texts in particular, the *Daxue* and the *Zhongyong* (Doctrine of the Mean). In the tenth month of that year, Yŏngjo visited the Sŏnggyun'gwan, the National Confucian Academy, where he gave a lecture on the *Daxue*. He even used the occasion of the lecture to write a preface for this Confucian classic, something no one had done since Zhu Xi, the founder of Neo-Confucianism.

---

7. Kwŏn Yŏn'ung, "Chosŏn Yŏngjodae kyŏngyŏn" (The royal lectures of King Yŏngjo's era), *Tonga yŏn'gu* 17 (onŭl ŭi Han'guksa yŏn'gu) (1989), pp. 370–73.

Yŏngjo asserted that the essence of the *Daxue*, which he considered to be study for the spirit and for the mind, was encapsulated in the concept of *myŏngmyŏngdŏk* presented in the first part of the book. Yŏngjo believed that by attaining that level of virtue, it would follow that he could become as worthy of the throne as the legendary Emperor Shun of China. Yŏngjo's keen interest in the concept of *myŏngdŏk* profoundly influenced his successor Chŏngjo.

Chŏngjo was appointed crown prince in Yŏngjo's thirty-fifth year, the year after Yŏngjo began to study the *Daxue* in depth. Chŏngjo began his formal studies (*kanghak*) in the first month of Yŏngjo's thirty-sixth year. After Chŏngjo finished the first book, the *Xiaoxe* (Lesser Learning), Yŏngjo personally selected the *Daxue* as his next text. Chŏngjo pursued his studies of the *Daxue* earnestly. According to the *Ch'unjŏrok* (Record of the days of the Crown Prince), a record of the discussions he had with the lecture officials (*siganggwan*), Chŏngjo questioned why Zhu Xi only discussed human nature in general in his foreword to the *Daxue* and made no reference to *myŏngdŏk* at all. He presented his own interpretation of this fact. Chŏngjo also believed that the concepts of *myŏngdŏk* and *sinmin* (renewing the people) were not mutually exclusive but that a ruler who attained the former would naturally encourage the formation of the latter. If a person were so inspired by the example of his monarch that he became a wholly new person himself, then the king's role would merely be to provide stimulation and encouragement to the people. Accordingly, Chŏngjo expected that his people would take an active role in their own cultivation.

After succeeding Yŏngjo to the throne, Chŏngjo continued debates over *myŏngdŏk* during the royal lectures. Even after he replaced the *kyŏngyŏn* with the *cho'gye munsin* system, Chŏngjo frequently discussed *myŏngdŏk* with the scholar-officials selected for the program. According to the synopsis of *Daxue* compiled in *Kyŏngsa kangŭi* (Lecture on the Classics), Chŏngjo again raised questions about Zhu Xi's preface. Chŏngjo considered the first volume of *Daxue* to be a "guide to learning and a charter for governing the world." On the central issue that had intrigued him for so long, the relationship between *myŏngdŏk* and human nature, Chŏngjo concluded that "man's inherent virtue (*myŏngdŏk*) controls his nature." As part of his lifelong study of the *Daxue*, in his twenty-third year on the throne, Chŏngjo edited and published a new book called *Taehak ryuŭi*, a compilation of key passages from three texts: the *Daxue*, *Daxue yanyi* (Further explication of the *Daxue*), and *Daxue yanyibu* (Supplement to *Daxue yanyi*). Shortly before publishing *Taehak ryuŭi*, Chŏngjo had published the aforementioned "Chasŏ," which originated from his years of studying the *Daxue*. The passage below is the first paragraph of "Chasŏ":

> The master of ten thousand rivers and the bright moon (*manch'ŏn myŏngwŏl chuingong*) speaks. In the beginning was the *t'aegŭk* [the Great Ultimate] and then the yin and yang came into being. Therefore, the Emperor Yao was able to reveal *li* [Principle] with the yin and yang. After the yin and yang, the five elements of which all nature is composed [water, wood, metal, fire, and earth] came into being and the Emperor Yu governed with these elements. As I observed the water and moon, I began to comprehend the logic of *t'aegŭk*, of the dualistic nature of the cosmos (yin and yang), and of the five elements. There is but one moon, and there are countless streams of water. The water is the moon, and behind the water is also the moon. The moon in the water and the rivers is the same, even if there are ten thousand rivers. This is so because there has only ever been one moon in the sky.

The essence of the first paragraph is the emphasis on the oneness between the moon and water. The moon may cast its reflection on countless bodies of water, but because it is the origin, it is as though the moon were filling up every single body of water. In the latter part of the book, Chŏngjo refers to the moon as *t'aegŭk*, and likens himself to the moon. He comes to this conclusion after observing the moon and its relationship to water and understanding the logic of *t'aegŭk*, of yin and yang, and of the five elements. The rest of his text explains his thoughts on the relationship among these three.

Chŏngjo explained the principles that he had followed after his coronation: "The *dao* (in Korean, *to*; moral principle) of the heavens and the earth is to view the world honestly (*chŏnggwan*); the *dao* of the sun and the moon is to shine righteously (*chŏngmyŏng*)." By following the counsel of the sages to rule seeking brightness, he conceived of an "ambitious scheme to rule the world" and thus was able to lead thousands of types of officials for nearly twenty years. He recalled that he had been guided by his heart when he selected officials, and he trusted them to follow him. He taught them to resolve difficulties. He melted them in fire and recast them in the proper mold so that they became pure. He united them like a chieftain reigning in rival feudal lords, responding to their every countermove. Fortunately, after he came to understand the order and the principles that governed *t'aegŭk*, yin and yang, and the five elements, he was able to look at a person with such clarity that he knew to treat the strong man with a velvet glove, and the mild man with steel. With the dull-witted man, he was very clear and thorough. He made up for others' shortcomings and flaws so that all were able to become complete, and he proudly compared them to cranes and ducks that formed flocks, not unlike the three thousand followers of Confucius. What Chŏngjo meant by understanding the principles of *t'aegŭk*, yin and yang, and the five elements was both the efforts of ruling and the result of that effort.

Chŏngjo felt that his achievements were similar to those of the legendary emperor Shun. As he tried to embody the concept of *myŏngdŏk*, he found that being virtuous came easily, like King Wen's rule of Western Zhou, and he could see all things in terms of the grander scheme of *t'aegŭk*. And finally, although he left all things according to their nature, they all became his own "possessions." He explained the process that led to these conclusions in terms of the principles found in the *Yijing* (Book of Changes). *T'aegŭk* produces two halves (yin and yang). *T'aegŭk* remains *t'aegŭk*, while the yin and yang produce the Four Forms, by which both yin and yang become *t'aegŭk*. The Four Forms in turn produce eight signs of divination. Each of the Four Forms then also becomes *t'aegŭk*. Chŏngjo felt that if he endeavored to achieve *myŏngdŏk*, it would be possible for all of his subjects to "enjoy the Five Blessings [longevity, health, wealth, love of virtue, and a peaceful death], to be at peace in mind and body, and to be bright in countenance." What is noteworthy about his reference to the *Yijing* is that in contrast to Zhu Xi, who considered the 16,770,000 divinations produced from all possible combinations of trigrams and hexagrams to be "limitless divination" in his *Yixue qimeng* (Enlightenment through Divination), Chŏngjo maintained that the number of combinations corresponded to the "number of my subjects." He went on to say that his own *myŏngdŏk* directly influenced the *sŏmin*, or common people, thus reinforcing his basic tenet that the monarch and his subjects are one. He summarized his thoughts on this issue as follows:

> My thoughts regarding the monarchy are based on the thoughts held by the Confucian sages. In the very beginning of the *Yiji* (The Twisting of Divinations), Confucius introduces the idea of *t'aegŭk*, with which to educate succeeding generations. In *Ch'unqiu* (The Spring and Autumn Annals), he revealed the universality of right-

eousness, how every nation is united under the king, how a thousand streams and a hundred waves converge into one sea, and how a thousand purples and ten thousand reds form one *t'aegŭk*... What I seek is to learn about the sages. If I compare this to the moon in the water, the nature of the moon is to emanate light (wisdom, purity), but its light is transmitted only when it is reflected in the water below. The vast waters of the Longmen River flow swiftly; the Huanghe River (Yellow River) is salty; the Jing River is muddy; and the Wei River flows clear. Since the water reflects the moon, the moonlight depends on the course and flow of the river. If the stream ceases, so too does the moonlight... If water swirls, so does the moon. If I can grasp the essence of water, it is the purity (*chŏng*), the essence of the moon. I see the water as people, and the reflections cast by the water are the faces and types of people. The moon is the *t'aegŭk*, and the *t'aegŭk* is I. Is this not what the sages meant when they compared the ten thousand faces of the bright moon to the reflection cast on the *t'aegŭk*? The true light of the moon is proper; if there is anyone who seeks to grasp the *t'aegŭk* (i.e., kingship) or peek from the aura of the *t'aegŭk*, I tell him that his efforts are in vain. It is as futile as trying to catch the moon in the water.

Thus, in "Chasŏ," Chŏngjo argues that a monarch can improve the welfare of his people through wise policies based on the concept of *myŏngdŏk* as described in the *Daxue*. These principles may be applied to all things in the same way that *t'aegŭk* is equally applied to all things and makes everyone pure. These were the basic teachings of the sages and illustrious rulers such as the Emperors Yao and Shun. Toward the end of "Chasŏ," Chŏngjo cautions against those who covet the throne as "though they were waiting at the edge of *t'aegŭk* for a chance." He says it is as futile and unattainable as grasping for the moon in the water. To become a proper monarch, he emphasized, one must expend a great deal of effort and preparation to attain *myŏngdŏk*.

Before Chŏngjo came to power, there had been no theory of monarchy that described the relation between the king and his subjects in this manner. Even if a case could be made that Yŏngjo laid the foundation for his ideas, "Chasŏ" was nevertheless the first systematic and rational exposition of this theory. Another unique aspect of the text is that Chŏngjo downplays the role of government officials and functionaries. In the traditional view of monarchy, if the king were a boat and the subjects the water, then the prime minister was the ferryman. Chŏngjo's theory of the monarchy was rooted, in part, in his opposition to factionalism, which gave officials immense influence. In the eighth year of his reign, Chŏngjo wrote an essay titled *P'abungdang* (Anti-factionalism), which appears in the first part of the *Hwanggŭkp'yŏn* (Book of Emperors). Although Ou Yangxiu and Zhu Xi Han contended that it was the duty of superior men (*kunja*) to associate with each other and overcome the factions of inferior men (*soin*), Chŏngjo argued that since factions of his day included both *kunja* and *soin*, the original meaning and purpose of factions had been lost. He believed that factions should be dissolved and that it was more appropriate for people to support the policies of the monarch as individuals. Chŏngjo was so firm in his conviction that he claimed he would not change his mind even if the sages appeared today and disagreed with him.

Chŏngjo's political philosophy as described in "Chasŏ" can be encapsulated in the concept of "virtuous absolute monarchy." This model of government bears many striking similarities to the enlightened absolute monarchies in Europe at the time. Europe's enlightened monarchs held intellectual debates on and investigations into what constituted the ideal man, the model upon which their absolute political authority was founded.[8] The idea that within the country, the monarch must come the closest to attaining perfection is no different from Chŏngjo's view of monarchy. In Europe, the enlightened absolute rulers attempted to achieve this goal by establishing the rule of law; as we shall see later, Chŏngjo tried to do the same thing. It is not inaccurate to say that Chŏngjo's philosophy was a Confucian version of enlightened absolute rule. Voltaire may have advised King Frederick of Prussia that Emperor Qianlong of the Qing dynasty was an example of such an enlightened ruler, but in terms of actual achievement, Chŏngjo may have come closer to the Confucian ideal.

THE ABOLITION OF SLAVERY

In theory, Chŏngjo believed that a monarch and his subjects were one, just like the moon and water, but what did this mean in practice? As mentioned above, Chŏngjo reformed the *sangŏn* and *kyŏkjaeng*

---

8. Kim Ŏnsik, "Kyemong chŏldaejuŭi ŭi sŏngkyŏk" (The character of enlightened absolutism), in *Togilsa ŭi che kungmyŏn* (Diverse aspects of German history), by Yi Min-ho et al. (Seoul: Zelkova, 1991).

systems in order to ascertain the opinions and sufferings of the people more directly and on a wider basis. His frequent travels outside the palace and city gates allowed ordinary people far more opportunity to take advantage of the new petition system. Based on what he wrote in the "Chasŏ," he purposely planned the many royal visits to the tombs of the former kings. Wanting to be like the moon that reflects on ten thousand rivers, Chŏngjo sought to leave the palace compound as often as he could.

The concept of serving the people was the goal of Confucian politics. It was by no means unique to Chŏngjo, but in terms of achieving that goal, the monarchs of the Chosŏn dynasty had a mixed record. Chŏngjo's revolutionary approaches to the *sangŏn* and *kyŏkjaeng* systems came the closest to achieving the Confucian ideal of *winmin* (literally, "serving the people"). However, these were not the only manifestations of Chŏngjo's political philosophy. Records of Chŏngjo's life written by Yi Mansu show many examples during his reign in which he put the concept of *wimin* into practice.

Yi termed Chŏngjo's love for his people *shiji yŏsang*, meaning that Chŏngjo's concern for them extended to the point that he worried about whether they would come to harm. He instructed governors and local officials to observe the people and to actively help them when needed. He also dispatched royal emissaries throughout the country to uncover corrupt or unjust laws and false charges. In addition, Chŏngjo solicited the opinions of high-ranking provincial officials and held audience with the people to ask about their sufferings. As part of his agricultural policy, he bolstered programs to help alleviate impoverished farmers during years of poor harvest and installed rain gauges and windmills, even using funds from the royal treasury to do so—measures that set him apart from his predecessors. For city residents, he abolished the practice of conducting business and trade transactions on palace grounds and eliminated abuses committed by royal slaves. On behalf of slaves, Chŏngjo eliminated the *ch'uswaegwan*, which hunted down runaway slaves, and rectified the Sŏnduan, the official register of official slaves owned by the government. For those who dwelled in the mountains and wilderness, he also eliminated the *yŏpkun*, the hunting brigade that caught pheasants on royal lands to present to the king. For the "people of the river and sea" (mainly people living near rivers in the Seoul region), he instituted a new fleet system for ferrying the grain tax, and he implemented a new method of selecting dried fish for tax payments. The diversification of people's occupations was a social consequence of developments in commerce and industry in the eighteenth century. Chŏngjo felt it was an important part of his obligation as monarch to resolve the social problems facing all the people. Yi Mansu recounts further anecdotes of Chŏngjo aiding people in all regions and of all ages. He reduced the quantity of abalone which Cheju Island inhabitants were required to send as tribute; he also lightened the burden of residents of the western provinces who sent him ginseng. Concerned about the welfare of children, Chŏngjo implemented the Chahyul chŏngch'ik, a welfare law for abandoned children or the needy in years of famine. He also reformed burial rites and procedures. It may be said that his solicitude extended from the cradle to the grave. There was virtually no segment of the population that did not benefit from his munificence.

Chŏngjo was particularly concerned about criminal justice and sought to eradicate any injustice committed against any individual. He is said to have diligently pored through judicial decisions in all provinces, sometimes all through the night, and would often append footnotes. To reach a judgment, he would examine the case no less than ten times, an indication of his unflagging dedication. Even in the second year of his reign, Chŏngjo acted decisively to halt executions carried out at the whim of administrative officials. He immediately dispatched secretaries from the criminal-law division of the Royal Secretariat to the Corrections Tribunal and the Ministry of Punishments to inspect instruments used for torture and execution for violations of legal standards. Not only did he enforce the proper implementation of these standards by the criminal offices, he also promulgated a new, more exacting standard (*Hŭmhyul chŏnch'ik*) for determining the guilt of prisoners, notifying officials in every province to comply with the standard or else face punishment themselves. In the seventh year, he chided the Corrections Tribunal and the Ministry of Punishments for lax record-keeping and ordered them to document the trial and punishment procedures of all offenders. These reports were to be complied together into book form and delivered to him on a regular basis. Chŏngjo would then spend the entire night reading the reports, adding notes and retrying the cases repeatedly. He felt that such keen interest in criminal-justice administration and strict oversight were required as part of the monarch's obligations to his subjects. Indeed, Chŏngjo felt it was his personal duty to correct injustices suffered by the ordinary people; it was the reason he set about reforming the existing system.

As mentioned earlier, Chŏngjo aided the slave class by abolishing the *ch'uswaegwan* and by establishing the *sŏnduan*, but he actually considered more far-reaching reforms. He entrusted to longtime confidant Yun Haengim the task of compiling *chuch'ŏng* (petitions to the throne) and *kyesa* (submissions to the throne), which were written by his maternal grandfather, Hong Ponghan. Yun Haengim was a man of many accomplishments who served in various posts for three generations of monarchs from Yŏngjo's reign, through the Crown Prince's brief regency, to the beginning of Chŏngjo's reign. By compiling his grandfather's papers, Chŏngjo intended to reveal the solidarity of the three administrations. The volume was completed early in the twenty-fourth year of his reign, just months before his death, under the title *Hongikchŏnggong chugo*. The book was not simply a series of related papers. Chŏngjo himself wrote an introduction and treatise for each section. Under the topic "slaves," Chŏngjo wrote of his conviction that the abolition of slavery was inevitable and declared his firm resolve to pursue abolition himself.

Chŏngjo believed that of all the injustices suffered by his people, slavery was the worst. Slaves were not only purchased and sold like livestock, but like land, slave status was passed down from generation to generation. Under the inhumane slavery system, slaves had no identity; they were not allowed to take their father's last name, much less marry. They were forced to do backbreaking labor until the day they died. Chŏngjo wondered how any fellow human being could accept the system as the status quo. The common justification was that Kija, the legendary founder of Kija Chosŏn who migrated from China at the end of the second millenium B.C., had introduced slavery, and so as an institution it was immutable. To that argument, Chŏngjo responded that the law most likely stipulated enslavement as a temporary form of punishment and not as a condition transmitted from generation to generation. He declared that the precedent of Kija would no longer be valid justification for maintaining the institution of slavery. Chŏngjo intended to abolish slavery in the following manner. For privately owned slaves, he intended to eliminate all rules and regulations regarding slavery and to replace them with new laws for employment. The relationship between slave and master would be transformed into one between employee and employer. This new obligatory relationship would apply only to the former slave; it would not carry over to the children of the ex-slave. As for losses in national revenues incurred by losing labor-remission fees collected from the freed slaves, Chŏngjo believed it would not be difficult to make up these losses through other financial sources.

Chŏngjo held many debates over whether to abolish slavery in the royal court, and because of the complexity of the arguments on both sides, he was unable to reach a quick decision. Apart from these official debates, however, Chŏngjo himself conducted detailed studies, together with "one or two followers," and came to the final decision as stated above. He wrote that just before declaring the abolition of slavery, he once again deliberated upon the social turmoil that would result from the elimination of such a deep-rooted institution. He believed the situation could be controlled by instituting new rules and regulations and that potential turmoil was not sufficient reason to perpetuate the misery of the slaves. This reasoning led him to the final conclusion that slavery had to be abolished. Chŏngjo ended his treatise by asserting that "people should be allowed to mingle with each other regardless of their status, but codes or classes should be strictly followed lest the people behave contrary to reason. Therefore, the abolition of slavery should be carried out without any reservation henceforth."

Had Chŏngjo's lofty resolution to abolish slavery been carried out according to his original intention, this might have been a shining chapter in Korean history. Unfortunately, shortly after making the resolution, Chŏngjo died from a chronic skin disease. According to royal records, Chŏngjo had contracted tumors that had destroyed his skin years before, and this disease never abated. His condition was exacerbated in early June of the twenty-forth year of his reign from overwork, and he died weeks later on the twenty-eighth day of the month, at the age of forty-nine.

After Chŏngjo's death, his supporters continued to press for the abolition of slavery. However, in the first month of the following year, the royal court entered into a turbulent period under the regency of the Queen Dowager Kim (second queen of Yŏngjo), who ruled on behalf Chŏngjo's son Sunjo. The *Shinyu saok* (The Purge of 1801) was originally a crackdown on Catholics, but ultimately many of the officials who had been cultivated by Chŏngjo became targets. In the midst of this bloody purge, a measure was adopted for the complete reform of the social class system. Under the reforms, the illegitimate offspring of concubines were finally allowed to take the civil examination for government office, and the system of official slaves was to be abolished. Based on this fact, some scholars have attributed the abolition of slavery to the regency of the Queen Dowager and the ascendent Old Doctrine faction (Noron),[9] without giving any credit to Chŏngjo's longstanding efforts for abolition.

Chŏngjo's reign laid the groundwork not only for the abolition of slavery but also for the elimination of restrictions against illegitimate offspring. All that remained was for the reforms to be implemented. In other words, Chŏngjo initiated both reforms, but they were only partially carried out by the Old Doctrine faction, which came to power after Sunjo ascended the throne. Thus, the abolition of slavery cannot be credited to the Old Doctrine faction. Chŏngjo's supporters would naturally have advocated the fundamental abolition of slavery, while the opposing faction would have adopted a more passive and limited stance. To gain hegemony, the Old Doctrine faction launched the Purge of 1801 in the name of suppressing Catholicism, but also to eradicate Chŏngjo's supporters. The new ruling faction recognized the need to adopt measures to curry popular support[10] and thus announced the freeing of official slaves and the elimination of restrictions on the illegitimate offspring of concubines, claiming that this too was the will of the late Chŏngjo. However, the measures proved to be a sham. The Old Doctrine faction excluded private slaves entirely, and among official slaves, those working in government offices were excluded. The abolition of official slaves was carried out only for slaves in the Naesusa and similar places; as a result, only 66,067 slaves were freed. Furthermore, the Old Doctrine faction restored the deficit that resulted from emancipation by dissolving the Changyongyŏng, the garrison that Chŏngjo had labored so hard to build up. The freeing of official slaves simply became another means of destroying Chŏngjo's political base.

One of the victims of the Purge of 1801 was Yun Hyaengim, who, as mentioned above, had been entrusted with the compilation of *Hongikchŏnggong chugo*. He was convicted of proselytizing Catholicism together with Hong Nak'an, the younger brother of Chŏngjo's mother, Lady Hong of the Hyegyŏng Palace, and was killed in the ninth month of that year. Yun was one of the "one or two followers" who were privy to Chŏngjo's discussions and studies regarding the abolition of slavery. His death is proof that the new ruling faction, which centered around the Queen Dowager Kim's brother (of the

---

9. Chŏn Hŏngt'aek, *Chosŏn hugi nobi sinbun yŏn'gu* (A study of the status of slaves in the late Chosŏn) (Seoul: Ilchogak, 1991), pp. 238–39.

10. Han'guk Yŏksa Yŏn'guhoe 19segi chŏngch'isa yŏn'guban, *Chosŏn chŏngch'isa 1800–1863* (The political history of Chosŏn, 1800–1863), vol. 1 (Seoul: Ch'ŏngnyŏnsa, 1990).

Kyŏngju Kim clan), was fundamentally opposed to Chŏngjo's plan for the completion abolition of slavery. The reactionary politics of the *sedo chŏngch'i* (government by royal in-law families) in the nineteenth century originated from this opposition to the total emancipation of slaves.

CONCLUSION

Korea's agrarian-based economy experienced phenomenal growth toward the end of the seventeenth century due to the introduction of new methods of rice-planting and an expansion in the commercial cultivation of crops. Commerce and industry also experienced both quantitative and qualitative development. This is evident in the burgeoning industrialization of Seoul and its outlying areas and other centers of political importance. In Seoul, peasants who left farming for the city settled in Yongsan, Map'o, Sŏgang, and other areas that had originally been storehouses for grain, turning them into thriving centers of commerce and industry. By the end of the seventeenth century, Seoul had expanded well beyond the city walls that had once defined its limits. Its population increased from one hundred thousand to over two hundred thousand, and its administrative scale and geographical size expanded as well. The end of the century marked a paradigm shift from a wholly agrarian economy to the beginnings of commercial capitalism.

These socioeconomic developments were accompanied by a sea change in politics as well. Just as socioeconomic developments were largely urban, political changes were mainly manifested in the city. Until that point, factional politics had centered on the interests of the land-owning class, but by the end of the seventeenth century it was becoming increasingly difficult for rival factions to coexist peacefully. In the interests of the monarchy and political stability, a new policy was introduced to promote impartiality among the factions, the *t'angp'yŏngch'aek*. The need for such a policy was first discussed in Sukjong's reign, and the groundwork was laid during Yŏngjo's reign. But it was not until Chŏngjo's rule that the policy took root, developing simultaneously with the propound shift in the economy.

The monarchy faced numerous challenges in the implementation of *t'angp'yŏngch'aek* policy in the eighteenth century. One challenge was the matter of dealing with officials who favored the former policy of factionalism. Another was the problem of resolving conflicts arising from a new, more diverse social structure in which the landed gentry were no longer the focus of politics. There was also the more mundane problem of unifying and systematizing bureaucracy so that officials could address issues in a way that reflected the new socioeconomic and political situation. Such complex problems could hardly be resolved without trial and error and suffering, and the monarchs of the eighteenth century did make their share of mistakes. Even though the Chosŏn monarchs absolutely supported the *t'angp'yŏngch'aek* policy, it was not fully implemented until much later.

The monarchy's efforts at reform had to take into account the role of Confucianism, the ideology that was at the very heart of Chosŏn's politics and whose influence on government administration remained strong up to that time. They had to find new interpretations of Confucian doctrines, imparting to them fresh meaning and relevance, especially since many precepts were ignored or neglected despite being widely known. Through a renewal of Confucianism, the monarchs could strengthen their legitimacy and their power base as well. If the monarch himself could embody their highest ideal of Neo-Confucianism, *sugi ch'iin* (which roughly translates to "one who could govern himself and thus govern others"), he would also embody the ideal of the *sŏnggun* (virtuous ruler). In other words, to ideally govern others (*ch'iin*), the king would have to achieve self-discipline and self-edification (*sugi*), thereby strengthening political stability. However, the kind of self-discipline or self-improvement that the *t'angp'yŏngch'aek* rulers willingly undertook to embody the ideal of *sŏnggun* contrasted sharply with the passive nature of previous rulers whose study of *sŏnghak* had been imposed on them by their subjects. In theory, the virtuous ruler who attained perfection could exercise absolute authority. There was also the practical purpose of cultivating the skills and talent necessary to tackle many challenges. It is interesting how similar the new ideal of monarchy as envisioned by Chŏngjo toward the end of the eighteenth century was to the ideal of enlightened absolute monarchy that prevailed in Europe at roughly the same time.

In sixteenth- and seventeenth-century Europe, monarchs entertained pretensions of acting as "representatives of God" and arbitrarily exercised absolute rule. By the eighteenth century, however, the concept of monarchy had changed, largely due to the influence of the Enlightenment. Rulers began to see themselves as the utmost "public servants of the people."[11] This change in philosophy emerged as rulers faced a host of new challenges in the course of resolving the inherent contradictions of feudalism. However, dismantling the legacies of feudalism did not necessary lead to the emergence of enlightened rulers. In England, France, the Netherlands, and other economically advanced nations with active citizenry, it was only through a popular revolution against the absolute monarchy that they developed into a republican form of government. Elsewhere in Europe, in nations like Prussia, where the economy was still largely agrarian and there was no citizen class, enlightened absolutism had to grapple with remnants of feudalism and a backward economy. The problems that faced the enlightened rulers of Europe were quite similar to those of Chŏngjo, especially in the way the monarchy's authority was regarded. Although there was as yet no challenge to the concept of monarchy as a hereditary right, a ruler had the responsibility to "do his best and strive to be the most perfect person in the country," in the words of Prussian King Frederick. Furthermore, a monarchy could enjoy legitimacy only to the extent that it was based on legalism or the rule of law. We can draw a parallel between Frederick and Chŏngjo as Chŏngjo, guided by the concept of *myŏngdŏk*, sought to become an enlightened and virtuous king and to create a just and humanitarian society in which all subjects were treated fairly. He also tried to reform the legal system through efforts such as the compilation of the *Taejŏn t'ongp'yŏn* (Comprehensive National Code of Laws). The striking similarity between the two contemporaneous monarchs, despite being half a world apart, is most likely due to the fact that both nations were undergoing similar socioeconomic and political changes. Even Confucian ideology called for a new kind of rule as demanded by the advent of capitalism.

Historians recognize that European enlightened absolutism, inherently unable to sustain itself, served as a bridge in the transition from feudalism to republican forms of government. However, in Korea, the Confucian ideal of enlightened absolutism and virtuous absolutism that had reached its summit under Chŏngjo collapsed with his death. Chŏngjo's vision failed to take root not because of its inherent limitations but because of the concentrated efforts of his political enemies to eradicate his legacy. Chŏngjo's lofty ideals were displaced by *sedo chŏngch'i* (government by royal in-law families). Reactionary in both form and policy, the government was unable to cope with the

11. Kim Ŏnsik, "Kyemong," op. cit.

various conflicts and contradictions arising from a changing society. It was almost preordained that under *sedo chŏngch'i*, popular discontent would foment revolts in the nineteenth century. Does this mean that the Confucian-based enlightened absolute monarchy that reached its peak in Chŏngjo's reign passed away completely with Chŏngjo? The answer is not simple. It requires further research into what positions successive monarchs took under the *sedo chŏngch'i*, how the leading intellectuals of the time conducted themselves, and how ordinary people themselves who benefited from Chŏngjo's *wimin* policy remembered Chŏngjo, who carried out an unprecedented policy for the welfare of the people.

translated by Edward Park

CHAPTER 10

# Seoul's Modern Urban Development During the Eighteenth and Nineteenth Centuries

THE TRANSFORMATION OF SEOUL, the capital of Korea during the Chosŏn dynasty (1392–1910), into a modern city is significant not only for the history of Seoul but also for the history of the nation. One well-known interpretation on this subject holds that Seoul's modern urban development began with Japan's colonization of Korea. This view first appeared in *Keijo hattatsu shi* (A History of the Development of Keijo [Seoul]), published by the Japanese Settlement Corporation in Korea in 1912, and was further elaborated in *Keijo-fu shi* (A History of Keijo Prefecture) published in 1930.

Since Korea was liberated in 1945, the history of Seoul has been the subject of numerous studies that have tried to refute the colonialist interpretation of Korean history. Although many facts about Seoul have been uncovered, there is still no interpretation of Seoul's modernization that has successfully challenged the existing ones. While these studies were initiated from a different viewpoint,[1] they did not treat the changes in Seoul after the opening of Korea's ports. Nonetheless, they are important because they have challenged the view that the modernization of Seoul was mainly thanks to Japan's efforts. On the occasion of the 600th anniversary of Seoul becoming the capital of Korea, this chapter will examine previous research on Seoul and

1. Yi Usŏng, "Sip'al segi Sŏul ŭi tosijŏk yangsang" (The urban development of Seoul in the eighteenth century), *Hyangt'o Sŏul* 17 (1963).

present a new interpretation arguing that Seoul underwent fundamental changes during the eighteenth century and at the end of the nineteenth century, which had a profound impact on the city's modernization.

In the past, studies on Seoul during the eighteenth century were undertaken in the context of the debate on the "sprouts of capitalism" in the 1960s. These studies asserted that with the internal development of capitalism, commerce developed during the eighteenth century, having an influence on the development of Seoul.

My work aims to build on the work of scholars who have advocated the "sprouts of capitalism" thesis by introducing the idea of the "general crisis of the seventeenth century." This topic has stimulated much research by modern European historians, and I will undertake a comparative analysis of Seoul and European cities during the seventeenth century to eliminate negative biases and misconceptions and produce an objective interpretation of Seoul's development.

In addition, recent research on the social and political history of the eighteenth century will enable me to examine not only the changes in Seoul's economy but also the monarchy's policies toward the capital's citizens. During that period, the kings began to meet the residents of Seoul often, regardless of their social status. I argue that such actions represented an effort to modernize the city by realizing the political ideals of Confucianism, though more research on this topic will be necessary in the future.

In analyzing changes in Seoul during the late-nineteenth century, I will focus on city-improvement projects carried out before the Russo-Japanese War (1904–1905). These projects were based on the notion of *tongdo sŏgi* (literally, "Eastern Ways, Western Technology"), the theory of modernization of the Great Han Empire (Taehan Cheguk), which advocated the introduction of Western technology while preserving the country's traditional beliefs and systems of thought. The view that Japanese colonial rule was responsible for Seoul's modernization has completely ignored the developments of this period. I argue that the Japanese simply claimed responsibility for carrying out urban-development projects which had actually been completed prior to colonization. Japanese propaganda praised their administrative and political achievements to conceal and rationalize their forceful seizure of Korea's sovereignty.

The primary objective of this study is to demonstrate that Seoul's urban development was based on the Great Han Empire's ideology of "Eastern Ways, Western Technology," the desire to acquire the benefits of modern Western civilization and to maintain the relative prosperity achieved during the eighteenth century. Furthermore, the promotion of close interaction between the king and the citizens in the eighteenth century had a significant impact on the development of commerce at the end of the nineteenth century and also on the modernization of Seoul.

## OVERCOMING THE "GENERAL CRISIS OF THE SEVENTEENTH CENTURY" AND THE NEW IMPETUS FOR THE DEVELOPMENT OF COMMERCE

The capital of the Chosŏn, then called Hansŏng, was established in the early fifteenth century, and it was originally a fortress city encompassing approximately seventeen kilometers. It held approximately 20,000 households, with a total population of about 100,000. Though thousands more people lived within a ten-*ri* (four km) radius of the fortress, there were no drastic changes in population during the sixteenth century. After the Hideyoshi Invasions began in 1592, the population drastically fell, dropping to 39,931 (see Table 1). However, the population quickly recovered to its former level, increasing to 95,569 by 1648 and decreasing slightly to 80,572 in 1657.

The recovery in population levels was surprisingly rapid considering that the Hideyoshi Invasions lasted for seven years and the Jurchens invaded twice in 1627 and 1636. Even more remarkable was the dramatic increase in population that was recorded in the 1669 census, reaching 23,899 households and 194,030 people.

The population in 1428, toward the beginning of the Chosŏn dynasty, was 18,522 households and 109,372 people; thus, the 1669 census recorded an increase of 5,377 households and 84,658 people. The population more than doubled since the national census in 1657. What were the causes behind such a drastic increase?

In my previous work, I have introduced the idea of the "General Crisis of the Seventeenth Century" and argued that the population increase was the result of a starving population migrating from farmlands to the city in order to receive the benefits of the government's emergency-relief policies.[2] Similar migrations took place in major cities in Europe during the same period and under similar conditions, and it would thus be interesting to compare the situation

---

2. Yi Tae-jin, "Chosŏn sidae Sŏul ŭi tosi paldal tan'gye" (The stages of Seoul's development during the Chosŏn period), *Sŏulhak yŏn'gu* 1 (1994).

of Seoul with that of European cities. The rapid population increase in Seoul paralleled the huge increases recorded in Madrid (55,000 people in 1497 to 140,000 in 1646) and in London (25,000 around 1500 to 575,000 around 1700).[3]

Recent studies on the general crisis of the seventeenth century in the West maintain that a phenomenon known as the "Little Ice Age" occurred because of global meteorite collisions. It resulted in continued, unusual climactic conditions and natural disasters such as earthquakes, tidal waves, hurricanes, hail, unseasonal snowstorms, floods, and droughts, which led to a severe drop in agricultural production. There were frequent famines and epidemics that caused a well-documented population reduction, and the starving population flocked to the cities in search of food. Because of such unrest and social instability, structural and political conflicts escalated between different regions of Europe and led to widespread revolts, revolution, and war.

Since the primary cause of the general crisis was a natural phenomena related to global meteor fallings, the "Little Ice Age" must have been a global phenomenon. The "Little Ice Age" must be taken into account to achieve a complete understanding of Korean history in the seventeenth century. The effect of the "Little Ice Age" is demonstrated by the southward movement of the Jurchens from the colder northern regions, leading to a dynastic change from the Ming to the Qing. It is clear that the drastic increase in the population of Seoul in 1669 was the result of a massive migration of starving people due to the "crisis of the seventeenth century." This migration was different from the simple influx of people that occurred in Europe. With the continual occurrence of natural disasters, the Chosŏn dynasty enacted special emergency measures, and the uprooted population from the farmlands converged on the cities to get access to the benefits of these measures.

In 1612 (4th year of Kwanghaegun, the fifteenth king of the Chosŏn period), the dynasty established a special agency called the Chinhyulch'ŏng (Office of Relief Works), which was responsible for managing relief projects and in charge of economic agencies such as the Hojo (Ministry of Taxation), Sŏnhyech'ŏng (Agency to Bestow Blessings, in charge of collecting the Uniform Land Tax), and

---

3. Geoffrey Parker, "Introduction," *The General Crisis of the Seventeenth Century*, G. Parker and Lesley M. Smith, eds. (London: Routledge & Kegan Paul, 1978), p. 10.

Sangp'yŏngch'ang (Ever-Normal Storehouses, an office to regulate the prices of goods). The main functions of the Chinhyulch'ŏng were to provide free food to starving people and to set up a labor system in which workers would be paid in food. The latter proved to be a much more important part of the office's activities. The corvée labor system, which had been used to procure the labor needed for large public projects such as building royal tombs or governmental offices, was converted to a subcontracting-wage system in which labor was paid by food.

While the establishment of the Chinhyulch'ŏng did cause a fundamental change in the administrative policies of the country, it was also an unavoidable measure taken to save the country's starving masses. To carry out its functions, it was necessary for government offices to procure a sufficient amount of rice to distribute as wages. From the beginning of the dynasty, grain was collected for storage in the Kunjach'ang, P'ungjŏch'ang, and Kwanghŭngch'ang granaries in the Yongsan-gang and Sŏgang areas along the Han River in Seoul. All three of these granaries were under the administration of the Hojo. Only the Kunjach'ang granary was designated for emergency use; the other two had separate functions, making it difficult to implement relief measures. To procure more revenue, the government replaced the tribute and corvée labor taxes with a land tax. This new taxation system had been proposed several times in the past but could not be implemented because of strong opposition; however, the "crisis of the seventeenth century" made its implementation look relatively desirable.

The Taedongbŏp (Uniform Tax Law) was gradually implemented in regions where it was the most feasible; it took more than half a century to be implemented in all eight provinces. The *taedongmi*, rice collected under the Taedongbŏp, was managed by the Sŏnhyech'ŏng, and its storage facilities were built around the Yongsan-gang area. Since coordination between various government agencies was necessary to implement these new policies, the Chinhyulch'ŏng was designed to work in coordination with the Hojo and the Sŏnhyech'ŏng. To maximize the utilization of the stored grain that was procured for relief measures, the cooperation of the Sangp'yŏngch'ang was also necessary since it controlled the regional price differences of rice and cloth.

The large increase in the number of households in the 1669 census is evidence of the effective implementation of the Chinhyulch'ŏng system. There was little reason to oppose the system since it provided food and ended the tribute and corvée-labor taxes. In the 1660s, the corvée-labor system was systematically abolished after its use was discontinued for the maintenance of royal mausoleums. As a symbolic gesture, even corvée labor for state funerals was changed to the subcontracting-wage system.[4]

The 1669 census calculated the population by counting individuals, not households, since taxation was assessed on individuals. Of the 194,030 residents of Seoul, since around 100,000 resided within the fortress, the remaining 94,000 must have lived outside. According to the 1789 census of Hansŏng-bu (Seoul prefecture), whose figures are more accurate for households since taxation at the time was assessed on a household basis, 22,094 households with 112,371 people lived inside the fortress, while 21,835 households totaling 76,782 people lived outside. These figures make it evident that the increased population of Seoul after 1669 mainly resided outside the city walls. The census of 1789 clearly showed that among the areas outside the fortress, people were concentrated in riverside areas and areas in or near the government's granaries: Tumo-bang, Han'gang-bang, and Tunji-bang in the south (total of 9,218 people) and Pansŏk-bang, Pansong-bang, Yongsan-bang, and Sŏgang-bang in the west (48,007 people) (see Table 2).

The Chosŏn government enacted policies to convert the corvée-labor system into a subcontracting-wage system and to change the tribute-tax system for procuring goods needed by the government into a system of purchase. Their purpose was to overcome the "crisis of the seventeenth century," and they served as the basis for the development of the economy not just of Seoul but also of the whole country. As unusual climatic conditions and natural disasters subsided somewhat in the late-seventeenth century, the newly implemented relief policies began to act as a catalyst for economic development. At the beginning of the eighteenth century, commercial development occurred primarily around the riverside areas of Seoul along the Han River, where emergency relief measures were carried out.[5]

---

4. The discussion of the change from the corvée labor system to the subcontracting wage system is largely based on Yun Yongch'ul, "17-18 segi yoyŏkje ŭi pyŏndong kwa morije" (The change of the corvée system into the subcontracting-wage system during the seventeenth and eighteenth centuries) (Ph.D diss., Seoul National University, 1991).

5. The discussion of the commercial development of areas of Seoul along the Han River is largely taken from Ko Tonghwan, "18-19 segi Sŏul kyŏnggang chiyŏk ŭi sang'ŏp paldal" (The commercial development of Seoul's riverside areas

Originally, the "capital river" (Kyŏnggang) region centered on the three rivers of Yongsan River, Sŏ River, and Hangangjin (now Hannam-dong). New residents first settled in these areas, and in the early eighteenth century, they officially became *pang* (neighborhood, district) of Hansŏng-bu. In the latter half of the eighteenth century, downstream regions such as Mangwŏn and Hapjŏng and areas outside of Tongdaemun also became incorporated into Seoul as *pang*. With the expansion of administrative districts, the name for the capital river region also changed from *ogang*, to *p'algang*, and to *sip'igang* (Hangang, Tumop'o, Ttuksŏm, Wangsimni, Anam, Chŏnnong, Sŏbinggo, Yongsan, Map'o, Sŏgang, Mangwŏnjŏng, and Yŏnsŏ).

As time passed, ports with active commerce increased in number. Originally, the capital river region was mainly for fishing and the collection of tax grain, but in the mid-eighteenth century, the ports thrived as each specialized in a particular business or a few businesses. For instance, Ttuksŏm specialized in the buying and selling of wood products; Sŏgang and Yongsan, in the collection of grain tax; Map'o, in the circulation of goods; Yŏŭi Island and Pam Island, in the cultivation of commercial agricultural crops, fishing, and shipbuilding. Commerce developed in the capital river region through the activities of private merchants (*sasang*). This commercial development had the potential of undermining the circulation system centered on the merchants (*sijŏn sang'in*) in the capital who had received a monopoly from the court and the government since the beginning of the dynasty.

## THE RELATIONSHIP BETWEEN THE KING AND THE RESIDENTS OF THE WALLED CITY DURING THE EIGHTEENTH CENTURY

As the "crisis of the seventeenth century" diminished, the capital of Chosŏn underwent a transformation as the riverside regions outside the fortress became developed. This change was reflected in a popular phrase of the time, "People in Seoul live on money, and the people in the eight provinces live on grain." Accompanying these changes, there was a great increase in maps of Seoul as well. Until that time, there were no individual maps of Seoul, and information on Seoul could be found in the sections in the national topographies on the capital or

along the Han River during the eighteenth and nineteenth centuries) (Ph.D. diss., Seoul National University, 1993).

Hansŏng-bu. As Seoul diversified and expanded in size, these traditional methods of providing information proved to be inadequate.

The most notable of the new maps was an individual map of the Seoul area. Until that time, the most detailed map of Seoul was the *Tosŏng samgunmun pun'gyejido* (map of three army garrisons assigned to defensive districts of the capital wall), which was made during the mid-eighteenth century during King Yŏngjo's reign. The map showed how Seoul was divided into three walled regions, each of which had a military garrison that was responsible for the region's supervision and defense. It was the result of Yŏngjo's new policies on the administration of the city's fortress.

Many other kinds of maps appeared as well. There were maps that depicted revised administrative districts, maps that showed the arrays of houses both inside and outside the fortress, and maps that depicted the ports that had been built along the Han River. Although each map had a different purpose, they all included the beautiful rivers and mountains surrounding Seoul.

According to *Sŏngshi chŏndo shi*, a poem about life within the walled city, written by late-eighteenth-century scholar Pak Chega (1750–1815), the King ordered the construction of a folding screen on which 40,000 houses both inside and outside of the city were painted in detail. Although a copy of that map does not exist today, the appearance of Seoul at the time can be deduced from the poem. There were also many others who composed poems about the capital city.

The painter Chŏng Sŏn (1676–1759) was famous for his realistic landscape style, and his numerous paintings of the surrounding mountains and rivers of Seoul are well known for their depictions of Seoul. Around the same time, the *Hanyangga* (Song of Seoul) was written in 1844 (10th year of King Hŏnjong's reign), and the *Han'gyŏng chiryak* (Summary of Records on Seoul), published during the early nineteenth century, is thought to be the first book published on Seoul's topography.

As life in Seoul became more and more complex, problems in city-planning began to arise that led to a discussion on how to use its space. In his famous work *Pukhak'ŭi* (Discourse on Northern Learning), Pak Chega wrote a section on city streets and made many suggestions on how to solve problems in Seoul.

First, he agreed with the following proposal by Ch'ae Chegong (1720–1799). Since the northern part of Chonggak had much traffic because of the proximity of Unjong Street, the center of commerce in Seoul, the street in that part of Chonggak should be widened to the same width as Unjong Street. He also suggested that stores be required to post a visible house number, with signs specifying the goods that were being sold. Countless flimsy and makeshift stores cluttered the main street, and he urged that this problem needed to be addressed in order to enable transport of goods and the city's development, even if it required the exercise of legal authority to do so. He even proposed that the contamination of the city's streets with ashes and human feces be dealt with, by using such waste as agricultural fertilizer. Ch'ae Chegong is well known as a scholar who advocated mercantilist ideas, and many city improvements were implemented during King Chŏngjo's reign, such as the rearrangement of stores, widening of streets, and paving of roads between Kanghwa and Suwŏn—almost as if the government were listening to his proposals.

The most important development in Seoul during the eighteenth century was probably the king's meetings with its residents. The king frequently left the palace and met with ordinary citizens on market streets or outside the palace walls to ask ordinary citizens about their lives and hardships. Before Yŏngjo's reign, these royal visits usually occurred only once every few years. It was only after the mid-eighteenth century that these trips became frequent. Furthermore, during this period, such trips came to be considered an important duty of the king.

In 1750 (26th year of his reign), Yŏngjo used skillful political maneuvering to end a decades-long debate on corruption in the *yangyŏk* (*kunyŏk*; military service) system. When several ministers refused to follow his opinion, Yŏngjo went to Honghwamun, the main gate of Ch'anggyŏng Palace, and gathered the *pangmin* (commoners) of Seoul to listen to their opinions. He then returned to the palace and ended the debate by telling the ministers who opposed him that what the people wanted was the same as what he was proposing.[6]

Afterward, Yŏngjo visited Chongmyo (Royal Shrine), secondary palaces, and shrines inside Seoul. On the road and in front of palace and city gates, he met various classes of the city's residence, including *kongin* (tribute merchants), *simin* (*sijŏn sang'in*; licensed merchants) *pangmin*, peasants, and Confucian scholars. After asking about their problems, he would order the relevant office to address whatever needed to be rectified. Over the course of twenty-five years, he made fifty such trips, establishing a new custom.

6. Ja Hyun Kim Haboush, *A Heritage of Kings* (New York: Columbia University Press, 1988).

Succeeding his grandfather Yŏngjo, King Chŏngjo (r. 1776–1800) expanded the practice that his predecessor had started. Just like his grandfather, Chŏngjo met with citizens within the walls of Seoul; however, he also established a new practice of visiting the tombs of past kings and queens, making trips outside of Seoul. Before Chŏngjo, there were kings who paid their respects at the royal tombs, but such visits were made only once or twice every several years. By contrast, Chŏngjo visited every royal tomb during his reign and made multiple trips to the tombs of his predecessors going back five generations.

Not only were the royal tombs located not only in villages north of the Han River such as Yangju, Koyang, and P'aju, but there were also four in areas south of the Han River in Kwangju (Sŏnnŭng and Chŏngnŭng) and Yŏju (Yŏngnŭng [Sejong] and Yŏngnŭng [Hyojong]). Since he visited Kwangju and Yŏju only one time each, his royal processions went mainly to areas north of the Han River. After Chŏngjo moved the tomb of his father to Suwŏn in the thirteenth year of his reign (1789), his trips south of the Han River became more frequent, reducing the geographical disparity.

Around the same time, Chŏngjo had the new city of Hwasŏng (now Suwŏn) constructed near his father's new tomb site. A royal villa was built in Hwasŏng, and he visited once a year to pay his respects at his father's tomb. The royal visits now extended one hundred *ri* (approximately forty kilometers) south of the Han River. Up to this time, the main difficulty in making royal visits south of the Han River was the difficulty in crossing the river. To facilitate visits to Hwasŏng, Chŏngjo established the Chugyosa (Bureau of Boat Bridges). Merchants in the Han River area were required to register their large boats with the new bureau, and in return to granting them the rights to transport a portion of the tax grain, they had to create boat bridges for crossings of royal processions. During his reign, Chŏngjo made sixty-eight visits just to the royal tombs. Adding his trips outside the palace within Seoul brings the total to over 110. He started these trips in the third year of his reign, averaging more than five visits per year.

Chŏngjo's successors continued these trips to the royal tombs. According to the dynasty's official records, his successors made the following number of trips: Sunjo, forty-seven times during his thirty-four-year reign; Hŏnjong, twenty-one times in thirteen years; and

Ch'ŏljong, twenty-nine times in fourteen years.[7] After King Sunjo, the reasons for the trips to the royal tombs changed. Although the visits continued, petitions were either not made or not heard, and the system was virtually discontinued. During Sunjo's reign, there were twenty-four cases recorded;[8] however, most of the petitioners were the offspring of well-known *sadaebu* (high-ranking government officials). In existing records, there are petitions made by the children of well-respected government officials such as Ch'ae Chegong, Chŏng Yagyong (1762–1836), and Yi Sŏgu (1754–1825). The motivation for all the petitions was to exculpate ancestors who had suffered some form of political injustice. Their ancestors belonged to a political faction loyal to Chŏngjo, who were later purged in the early years of Sunjo's reign. The king was the only person they could turn to for their ancestors' exculpation.

From Sunjo's reign, there is no evidence of petitions made by people of low social status, only by the descendants of *sadaebu*; and during the reigns of Hŏnjong and Ch'ŏljong, there were not even any petitions by descendants of *sadaebu*. Royal tomb visits became merely a ceremony that the king performed to worship the royal ancestors, especially ancestors going back five generations.

Since in-laws of the royal family occupied important positions in the Border Defense Council (Pibyŏnsa) and controlled the government bureaucracy, the king's role in politics declined. Consequently, his contact with the people was hindered, and the result was political chaos. In-law families that exploited and oppressed the people began to face resistance in various regions beginning in the late 1830s. The disorder of rule by in-law families and resistance to it began to decrease gradually with the Taewŏngun's attempts to restore the traditional order of the Chosŏn dynasty.

---

7. If these figures are recalculated based on the number of visits to individual tomb sites, the results are eighty-seven, thirty-seven, and fifty-five visits, respectively. Thus, sometimes several tomb sites were visited on a single trip.

8. These statistics were gathered from the *Sunjo sillok* (The Veritable Records of King Sunjo).

## THE CITY PLAZA AND URBAN-DEVELOPMENT PROJECTS IN THE LATE-NINETEENTH CENTURY

After the "Treaty of Amity and Commerce between the United States and Corea" was signed in 1882, Westerners visited Korea more frequently and began to write many books about the country as well. The descriptions of Seoul in these books varied considerably according to when the visits were made. Everyone who visited Seoul before autumn 1896 noted that the city was filthy with narrow streets. On the other hand, those who visited Seoul after autumn 1896 had only praise for the city. Isabella Bird Bishop, who visited Korea as a member of the British Royal Geographic Society in February 1894, January and October 1895, and October 1896 wrote the following about her last visit to Seoul in her well-known book *Korea and Her Neighbors*:

> Seoul, in many parts, especially in the direction of the south and west gates, was literally not recognizable. Streets, with a minimum width of 55 feet, with deep stone-lined channels on both sides, bridged by stone slabs, had replaced the foul alleys, which were breeding-grounds of cholera. Narrow lanes had been widened, slimy runlets had been paved, roadways were no longer "free coups" for refuse, bicyclists "scorched" along broad, level streets, "express wagons" were looming in the near future, preparations were being made for the building of a French hotel in a fine situation, shops with glass fronts had been erected in numbers, an order forbidding the throwing of refuse into the streets was enforced—refuse matter is now removed from the city by official scavengers, and Seoul, from having been the foulest is now on its way to being the cleanest city of the Far East![9]

Ever since her first visit to Korea, Mrs. Bishop had a special affection for and attachment to the country. She visited not only Seoul but also various regions in the countryside, recording her impressions about the lives of the Korean people. In her writings, she had always expressed her discontent with the filthiness of Seoul. However, in her last visit, she was immensely surprised by the changes in the city. How did these changes occur?

---

9 . Isabella L. Bird, *Korea and Her Neighbours* (Rutland, Vermont, and Tokyo, Japan: Charles E. Tuttle Company, Inc., 1986), pp. 265–66.

Mrs. Bishop credited the changes to two people: McLeavy Brown, the British standing advisor to the T'akjibu (Ministry of Finance) and head of the Revenue Office, and Yi Ch'aeyŏn, the mayor of Seoul (Hansŏng-bu). Yi Ch'aeyŏn had accompanied the first Korean Ambassador to the United States, Pak Chŏngyang, to Washington, D.C., and served as mayor of Seoul from October 1896 to November 4, 1898. Brown had worked for Korea for many years since 1892, serving as tax accountant of the Chosŏn Maritime Customs Office (November 1892–November 1905) and as standing advisor to the T'akjibu (October 1893–November 1897 and March 1898–November 1905). Mrs. Bishop wrote about their accomplishments as follows:

> This extraordinary metamorphosis was the work of four months, and is due to the energy and capacity of the Chief Commissioner of Customs, ably seconded by the capable and intelligent Governor of the city, Ye Cha Yun [Yi Ch'aeyŏn], who had acquainted himself with the working of municipal affairs in Washington, and who with a rare modesty refused to take any credit to himself for the city improvements, saying that it was all due to Mr. McLeavy Brown.

There is no doubt that these two men played a key role in changing Seoul's appearance in the autumn of 1896. However, while these men were in charge of the administrative matters, they did not have the power to make policy decisions. Matters of great importance, such as urban improvements in the capital, were decided by the King or, at least, required his permission. However, research on this period has given all the credit for modernizing projects to the reformists or the Independence Club (Tongnip hyŏphoe), as if the king had nothing to do with them. The main reason is that Kojong has been regarded as a ruler who did not possess the determination or will to modernize the country. The decisions Kojong made in 1896 on urban-improvement projects clearly demonstrate that he had both determination and will from the very beginning.

On February 11, 1896, the King, along with the Crown Prince, moved from Kyŏngbok Palace to the Russian legation in Taejŏng-dong.[10] The King resided there while the Crown Prince and Princess stayed in Kyŏng'un Palace, which was next to the legation. In Korea,

---

10. Kojong sillok (The Veritable Records of King Kojong), vol. 34 (Seoul: The National History Compilation Committee, 1970).

this incident is known as the Agwan P'ach'ŏn (literally, "the King's flight to the Russian legation"). Many scholars have viewed this event negatively since Kojong's sudden decision to move to the Russian legation appeared as if he was too reliant on the foreign powers. Such a position was unacceptable for a king, and it was regarded as an act that would bring the country to ruin. However, this interpretation differs from the one contained in the *Kojong sillok* (Veritable Records of King Kojong).[11] The official record did not use the term *p'ach'ŏn* ("flight from the royal palace"), and it noted that even after moving to the Russian legation, the King made visits outside the legation and even frequented Kyŏng'un and Kyŏngbok Palaces. The King and Crown Prince visited Kyŏngbok Palace often because it contained the shrine of Queen Min, who had been assassinated by the Japanese a few months earlier. The King's decision to move to the Russian legation was an act of resistance against Japan, which was already planning to annex the country. Soon after its victory in the Sino-Japanese War, Japan had already killed the Queen and turned the King into a figurehead. This strategy was successful in giving Chosŏn some breathing room to establish itself as an independent nation.

After the Sino-Japanese War, Japan was already considering turning Chosŏn into a protectorate and was scheming to undermine the authority of the throne. Their greatest obstacle was Queen Min and the people loyal to her; to eliminate her influence, Japan had her assassinated on August 23, 1895. The King could not overlook such an incident and tried to find a way to punish those who were involved in the assassination. This was the reason that he decided to move to the Russian legation. Of course, the decision was made with the prior agreement of the Russian legation. As intended, this bold move completely reversed the political situation. On the day the King left the palace, Yi Chaemyŏn, the Minister of the Royal Household, submitted his resignation, taking responsibility for the incident. All government ministers, including pro-Japanese officials, were then obliged to follow and submit their resignations as well. The King accepted the resignation of all officials including, Kim Hongjip (1842–1896), the prime minister, and reorganized the cabinet. The next day, Kim Hongjip and Chŏng Pyŏngha (?–1896), the Minister of Agriculture, Trade, and Industry, were assassinated. In a decree, the King declared that the two officials who were assassinated were deeply

---

11. This description of events was drawn from the relevant records of the *Kojong sillok*.

involved in the murder of the Queen and that their death was a punishment sent from heaven. The King added that the two officials had disobeyed the King by hiding the assassination of the Queen from the public for over three months and had even falsely announced at the time that the King had deposed the Queen.[12] The King's move to the Russian legation panicked the Japanese government, which was already being pressured by the international community because of the assassination of Queen Min,[13] leading them to change their ambassador to Korea. Though there were difficulties, the move to the Russian legation was beneficial to the King, whose government was in peril. Kojong began to use the reversal in the political situation as an opportunity to establish a foundation to turn Korea into an independent state.

Kojong returned to Kyŏng'un Palace on February 20, 1897, after residing at the Russian legation for a year. During that year, Kojong attempted many state reforms, but his most significant effort was the decision on September 24, 1897, to adopt the Ŭijŏngbu (State Council) cabinet system with the King as an executive with decision-making powers. Then it was announced that the King, who controlled the affairs of state, had decided to form a new government. The new government was organized with the King as its head, who would participate in all decisions and oversee state affairs.

The new political system established by the King needed to construct a suitable palace and capital city. Before his decision to restore the Ŭijŏngbu system, the King ordered the transfer of the court from Kyŏngbok to Kyŏng'un Palace (now known as Tŏksu Palace) on September 4 with the intention of using it as the main palace. The shrine of Queen Min was also moved to Kyŏng'un Palace. One of the reasons for the King's delay in leaving the Russian legation was the time it took for construction work at the palace. Construction continued even after the King began residing at the palace.[14]

12. The unprecedented regicide of Queen Min by the Japanese mob of August 22, 1895 (by the lunar calendar), had been actually covered up for nearly three months until King Kojong presented evidence of the murder on October 15. *Kojong sillok*, vol. 33, Oct. 15, 1895.
13. Japanese Minister Komura Jutaro left Seoul on May 29, and the new Minister Harakei began his post on July 16.
14. According to the Kojong sillok, the total cost of construction of Kyŏngun Palace, proposed by the State Council and paid for by the King, was 463,122 wŏn. The dates of the propositions were December 6, 1896; June 4, July 15, September 14, September 29, and November 1, 1897; and February 9 and November 2, 1899.

On August 4, 1896, just before construction work on Kyŏng'un Palace began, the local government system was also reorganized. In the Kabo Reforms of 1894, the country had been divided into twenty-three *pu/bu* (prefectures or districts), but now the former division into thirteen *do* (provinces) was restored. However, Hansŏng-bu (Seoul), the seat of the national government, remained a separate administrative unit, as it had been in the past. The pro-Japanese Kabo cabinet had implemented a Japanese-style system of local government, eliminating the administrative distinction between Hansŏng-bu, the capital, and *bu* in the provinces. This reform had lowered the status of the capital, and the reorganization of local administration was intended to rectify this situation.

The restructuring of the government facilitated efforts to turn Hansŏng-bu into a capital befitting the new monarchical system. Chinjŏn, the hall where the portraits of the current monarch were kept, was moved from Kyŏngbok to Kyŏng'un Palace. Immediately afterward, on September 28, the Home Ministry promulgated Order No. 9 (Naeburyŏng che 9 ho), announcing plans for the redevelopment of Hansŏng-bu. It ordered the removal of all houses that jutted into the main roads from Hwangt'ohyŏn hill to Hŭnginjimun (East Gate) and from Taegwangt'on Bridge to Sungnyemun (South Gate). The purpose was to broaden the roads from their original width of fifty *cha* (about 50 feet) to seventy-to-eighty *cha*. This government order brought about the transformation of Hansŏng-bu that surprised Isabella Bird Bishop.

The government restructuring that the King carried out in 1896 during his stay at the Russian Legation clearly shows that the urban improvement projects for Seoul were part of the King's plan to reform the entire nation. The King also had a plan to reorganize national finances in order to provide the money needed for the rebuilding of the capital and the palaces. The King entrusted this task to McLeavy Brown, who was the standing advisor to the Ministry of Finance and head of the Revenue Office. On July 12, 1896, the King ordered strict supervision of all budgetary expenses from the Ministry of Finance by pertinent officials and that all matters had to receive prior approval from Brown. The King was aware that the corruption and irregularities within the government were undermining the state's finances. This was the reason that this important task was entrusted to Brown, who had not only experience in such affairs but also the trust of the King.

The King appointed Yi Ch'aeyŏn as mayor of Seoul on October 6 of the same year.[15] The King himself was in charge of the redevelopment of Seoul; through the appointment of these two officials, he controlled both the administrative and financial aspects of the project.

What were the basic ideas behind the redevelopment of Hansŏng-bu as planned by the King? The Home Ministry Order, mentioned above, only concerned the widening of the two main roads, and it is difficult to discern what the overall plan was through that order alone. In her book, Isabella Bird Bishop mentioned that the streets leading to Sŏdaemun (West Gate) were also transformed almost beyond recognition. It is evident that the redevelopment of Seoul was not limited to the widening of the two main roads.

Kim Kwang'u, an expert on city planning, has done an important study on this topic.[16] Based on a map of Seoul made by the Japanese in 1903, he concluded that the redevelopment plan for Seoul sought to make Kyŏng'un Palace the center of the city with radial roads extending from it and with a circuit road connecting the radial roads with outside feeder roads (see Map 1). He pointed out that this plan was fundamentally different from the draft plans of the Japanese Resident-General in Korea (1905–1910).[17] In those draft plans, the central district of Seoul was located just north of the Resident-General's office, which was located at the foot of Namsan (South Mountain). It was also different from the city plan announced by the Japanese Government-General in 1919 that proposed, among other things, the construction of a road starting in front of Kyŏngbok Palace, passing through Namdaemun (South Gate), and leading to the new municipal district in Yongsan.[18]

Kim Kwang'u's conclusions correspond almost perfectly with the way the palace was actually constructed as envisioned by Kojong as well as with his plans for the restoration of royal roads, which was carried out at the same time. Because Kim Kwang'u is not a historian,

15. Yi Ch'aeyŏn was appointed to the post of mayor of Seoul after being placed in charge of supervising the construction of the Seoul-Inch'ŏn railroad as an official of the Ministry of Agriculture and Commerce.
16. Kim Kwang'u, "Taehan Cheguk sidae ŭi tosi kyehoek—Hansŏng-bu ŭi tosi kaejo saŏp" (Urban improvements in the Great Han Empire—the reconstruction of Seoul), *Hyangt'o Sŏul* 50 (1990).
17. "Kyŏngsŏng sigu kaesu yejŏng kyehoek nosŏndo," *Chosen sotokufu kanpo* (Gazette of the Chosŏn Government-General), November 6, 1912, quoted in Kim Kwang'u, p. 118.
18. "Kyŏngsŏng sigu kaesu yejŏng kyehoek nosŏndo," *Chosen sotokufu kanpo*, June 25, 1919, quoted in Kim Kwang'u, p. 119.

he mistakenly gave the credit for the plan to the reformists and the Independence Club. Despite this understandable error, Kim Kwang'u deserves credit for his detailed analysis and understanding of urban structure, which was the objective of his study.

Up to now, scholars have had a negative view of Kojong's decision to use Kyŏng'un Palace as his main palace. Just as the Agwan P'ach'ŏn was viewed negatively because the King had escaped to a foreign legation and appeared to rely too much on foreign powers, the decision to move the court to Kyŏng'un Palace was also viewed disapprovingly. However, this is a superficial judgment that ignores the true nature of this decision. It is true that foreign missions or legations can provide shelter or support in times of crisis. However, this was not the King's purpose in moving his court to Kyŏng'un Palace. Kojong was also planning on strengthening the military troops that would guard the palace. A training facility for military officers was built at Kyŏnghŭi Palace, which was located at the very rear section of Kyŏng'un Palace, and lodgings for palace guards were built in front of the eastern P'odŏkmun gate of Kyŏng'un Palace.[19] Furthermore, on June 29, 1898, Emperor Kojong restructured the government so that the Emperor was the supreme commander of the armed forces, including the army and navy, with the crown prince as his chief commander. The Chief Commander's Headquarters were built next to the Kungnaebu (Ministry of the Royal Household) located on the main road toward the east right in front of Taean Gate (Taeanmun) of Kyŏng'un Palace. When the Great Han Empire was proclaimed in October 1897, Emperor Kojong managed state affairs through these two agencies. The Wŏn'gudan, the symbolic place where the ceremony declaring the Great Han Empire was held, stood behind these two buildings.

From the very beginning of the expansion of Kyŏng'un Palace, Kojong was planning various measures to strengthen the self-defense forces as well as to enhance the dignity of his empire. Significantly, Kojong held the funeral for the assassinated queen only after all these policies were enacted. It was highly unusual to hold the state funeral two years and a month after the queen's death was announced. Kojong elevated the status of his queen to that of an empress and held

---

19. The official records from the *Kojong sillok* show that on July 15, 1897, a requisition order was made for the construction and repair costs for these billeting facilities as part of the palace's overall expenditures.

a funeral befitting her new status; he also used this opportunity as a turning point to reconstruct the Empire.

Through his move to the Russian legation, Kojong carried out sweeping reforms to build an independent, self-reliant nation. Such efforts were accelerated with the founding of the Great Han Empire. Until now, historians have generally regarded the Great Han Empire as conservative; however, this view needs to be reexamined.

The Kwangmu (1897–1907) Reforms, personally led by the Emperor, were rooted in the notion of *tongdo sŏgi* (Eastern Ways, Western Technology). The emphasis on "Eastern Ways" was intended to promote national pride in the country's traditions and to preserve national independence. Kojong repeatedly made clear his willingness to accommodate the progressive reforms demanded by the Independence Club and the Manmin Kongdonghoe (mass assemblies).[20] Because he gave top priority to building an independent nation, he promulgated a royal edict, calling for a military-conscription system on March 15, 1903, the year before the outbreak of the Sino-Japanese War.

Emperor Kojong noted that the weakening of the military was caused by the collapse of the "one farmer–one soldier" system and that there was a similarity between the conscription system in the West and the country's traditional Five Military Commands (Okun'yŏng) system. He instructed his ministers to make sweeping reforms of the military by combining the best of both systems and urged all Koreans to devote their energy, hopes, and patriotism to that end.[21] Out of a total annual expenditure of 9,697,000 wŏn in 1903, 4,123,000 wŏn went toward military spending,[22] demonstrating how important military reform was to the empire. By 1903, the monarchy had increased the size of the guards to 12,000 men and constructed a gun-manufacturing factory in Yongsan.[23] It was not the incompetence

20. The term literally means "convocation of ten thousand people."
21. "Choch'ik pŏmnyul" (Royal Edicts and Laws), Kŭmho Series kŭndae pŏpryŏng p'yŏn (Kyujanggak charyo ch'ongsŏ) (Seoul: Hau kihoek ch'ulp'an, 1991), pp. 314–15.
22. *Nihon gaiko bunsho* (Documents of Japanese Diplomacy), vol. 37, no. 1 (Tokyo: The Ministry of Foreign Affairs of Japan, 1958), p. 353.
23. There were imperial and governmental bureaus, factories, and plants such as the Mint Bureau (1898), the Printing Bureau (1900), the Measuring Instruments Factory (1902), the Silk Thread and Fabric Factory (1902), the Power Plant Station of the Hansŏng Electric Co. (1903), the Rice Mill of the Ministry of the Royal Household (1903), the Small Fire Arms Factory of the Military Authorities (1903), the Brick Factory, and the Glass Factory in the

of the Great Han Empire, but the apparent progress in Korea's modernization that made Japan worry that it was losing its opportunity to annex the country.

In the spring of 1898, a few months after Chosŏn became the Great Han Empire, new Western inventions such as the telegraph, the telephone, electricity, and streetcars began to appear in the streets of Seoul. The Emperor advocated the "Eastern Ways, Western Technology" program by actively accepting Western civilization in an effort to build a foundation for the country's modernization. Genthe, a reporter from Cologne, Germany, visited Seoul in 1901 and noted the city's changing appearance:

> Among all the Asian capitals, Seoul, which is the residence of the so-called Emperor of the Great Han Empire, has nowadays perhaps the strangest outlook. It is strange because it is so different from what one would expect from the capital of an Asian sovereign, and on the other hand, because it shows such harsh contrasts between old and new barbaric Asiatic primitive states and Western innovations, such contrasts would probably be hard to find elsewhere on earth. (translated from German to English)[24]

Genthe also wrote about his impression of Koreans:

> The King and his progressive counselors were luckier with other innovations, because from the bottom of his heart, the Korean is neither xenophobic nor against innovations. Therefore, it might be possible to convert him completely without difficulty to become a modern man in the Western sense. The King himself almost always took up the progressive thoughts and suggestions of his foreign counselors with eagerness and comprehension. (translated from German into English)

One notable development in Seoul after October 1896 was the construction of parks and public squares. T'apkol (Pagoda) Park was built around this time, and the credit for it is sometimes given to the Englishman McLeavy Brown, perhaps because of the fact that Brown

---

Yongsan area south of the walls of Seoul before the Russo-Japanese War of 1904–1905. *Keijo-fu shi* (1930), pp. 1007–29.

24. "Band 1 Korea," *Genthes Reisen* (Berlin: Allgemeiner Berlin fuer Deutsche Literatur, 1905), pp. 201, 222.

and Yi Ch'aeyŏn were both actively working on city planning in Seoul after 1896. However, it should be emphasized that the creation of the park was part of the Emperor's overall plan for urban development. Why was T'apkol chosen as the location for the first public park? Photos taken in the 1880s show thatched-roofed houses clustered around a thirteen-story pagoda standing on the site of Wŏn'gak Temple in T'apkol (see Photo 3). The thatched-roofed houses were a result of the rapid influx of people into the city from the eighteenth century onward. In 1896, the houses were removed in order to restore the compound of Wŏn'gak temple to its original state, so that it could be used as a place for public gatherings and leisure activities. Why was a park built on a site crowded with such houses?

It is natural for a downtown park to be located in an area with dense pedestrian traffic. Pagoda Park bordered on Chongno, one of the two main streets of Seoul, and was located in the center of a busy market area. These two factors alone were sufficient to make the area an ideal location for a park. The district was named "Ch'ŏlmulgyo" and was one of the places during Chŏngjo's reign where the royal carriage would stop for people to present petitions to the king. It was an area associated with the benevolent rule of the king and a place where the government listened to popular opinion and the people's sufferings.

When the petition system was in effect during Chongjo's reign, there were three areas in Seoul that were designated as places where people could petition the king:[25] the P'ajagyo district where the royal procession would pass on its way from Tonhwamun gate of Ch'angdŏk Palace to Chongno; the Ch'ŏlmul Bridge district near T'apkol with Kyŏngbok and Kyŏnghŭi palaces to the west; and the Hyejŏng Bridge district further west where the six government offices were located. The first district was a commercial area that developed in the eighteenth century; the second was the center of the city's commerce; and the third had the six main government offices which were adjacent to shops and markets. It was of great historical significance that one of these districts was chosen as the site of the country's first public park.

---

25. Han Sanggwŏn, "Chosŏn hugi sahoe munje wa sowŏn chedo ŭi paldal—Chŏngjo tae sangŏn-kykjaeng ŭi punsŏk ŭi chungsim ŭro" (Social issues and the sowŏn system of the late Chosŏn dynasty—an analysis of Chŏngjo's sangŏn and kyŏkjaeng systems) (Ph.D. diss., Seoul National University, 1993), pp. 47–49, 82–83.

After in-law families undermined royal authority by seizing power during Sunjo's reign, the king continued to make regular visits to the tombs of the royal ancestors, but people were no longer given access to the king. This situation persisted until Kojong's reign. He visited the tombs of royal ancestors going back five generations, but there is no record of his meeting with petitioners on these trips. However, he often used his outings in the city as opportunities to talk with the common people.[26]

Restoring royal authority was not an easy task. The Taewŏn'gun, a title for the living father of the king, was the first to attempt such a task, but there were limits to what he could accomplish since he was not a king. Kojong assumed personal control of the government ten years after he had ascended the throne. In 1886, the 23rd year of his reign, he honored the wishes of Chŏngjo by declaring the abolishment of hereditary slavery. Even though he failed to restore the petition system, he showed his willingness for closer contact with the people through his preference for the word *minguk* ("people and country") over the term *pangga* ("country and family").[27] Kojong was a spiritual successor to Chŏngjo in his belief that the relationship between the monarch and the people was like that between the ten thousand rivers and the full moon.

In his desire to be a benevolent monarch, he must have been more than willing to approve the construction of a public park in the

---

26. I plan to do a separate study regarding King Kojong's practice of visiting the royal ancestral tombs and meeting with petitioners.

27. The earliest source shows that King Kojong instructed his Second High-State Councillor on August 25, 1879, as follows: "The painful problems facing the people of the country cannot be counted on the fingers of both hands. The country is like a patient suffering from an ailment of *kohwang* (the part between the heart and the cornea which cannot be treated with either acupuncture or medicine) who must receive good treatment from a skilled doctor" (*Kojong sillok*, vol. 16, August 25). Emperor Kojong made a similar statement in an admonition to Prime Minister Cho Pyŏngse on November 10, 1898: "Despite your function as the state's and the public's ear, nothing has kept me from being isolated from my people. You have disappointed me by placing the greatest importance to your need for self-preservation. The people should not have to present their petitions directly to the royal carriage in order to have them heard. You shall listen to what the people have to say and act for the long-term interest of the nation" (*Kojong sillok*, vol. 38, November 10, the 2nd year of Kwangmu). However, further study is needed to determine whether this term came from Confucian thought or was a translation of a Western concept into Korean via a Confucian background. Emperor Kojong frequently used this term until he was forced to abdicate in 1907 by the Japanese.

T'apkol area when it was proposed by Yi Ch'aeyŏn and Brown, the principal engineers of the urban development project. A report sent by the American Horace Allen to Washington, D.C. in September 1897 included a map showing the location of the American legation (see Map 2). This map indicated a public park that was adjacent to the west gate of the newly-built Kyŏng'un Palace—evidence of the king's desire to construct parks for the benefit of the people.

What about the other two districts? During the March First Movement and the celebration after liberation, people gathered in front of Taeanmun gate of Kyŏng'un Palace, around Hyejŏng Bridge (now the Kwanghwamun intersection), and at Pagoda Park. The Kwanghwamun intersection where the cenotaph used to be was the area in front of Hyejŏng Bridge where petitioners had audiences with the king in the late eighteenth century. It was no coincidence that the area where the people had audiences with the king became the place where people gathered when the country suffered from foreign oppression.

Photographs taken by Westerners who visited in the 1880s show pedestrians milling in the street going from Kwanghwamun to Hyejŏng Bridge, where the offices of the six ministries were located (see Photo 4).[28] The relaxed attitude of the people in the photos suggests that the people were not intimidated by the presence of the government offices. This was the place where Tonghak followers knelt on the ground for three days in February 1893 to request amnesty for their arrested leader.[29] The Hyejŏng Bridge district had historically served as a gathering place for mass rallies. It was not coincidental that a cenotaph commemorating the 40th year of Kojong's reign (the 6th year of Kwangmu) was erected here in 1902 (see Photo 2).

The area in front of Taean Gate of Kyŏng'un Palace became a new gathering place after the palace became the main palace of the Great Han Empire (see Photo 5). Originally, the gathering place was located in front of the south gate (Inhwa Gate) of the palace,[30] and it was through this gate that Kojong moved into the new palace.

---

28. Professor Kim Kiho of the University of Seoul (Sŏul sirip taehakgyo) has argued that the area should be viewed as a plaza. Kim Kiho, "Kyŏngbokkung pogwŏn ŭi tosi kyehoekjŏk ŭimi" (The significance to city planning of the Kyŏngbok Palace restoration), *Kŏnch'ukga* (1993), p. 54.

29. *Kojong sillok*, vol. 2, p. 449, February 21, 1893.

30. More research should be done on whether there is a relationship between the traditional petition system and the sites of public parks on the guide map.

In November 1898, the Independence Club held a series of meetings of the Manmin Kongdonghoe on Chongno Street and also used the area in front of Inhwa Gate as a place to submit petitions to the Emperor. This was the place that the Hwangguk Hyŏphoe (Imperial Association) mobilized two thousand itinerant merchants to attack the Convocation on November 21. This was also the place where the Emperor called for a truce between the members of the Convocation and the Imperial Association and personally gave assurances to the heads of foreign legations in attendance in order to defuse the tense situation between the two groups on Chongno. Kojong granted the Independence Club's request to give the Chungch'uwŏn (Privy Council) legislative functions and to legalize the Independence Club.[31] Such decisions are well-known examples of the emperor's concern for the will of the people.

Taean Gate became the meeting point for mass rallies as a result of being the hub of a number of streets that radiated away from it, and after the meetings of the Convocation came to an end. Because of the country's internal strife, there are few records about the mass rallies held there. It was not until after the Russo-Japanese war, when Japan increased its efforts to take over the country, that people rallied here again, this time to protect the emperor from the aggressions of the Japanese (see Photo 6). These rallies can be viewed as the beginning of the anti-Japanese resistance movement.

The largest rally was held during the March First Independence Movement. The funeral for Emperor Kojong was the impetus for the movement since there were persistent rumors that the Japanese had poisoned him (see Photo 7). After the movement, the Japanese carried out a reorganization of the city based on a plan drafted by the Government-General's office. It called for the construction of a new road leading from the Kwanghwamun intersection through the Namdaemun (South Gate) area to the newly constructed town of Yongsan. The road was strategically important to the Japanese since it was the most effective route to move troops within the city. The headquarters of the 60th regiment, the garrison stationed in Yongsan, was located near Taean Gate, and the Japanese military police and two battalions of troops were stationed in front of Kwanghwa Gate. The offices of the colonial government and the Seoul municipal

---

31. Yu Yŏngnyŏl, "Kaehwagi ŭi minjujuŭi chŏngch'I undong" (Democratic political movements in the Enlightenment Period) in Yi Chong'uk, et. al., *Han'guk sasang ŭi chŏngch'i hyŏngt'ae* (Seoul: Ilchogak, 1993) pp. 272–73.

government were also within the city limits. Because of the new road, people could no longer gather in the Hyejŏng Bridge district in front of Kwanghwa Gate nor in the plaza in front of Taean Gate. The Government-General's plans for city development were clearly designed to strengthen the Japanese military's control of the capital. When Korea was liberated, it was natural that crowds gathered in the places where they had demonstrated in the past (see Photo 8).

CONCLUSION

This chapter has examined the development and diversification of Seoul and its surrounding areas from the second half of the seventeenth century to the end of the nineteenth century. The "Little Ice Age" was a global phenomenon in the seventeenth century, and efforts to overcome the "general crisis" led to comparable developments in Seoul and Western cities in this period. The resulting prosperity of the eighteenth century led to changes in the monarchy, as the king began to make visits outside the palace walls to meet with the people directly, since a true Confucian monarch should respond to changes in society. Seoul was at the center of these historical changes toward modernization.

The development and prosperity of the eighteenth century were difficult to maintain. The rise of in-law politics during the early- and mid-nineteenth century undermined the authority of the monarch and reversed the advances made in the previous century. The common people resisted strongly and rose in protest against the corrupt bureaucracy. In the midst of this internal unrest, Korea opened its ports to the West, leading to an influx of foreign influences. These events resulted in increased confusion and repeated political disturbances, causing Korea to lose its attractiveness as a market for foreign capital.

In order to overcome the internal and external crises, King (later Emperor) Kojong tried to modernize the country according to the idea of "Eastern Ways, Western Technology." As part of these reforms, the appearance of the capital, Seoul, was completely transformed. City improvements, begun in October 1896, were a literal realization of the ideas of "Eastern Ways, Western Technology" by combining the country's traditions with the fruits of Western civilization. Roads were built to converge on the center of the city at Kyŏng'un Palace, which Kojong decided to use as his main palace. Places where the people had gathered to express their opinions since the end of the eighteenth century were turned into public parks and plazas. When the Japanese tried to undermine Korea's sovereignty after the Russo-Japanese War, crowds of people would gather in front of the main gate of the palace; it served as an arena for the people to express their desire to preserve their sovereignty and protect their emperor.

Among the many changes in this period, the most significant in terms of the modernization of both Seoul and Korea was probably the development of ways to express public opinion. Although expressions of public opinion were temporarily suppressed during Japan's colonial rule, they were revived after liberation.

People today seem to be unaware that plans were continually being drawn up to expand the roads and make improvements to the city. Seoul's celebration of its 600th anniversary is a good opportunity to reflect upon the significance of the parks, public squares, and other historic sites of Seoul and how they are being thoughtlessly removed from the landscape of Seoul.

translated by Edward Park

Seoul's Modern Urban Development    261

Table 1

SEOUL'S POPULATION DURING THE CHOSŎN PERIOD

| Year | Housholds | Persons | Year | Households | Persons |
|---|---|---|---|---|---|
| 1409 | 11,056 | 109,372 | 1771 | 38,497 | 196,219 |
| 1428 | 18,522 | 39,931 | 1774 | 38,531 | 197,558 |
| 1432 | 18,830 | 95,569 | 1777 | 38,593 | 197,957 |
| 1435 | 21,891 | 80,572 | 1780 | 38,742 | 201,070 |
| 1438 | 20,352 | 194,030 | 1783 | 42,281 | 207,265 |
| 1593 | 16,006 | 167,406 | 1786 | 42,786 | 195,731 |
| 1648 | 15,760 | 185,872 | 1789 | 43,929 | 189,153 |
| 1657 | 23,899 | 199,018 | 1792 | 43,963 | 189,287 |
| 1669 | 22,740 | 188,597 | 1795 | 43,890 | 191,501 |
| 1678 | 28,356 | 186,305 | 1798 | 44,945 | 193,783 |
| 1717 | 31,859 | 207,733 | 1807 | 45,707 | 204,886 |
| 1723 | 32,747 | 187,756 | 1837 | 45,640 | 203,925 |
| 1726 | 32,372 | 194,432 | 1852 | 45,678 | 204,053 |
| 1729 | 35,768 | 189,985 | 1863 | 45,162 | 204,624 |
| 1732 | 33,836 | 182,584 | 1864 | 47,565 | 202,639 |
| 1735 | 35,576 | 180,090 | 1865 | 46,662 | 206,980 |
| 1738 | 34,886 | 174,203 | 1866 | 45,646 | 200,059 |
| 1741 | 34,153 | 197,452 | 1867 | 45,605 | 207,271 |
| 1747 | 34,652 | 172,166 | 1868 | 45,598 | 207,206 |
| 1750 | 34,953 | 183,782 | 1869 | 45,898 | 206,967 |
| 1753 | 38,108 | 194,634 | 1870 | 45,928 | 207,062 |
| 1756 | 36,467 | 188,884 | 1871 | 46,503 | 200,804 |
| 1759 | 39,926 |  | 1872 | 46,556 | 200,819 |
| 1762 | 39,344 |  | 1873 | 45,734 | 197,377 |
| 1765 | 38,770 |  | 1874 | 45,301 | 191,445 |
| 1768 |  |  | 1875 | 45,299 | 200,951 |
|  |  |  | 1876 | 44,607 | 198,372 |

SOURCE: Ko Tong-hwan, "18-19 segi soul kyŏnggang chiyŏk-ŭi sangŏp paldal" The Commercial Development of Seoul's Riverside Areas along the Han'gang River During the 18th and 19th Centuries (Ph.D. diss., Seoul National Univ., 1993).

262   Chapter Ten

## Table 2
### SEOUL'S POPULATION IN 1789 BY DISTRICT/WARD

| District | Within the city walls | | | Outside the Walls | | |
|---|---|---|---|---|---|---|
| | Ward | Household | Persons | Ward | Household | Persons |
| Middle | Chŏngsŏn-bang | 779 | 4,001 | | | |
| | Kwanin-bang | 450 | 2,123 | | | |
| | Kyŏnp'yŏng-bang | 512 | 2,535 | | | |
| | Sŏrin-bang | 300 | 1,216 | | | |
| | Changt'ong-bang | 791 | 4,169 | | | |
| | Sujin-bang | 498 | 2,271 | | | |
| | Kyŏnghaeng-bang | 515 | 2,859 | | | |
| | Chingch'ŏng-bang | 237 | 1,012 | | | |
| Subtotal | 8 | 4,082 | 20,186 | | | |
| East | Yŏnhwa-bang | 1,175 | 5,545 | Sung-shin-bang | 1,241 | 3,886 |
| | Kyŏngmogung-bang | 776 | 4,026 | | 2,511 | 7,683 |
| | Sunggyo-bang | 839 | 4,276 | | | |
| | Kŏndŏk-bang | 471 | 1,868 | | | |
| | Changsŏn-bang | 689 | 2,426 | | | |
| Subtotal | 5 | 3,950 | 18,141 | 2 | 3,752 | 11,569 |
| South | Myŏngch'ŏl-bang | 1,614 | 5,371 | Tumo-bang | | |
| | Hundo-bang | 1,027 | 6,095 | | | |
| | Naksŏn-bang | 1,168 | 6,021 | Han'gan-g-bang | | |
| | Kwangt'ong-bang | 372 | 2,176 | | | |
| | Myŏngnye-bang | 571 | 3,821 | Tunji-bang | | |
| | T'aep'yŏng-bang | 343 | 2,343 | | | |
| | Hoehyŏn-bang | 989 | 6,550 | | | |
| | Sŏngmyŏng-bang | 814 | 5,189 | | | |
| Subtotal | 8 | 6,898 | 37,566 | 3 | 3,072 | 9,218 |
| West | Yangsaeng-bang | 687 | 3,394 | Pansŏk-bang | 2,965 | 13,882 |
| | Indal-bang | 798 | 4,110 | | | |
| | Chŏksŏn-bang | 689 | 3,306 | Pan-song-bang | 2,791 | 12,971 |
| | Yŏgyŏng-bang | 706 | 3,402 | | | |
| | Hwanghwa-bang | 950 | 5,975 | | | |
| | | | | Yong-san-bang | 4,617 | 14,915 |
| | | | | Sŏgang-bang | 2,186 | 6,239 |
| Subtotal | 5 | 3,830 | 20,187 | 4 | 12,541 | 48,007 |
| North | Sunhwa-bang | 1,167 | 5,917 | Sangp'yŏng-bang | 560 | 1,939 |
| | An'guk-bang | 229 | 1,275 | | | |
| | Kahoe-bang | 252 | 1,765 | | | |
| | Ŭit'ong-bang | 158 | 865 | Yŏnhŭi-bang | 1,279 | 4,173 |
| | Kwan'gwang-bang | 652 | 2,297 | | | |
| | Chinjang-bang | 346 | 1,578 | Yŏnŭn-bang | 631 | 1,876 |
| | Yangdŏk-bang | 124 | 908 | | | |
| | Chunsu-bang | 204 | 994 | | | |
| | Kwanghwa-bang | 202 | 692 | | | |
| Subtotal | 9 | 3,334 | 16,291 | 3 | 2,470 | 7,988 |
| TOTAL | 47 | 22,094 | 112,371 | 12 | 21,835 | 76,782 |

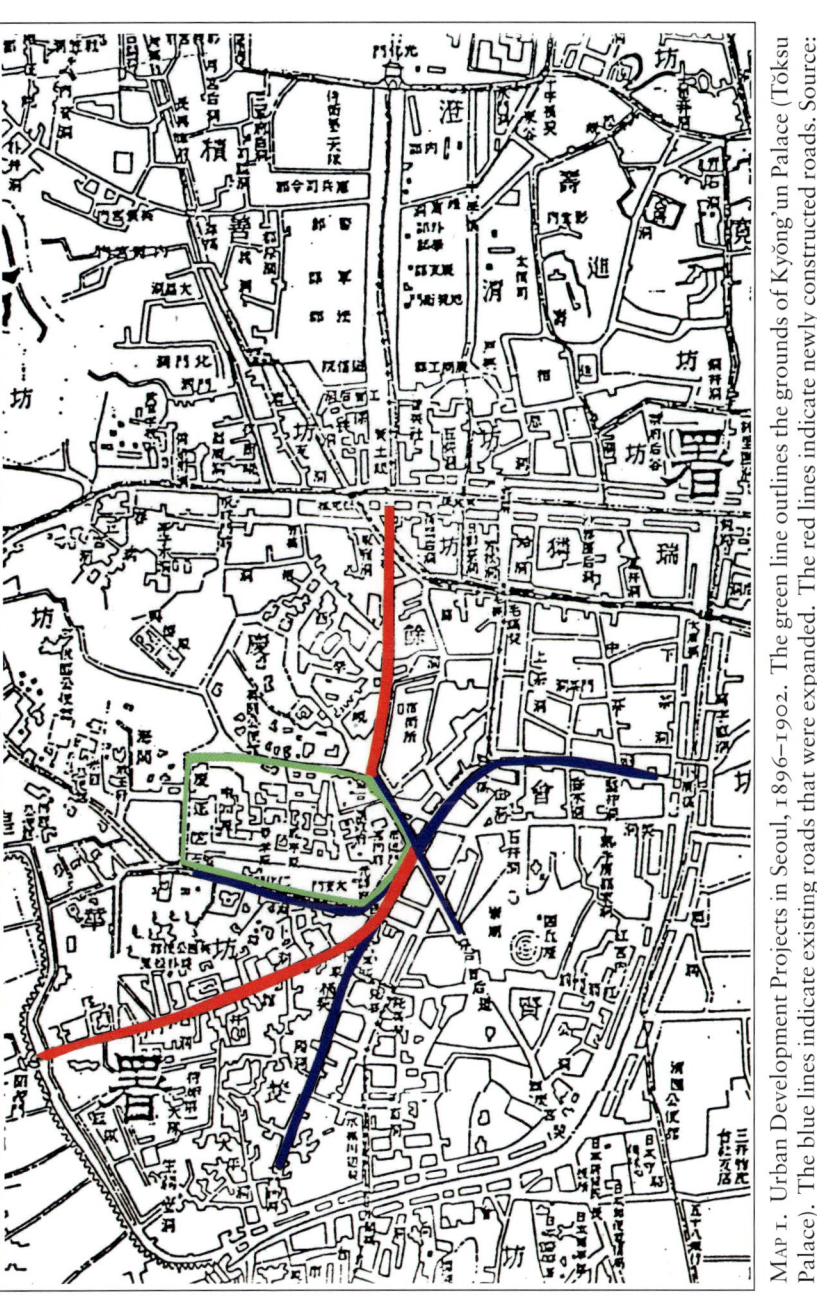

MAP 1. Urban Development Projects in Seoul, 1896–1902. The green line outlines the grounds of Kyŏng'un Palace (Tŏksu Palace). The blue lines indicate existing roads that were expanded. The red lines indicate newly constructed roads. Source: Kim Kwang'u, "Taehan Cheguk sidae ŭi tosi kyehoek—Hansŏng-bu ŭi tosi kaejo saŏp," *Hyangt'o Sŏul 50* (1990).

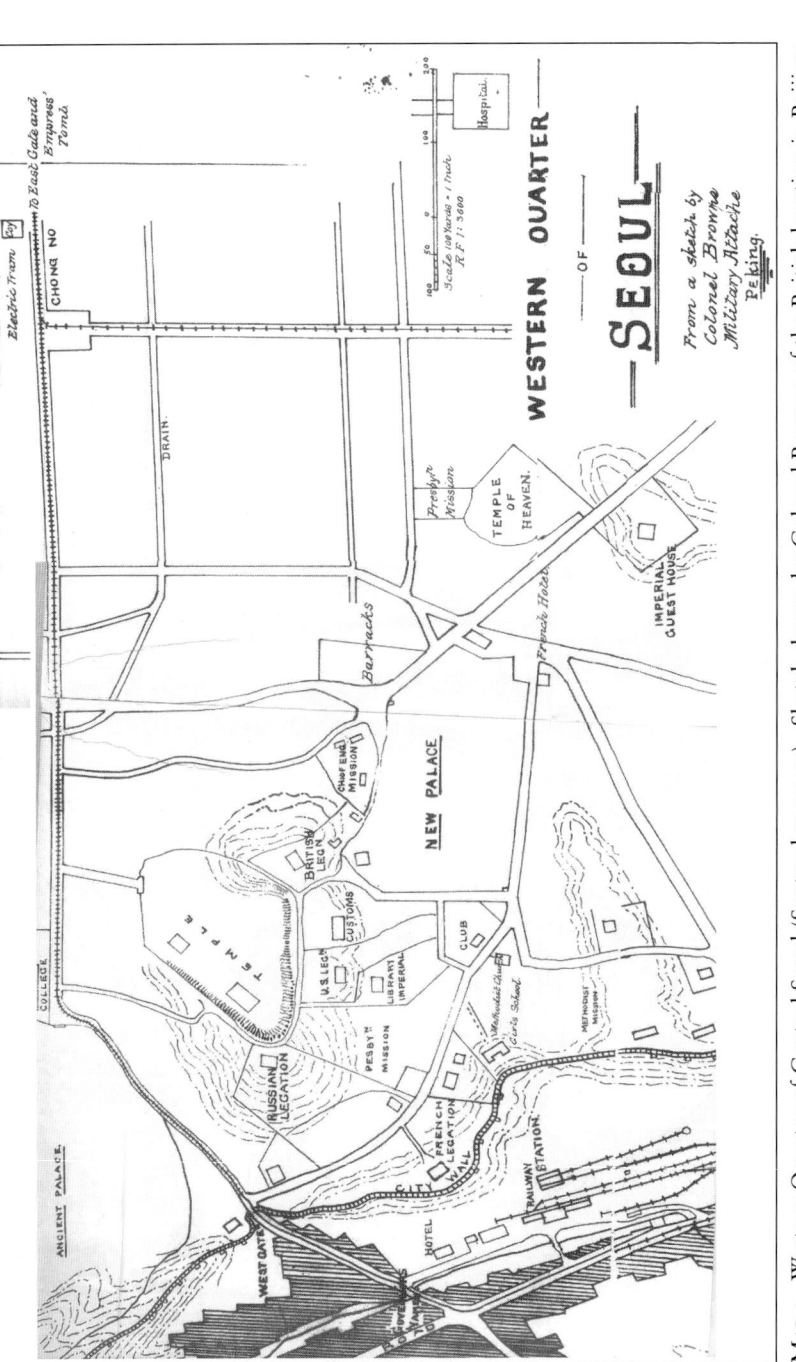

MAP 2. Western Quarter of Central Seoul (September 1901). Sketch drawn by Colonel Browne of the British legation in Beijing. Image slightly altered to fit on the page. Source: Kim Chŏngdong, (*Kojong Hwangje ka saranghan*) *Chŏngdong kwa Tŏksugung* (Seoul: Palŏn, 2004). The original is kept in the Toyo Bunko in Tokyo.

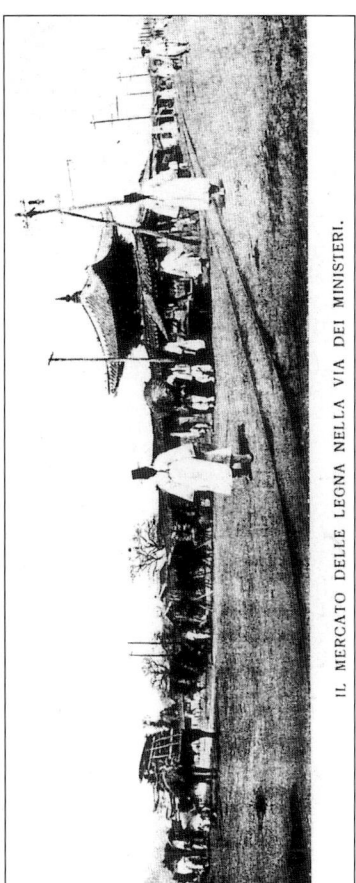

IL MERCATO DELLE LEGNA NELLA VIA DEI MINISTERI.

LA GRAN STRADA DELLA PORTA DI LEVANTE COLLA SEDE DELLA « SEOUL ELECTRIC CO. ».

PHOTOS 1-1 and 1-2. Unjong Street (present-day Chongno) after the urban improvement projects. Source: Carlo Rossetti's *Corea e Coreani: impressioni e ricerche sull'impero del gran Han* (Bergame: Istituto Italiano d'Arti Grafiche, 1904)

Photo 2. Monument commemorating the 40th year of Kojong's reign in the Hyejŏng Bridge district.

Photo 4. Street going from Kwanghwamun to Hyejŏng Bridge, where the offices of the six ministries (Yukcho) were located.

PHOTOS 3-1, 3-2 and 3-3. Thirteen-story pagoda on the site of Wŏn'gak Temple.

SOURCE: *Carlo Rossetti's Corea e Coreani: impressioni e ricerche sull'impero del gran Han* (Bergame: Istituto Italiano d'Arti

Photo 5: Taean Gate of Kyŏng'un Palace (present-day Tŏksu Palace).

Photo 6: Funeral procession for Empress Min passing through the main gate (Taean Gate) of Kyŏng'un Palace (November 1897).

PHOTOS 7-1, 7-2 and 7-3: Funeral for Emperor Kojong (1919).

Photo 8: Crowd in front of Taean Gate after Korea's liberation on August 15, 1945.

CHAPTER 11

# The Leaders and Objectives of the Seoul Urban Renovation Project of 1896–1904

SEOUL HAS BEEN DESIGNATED the capital of Korea three times since the establishment of the Chosŏn dynasty. It first became the capital in 1394 with the founding of the Chosŏn dynasty, then again in October 1897 with the establishment of the Great Han Empire, and once more in 1948, when the government of the Republic of Korea was officially inaugurated. For the second instance, most people believe that Seoul's designation as the capital was merely a logical consequence of the change in the country's name. In fact, its historical significance is no less than that of the first designation, since the second came as the result of the modern urban development project which began in 1896 to make Seoul into a suitable imperial capital.

However, this is not a well-known fact. The year 1996 marked the 100th anniversary of this significant event, but there were no activities to commemorate it. This contrasted with all the festivities held in 1994 to mark the 600th anniversary of Seoul as the Chosŏn Dynasty's capital.

The prevailing view about the Great Han Empire was that it was simply an extension of the Chosŏn dynasty or a last desperate attempt to save the kingdom before colonization by Japan. In reality, the Great Han Empire pursued many modernization projects to strengthen the empire's independence and had some notable achievements, the urban development of Seoul being one of them. However, these accomplishments were distorted by the Japanese during their colonial rule. The urbanization of Seoul began after King Kojong moved from the royal palace to the Russian legation in 1896 (Agwan P'achŏn), and it is significant not only to the history of the city, but to that of the country as well.

## THE ORIGINS AND LEADERS OF SEOUL'S URBAN DEVELOPMENT PROJECT

Kim Kwang'u was the first to draw attention to 1896 as a milestone in the urban development of Seoul.[1] His view is all the more notable, considering that he is not a historian.[2] According to Kim, Seoul's modernization and urbanization began with the Kabo Reforms of 1894 and lasted until the Chosŏn suburban development plan of 1936, with the earlier phase considered the suburban management period. He divided the period afterward into the suburban development period and the national land-development period.[3] But Kim locates the roots of Seoul's urban development in the first period, which he breaks down further into two stages, as follows:

(1) From Kim Okgyun and Pak Yŏnghyo's law regarding provincial government (1882–1883) until the Independence Club's project for the administration of Hansŏng-bu (Seoul prefecture) (1896–1899).

(2) From Resident-General Ito Hirobumi's city blueprint project (1906–1909) to the Government-General's city blueprint (since 1911).

Keeping (1) and (2) in mind, Kim cites Interior Ministry Order No. 9 of September 28, 1896, a plan to widen the roads of Hansŏng (Seoul), as a specific example of how Seoul was developed into a modern urban city. Kim analyzes the main features of the Interior Ministry Order as follows:

First, houses that jutted into the main roads of Hansŏng-bu, such as Chongno (from Hwangt'ohyŏn hill to Hŭng'injimun [East

---

1. Kim Kwang'u, "Taehan Cheguk sidae ŭi tosi kaehoek—Hansŏng-bu tosi kaejo saŏp" (City planning during the Great Han Empire period—the city improvement projects of Seoul), *Hyangt'o Sŏul* 50 (1990).
2. The writer has already praised the importance of Kim's research in "The Nature of Seoul's Modern Urban Development During the Eighteenth and Nineteenth Centuries," *Korea Journal* 35, no. 3 (Autumn 1995).
3. Kim Kwang'u, op cit., pp. 96–97.

Gate] and Namdaemun road (from the Taegwangt'ong Bridge to Sungnyemun or South Gate), were torn down to expand the roads from their original width of 50 *cha* (about fifty feet) to 70–80 *cha*, reestablishing the original scale of the main roads.

Second, after the Agwan P'achŏn, roads were created centering around the main gate of the new Kyŏng'un Palace (Kyŏngungung; today's Toksu Palace). These new roads were connected to existing ones, changing the city's road structure with radial roads, ring roads connecting outside feeder roads, and circular roads connecting the city to the outskirts of Seoul.

Third, buildings of political importance were built in Western styles and located along main roads, contributing to a more systematic urban layout. These buildings included various government offices, missions, and legations near Kyŏng'un Palace; Queen Min's grave at Ch'ŏngnyangri; the Hwan'gudan (Round-Mound Altar) and adjacent buildings; the Taekwanchŏng for foreign dignitaries; Independence Gate and Independence Hall; and Chŏnhwan'guk in Yongsan.

As Kim's analysis demonstrates, the city-development plan involved a great many changes, playing an important role in the history of the Great Han Empire. But in addition to uncovering these facts, it is necessary to analyze the meaning behind the developments.

First, it is important to understand the basic concept behind the redevelopment plan. Kim Kwang'u identifies four key figures—Kim Okgyun (1851–1894), Pak Yŏnghyo (1861–1939), Pak Chŏngyang (1841–1904), and Yi Ch'aeyŏn (?–?)—behind Seoul's development. Their achievements are described below:

(1) Kim Okgyun: Wrote a treatise on principles and regulations of road construction and maintenance (1882–1883).
(2) Pak Yŏnghyo: Established the office of governing provinces when he was the city mayor in 1895, and when he became the Interior Minister, issued "eighty-eight directives" (*hunsi*) to local governors.
(3) Pak Chŏngyang: On the 6th day of the eighth lunar month of 1895, received approval for an internal ordinance that called for the revision of roads and the elimination of temporary housing. On September 30, 1896, he won approval for the Interior Ministry Order to expand and repair the roads in Hansŏng-bu.

(4) Yi Ch'aeyŏn: When Pak Chŏngyang's reform bill was approved, Yi was appointed the mayor of Hansŏng-bu (Seoul) and was actively involved in the city's development process for years.

According to Kim Kwang'u, all four had a keen interest in the problems of provincial government. Based on this common factor, Kim charts the development of urban ideology as follows: Kim Okgyun's Kapsin Coup of 1884 gave rise to the Kabo Reforms associated with Pak Yŏnghyo, and this, in turn, led to the independence movement, in which Pak Chŏngyang and Yi Ch'aeyŏn were actively involved. In the context of the traditional interpretation of the tumultuous events following Kojong's retreat to the Russian legation, that of distinguishing the reform movement from the conservative movement, it is easy to see how Kim could come to this conclusion. But more recent studies have questioned this interpretation, pinpointing several problems with it. This historical view also seems to clash with the basic ideology of the urban development plan.

Kim and Pak Yŏnghyo were the main leaders of the Kapsin Coup and were pro-Japanese, taking Meiji Japan as their model for reform. In contrast, Pak Chŏngyang and Yi were pro-American. When Pak became the first Korean Minister to the United States, Yi accompanied him as an interpreter. These differences alone are sufficient to separate the four figures into two groups.

Because Kim and Pak Yŏnghyo were exiled by the king for treason as the main leaders of the Kapsin Coup of 1884, they had almost no opportunity to implement their ideas. But Pak Chŏngyang and Yi were so-called moderates who pursued reforms within the framework of the monarchy.[4] Pak Yŏnghyo, who was a key member of the reformist movement, returned temporarily during the Kabo-Ŭlmi Reforms in 1894–1895 and tried to enact the reforms mentioned above. However, this reform was actually imposed by force by the Japanese and ended in failure. Pak was later accused of being part of a conspiracy to overthrow King Kojong and was ultimately forced to return to Japan again. However, Pak Chŏngyang and Yi distanced themselves from the pro-Japanese faction, even after the Sino-Japanese War. As a result, after the Agwan P'achŏn, they gained the trust of the monarch. By the end of September 1896, when Seoul's redevelopment

---

4. Regarding Pak Chŏngyang, see Yi Kwangnin's bibliographical introduction in *Pak Chŏngyang chŏnjip* (Seoul: Asea munhwasa, 1984). Up to now, there has been no research on Yi Ch'aeyŏn.

plans began to take hold, Kim Okgyun had already passed away, and Pak Yŏnghyo left for America in November, vowing never to return to Asia.⁵ Was Seoul's redevelopment directed solely by Pak Chŏngyang and Yi Ch'aeyŏn? The two undoubtedly played a vital role in carrying out the actual reforms, but it is important to remember that they could not have made any changes to the royal capital without the king's consent. As Kim Kwang'u noted, Park and Yi were deeply involved in the establishment of the Independence Club (Tongnip Hyŏphoe), which was founded on July 2, 1896. Pak supported the organization when he became the Deputy Prime Minister after the assassination of Prime Minister Kim Hongjip (1842–1896) and assumed Kim's duties. Yi Ch'aeyŏn was one of the founding members of the Independence Club. The organization was actually founded by supporters of the monarchy, who wanted to take full advantage of the new political situation that emerged after the Agwan P'achŏn. However, it would be a mistake to credit the reformists or the Independence Club with Seoul's redevelopment simply because Park and Yi were closely involved with the group. They were involved in the process from the beginning as high-ranking members of the cabinet (Interior Minister and mayor of Hansŏng-bu, respectively). Two years later, in February 1889, when some members of the Independence Club began to agitate against the monarchy, the two left the club and affirmed their loyalty to the King. As mentioned earlier, Pak Chŏngyang, then Minister of the Interior, passed a bill that called for revising the roads and eliminating housing on the main roads on the 6th day of the eighth moon in 1895, before the Agwan P'achŏn incident. However, this bill was never implemented. The starting point of Park and Yi's urban development plan was the monarchy's return to power after the Agwan P'achŏn and Pak's promotion from Minister of the Interior to Deputy Prime Minister. The two were able to implement their ideas only with the full support of the King, after he regained power.

To have a better understanding of the basic purpose and nature of Seoul's urban development plan, we must cast aside the negative historical perception of King Kojong and his flight to the Russian legation. Kojong believed in modernization based on the theory of *tongdo sŏgi*, which literally means "Eastern Ways, Western Technology." The theory is based on the idea that Korea should adopt modern techniques and technologies from the West without abandon-

5. *The Independent* (Tongnip sinmun), November 7, 1896.

ing traditional systems and philosophies. Concerned about the Taewŏngun's isolationist policy, Kojong became directly involved in the country's modernization process. His agreeing to sign the Treaty of Amity and Commerce with the United States was his way of trying to break away from the China-centered world order.[6] The king's intention was welcomed by the Americans and bore fruit, at least in the short term. But the treaty also angered the Qing dynasty so that when a military riot erupted in 1882, the Qing used it as an opportunity to increase its presence in Chosŏn. It tried to colonize the country, and in the process, Kojong's reform plan was attacked from all angles. The Treaty of Amity and Commerce with the United States was signed in 1882, but due to pressure and interference from Qing China, it took six years for the King to dispatch Pak Chŏngyang as the first Korean Minister to the United States.

The Qing dynasty withdrew from Chosŏn when it lost the Sino-Japanese War, but Japan immediately stepped into its place. When the Tonghak uprising broke out, the Qing dynasty immediately dispatched troops to Chosŏn, using the rebellion as a pretext to gain exclusive control over Chosŏn. Japan then stormed in, using the 1885 Tientsin Convention as justification for its decision. But Japan sent troops to Seoul, not to the Chŏlla province where the Tonghak movement had erupted, claiming that to control the farmers' revolt, they first had to reform the administration. The resulting Kabo Reforms were strongly influenced by Japan, beginning with the establishment of the Kun'guk Kimuch'o (Office of State Military Affairs). Japan's separation of the government and the monarchy was nominally in the interest of political modernization, but its actual goal was to make Chosŏn a protectorate and dismantle the throne. Japan also used the Triple Intervention in April 1895 as the pretext for assassinating Queen Min in October of that year, undermining the royal court's power and turning the king into a virtual figurehead. The Agwan P'achŏn was Kojong's way of escaping this life-threatening situation: he sought refuge at the Russian Legation and asked Russia and the United States for help.[7] The success of the Agwan P'achŏn

---

6. Kim Kyŏngt'ae, "Pulp'yŏngdŭng choyak kaejŏng kyosŏp ŭi chŏn'gae" (The negotiations for revision of the unequal treaties), *Han'guksa yŏn'gu* 11 (1975), pp. 202–3.
7. In the November 5, 1896 edition of the *The Independent*, the following passage clearly expresses what people at the time thought about the Agwan P'achŏn. This editorial was written in reply to Japanese criticism of the Chosŏn monarch's refuge at the Russian legation. "The King is at the Russian legation

meant that Japan had no choice but to retreat. After recovering its authority, the royal court decided to use this opportunity to build an independent state and strengthen itself. Developing the capital city was one of the projects implemented to achieve this goal.

As a result, the redevelopment of Seoul after the Agwan P'ach'ŏn incident was headed by Pak Chŏngyang, first Korean Minister to the United States, with the aid of experience and know-how of followers such as Yi Ch'aeyŏn, Yi Sangjae (1850–1929), and Yi Chongha (?–?). This will become clearer in the next section.

BASIC PLAN AND IMPLEMENTATION OF SEOUL'S URBAN DEVELOPMENT

Considering the importance of the 1896 Seoul (Hansŏng-bu) development plan, it would seem logical that there would be various blueprints and documents related to the project. Unfortunately, most of the documents were not preserved. The only materials left are some papers related to the bill that called for road expansion in Hansŏng-bu (end of September 1896) and editorials and articles in *The Independent* that reported the progress of the project.

For a project that required as much planning as this one, it is difficult to determine the overall scheme—for example, whether there was a master plan or whether the project was completed in parts—just from documents relating to its implementation. Documentation about Seoul's development projects from the fall of 1896 to the Russo-Japanese War in 1904 is incomplete and scattered, so it is difficult to grasp the overall picture. From surviving documents, we can determine the following aspects about the development plan:

A. Repair of roads and waterways
1. Repair of existing roads
2. Repair of sewers
3. Construction of new roads (roads radiating from the front of Kyŏng'un Palace)

by his own royal volition, not because he was asked to remain by the Russian minister. Therefore, there is no reason why the Chosŏn monarch should hate the Russian minister. Rather, we should be thankful to him for allowing the King to come here, when he was faced with a life-threatening situation. No one is more angered and upset about the King's situation than we. And the Japanese are to be blamed for driving our king to seek refuge at the Russian legation."

B. Construction of new buildings
1. Kyŏng'un Palace
2. Independence Gate
3. Hwan'gudan
4. Memorial pavilion celebrating the fortieth anniversary of Kjong's coronation

C. Construction of new parks
1. Independence Park
2. Public park to the west of Kyŏng'un Palace
3. T'apgol (Pagoda) Park

D. Public infrastructure
1. Electricity
2. Waterworks
3. Streetcars
4. Railroads

E. Designation of industrial production sites
1. Government-run industrial district in Yongsan
2. City market near Namdaemun (South Great Gate; today's Namdaemun market)

A-1: The repair of existing roads was one of the basic projects pursued in the earlier stage of the urban development plan. The roads surrounding the capital, such as present-day Chongno and Namdaemunno, were built fifty to eighty *cha* (1 *cha* = 33cm) in width. However, the roads became crowded after the eighteenth century as commercial business boomed and the population grew at an explosive rate. Toward the end of the eighteenth century, there were suggestions for change, but no specific plan was proposed, and the issue dragged on until 1896. The Interior Ministry directive, dated September 28, finally addressed the issue and restored the roads to their original width. According to a report in *The Independent*, the Hansŏng-bu government ordered the directive to go into effect on October 16, and the houses and stores that had crowded the street were torn down. By November 11, most of the work was completed, and the roads were repaired by the end of November.

The withdrawal of Japanese shops along the road from Namdaemun to Chongno was carried out amicably through friendly negotiations between Yi Ch'aeyŏn and the Japanese consulate, for which both

The Leaders and Objectives 277

sides were praised (according to newspapers dated November 12). On December 8, when work inside the royal palace was completed, newspapers reported that the construction department had set a budget to expand other roads: Namdaemun to Yongsan, Saemun to Samgae, and Yŏmch'ang Bridge to Samgae.

In an editorial published on November 7, *The Independent* stated that this project represented Chosŏn's move toward modernization and praised its supervisors. The paper praised Deputy Prime Minister Pak Chŏngyang, Mayor Yi Ch'aeyŏn, and other government officials such as Kim Chŏngsŏk, Yi Chongha, Yi Chaeu, Hong Chunp'yo, Chang Yunhwan, and Ku Pŏmsŏ for their dedication and hard work. No one from the construction department was specifically mentioned, but the head of the department was Yi Sangjae.

A-2: Work on the sewage system was generally carried out together with that of roadways. In its March 6, 1897 edition, *The Independent* stated that Deputy Mayor Ri Kyep'il was examining sewers with the American reporter W.M. Dye. Several months before, on November 3, 1896, the paper reported that a sewer had been built under the large three-way street in Kuri-gae. The government and the city suggested that the existing sewage system be removed or replaced by a smaller sewer. Based on this report, there may have been some construction work to build a smaller sewer or to change the flow of the sewage system.

A-3: The development of a radial-road plan brought about the clearest changes to the structure of the city. Roads were to originate from the main gates of the new palace, Kyŏng'un Palace, and the plan was similar to plans favored by many large cities in Europe and America beginning in the mid-nineteenth century. Kim Kwang'u first discovered this radial-road plan on a map of Seoul produced by the Japanese in 1903. It is noteworthy that Seoul implemented a road plan that was popular in the West at this time. The *Tongnip sinmun* carried two articles on this project. The April 6 edition reported that Yi Ch'aeyŏn had assessed road conditions on Sŏsomun with McLeavy Brown, who was the British standing advisor to the Ministry of Finance and head of the Revenue Office. The newspaper also wrote that two junior officials from the city and the government measured the side roads and counted the number of houses around Sŏsomun. An April 13 article praised the American Methodist mission and the German Karl Wolter, who owned a large part of the land along the Chŏngdong-Sŏsomun road, for giving up some of their property to help the city expand its road system.⁸ These articles once again affirm the view that the city-road development project was pursued with the cooperation that the mayor, Yi Ch'aeyŏn, received from foreign advisors.

Washington, D.C., where Pak Chŏngyang and Yi Ch'aeyŏn resided as diplomats for many years beginning in 1887, is well known for its radial-street plan. Not surprisingly, the king noted their suggestions and adopted Washington's layout, choosing centrally located Kyŏng'un Palace as the axis for a radial road plan.⁹ Sim Ŭisŏk, an engineer with the Interior Ministry who participated in the survey of the Sŏsomun area, also had an important role in the project. At the time, Shim was in charge of the expansion of Kyŏng'un Palace, and he was also in charge of the construction of Hwan'gudan and Independence Gate. His involvement in three important areas of the urban development project indicates that they were pursued according to a master plan. Sim Ŭisŏk was a close associate of Pak Chŏngyang, as shown by his appointment as an official architect (of the sixth grade) in the Interior Ministry on July 19, 1895 when Pak was the Interior Minister.¹⁰

The expansion plan for city roads can be summarized as follows: the first phase was to reestablish the original width of the main roads,

---

8. This story was also printed in English in *The Independent* (April 15, 1897).

9. One of Park's writings about Washington, D.C., shows the keen interest Korean officials had in the city. The following is a translation in one of his texts: "Washington is the capital of the U.S. In the eighty-eight years since its establishment, the population has grown and housing expanded so that now the city boasts a population of around 200,000 and the city uses various materials from wood to bricks to build houses. Some buildings are built 10 stories high, some have underground floors. Architects even use glass and steel for the exterior. The horizontal streets named according to the twenty-six letters of the alphabet and the vertical streets are numbered. Each house and building has its own number that corresponds with the horizontal and vertical street. It is an impeccable grid map of the city. Houses are divided into squares and they have a specifically designated area allotted for each house. Here and there, you can see trees, parks, and benches as recreational areas. The main intersections are named after famous military heroes (i.e., Washington Square) and have huge statues of them on horses. But this kind of city planning is found in other places as well, not just in D.C."—from *Pak Chŏngyang chŏnjip* 6, pp. 643–45.

10. *Pak Chŏngyang chŏnjip* 6, p. 34. In "Reconstructing Korea's Modern Architecture" (*Kŏnch'uksa*, May 1987–Feb. 1989, Korean Architects Association), Professor Kim Chŏngdong cites the Paejae school (1887), Independence Gate (1896), Chungdong church (1895–1898), Ewha school (1889), Kojong's fortieth anniversary memorial tower (1902), Sangdong church (1900), and Sŏkjojŏn (1900) as Sim Osŏk's outstanding works.

Chongno and Namdaemun, through the clearing of houses. They were then to be connected with the commercial districts from Namdaemun to Yongsan, from Saemun to Samgae, and from Yŏmch'ang Bridge to Samgae. Next, a radial-road system was established starting from the main gates of Kyŏng'un Palace. In addition, the plan called for connecting Namdaemun to Independence Gate to improve access between the royal palace and the surrounding areas. In this stage, it is clear that Ri Kyep'il, Sim Ŭisŏk, Dye, and McLeavy Brown were the main figures involved in the project.

B-1: The construction of Kyŏng'un Palace was the most important of the development projects, and it began the earliest. The layout of Chosŏn royal courts at this time was indirectly influenced by the popular theory of geomancy (*pungsujiri*), with the king's throne traditionally facing south. To place Kyŏng'un Palace in the center of the city and use this as the focal point for the radial-road plan contradicted the traditional principles of geomancy. Five days after Kojong took refuge at the Russian legation on February 16, he ordered Kyŏng'un Palace to be repaired. Even at this point, the king was not intending to use Kyŏng'un Palace as his main residence; it merely seemed that he was considering returning either to Kyŏng'un Palace or to Kyŏngbok Palace.[11] However, according to *The Independent* of August 15, the king gave the order on August 10 for the royal household and construction departments to carry out the repairs, and shortly thereafter, on August 25, he ordered the shrine of the assassinated Queen Min to be transferred to Kyŏng'un Palace.[12] These reports suggest that the official decision to make Kyŏng'un Palace the royal palace was made in August. During this time, road repairs and the construction of Independence Gate were proceeding at full speed. When the king moved to Kyŏng'un Palace a year later, in February 1897, most of the construction work had been completed, but repairs continued for many years, even after the king took up residence. In addition, the king continued to add new government buildings around the royal palace after the Great Han Empire was established.

11. Seoul National University Library, Kyujanggak (Royal Library) collection, Kŭmho series, "Constitutional Law," p. 60. Royal proclamation, 16th day of the second Month.
12. Yi Tae-jin (Yi T'aejin), "Kyujanggak Chunggukbon tosŏ wa Chip'okje tosŏ" (Kyujanggak-Chinese books and Chip'okjae royal collection), *Minjok munhwa nonch'ong* 16 (Yŏngnam University, 1996), pp. 177–78. The Chinjŏn pavilion was where portraits of the king were kept. Before this, the portraits were hung in the Kyŏngbok Palace, at the king's office.

B-2: The construction of Independence Gate was also an important project in the urbanization of Seoul. The purpose of its construction will be examined in detail later in this chapter, but the widespread belief that Sŏ Chaep'il or the Independence Club built the gate is completely unfounded. An editorial printed in *The Independent*, written either under Sŏ's direction or anonymously by Sŏ himself, clearly states that this gate was part of the government's urban planning project. According to this editorial, after the Agwan P'achŏn, the monarch wanted to raise the status of his people in the eyes of foreigners. To prove that the Great Han Empire was completely independent, the gate was constructed at the site of Yŏng'ŭn Gate, where envoys from China had been received in the past.[13] The Great Han Empire wanted to show to both foreigners and its subjects that it was on an equal footing with China and Japan, since both those countries now had taken the political form of an empire. The court felt that the project would have more meaning if it were undertaken by the people rather than by the ruler or the government. The monarch persuaded his closest ministers to create the Tongnip Hyŏphoe (Independence Club), with part of its objective being the construction of Independence Gate. The monarch tried to make it appear that funding for the gate had come from this organization, but in fact, 1,000 wŏn or one-third of the Club's total contribution was given in the Crown Prince's name.[14] Construction began with a ground-breaking ceremony on November 20, 1896, and took almost one year to complete.

B-3: The construction of Hwan'gudan had almost the same motive as that of Independence Gate. It was built on the site of Nambyŏl Palace, where Chinese envoys used to stay in Seoul after passing through Yŏng'ŭn Gate. The city development project intended to mark the inauguration of Korea as a truly independent country with the construction of these two structures. The actual construction of Hwan'gudan began around the time the monarchy became an empire. Discussions on reorganizing Chosŏn into an empire began in August

13. Ibid. p. 201.
14. For information about funding for the project, see Chu Chin'o, "Sipku segi huban kaehwa kaehyŏknon ŭi kujo wa chŏn'gae—Tongnip hyophŏe rŭl chungsim ŭro" (Modernization at the end of the nineteenth century: The structure and development of modernization centered around the Independence Club" (Ph.D. diss., Yŏnsei University, 1995), p. 85. According to this dissertation, the total amount mentioned in *The Independent* was 5,897 wŏn and the Crown Prince's 1,000 wŏn was 17% of the total amount. The Crown Prince's contribution was mentioned in the December 15, 1896, edition of the newspaper.

1897. But if construction of the Hwan'gudan had begun at this time, it could not have been completed in time for the emperor's coronation ceremony on October 12. The structure must have been completed by this date since part of the coronation ceremony was supposed to take place at the new Hwan'gudan. It may be surmised that the blueprint for the building was probably drawn up not long after January 15, 1897, the date that Chosŏn declared its independence (as announced in *The Independent*'s January 14 issue). As was discussed earlier, Yi Ch'aeyŏn, McLeavy Brown, and Sim Ŭisŏk were surveying the Sŏsomun area around the end of March and early April. With the radial-road plan centered around the Taeanmun, the main gate of the new palace, officials had probably already considered building Hwan'gudan at the site of Nambyŏl Palace. If this assumption is correct, the incorporation of the radial-road plan centered around the heart of the city should be recognized for its careful and detailed planning.

B-4: The memorial palace that was erected to celebrate the fortieth anniversary of King Kojong's rule had another function: to celebrate the emperor's upcoming sixtieth birthday. At the time, Kojong was fifty-one years old and by the standards of the time was considered long-lived. In Confucian society, age is one of the criteria that determines respect, and in that sense, Kojong's longevity held special meaning for the empire. According to Chosŏn dynasty tradition, officials also were permitted to join the Kiroso (Superannuation Bureau) when they reached the age of sixty. Occasionally, exceptions were made, and a ruler would join the Kiroso even before his sixtieth birthday. King Yŏngjo was the first person under the age of sixty to join (he was fifty-one). Emperor Kojong followed his example and joined the Kiroso in 1902, the first emperor to do so.

The location of the memorial palace also had special significance. It was built directly in front of the Kiroso, facing the south, which was considered to be the center of Seoul. This was also the site where, since the eighteenth century, kings had stopped to hear the petitions of the people, and it was a popular gathering point for crowds—whether to witness an execution or for some other purpose. Building a memorial celebrating Kojong's longevity and his entrance into the Kiroso in the fortieth year of his reign in this location was of great significance in a Confucian country.

C-1: The details of the plan show that the construction of parks was important to the city's redevelopment. The construction of Independence Park was discussed and decided together with that of

Independence Gate. The city designated land around Independence Gate and Independence Hall (the Independence Club's office building) for use by the park and banned citizens from cultivating the land for private use or disturbing the rocks, trees, and grass.[15]

C-2: The public park that adjoined Kyŏng'un Palace was documented in a map dated September 30, 1897, that was drawn by American consul Horace Allen and sent to his home government. On the map, he wrote "public park" in the space facing the west entrance of Kyŏng'un Palace (possibly the front of Chŏngdong Church).[16]

C-3: The fact that T'apgol Park was built in downtown Seoul is particularly significant. Construction on the park began in 1899. On March 29, 1899, an editorial in *The Independent* discussed rumors that the Minister of the Royal Household, Yi Chaesun,[17] had ordered the removal of houses in the T'apdong (T'apgol Park) area to make way for a park. Though some dismissed these rumors as nonsense, the article exclaimed that if those rumors proved true and if Minister Yi was indeed working on a large-scale project that would benefit thousands of citizens, then he was a worthy minister.[18] However, this project was almost derailed because of disputes among the State Council, the Finance Ministry, the Interior Ministry, and the Hansŏng

---

15. *The Independent*, April 8, 1897.

16. Yi Tae-jin, "Sippal-sipku segi Sŏul ŭi kŭndaejŏk tosi paldal ŭi yangsang" (The nature of Seoul's modern urban development in the eighteenth and nineteenth centuries), *Sŏulhak yŏn'gu* 4 (1995), pp. 29–30; the English translation appeared in *Korea Journal* 35, no. 3 (autumn 1995).

17. The Independence newspaper did not name Yi Chaesun but identified him by his rank. From an examination of available records from the period, Yi is referred to as "Minister of the Royal Household" in a document nominated as the "Adjutant-General of the Wŏnsubu" (The Supreme Military Council), dated May 14 of that year. (Seoul National University Library, Kyujanggak [Royal Library] Archives, Kŭmho Series, "Constitutional Law," Choch'ik, pŏbryŏng, p. 174). It is not certain why the Minister of the Royal Household would be involved in the construction of a park. From spring 1898, An Kyŏngsu and other pro-Japanese members of the Independence Club began to hold rallies of the Kwanmin Kongdonghoe (Joint Convocation of Officials and Common People) and the Manmin Kongdonghoe (Convocation of Ten Thousand People) at Chonggak, right in front of the future T'apgol Park. These rallies ultimately led to the demise of the Independence Club at the end of the year. There is a possibility that T'apgol Park was constructed in that location to eradicate such rallies.

18. Yi Chaesun was one of the key figures in an incident that later earned him the position of Minister of Royal Households. On October 11, 1895, he was caught climbing over the wall of Ch'unsaengmun to reach pro-American and pro-Russian officials, in an attempt to rescue Kojong, who was virtually being held captive at Kyŏngbok Palace by the Japanese.

city government over the problem of compensation for the houses that were scheduled for removal. The Tapdong area was densely populated at the time, packed with straw- and tile-roofed houses, in the midst of which stood the thirteen-story stupa of Wŏngak Temple. As Minister Yi and the Hansŏng city government undertook this task, not all of the directives were reported to the Interior Ministry. This led to confusion and conflict, bringing the project to a standstill. McLeavy Brown, director of the Custom House and standing advisor to the Finance Ministry, obtained the necessary funds from the Finance Ministry's budget, and the project was resumed.[19] On June 1, *The Independent* reported that the demolition of the houses had begun again. The construction of the park probably took at least two years.[20]

The fact that the city planners considered the construction of parks along with a radial road structure provides a clue to determining which city might have served as the model for the project. Earlier, it was mentioned that many of the leading figures in Seoul's urbanization had worked in Washington, D.C., under the first Korean Minister to the United States. This fact suggests that Washington was the inspiration for the new road plan, which radiated from an axis originating at the Kyŏng'un Palace. Indeed, Washington, D.C., is well known for its radial-road plan and many public gardens. Although a reference to Washington can be found in *Misok sŭpyu* (Brief Observations on American Customs) in Pak Chŏngyang's *Hwasont'on-gi* (On Washington, D.C.), contemporary urban historians have also pointed out these features as the city's defining characteristics: "Washington, D.C., was a special case, but the length and scale of its radial avenues marked a new stage in the application of the Renaissance example. With the avenue or broad street went, in some cases, the geometrical piazza or square. These could be combined with the public garden, and the park could be added to, or incorporated in, this pattern."[21] It is highly possible that Washington, D.C., was the model for Seoul's

19. The April 21, 1899, issue of *The Independent* reported that the Finance Ministry allocated 50,000 wŏn for the project.
20. Nowadays, all reference books and signs commonly credit McLeavy Brown with having built the park in 1897. Not only is it wrong that Brown spearheaded the work, but even the date is inaccurate. Browns' involvement in the project as a consultant to the Finance Ministry is limited. Credit needs to be given to the City Council, which was supported by the Minister of Royal Households Yi Chae-sun.
21. Anthony Sutcliffe, "The Origins of Urban Planning 1890–1914: Berlin, Paris, London, New York," *Sŏulhak yŏn'gu* 4 (1995), p. 82.

urbanization program, based on the experiences of its chief architects.[22]

D: The construction of infrastructure and public facilities completely changed the face of Seoul as they introduced Western civilization after the city was reorganized as described above. Work on a power grid, a streetcar system, and waterworks began in January 1898. Kojong signed a contract with the American Collbran-Bostwick Development Company and others to form a joint venture called the Hansŏng Electric Power Company, which was commissioned to build power lines, street lamps, water pipes, and telephone lines.[23] The fact that Mayor Yi Ch'aeyŏn was appointed president of this company indicates there were connections with the city development plan. In May 1899, the company built the first streetcar line from Sŏdaemun to Ch'ŏngnyangni; in April 1900, it installed three streetlamps along Chongno, the first of many sweeping changes to the city.[24] It is no coincidence that streetcars were running on Chongno by the time construction began on T'apgol Park. It is also significant that these innovations were built by a company founded jointly with Americans and that some of the key figures of Seoul's redevelopment plan had lived in the United States.

The introduction of electricity and the streetcar was meant to do more than make urban life more convenient. As part of the streetcar line construction, the main station was linked to Seoul's railroad station in an effort to join Seoul's transportation system with the national rail network. When the *Hansŏng sunbo* (a newspaper issued every ten days) and the *Hansŏng chubo* (a weekly newspaper) were in publication during the 1880s, there was already a great deal of information and discussion on the development of mining to supply fuel for railroads and streetcars.[25] Interestingly, the minister to the United States, Pak Chŏngyang, tried to find professional mining

---

22. At the time, the population of Washington, D.C., was 200,000, similar to that of Seoul.
23. No Inhwa, *Taehan cheguk sigi ŭi Hansŏng chŏn'gihoesa e kwanhan yŏn'gu* (A study of the Hansŏng Electric Power Company during the Great Han Empire period), *Ewha sawŏn* 17 (1980), p. 9.
24. Korea Electric Power Corporation, *Han'guk chŏn'gi paeknyŏnsa* (100 Years of Electricity in Korea) (Seoul: Han'guk chŏllyŏk kongsa, 1989).
25. "Discussion on Electricity," *Hansŏng sunbo*, November 1, 1883; November 10, 1883. Britain's Power Company (this is the first mention of streetcars); "The Advent of Electricity," *Hansŏng chubo*, May 14, 1887.

technicians who could develop coal and gold deposits and invite them to Seoul.[26] The monarch and government of Chosŏn took an active interest in the construction of a railroad and were in the midst of secret negotiations with the British to build a line between Seoul and Pusan, when the Japanese dispatched troops to Chosŏn and wrested away the concession rights. After the Agwan P'achŏn, Kojong was interested in independently developing the Honam (Seoul–Mokpo), Kyŏngwŏn (Seoul–Wŏnsan), and Kyŏng'ŭi (Seoul–Ŭiju) lines as the Kyŏng'in (Seoul–Inchŏn) and the Kyŏngbu (Seoul–Pusan) concessions had been taken by the Japanese and the Americans. Yi Ch'aeyŏn and McLeavy Brown worked on the feasibility studies for this project. Shortly before the opening of the Kyŏng'in line, the streetcar station for western Seoul was built right next to the Kyŏng'in station. The Collbran-Bostwick Development Company was contracted to build the Kumgok and Tŏkso feeder lines in April 1900. The Yongsan line was completed in December 1899 and connected to the Hongnŭng line; by July 1900, it was connected to the Kyŏng'in railroad line.[27] The development of the railway and streetcar networks was undertaken with the purpose of making Seoul the industrial center of the country.

By the latter half of the eighteenth century, the population of Seoul inside the city walls had reached 100,000, with another 100,000 residents outside. Commerce and handicraft industries flourished outside the fortress along the Han River in districts such as Yongsan, Map'o, Sŏgang, and Hangangjin (today's Hannam-dong). As part of the city's development plan, roads inside the fortress that had been widened in December 1896 were expanded to the same width in outlying districts. The Yongsan area was designated and developed as an industrial district. From 1898 to 1903, the following state-run factories were built in Yongsan: the state mint (1898), a printing press (1900), a factory which produced weights and measures (1902), a sericulture farm (1902), a power plant for the Hansŏng Electric Power Company (1903), a royal rice-polishing facility (1903), a munitions factory (1903), a brick factory, glassworks and more.[28]

26. Pak Chŏngyang concluded a contract with the mining engineer, Mr. Pearson, of New York City, whose work on behalf of Korea is documented in *Pak Chŏngyang chŏnjip* 4, pp. 209–20 (includes a copy of the contract and other data).
27. *No Inhwa*, p. 13. Hongnŭng was the tomb of Queen Min, Kojong's queen.
28. *Kyŏngsŏngbusa* (History of Seoul), pp. 1007–29.

## Chapter Eleven

### THE OBJECTIVES AND HISTORICAL SIGNIFICANCE OF SEOUL'S URBAN DEVELOPMENT

The reconstruction of Seoul as a modern capital began in 1896 as described above, but it continued for more than a few years. The basic project was initiated with the birth of the Great Han Empire and Kojong's inauguration as Emperor, but additional projects continued until the outbreak of the Russo-Japanese War in 1904. The urbanization of Seoul was intended to change the face of Seoul just as Chosŏn was embarking on a new beginning as a truly independent country which had thrown off the shackles imposed by the Qing Dynasty and Japan. These intentions were clearly expressed in an editorial discussing the construction of Independence Gate in the *Tongnip sinmun* on June 20, 1896. Though somewhat long, it is worth quoting at length:

> By Your Majesty's accession to the throne as Emperor, you have demonstrated your holy volition, your deep love for the country, by becoming the most supreme in a succession of kings, and by asserting that our country is independent, thereby taking your rightful place among sovereigns of other nations. For we believe that Your Majesty's new title was meant not only to elevate your rank, but to elevate the Chosŏn people as a whole. The people who know of your holy volition are prepared to sacrifice everything for Your Majesty. Your Majesty's new title raises hope that our nation will gradually become stronger and that we will not lose our rights as an independent state; that in fact our authority will become strengthened. Indeed, it may please Your Majesty to know that the expatriate community here reveres you, and that we consider it every citizen's duty to act, and that we hope to save the nation. We see the forthcoming construction of a new gate and its proposed name Independence Gate, on the site of what was until now [*sic:* what used to be] Yŏnju Gate [*sic:* Yŏng'ŭn Gate] at Mohwagwan, as a clear manifestation to the world that Chosŏn is an independent state. Furthermore, it is not enough to erase the shame that Yŏnju Gate represents to our history by razing it, but we must build the Independence Gate right over the spot. The construction of the Independence Gate will not only erase the shame of Yŏnju Gate, it will be the cornerstone of our

independence. We have heard that the Chosŏn people are overjoyed and delighted by this.²⁹

This editorial notes that the construction of Independence Gate raised the profile not only of the monarch but of the whole country as well, emphasizing that the idea came from the Emperor's patriotism and love for his people. This was the purpose behind not only Independence Gate but the whole urban development project.

In the July 2, 1896, issue of the *Tongnip sinmun*, the editorial was more forthright in its assertion of the purpose behind urban development. The editorial appears to have been written to refute an article in a foreign newspaper (possibly Japanese), which sarcastically mentioned that it was impossible to determine whether the cabinet was being run by reformists or diehard conservatives because of the lack of any visible accomplishments by the Chosŏn government since the Agwan P'achŏn. As the editorial noted, the Chosŏn army had grown a hundred times, and its finances were being managed by the American F. Neinstead. The advisor to the Finance Ministry, McLeavy Brown, had controlled the money supply and managed the national budget so that Chosŏn had no foreign debt. The construction of the Ŭiju railroad line was being negotiated just as the Kyŏngin and Kyŏngbu lines were due to open. Last but not least, the government had introduced many sweeping changes as part of its plan to redevelop Seoul. Roads had been cleaned up and widened, and the sewage channels drained. As a result, horses and oxen could travel easily on the roads, while the incidence of disease had fallen. The editorial stated that these were "the government's great accomplishments and a great benefit to the people." It went on to say, "If it were not for a sagacious monarch or a reform-minded government, who else could orchestrate such works?" The editorial noted that the populace was not content to stand by but took part in the construction of Independence Gate and Independence Hall, further noting a fund-raising campaign organized by the Independence Club. It said, "The Emperor and the Crown Prince and progressive members of the Cabinet wanted the best for the nation, and we hope that they were introducing such reforms in the interest of advancing the nation. If foreigners would bide their time, instead of blaming the government, they would naturally realize that the government has been reformed." Until recently, it was widely believed that the construction of Independence

---

29. The term "we" refers to Sŏ Chaep'il, who had American citizenship.

Gate was not the work of the government but the effort of Sŏ Chaep'il of the Independence Club. However, this editorial, written by Sŏ Chaep'il himself or with his approval, reveals that the government did indeed build the gate, and it is important to rectify this misconception.[30] The objective of urban development was to change the face now that it became an independent state, and it actively adopted the layouts, infrastructure, and facilities of Western cities in order to build up the strength necessary to maintain the country's independence. At the helm of the project was the monarch, but government officials who had worked in the United States, such as Pak Chŏng yang, did the actual implementation. Both the Emperor and the bureaucrats shared the philosophy of the reformists, which was expressed in the concepts of *tongdo sŏgi* (Eastern Ways, Western Technology) and *kubon sinch'am*, the belief that innovations must be based on established foundations. *Tongdo sŏgi* can be seen as the underlying principle of the Kwangmu Reforms of the Great Han Empire. The prevalent tendency to classify only groups that pursued *tongdo sŏgi* such as leaders of the Kapsin Coup as the Enlightenment Faction and to regard all others as conservatives must be abolished. This thinking was based on a conscious attempt to diminish the achievements of the enlightenment policies led by Emperor Kojong.

Among the many projects involved in building an imperial capital, endeavors such as moving the main palace to the city center and the care lavished on public parks have a deeper significance on the level of political ideology. It would be tempting to regard these two efforts as simple imitations of Western cities, but some consideration should be given to what made those Western ideas acceptable to Korean society. King Yŏngjo and King Chŏngjo, who ruled during the eighteenth century, often ventured out of the palaces and onto the streets of Seoul, giving the public more opportunities to air their grievances to their ruler. One study has shown that Chŏngjo went on seventy royal processions and listened to some 6,000 civil petitions during his twenty-four year reign.[31] Eighteenth-century rulers, in sharp contrast to their predecessors who mainly relied on the counsel of high-ranking

---

30. There is a possibility that Sŏ Chaep'il made the suggestion that the new Independence Gate be built on the site of Yŏng'ŭn Gate. But this conjecture was exaggerated and distorted such that Sŏ's Independence Club is credited with the actual construction of the gate, instead of the government.

31. Han Sanggwŏn, *Chosŏn hugi sahoe wa sowŏn chedo* (A study of late Chosŏn dynasty society and the petition system) (Seoul: Ilchogak, 1996).

officials, tried to have more direct contact with ordinary citizens. Because of economic and social changes, there was growing conflict between the social classes, which made it increasingly difficult for the king to rely solely upon or to side exclusively with the nobility. Monarchs realized that the dynasty could not be sustained without the support of ordinary citizens, who comprised the majority of society. They went beyond the traditional *wimin* (hierarchical view of the relationship between sovereign and subject) and developed the concept of *minguk* as a new theory of kingly rule which emphasized the unity of the king and his people.[32] Chŏngjo firmly established this political ideology, and though temporarily eclipsed during the period of in-law rule (*sedo chŏngch'i*) during the nineteenth century, it was restored by Kojong.

During their reigns, Yŏngjo and Chŏngjo received civil petitions at three places, all located in present-day Chongno in downtown Seoul. One of the locations is now a public park, and another was the site of a memorial commemorating the fortieth anniversary of King Kojong's ascension to the throne. It is no coincidence that they were built in locations of such historical significance. Considering the kings' custom of going into the streets to learn about public sentiment, moving the main palace to the city center suggests that they wanted to become closer to the people. The development of the *minguk* ideology and similar beliefs played an important role in facilitating the introduction of Western ideas.

CONCLUSION

The urban development of Seoul, which began after Kojong's retreat to the Russian legation in 1896, marks the first example of modern city planning in Korea, and its significance to the history of the nation is unquestioned. Not only did it signal the new beginning of the country as an independent nation, but it also served to reposition the emperor, the head and symbol of the state, as a reformer who sought to promote the further development of traditional political ideology through elements of Western civilization. The fact that the importance of Seoul's development in this light has not been widely known or credited until recently is due to the generally negative perception of Kojong and his reign. The Japanese did much to distort or conceal his

32. For more on this topic, see chapter 7 in this book.

achievements in an effort to justify their forceful occupation and subsequent colonization of Korea in 1910. In their rewriting of history, Kojong as king and later as emperor barely registers as a leading player, while his reign is characterized by conflicts with Queen Min and the Taewŏngun. The portrait that emerges from such distortions is that of a confused, weak-willed, ineffectual puppet caught between his father and the queen. Kojong's achievements were wrongly attributed to pro-Japanese reformists and the Independence Club.

The achievements of Seoul's redevelopment cannot be easily erased because it visibly changed the city's landscape. Nevertheless, the Japanese Resident-General and the Government-General did their best to alter these achievements. In the *Keijo shiku kaishu yotei keikaku rosen-zu* (Draft Plan to Restructure Kyŏngsŏng's [Seoul's] City Roads and Streets) pronounced in 1912 (prepared by the Resident-General before August 1910), the radial-road system originated from the base of Nam Mountain, just north of the Resident-General building, in an attempt to alter the original radial plan centered on Kyŏng'un Palace. For some reason, this proposal was never put into effect. It seems that Japan put so much effort into destroying Kyŏngbok Palace and other palaces to host the Chosŏn Mulsan Kongjinhoe (Chosŏn Industrial Exposition) in 1915 that it lacked the ability to attempt other projects. After the first stage of the destruction of Kyŏngbok Palace, a project to restructure the area around Kyŏng'un Palace was initiated according to a new plan drafted on June 25, 1919, soon after the March First Movement. A new axial road connecting Kyŏngbok Palace, Kyŏng'un Palace, Namdaemun, and Yongsan was expanded to accommodate the movement of Japanese troops, destroying the plaza in front of Kyŏngbok Palace, the area around the memorial to the fortieth anniversary of Kojong's coronation, and the plaza in front of Taean Gate at Kyŏng'un Palace, completely changing the face of the city.

In 1919, on the occasion of Kojong's funeral, mass rallies declaring Korea's independence had erupted on March 1st in three locations: in the plaza in front of Taeanmun at Kyŏng'un Palace, at Tapgol Park, and at Kojong's fortieth-memorial pavilion. The "Draft Plan for Restructuring Kyŏngsŏng's (Seoul's) Roads" that was formulated by the Government-General after the March First Movement proposed the demolition of two of those locations. It also provided for the rapid deployment of Japanese troops stationed at Yongsan to quell any further public gathering. Thus, the widening of roads was clearly designed to make it easier to suppress riots. Even though the Japanese posted troops in front of Kyŏngbok Palace and Kyŏng'un Palace, they built the new headquarters for the Government-General, City Hall, and all the administrative offices in those locations instead in the span of a few years. The Japanese systematically obliterated the physical landmarks of the urban development project that had been implemented by the emperor beginning in 1896, and the project itself was eventually forgotten. It is regretful that the project should have suffered such neglect, for its aims and strategies are of considerable importance in understanding the history of Seoul and of Korea.

translated by Edward Park

PART IV

# Overcoming the Distortions of Korean History

CHAPTER 12

# Why Has Yangban Culture Been Denounced?

A FEW YEARS AGO, one of my colleagues who specializes in education told me, "We [Koreans] have thrown away so much of what was uniquely ours that education no longer has anything to hold onto." The moment I heard this, I felt something akin to the despair one feels when standing at the edge of a cliff. Unlike historians who have been discussing their concerns for a long time, those of education scholars have a concrete, practical context. Indeed, during the past few years, there have been frequent stories in the news reporting that classes cannot function normally at times with students accusing their teachers of crimes and even students physically striking teachers.

Only a few decades ago, Koreans were the people who, more than any other in the world, heard talk of morality and ethics. Confucianism emphasizes morality and ethics, and thanks to its five-hundred-year-old tradition as the ideology of state and society, its echoes were heard for a long time even after the fall of the Confucian state. Confucianism emphasized the ethical and moral nature of humanity more than any other ideology or religion, and Koreans, who had spent nearly five hundred years engaged in Confucian cultivation, became more moral than any other people in the world. In the present day, however, the opposite is true. Koreans are denounced as examples of immorality that has even surpassed the "ugly Korean" stereotype. No matter how much the modern age celebrates the power of individuality, the loss of morality is unacceptable. Immorality and unethical behavior are clearly shameful.

The moral decline of Koreans, as my colleague pointed out, is related to the rash abandonment of those things that are ours. With the loss of the country's sovereignty in 1910, the educated tended to lay all the responsibility on the ruling-class yangban and the Confucian culture of the previous era. At the same time, Japan propagated the false idea that Korea's demise was due to the Confucian adherence to tradition and factional struggles among the yangban. With such a "consensus" developing internally and externally, the Chosŏn Dynasty, the yangban, and Confucian culture all began to be completely denounced. As a result, the march began to throw out everything that was ours. If the portrait of Koreans that remains at the end of this process is one of immorality and a lack of ethics, then we must seriously begin to reflect upon our past behavior.

THE LEGACY OF YANGBAN CONFUCIAN CULTURE

This chapter is not meant to be a conservative defense of yangban culture. The objective is to diagnose the various forms of regression brought about by its total rejection. It is first necessary to define "yangban culture." In this chapter, the term "yangban culture" refers to all of Confucian culture during the Chosŏn dynasty, the culture created by the yangban *sadaebu* (literati) who were the leading force during the five hundred year reign of the dynasty.

The term "yangban" originally referred to the two orders of officials, the civilian (*munban*) and military (*muban*). From the sixteenth century, it also signified the social class that was able to assume both civilian and military positions. The groups belonging to this social class were also called *sajok* (hereditary aristocratic families) or *sadaebu* (literati, scholar-officials). The term also referred to scholars studying Confucianism and those who became officials by passing the civil service examination (*kwagŏ*) in order to put the ideology into practice.[1] It would be no exaggeration to say that the yangban class was born through Confucianism. What, then, is Confucianism?

Confucianism is a religion and an ideology whose highest goal is to realize the will of Heaven (*ch'ŏndo*) in the world of humanity. In Confucianism, Heaven is the ruler with a great will that enables all

[1]. Yi Tae-jin (Yi T'aejin), "Chosŏn sidae ŭi yangban kaenyŏm kwa yŏn'gu tonghyang" (The concept of "yangban" in the Chosŏn period and research trends), *Hag'yeji* 3 (Military Museum of Korean Military Academy, 1993); Japanese translation published in *Chugoku: shakai to bunka*, no. 8 (1993).

things to live, and the essence of this great will is benevolence (*in*). As the lords of all creation, human beings have the duty of realizing benevolence in this world. Thus, the monarchy that rules over the world of humanity must rule benevolently, and officials must exist to assist the monarch. These were the central ideas governing all the behavior and conduct of the *sadaebu* of the Chosŏn dynasty—at least in principle.

The yangban *sadaebu* of the Chosŏn dynasty were well versed in the Song dynasty text, the *Great Learning* (K. Taehak). The *Great Learning* taught that the way to achieve benevolent rule was to cultivate oneself, to put one's house in proper order, to rule the country, and to bring peace to the world (K. *susinjega ch'igukp'yŏngch'ŏnha*). Though these words seem to provide an easy guide, the study of cultivation, the beginning of this process, was not so simple.

As is well known, the text begins with a passage stating that the Way of the *Great Learning* is to explain virtuous conduct (*myŏngdŏk*) and to transform the people (*sinmin*). The focus of self-cultivation was thus to understand virtuous conduct. In order to achieve benevolence in this world, it is necessary to engage in self-cultivation to understand the virtue bestowed by Heaven. In spite of the virtuous conduct bestowed by Heaven, many people became obsessed with prestige and desire, failing to conduct themselves in a virtuous manner. Therefore, scholars had to thoroughly engage in the study of self-cultivation to eliminate such desires, thus gaining the ability to participate in the realization of benevolent rule. Though the path of self-cultivation was not easy, it was a worthy endeavor for scholars to endure the suffering in order to transform the people, rule the country, and bring peace to the world. The minds of the *sadaebu* were to be hardened in the ideal of "bearing the concerns of the world before others and sharing the joys of the world after others."

Of course, there were many cases in which the actual lives of yangban *sadaebu* did not accord with this ideal type. In reality, there were far more people who, obsessed with obtaining wealth or power, abused the privileges of status that had been granted to them. The ideals of a Confucian monarchy could be achieved only through the bureaucratic system. *Sadaebu* were necessary in order to maintain the bureaucracy, but the integrity of those appointed as officials could not always be guaranteed. Self-cultivation was stressed in order to suppress the corruption of individual officials, and the government operated according to factional politics (*pungdang chŏngch'i*) in which political groups assumed responsibility for matters of state. But conflict among the factions once again brought about a situation in which officials caused suffering among the people. The eternal task of Confucianism was to resolve the contradictions between the ideals of the rule of the Three Dynasties (*samdae chich'i*) and the reality of the bureaucratic system.

The Confucianism of the Chosŏn dynasty had a number of problems due to its adoption of Zhu Xi's (Chu Hsi's) Neo-Confucianism as the sole orthodoxy. Another branch of Confucianism was the School of Wang Yangming, which offered a different interpretation of the *Great Learning* than that of Zhu Xi's. Wang Yangming opposed Zhu Xi's change of the phrase *ch'inmin*, as it appears in the *Book of Rites*, to *sinmin* (renovating or making new the people). He offered a different interpretation of the initial passages of the *Great Learning*. He regarded the "understanding of virtue" (*myŏngdŏk*) as the very constitution (K. *ch'e*) of all creation and "being close to the people" (*ch'inmin*) as the use (K. *yong*) of all creation. In his view, even people who were not literati (*sa*) could become exemplars of virtuous conduct on their own. Wang Yangming's work was a reaction to the fact that Zhu Xi Neo-Confucianism saw only the *sadaebu* as models of virtuous conduct and did not discuss commoners' potential for virtue. There were *sadaebu* in Korea who undertook serious study of the Wang Yangming School in the sixteenth century; nonetheless, Korea was a world of Zhu Xi Neo-Confucianism in which the *sajok* and *sadaebu* were dominant.[2] A strong class barrier had been created to protect the status of the yangban *sadaebu*.

However, the Confucian culture of the Chosŏn dynasty was not a product of the ancients. In the eighteenth century, kings such as Sukjong, Yŏngjo, and Chŏngjo, were concerned about the ill treatment of the common people, even by the political factions of the day. Under the slogan of protecting the common people, they called for the end of factional politics and asserted the legitimacy of direct rule by the monarch. They argued that it was necessary for them to rule directly, as Yao and Shun had done, in order to create the world of impartiality (*t'angp'yŏng*) that had existed during the rule of the Three Dynasties.[3] The *t'angp'yŏng* kings' policy of protecting the common

---

2. Chŏng Chaehun, "Chosŏn chŏngi yugyo chŏngch'i sasang yŏn'gu" (A study of Confucian political thought in the early Chosŏn period) (Ph.D. diss., Seoul National University, 2001).

3. See Yi Tae-jin, "Chosŏn sidae ŭi 'minpon' inyŏm ŭi pyŏnch'ŏn kwa sippal segi 'min'guk' inyŏm ŭi taedu," in Pak Ch'ungsŏk, et al., *Kukka inyŏm kwa*

people went beyond the concept of *minbon* (people as foundation). The term *minbon* referred to the idea that the people (*min*) are the foundation of the country, but in the world of Neo-Confucianism, where kingly rule is achieved through the counsel of the *sadaebu*, the people were not the rulers of the country but were always the object of rule. Just as the character *kalga* (family) was emphasized in the word *kukga* (state), the royal family (*wangga*) and the families of the *sadaebu* (*sadaebuga*) were the rulers of the country. The concept of *minbon* simply emphasized the lesson that although the king and *sadaebu* conducted politics, they were not to forget that the people constituted the foundation of the country.

In the eighteenth century, the *t'angp'yŏng* monarchs began to use a newly coined term, *minguk* (republic); the meaning of the term was that both the people and the king (equated with *kuk* as state) were the rulers of the country.[4] King Chŏngjo the Great even went so far as to declare that the people were the incarnation (*punsin*) of the ruler. Of course, he did not eliminate the *sadaebu* or deny their role; however, his attitude was that if a *sadaebu* did not endorse the idea of *minguk*, he was not needed at court. The *t'angp'yŏng* monarchs felt that this was the only way to protect the people from exploitation by the yangban *sadaebu*. For instance, King Chŏngjo decided to abolish public and private slaves (*kongsa nobi*) completely in order to eliminate inequalities among the people. These goals of *t'angp'yŏng* politics were closer to the position of the Wang Yangming School, which viewed the people as having the potential to be exemplars of virtue, than to that of the Zhu Xi School, which regarded only the *sadaebu* as the leaders of the transformation of the people (*sinmin*).[5] This transformation was a unique development undertaken by the Confucian monarchy of Chosŏn. *T'angp'yŏng* politics and the concept of *minguk* in the eighteenth century were efforts to resolve the problems caused by a social system centered on the *sadaebu* and *sajok* without rejecting Neo-Confucianism itself.

The concept of *minguk* in the eighteenth century was not the product of magnanimous thinking by the monarchy. The development

---

*taeoe insik* (Seoul: Ayŏn ch'ulp'ansa, 2001); published in Japanese as Yi Tae-jin "Chosen jidai no 'minpon' rinen no hensen to jyuhachi seki 'minkoku' rinen no taito" (Changes in the concept of *minpon* in the Chosŏn period and the emergence of the concept of *minguk* in the eighteenth century), *Kokka rinen to taigai ninsiki* (Tokyo: Keio University Press, 2001).
4. Ibid.
5. See Chŏng Chaehun, op. cit.

of commoner society made such new ways of thinking possible. With social and economic development, the number of commoners who became as wealthy as the yangban increased, enabling them to exert social influence. The rivalry between existing yangban and the newly rising class contributed to the impoverishment of the commoners. The monarchs felt that the concept of protecting the common people could be at once a goal and the first step toward solving this problem. What is significant is that as the newly rising class began to assume yangban status, the nature of the yangban class itself began to break down.[6] Many cases arose where it was difficult to distinguish between true yangban and commoners using family registers (*hojŏk*). This change signified a decrease in the social influence of the "real" yangban. The increase in the number of yangban of commoner birth decreased the prestige of yangban status. As commoners began to use expressions such as "this yangban" or "that yangban" casually, the terms *sa* and *sain* (person of letters) became the more prestigious way to designate those of scholarly achievement. As the number of commoners who became yangban increased in the nineteenth century, a new issue that emerged was how and to what extent they would engage in Confucian self-cultivation.

Since the history of the yangban in the Chosŏn period was characterized by such social dynamism, there is no reason for yangban culture to be rejected. In the fifteenth and sixteenth centuries, the yangban *sadaebu*'s Confucian sense of responsibility to society and the government left them open to the possibility of historical change. The rise of commoners from the eighteenth century and the monarch's support for the concept of *minguk* were changes that demonstrated the emergence of a different historical dynamic. If the yangban of commoner origin—whose numbers increased in the nineteenth century—absorbed Confucian norms, then it is necessary to see this phenomenon as the social diffusion of an elite humanism. In the context of such cultural vitality, it is difficult to believe that Korea was powerless to act in the face of Western material civilization.

---

6. Yi Tae-jin, "Chosŏn hugi yangban sahoe ŭi pyŏnhwa" (Changes in yangban society in the late Chosŏn period), *Han'guk sahoe paljŏnsaron*, Hallim kwahagwŏn chongsŏ 8 (Seoul: Ilchogak, 2000).

## THE UPSIDE-DOWN MODERN VIEW OF HISTORY

The general view of the last years of yangban society and culture has been that the Chosŏn dynasty was so immersed in the exclusionist thinking of Confucianism that it rejected the opportunity of opening to the new international order, and eventually it surrendered its sovereignty to a Japan that had already succeeded in Westernization. Was this indeed the case?

During the rule of the Taewŏngun (1864–1873), it is true that Korea suppressed Catholicism and was hostile to France, America, and other countries. However, the young King Kojong, who assumed direct rule in December 1873, took a very different approach. Believing that continuing isolation would only bring about the country's downfall, he hastened to establish diplomatic relations with Japan, which was experiencing a period of disorder. He sent missions to Japan and China and had them report on the introduction of Western civilization there. When the Treaty of Amity Between Chosŏn and Japan was signed in 1876, the Japanese Ambassador Extraordinaire and Plenipotentiary was rather bewildered by the degree of openness displayed by Chosŏn. Of the thirteen articles of the draft treaty prepared by the Japanese, nine were modified at Chosŏn's request, and the thirteenth article regarding most-favored nation status was removed. Japan accepted all of Chosŏn's demands, content simply to conclude a treaty with Chosŏn.[7] This version of events differs from the prevailing view that Chosŏn was stubbornly isolationist because of its ignorance of international affairs and was opened by Japan. The view of history that emphasized Japan's role in opening Chosŏn was developed around the time of annexation to justify Japan's actions.[8]

The signing of the Treaty of Amity and Commerce between the United States of America and Corea in April 1882 was one of the achievements of the early years of Kojong's enlightenment policy. He felt that the advance of the West into East Asia would bring the Sinocentric world order to an end; in this global change, the path for Chosŏn was quickly to establish new international relationships with

---

7. See Yi Tae-jin, "Kŭndae Han'guk ŭn kwayŏn 'ŭndunguk' iŏttŏnga?" (Was early modern Korea really a "hermit nation"?), *Kojong sidae ŭi chaejomyŏng* (Seoul: T'aehaksa, 2000). The English translation of this text can be found in chapter thirteen of this book.

8. See Yi Tae-jin, "Kojong hwangje amyaksŏl pip'an" (A critique of the theory of Emperor Kojong's ignorance and weakness) in *Kojong sidae ŭi chaejomyŏng*.

the Western powers.[9] He dispatched officials to Japan to collect materials relating to treaties as defined by international law (*Man'guk kongbŏp*) and searched for new ways of dealing with the new international situation. At this time, an opportunity arose to open relations with the United States, and after negotiations this treaty was formalized. Since the treaty applied a ten to thirty percent tariff to goods imported from the United States, Japanese newspapers offered high praise, saying it was the first equal treaty in Asia.[10] The view that this treaty was concluded on the advice of Li Hongzhang of Qing China was a distortion meant deliberately to emphasize the incompetence of the Chosŏn government. It is true that Li Hongzhang's influence played a role, but the Chosŏn monarch already had a plan in place prior to his involvement. Moreover, Li's request that the treaty contain language about Chosŏn's suzerain relationship to China was completely rejected.

However, the Imo Soldiers Riot that broke out on June 9, 1882, ruined plans for the implementation of King Kojong's enlightenment policy (*kaehwa chŏngch'aek*). More than any other country, Qing China responded strongly to this incident. China had concluded that Chosŏn was using the Chosŏn-American Treaty to try to break away from Chinese influence. When riot broke out, China took advantage of the opportunity to block Chosŏn's plans. China declared that the Emperor could not stand idly by as a military revolt caused distress to the Chosŏn ruler, whose title had been vested by the Emperor himself. It dispatched troops to Chosŏn under the pretext of hunting down the instigators of the riot. However, even after capturing the Taewŏngun and sending him to China, Chinese troops remained in Chosŏn to exert their influence in the country's internal affairs.

Japan also used this incident as an opportunity to apply pressure on Chosŏn. Denouncing the fire that broke out at the Japanese legation during the riot as a profaning of the Japanese flag, Japan demanded a huge sum in damages from the Chosŏn government and also obtained numerous concessions, such as an increase in the number of treaty ports and an expansion of its rights of passage. Prior

---

9. See Yi Tae-jin, "Kojong hwangje amyaksŏl pip'an" and "Kŭndae Han'guk ŭn kwayon ŭndunguk iŏttŏnga?" in *Kojong sidae ŭi chaejomyŏng*.

10. Kim Kyŏngt'ae, "Kaehang chikhu ŭi kwansegwŏn munje" (The problem of the restoration of tariff rights immediately after the opening of the ports), *Han'guksa yŏn'gu* 8 (1972); Kim Kyŏngt'ae, "Pulp'yŏngdŭng choyak kaejŏng kyosŏp ŭi chŏn'gae" (The progress of negotiations for the revisions of the unequal treaties), *Han'guksa yŏn'gu* 10 (1975), p. 199.

to this incident the Japanese had not been able to overcome Chosŏn's opposition to gain these concessions.

It would be no exaggeration to say that the chaos of Korea's modern history began with the Imo Soldiers Riot, the major incident that undermined the initial measures of the enlightenment policy. Kojong, however, did not deviate from his objective of implementing the enlightenment policy, even in the midst of these difficulties. On August 5, 1882, just ten days after the Qing soldiers had arrived, the king strengthened his resolve for enlightenment by handing down the following edict (*kyoyumun*). The edict was divided into three parts and addressed the inevitability of the country's opening to international relations and modern civilization:

> First, if we respond to the foreign powers who are pressing at our door in a hostile manner as we did in the past, it will only result in war; thus, as a result, we will be destroyed by our own hand, isolated and helpless; and even if we were to fight and be victorious for a day, we would find ourselves in a situation from which we could not return.
> Second, some say that if we succeed in opening and enlightening our country, we must be concerned about heresy, namely the spread of Christianity, but the suppression of heresy and the entering into amicable relations are separate issues based on international law, and even if we are to commit to trade relations, it is not the case that we would be abandoning our orthodoxy [*chŏnggyo*; i.e., Confucianism] overnight.
> Third, some say that if we accept and study Western machines and manufacturing technology, we will be inviting heresy, but it is not impossible for the two to progress side by side. The paths of the strong and the weak are widely different, but how are we to stop others from scorning and overlooking us unless we learn from them?[11]

At the end of the edict, the young King Kojong noted that the soldiers' riot in June had endangered the country's situation, made Chosŏn the laughing stock of the world, and cost it the trust of its neighbors. Despite this, Chosŏn restored diplomatic relations with Japan and successively signed trade agreements with the Western

---

11. *Kojong sillok*, Vol. 19, 19th year of Kojong's reign, fifth day of the eighth month.

powers. After Kojong implored the people not to incite disturbances against foreigners, whether Japanese or Western, he ordered the removal of all the anti-Western monuments (ch'ŏkhwabi) that had been erected during the Taewŏngun's rule.

At the end of December 1882, Kojong also issued an injunction to the people concerning the creation of the internal conditions necessary to open the country and introduce Western civilization. On the commercial trade agreements with the West, he explained, "If we intend to regain harmonious rule, we must first shatter our preconceived notions." Under this premise, he urged people to abandon the traditional class hierarchy of scholars, farmers, artisans, and merchants (sa-nong-kong-sang) and exhorted all yangban to devote themselves to creating wealth. He also stated that the children of yangban should attend school together with commoners, such as farmers, artisans, and merchants; that priority be given to talent over birth; and that no distinctions should be made between commoners and yangban. He wrote that these reforms were the path to increase the wealth of both the country and individual families.[12] This official proclamation was significant because the king was trying to abolish the class distinctions that had existed for nearly five hundred years.

The groundwork for this surprising proclamation was laid by the earlier emergence of the concept of *minguk* during Chŏngjo's reign. Chŏngjo was the predecessor whom Kojong most admired, and Kojong attempted to continue the ideals of *minguk* politics and enrich the country by importing the new technological civilization of the West. Four years later, in 1886, Kojong's proclamation on the abolition of the hereditary system of private slaves represented the achievement of what Chŏngjo's had decided to do in 1800 but failed to implement because of his sudden illness and death.[13]

Anyone familiar with Korean history may feel some confusion at this point. According to the commonly held view of this period, it was Kim Okgyun and other leaders of the Kapsin Coup of 1884 who accomplished these radical measures; how could it have been Kojong? The abolition of the social status system was supposed to have occurred in 1894 as part of the Kabo Reforms; how could Kojong have already accomplished it in the 1880s? The view of history that

---

12. *Kojong sillok*, Vol. 19, 19th year of Kojong, twenty-eighth day of the twelfth month.

13. Yi Tae-jin, "Kojong ŭi kukki chejŏng kwa kunmin ilch'e ŭi chŏngch'i inyŏm" (Kojong's establishment of a national flag and the political ideal of *kunmin ilch'i*), in *Kojong sidae ŭi chaejomyŏng*, p. 263.

sees the Kapsin Coup and the Kabo Reforms as defining moments in Korea's modernization provided the framework needed by Japan to justify its takeover of Korea in 1910. This reasoning is similar to the view that the Kanghwa Treaty of 1876 was accomplished by Japan. Japan's claim to have seized Korea's sovereignty for the purpose of reforming its government would have been untenable if Kojong were to have appeared even slightly competent or eager to modernize the country. Thus, Japan hastened to destroy Kojong's image and instead highlighted events such as the Kapsin Coup and the Kabo Reforms, incidents that Japan supported or was directly involved in, as opportunities that demonstrated a potential for modernization.

At the time of the Kapsin Coup, there were around four thousand Qing soldiers stationed in the Seoul area. In contrast, the Japanese legation garrison, which Kim Okgyun (1851–1894) and others were relying upon to support their coup, was comprised of just a single company.[14] Undertaking a coup with knowledge of this fact was an extremely reckless act. How could it be said that this coup d'etat was the origin of modernization? The tragedy of the coup went beyond the actual event itself. Since the coup was anti-Qing, it provided the pretext for China to intervene directly in Chosŏn's internal affairs. In actuality, it was Yuan Shikai (1859–1916), the Director-General Resident of Diplomatic and Commercial Relations in Chosŏn, who created the system to enable Chinese intervention in Chosŏn immediately after the attempted coup. Chinese intervention continued for nearly ten years and inflicted a fatal blow to Korea's ability to modernize on its own.

Japan had supported the coup d'état and was on the losing side, as were the coup's Chosŏn leaders, but in the aftermath, the Japanese gained many benefits. The Japanese legation had initially distanced itself from Kim Okgyun, Pak Yŏnghyo, and the other coup plotters, thinking that there was no reason to aggravate relations with Qing China. The consul Takezoe Shinichiro (1842–1917) was then summoned to Tokyo, and on his return to Chosŏn, he suddenly became very close with the plotters in the days and weeks leading up to the coup. The Japanese legation was well aware that its forces were at a complete disadvantage compared with the Qing troops. Nonetheless, there was another reasoning behind their decision to support the plan

14. For a description of the rest of the events of the Kapsin Coup, see Yi Tae-jin, "1884nyŏn Kapsin chŏngbyŏn ŭi hŏwisŏng—Ilsa naewi ŏsŏ wijo ŭi kyŏngwi" (The falsehoods of the 1884 Kapsin Coup—the fabrication of the official document "Ilsa naewi") in Kojong sidae ŭi chaejomyŏng.

of Kim Okgyun's group to instigate a coup. If a situation arose in which Japan suffered damage during the coup, as had happened during the Imo Soldiers Riot, Japan decided that it could possibly serve as the pretext to secure the right to intervene in Korea's affairs.

After Chinese troops entered the Korean peninsula, Japan's influence declined, but they could do nothing about it given the strength of their country at the time. Despite their disadvantage, Japan wanted to make a dramatic move to enable itself to exert its influence in Korea, and they thought that Kim Okgyun's planned coup could make this possible. When the Japanese fled Korea just three days after the coup, the Japanese legation staff secretly set fire to their own building. After maneuvering themselves into the position of a victim, Japan gained the right in the Convention of Tianjin (April 18, 1885) to send troops to Korea together with China in the event of an emergency on the peninsula, declaring that it was important to prevent a repetition of such events. Kim Okgyun's group was so fixated on gaining power that they ended up being completely used by the Japanese. How can a person like Kim be called a pioneer of modernization?

Around the time Korea lost its sovereignty in 1910, Japanese *ronin* began an effort to glorify Kim Okgyun as a hero.[15] Their objectives were as follows. First, Kim's lionization as a pioneer of modernization would make it possible to obscure the accomplishments made under Kojong's leadership. Second, it would be possible to portray Queen Min, who was restored by Qing forces after the Imo Soldiers Riot, as a staunch conservative by contrasting her with the anti-Qing position of Kim Okgyun. This disparagement was useful in providing a justification for the queen's assassination. The Japanese wanted to convince people that the queen had to be eliminated, despite her status, because her power was backed by the support of China. It is important to remember that among the leaders of the effort to discredit the queen were many who were also involved in her assassination.

During the period of Chinese interference under Yuan Shikai, Chosŏn's politics and the economy worsened. Having obtained the right to dispatch troops to Chosŏn through the Convention of Tianjin, Japan focused on building up its military, while outwardly maintaining cordial relations with China. Japan's policy of pursuing capitalist

---

15. See Kim T'aeŭng, "Ilche kangjŏmgi Kim Okgyun ch'uang kwa wiin kyoyuk" (The lionization of Kim Okgyun during the Japanese occupation period and the education of heroes), *Yŏksa kyoyuk* 74 (2000).

## Why Has Yangban Culture Been Denounced? 307

development after the Meiji Restoration began to bear results around 1885; from this time, the Japanese government devoted many of its resources to promoting military industries. Within ten years, the opportunity came to exercise its right to dispatch troops to Korea, one of its spoils from the Kapsin Coup. In 1894, when the Tonghak peasant army rose in revolt, Yuan Shikai forced the Chosŏn government to request troops from China.[16] His purpose was to strengthen China's ability to intervene in Korea's affairs and to chastise the people of Chosŏn for their resistance to Chinese intervention. The Japanese legation closely followed the nearly twenty-day dispute between the Chosŏn government and Yuan Shikai. As soon as the Chosŏn government, unable to defy Yuan Shikai's demands, sent an official request for Chinese troops in the name of the Minister of the Left, the Japanese government, whose troops were standing ready, dispatched a brigade as soon as China's notification arrived in Tokyo. Japanese troops arrived in Inch'ŏn before the Chinese forces.

With its built-up military, Japan intended to establish exclusive control over the Korean peninsula even if it meant starting a war with China. Unlike the Chinese forces, the Japanese army avoided areas where the Tonghak peasant army was and headed to Seoul. Their plan for dealing with the peasant uprising was to surround the royal palace and force the Korean government to enact the reform agenda they had already prepared, all under the pretext of reforming domestic politics. This was the beginning of the Kabo Reforms in 1894. The Office for Military and State Affairs (Kun'guk kimuch'ŏ) was hastily created as the central organ for reform. There were officials appointed to this office who attempted to eliminate Japan's influence and to implement reforms already planned by the government, but the Japanese quickly suppressed them. Is it possible to regard "reforms" that were pursued under coercion as the essence of Korean modernization?

The simultaneous entry of Chinese and Japanese forces into Chosŏn developed into an all-out military confrontation. Victorious in the Sino-Japanese War, Japan wanted to use its military might to undermine Chosŏn's sovereignty and turn the country into a protectorate. Minister of Foreign Affairs Inoue Kaoru (1835–1915) was appointed as the minister to Korea and took control of all matters in Seoul. Japan retreated on its plans to turn Chosŏn into a protectorate

16. See Yi Tae-jin, "1894nyŏn 6-wŏl Ch'ŏnggun ch'ulbyŏng kwajŏng ŭi chinsang—chajin ch'ŏngbyŏngsŏl pip'an—" (The truth about the dispatch of Chinese troops in June 1894—a critique of the theory of the voluntary request for troops), in Kojong sidae ŭi chaejomyŏng.

at the time of the Triple Intervention in April 1895, which forced Japan to return its war spoils to China, including the cession of the Liaodong peninsula. However, Japan then had Queen Min assassinated in October 1895, as if in retaliation for this unfavorable turn of events. The Queen had been covertly seeking the assistance of the Russian and the United States legations in order to save the monarch, who was practically imprisoned by Japanese forces. After the queen's assassination, King Kojong together with the crown prince and other members of his family fled Kyŏngbok Palace with the help of both the Russian and the United States legations. He took up residence in the Russian legation on February 11, 1896, and this incident is known as the "Agwan P'ach'ŏn." He then disbanded the pro-Japanese cabinet and restored the power of the monarch.[17]

For the moment, Kojong had succeeded in escaping from Japanese interference. In 1897, he officially renamed the country the "Great Han Empire" and pursued a self-strengthening modernization policy, which had been adrift until then. To involve the citizens in this new beginning, he also launched the Independence Club (Tongnip hyŏphoe) as a quasi-governmental organization. In the context of emergence of the concept of *minguk*, it is significant that the first social organization in Korean history was launched at the initiative of the emperor. However, the Independence Club could not operate freely due to the interference of the Japanese legation. Its anti-Russia movement and citizens' assemblies with officials are considered to be the beginnings of the popular rights movement in Korea; however, in reality, some of the Club's leaders were pro-Japanese and were working with the Japanese legation to undermine the emperor's authority.[18] Although the emperor understood the importance of popular rights, he felt that national sovereignty should take precedence at a time when foreign powers were posing a threat, and he repeatedly called for calm. In the end, however, he ignored what people said and issued an order for the Club to suspend all its activities, in order to bring the unrest to an end.

The Kwangmu Reforms, as the Great Han Empire's modernization policies have been called, began to bear fruit as the political situation stabilized. Since Japan began its colonial rule over Taiwan in 1895, it made no further encroachments on Korea. This was an

---

17. Yi Tae-jin, "Kojong sidaesa hŭrŭm ŭi chaejomyong" (A reexamination of the trends of the history of the Kojong period) in *Kojong sidae ŭi chaejomyŏng*, pp. 31–33.

18. Ibid., pp. 50–67.

important international factor behind the accomplishments of the Kwangmu Reforms. However, Japan established its rule in Taiwan by 1900, and from 1901, it turned its attention again to the Korean peninsula. Following an expansionist strategy, Japan instigated the Russo-Japanese War in February 1904 and began the process of seizing Korea's sovereignty.

Though the objective of this section was to trace the development of yangban culture in the nineteenth century, it was necessary to undertake a lengthy examination of Kojong's reign. It would be almost impossible to understand yangban culture properly when prevailing views on that period have been distorted. Since the negative prejudices against yangban culture emerged from an erroneous view of history, it is impossible to take even a single step toward historical truth without first correcting these misconceptions. In the context of the development of *minguk* politics since the eighteenth century, the main agents of history in the Kojong era were the ruler and the people. While developments among the common people are important to understand this period, developments in the monarchy should not be ignored or excluded. Views on this period up to the present have ignored the monarch for his supposed incompetence, and in his place flickered the image of a successfully modernized Japan and its agents. In such circumstances, how can traditional culture, as represented by Confucianism and the yangban, be judged properly?

## THE MODERN TRANSFORMATION AND ORIENTATION OF YANGBAN CULTURE

### (1) The Tale of Ch'unhyang

Confucianism is generally thought to be a feudal or medieval ideology. In fact, criticizing or rejecting Confucianism seems to be a prerequisite for being progressive. However, in Western history, feudal and medieval things are not targets of total condemnation. The historical role and contribution of feudal ideologies and religions have always been acknowledged. In the case of Korean Confucianism, it is difficult to achieve a balanced view because of the strong prejudice that it was the main obstacle to modernization. Since Confucianism has become a sacrificial offering to a sacred modernity, Korea's modernity has necessarily become severed from its tradition. How can Korea endure such a loss?

Japan's Meiji Reformation is generally regarded as the only case of successful modernization and Westernization in Asia. No critic of Confucianism would disagree with this view. What these critics overlook is the fact that the goals of the Meiji Reformation were deeply rooted in both Japanese and East Asian traditions. A good example is the Imperial Rescript on Education (*Kyoiku chokugo*) of 1890. As is well known, the purpose of this edict was to create new citizens in the process of establishing a nation-state under the emperor system. Its message was that all citizens must observe closely the Three Ethical Bonds (K. *samgang*; J. *sanko*) of Confucianism. If Confucianism is equated with what is feudal, then it could be said that Meiji Japan promoted feudal ethics in order to produce modern citizens. Such logic is untenable.

Confucianism was categorized as feudal because the only class that could partake of Confucian culture during the Chosŏn dynasty was the "feudal" status group of the yangban *sadaebu*. Confucian ideology, in and of itself, is not necessarily feudal. Perhaps if Confucianism could eliminate its class restrictions and become the culture and ideology of all classes, there would be no reason to see it narrowly as feudal or medieval. Originating in the early Chin dynasty, Confucianism was adopted as an "ancient" ideology in the Han and Tang periods, and it was reformulated into a medieval ideology during the Song and Yuan periods. It was this Confucianism that was adopted by the Chosŏn dynasty. Since Confucianism contains trans-historical truths like any other religion, it is capable of historical change and adaptation. It is incorrect to categorize it definitively as feudal simply because it was dominant during the Chosŏn dynasty.

As is well known, the major works of popular literature from the late Chosŏn period are *p'ansori* such as *Ch'unhyangjŏn* (The tale of Ch'unhyang) and *Simch'ŏngjŏn* (The tale of Simch'ŏng). It is interesting in the context of the modern aspects of Confucianism that all these works extol the values of the Three Bonds and Five Moral Rules of human relationships (*samgang oryun*). The *Tale of Ch'unhyang* is about the romance between Ch'unhyang, the daughter of a retired *kisaeng* (female artist-entertainer), and Yi Toryŏng, the legitimate son of a yangban scholar-official. The story shows how their marriage was able to persevere because of Ch'unhyang's complete faithfulness, for which the king highly esteems and rewards her. The heroine of the *Tale of Simch'ŏng* is the daughter of a poor commoner who is blind. Through her deep filial piety to her blind father, Simch'ŏng becomes a queen and is able to restore her father's sight. A marriage between the

## Why Has Yangban Culture Been Denounced? 311

daughter of a low-born *kisaeng* and the son of a *sadaebu* would have been unthinkable in a hierarchical class society dominated by the yangban. Though the *Tale of Simch'ŏng* takes place in the undersea world of the dragon palace, it was equally unimaginable for the daughter of a commoner to become a queen. What is the significance of the fact that stories and *p'ansori* with such content were so widespread in commoner society? At a time when orthodox yangban *sadaebu* were trying to maintain their status privileges, what does it mean that the king was encouraging works that they could never accept?

There are many stories of kings during the period of *sedo chŏngch'i* (rule by in-law families) who invited *p'ansori* singers to the palace or supported them financially. Kings Sunjong, Hŏnjong, and Ch'ŏljong all did so, and the Taewŏngun, who ended *sedo chŏngch'i*, was also a patron of *p'ansori*. When he assumed direct rule of the country, Kojong continued this tradition. In 1902, the fortieth anniversary of his ascension to the throne, Kojong established Hyŏmnyulsa (a Western-style amphitheater) in Seoul as the royal theater, and it was used for performances of *p'ansori* and Korean classical music. The kings' patronage of *p'ansori* suggests that the nineteenth-century rulers favored the commoners over the leaders of the yangban *literati*, supporting them in their desire for social mobility. These efforts by the monarchs were an attempt to realize the *minguk* ideal of "unity between the ruler and the people" (*kunmin ilch'i*) established by the eighteenth century *t'angp'yŏng* monarchs; the general trend of the time was for kings to turn to the people for their base of support. Until that time, the ethics of the Three Bonds and Five Moral Rules had been the sole province of the yangban *sadaebu*; they were to be exemplars of these ethics, and the commoners were to follow their example. In the eighteenth and nineteenth centuries, the people became the main agents of ethics, and monarchical authority came to be based on the will of the entire people. In substance, this conception is no different from goals of the Imperial Rescript on Education of Meiji Japan. If anything, the imperial rescript's conception of the emperor's relationship to his people as one of father and son seems to be less progressive than the Chosŏn dynasty's notion of the ruler as the incarnation of the people. In any event, it is very important to note that yangban culture did not become a target of attack but rather proliferated among the masses during the breakdown of feudal society. Even though there were critiques and condemnations of the yangban themselves, yangban culture, which was based on Confucianism, was not rejected.

## (2) The Case of Pak Ŭnsik

During Kojong's reign, the foreign powers were not the only problem, for there was also internal strife and disruption. In this period, the term *oran* (five confusions) was widely used, and it referred to Catholicism (*sŏran*), Tonghak (*tongnan*), general immorality (*chapnan*; i.e., wine, women, and gambling), refugees (*iran*), and lawsuits about graveyards (*sallan*).[19] The phenomenon of *chapnan* is especially interesting in relation to yangban culture. The term *chapnan* referred to the phenomenon of scholars indulging in vices and bringing themselves and their families to ruin out of their despair at losing all opportunities for political advancement and economic gain because of the *sedo* families in Seoul and their children. They lacked opportunities for political advancement because the civil service examinations were not being conducted fairly and provincial scholars were being excluded. Pak Ŭnsik (1859–1925), one of the most important intellectuals of this period, described the changes in scholars during this time as follows:

> A hundred years ago, scholars practiced benevolence and justice (*inŭi*), immersed themselves in the study of great deeds, and thought of the country's affairs as their own. But during the past hundred years, even if scholars lived in solitude in rural villages and read the works of Confucius and Mencius to prepare for the civil service examination, they failed to discover meaning in their works. Recently scholars have put away all their books, compete to seek profit, and do not even hesitate to turn their backs on their king and their country.

In the 1890s, Pak Ŭnsik was the editor-in-chief of the newspaper *Hwangsŏng sinmun* and played a leading role in enlightening the masses. After the country's loss of sovereignty in 1910, he went to Manchuria and then to Shanghai where he devoted himself to the independence movement. In 1919, the Korean Provisional Govern-

---

19. This section on Pak Ŭnsik and social conditions of the time is mainly taken from No Kwanbŏm, "Pak Ŭnsik (1859–1925) ŭi kusŭp kaeryangnon kwa Yangmyŏnghak chech'ang" (Pak Ŭnsik's reform of old customs and advocacy of Wang Yangming [Neo-Confucianism]) (M.A. thesis, Seoul National University, 1999).

ment was established in Shanghai, and he became its second president in 1925. He was undoubtedly an individual of the highest integrity among intellectuals during this period. How did he view yangban culture? When he was young, Pak Ŭnsik was immersed in a traditional view of education. He devoted himself to studying Neo-Confucianism and quickly made a name for himself. It is known that he associated with the disciples of Chŏng Yagyong (1762–1836; *ho* Tasan) and studied Silhak thought. To overcome *chapnan*, he was initially interested in things closest to traditional ways. For instance, he felt that it was sufficient to instill in scholars the sense of duty to "cultivate oneself in order to rule over others" (*sugi ch'iin*). Because the civil service examination was not conducted in an impartial manner, he proposed establishing a recommendation system for nominating men of ability in each region of the country. Although the category of scholar had already extended beyond that of legitimate yangban, he developed this plan in order to overcome the *sadaebu*'s de facto monopolization of exam passers by in Seoul.

Pak Ŭnsik first mentioned the introduction of new learning (*sin hangmun*) in his 1901 book *Hŭnghaksŏl* (A Theory of Emerging Learning). In this text, he argued that the strength of a country depends on the promotion of learning (*munhak*) and the achievement of civilization. The term *munhak* referred to new learning in fields of practical benefit to people's welfare, such as agriculture, commerce, mining, medicine, military science, and physics. As a concrete plan for development, Pak discussed proposals such as establishing schools, publishing books, sending students to study abroad, and training teachers. The basic plan of this text was to encourage the involvement of scholars in politics through the promotion of new learning and the training of people necessary for the administration of the state. It could be said that these ideas were similar to those of his previous framework. However, not only had the content of education changed, but a new idea had also emerged of the state being founded upon its citizens and citizens being perfected through *munhak*, that is, new learning. He was concerned with producing the citizens of a modern nation-state.

In his 1904 text *Hakgyu sillon* (New Theory of Academic Rules), Pak Ŭnsik advocated the teaching of new learning for the education of provincial scholars. He also expected the imperial family to establish imperial schools and supervise the teaching of *munhak*—the new Western learning. The Department of the Imperial Household, directly under the control of the Emperor, had already established around twenty offices and was in charge of modern industrialization projects. Pak felt that in order to train the people needed for these projects, it would be necessary to establish and operate various kinds of schools. His position was that such reforms needed to be pursued even further.

Even more important, *Hakkyu sillon* contained the idea that traditional Confucianism should move from the domain of politics to that of religion and that politics should be centered on the new learning. Pak's proposal was to put the Imperial Household in charge of spreading the new learning and to turn Confucianism into a state "religion" by translating the *Elementary Learning* and the Four Classics into Korean and teaching them to farmers, artisans, and merchants, as well as women, who constituted the foundation of the country. These ideas were based on the belief that the fortunes of the country depended on the new learning and that the preservation of the country's vitality relied upon the maintenance of religion. His thinking was based on the concept of *tongdo sŏgi* (Eastern ways, Western technology). These ideas can also be seen as a search for a concrete way of fostering the national consciousness necessary for the establishment of a modern nation-state among the people. Similarly, in Meiji Japan, Ito Hirobumi created state Shinto and had it included in the Constitution adopted in 1890. There was a fundamental difference between Confucianism and state Shinto as religions; however, they had in common the fact that both were felt to be necessary to foster a national spirit at the time when a modern nation-state was being established.

Pak Ŭnsik's *Hakgyu sillon* was a reflection of its times. The Great Han Empire had been inaugurated in October 1897 and had begun the Kwangmu Reforms to lay the foundation for modernization. The text was suffused with great expectations for modernizing reforms based on the idea of *tongdo sŏgi* that were being pursued by Kojong. The fundamental objective of the effort to promote national consciousness by turning Confucianism into a state religion was to develop solidarity and a sense of duty among the empire's subjects. However, when the Russo-Japanese War began in February 1904, Japan used its military to begin undermining the sovereignty of the Great Han Empire. In such a critical turn of events, Pak's thinking changed rapidly. From 1907, he began to emphasize strongly the development of "society." For him, society was "a mutual union of the general populace to pursue and cooperate on projects for the public good for the state and the nation." He argued that in an age of competition, survival depended on solidarity—i.e., the union of organizations—and he saw the incomplete elimination of negative customs and the incomplete achievement of a new civilization as obstacles to social development.

Pak Ŭnsik's 1907 work *Kusŭp kaeryang* (Reforming Old Customs) criticized the Korean people's lack of interest in the development of knowledge and the expansion of rights and urged people to devote greater effort to national self-strengthening (*punbal chagang*). He felt that in the face of a crisis of national sovereignty, it was necessary for the people to unite as a "society" on their own and carry on a self-strengthening movement themselves, rather than the government. Pak pointed out that the notion of "society" was not completely unfamiliar to Koreans but had been exemplified by the *sarim* (Neo-Confucian literati) of the Chosŏn dynasty. His concern was to raise awareness of tradition and to instill confidence in its realization.[20] Many intellectuals at the time, surprised by Japan's victory in the Russo-Japanese War, urged national self-strengthening and argued that knowledge of foreign civilizations should be spread among the people as well. However, Pak Ŭnsik thought differently. He argued that priority had to be given to achieving the inherent unity (*sŏnch'ŏnjŏk tanhap*) that the people would realize through their own efforts.

In the face of an imminent international crisis, it would be logical to expect that the internal unity of the country would automatically be strengthened, and Pak Ŭnsik's conception of "inherent unity" was initially not much different. By 1909, however, when he founded the Taedong religion (Taedonggyo), his ideas seemed to have underdone a significant change. He explicated the essence of human unity in terms of the Wang Yangming School of Neo-Confucianism as "the benevolence (*in*) of the unity of all things in the world." He regarded unity as a matter concerning the Way of Heaven or the Mandate of Heaven for survival. As discussed above, the Wang Yangming School had its own interpretation of the initial passages of the *Great Learning*; they regarded the understanding of virtue (*myŏngdŏk*) as the very constitution (K. *ch'e*) of all creation and "being close to the people" (*ch'inmin*) as the use (K. *yong*) of all creation. In contrast to Zhu Xi Neo-Confucianism, which saw only the *sadaebu* as having the potential to be exemplars of virtuous conduct, the Wang Yangming

---

20. "Kŭnŏmi wa mua ranŭn yŏnsŏl," *Sŏbuk hakhoe wŏlbo* 1, no. 5 (Oct. 1908).

School felt that it was necessary to include all the people in order to fulfill the notion of *ch'inmin*. Pak Ŭnsik defined the essence of unity as the "benevolence of the unity of all things in the world" because he believed it was a matter of the Way of Heaven (*ch'ŏndo*), which was the object of the explication of virtuous conduct. He felt that each person needed to see himself or herself as a subject capable of understanding the Way of Heaven in order to break completely with the old customs (*kusŭp*) whose existence depended on the monarch, the government, and political factions. He turned to the Wang Yangming School of Neo-Confucianism because it provided an ideology that could make it possible to achieve these goals within the bounds of tradition. His objective in founding the Taedong religion was precisely to put these ideas into practice.

To Pak Ŭnsik, traditional yangban culture, which was based on Neo-Confucianism, was something to be surpassed but was not the object of denunciation. Most advocates of national self-strengthening denounced tradition, convinced that the only path for survival was the introduction of Western civilization. By contrast, Pak believed that the acceptance of a new civilization lacking in national spirit was virtually suicidal. He acknowledged the contributions of scholars of previous eras to the country's development, and he felt that the most pressing task of the times was to instill a sense of duty in all the common people. For him, the value of Wang Yangming Neo-Confucianism was that it provided a logic that would make the achievement of this task possible. It is clear that all of his efforts were dedicated to the rebirth of the people as modern citizens. While he served as the leader of the Taedong religion, he began to compile an anthology (*munjip*) of Chosŏn period Neo-Confucianists, such as Yi Hwang (T'oegye) and Yi I (Yulgok). He planned to publish it in an edition called the *Kukjo hak'an* and send it to the Wang Yangming Neo-Confucian Society (Yomei gakkai) in Japan. This plan is evidence of Pak's conviction that the yangban culture of the Chosŏn dynasty had universal value.[21]

WESTERNIZATION AND THE DENUNCIATION OF YANGBAN CULTURE

After the opening of the ports, there were three types of responses to Western civilization. They were *ch'ŏksa wijŏng* (reject heterodoxy and defend orthodoxy), *tongdo sŏgi* (Eastern ways, Western technology),

21. No Kwanbŏm, Ibid.

and *sŏdo sŏgi* (Western ways, Western technology). First, the advocates of *ch'ŏksa wijŏng* saw Christianity as the essence of Western civilization and felt it was necessary to reject it completely since its adoption would result in the demise of Confucianism. As is well known, the notion of *ch'ŏksa wijŏng* was the foundation of the Taewŏngun's foreign policy. However, after the Imo Soldiers Riot, many of its advocates began to feel it was necessary to adopt Western technological civilization, influenced by Kojong's 1882 edict.

Second, the advocates of *tongdo sŏgi* believed that in order to achieve national self-strengthening, it was necessary to adopt the new technology of the West while maintaining the Confucian tradition of the Chosŏn dynasty. After assuming direct rule, Kojong and reformist officials constituted a vanguard force, and after the 1882 edict, reformist Confucianists began to emerge and became the base of support. Of course, Pak Ŭnsik was also a supporter of *tongdo sŏgi*. In August 1897, shortly before the inauguration of the Great Han Empire, Kojong noted that "the code of laws of the country originally could not be completely changed, and even if all Western ways could not be adopted, they do deserve serious consideration." These ideas could be said to express the essence of *tongdo sŏgi*.

Third, the advocates of *sŏdo sŏgi* viewed Confucian culture as barbaric and semicivilized and felt it was necessary to adopt the ways and technology of the West fully in order to become truly civilized. Obviously, as *sŏdo sŏgi* completely rejected the traditional yangban and their culture, it played the largest role in the denunciation of yangban culture.

From the very beginning, the notion of *sŏdo sŏgi* was influenced by Japan. Fukuzawa Yukichi (1834–1901) was a famous thinker and commentator in Japan at the time, and the idea of *sŏdo sŏgi* originated with his assertion that the rapid adoption of Western civilization was essential in order to overcome barbarism and a semi-civilized state. Among the young Chosŏn intellectuals, there were many who were influenced by his ideas; most importantly, Kim Okgyun and the other leaders of the Kapsin Coup. Interestingly, the idea was promoted that the quickest way to introduce Western civilization was not through Western countries but through Japan. During the Sino-Japanese War (1894–1895), many Chosŏn intellectuals were astonished by the rapid growth of Japan's military strength. During the Russo-Japanese War (1904–1905), their shock at seeing Japan defeat a great power like Russia was even greater. The notion of *sŏdo sŏgi* became popular in the form of a discourse on national self-strengthening (*chagang*), and it developed into a logic that supported Japanese rule as it became intricately connected with the Residency-General's improvement of administration (*sijŏng kaesŏn*). After the Russo-Japanese War, the notions of *tongdo sŏgi* and *sŏdo sŏgi* ultimately came to represent, respectively, support for independence and for foreign rule.

After the Russo-Japanese War, the movement for national self-strengthening (i.e., *sŏdo sŏgi*) devoted much energy to the elimination of old customs (*kusŭp*), and the Resident-General's effort to improve administration took charge of the civilizing process. The dependent nature of Koreans and Korean society was one of the old habits that was emphasized and came under criticism. The dominant dynamic underlying Korean society was the mutual relationship between oppression and dependence; the upper classes oppressed the lower classes, and the lower classes were dependent upon the upper.[22] Advocates of self-strengthening criticized the fact that the Korean way of life was too subject to power and arbitrary tastes as society was structured according to a hierarchy based on various forms of discrimination: status (high vs. low), region (capital vs. countryside), gender (male vs. female), and age (old vs. young). They pointed out that even in economic life, the habit of dependency was strong since people were idle and lazy (*yuŭi yusik*). They noted that the working population amounted to only one-fourth of the total population, and most people lived off of others like parasites. The habit of dependency was not regarded as a temporary condition but as a part of the Korean national character that had existed for generations. The discourse on *sadaejuŭi* (serving the great) had already begun to emerge at this time, with the claim that Korea's tendency to depend upon foreign countries had developed in the distant past when Kim Yusin of the Silla kingdom used troops from Tang China to defeat Koguryŏ and Paekche.

Since the advocates of national self-strengthening ceded the initiative in reform efforts to the Japanese, their main role was to criticize the negative aspects of Korea. This kind of criticism clearly did nothing but justify Japan's aggressive intentions toward Korea. The natural result was that large numbers of Koreans became pro-Japanese collaborators. One of the most well-known collaborators, Yi Kwangsu, published his controversial treatise "Minjok kaejoron" (On National Reconstruction) in the May 1922 issue of *Kaebyŏk*; it was a reformulation of the ideas of *sŏdo sŏgi* and national self-strengthening

22. No Kwanbŏm, Ibid.

after the March First Movement. In its simplistic discussion of reforming old customs, yangban culture came under relentless attack. Yi felt that the Japanese assertion that the cause of the Chosŏn nation's decline was maladministration was an insufficient explanation. He argued that the true cause was the lack of morality among the ruling class; i.e., the king and the yangban. In other words, it was a politics of corruption whose goal was not the country's benefit or the people's welfare but the pursuit of profit by the king and political factions. Though this text can be considered a form of critical self-reflection, it is still difficult to understand how Yi Kwangsu could slander his ancestors more severely than the Japanese who had taken over his country.

Now let us return to the *Tale of Ch'unhyang*. In 1902, as mentioned above, Emperor Kojong established the *Hyŏmnyulsa* as a theater for performances of traditional Korean music, but it was shut down in April 1906 because of the rush to promote education. The emperor's heart was moved by the urgent cries for education. Their argument was that at a time when the Resident-General was established (February 1902) and the country's sovereignty was being threatened, it was necessary to hurry to build primary schools, high schools, and colleges to raise the educational level of the people; it was not a time for men and women to mix socially and enjoy *p'ansori* performances until late at night.[23]

In 1908, the privately owned theater Wŏn'gaksa was built, and it began performing a new style of drama called *ch'anggŭk*. Unlike *p'ansori*, *ch'anggŭk* used a cast of performers rather than a single singer, and it stirred peoples' curiosity as a new cultural form that had come from Japan. The *p'ansori* version of "The Tale of Ch'unhyang" was adapted and performed as *ch'anggŭk*. Yi Haejo's "Okjunghwa" ("Imprisoned Flower," 1911) was based on the *ch'anggŭk* version of the *Ch'unhyang* story. Yi also rewrote and adapted other traditional tales and attempted to transform *p'ansori* performance into *ch'anggŭk*. "The Tale of Simch'ŏng" became "Kangsangryŏn" (A Lotus Flower on the River, 1912); "The Tale of the Water Palace" (*Pyŏljubujŏn*) became "To ŭi kan" (The Liver of the Rabbit, 1913), and "The Tale of Hŭngbu" became "Yŏn ŭi kak" (Leg of the Swallow, 1913).

"Imprisoned Flower" was an adaptation of "The Tale of Ch'unhyang" mainly based on Sin Chaehyo's "Namch'ang

---

23. *Kojong sillok*, Vol. 47, 10th year of Kwangmu, twenty-fifth day of the third month and seventeenth day of the fourth month, Yi P'ilhwa's memorial.

Ch'unhyangjŏn" (a version for a male singer) and the Seoul woodblock-print version of "Namwŏn kosa" (Old Song of Namwŏn), but its themes were entirely different. In the original *p'ansori* versions, the plot focused on Ch'unhyang's faithfulness, the punishment handed down by the secret royal inspector, her marriage to the secret inspector, and the king's reward for her fidelity. But the *ch'anggŭk* version, strangely, emphasized free love (*chayu yŏnae*) and the reconciliation of the male protagonists, Yi Mongnyong and Pyŏn Hakto, the newly appointed governor.

In Sin Chaehyo's version, Ch'unhyang was portrayed as the daughter of a family of some status with some members having served in official posts. Taking its cues from this portrayal, "Imprisoned Flower" made her even more accomplished: she began learning calligraphy from the age of seven, read the *Elementary Learning*, and was an expert in the rules of etiquette. It also depicted Yi Mongnyong as the son of a famous *sedo* family in Seoul. His family was the wealthiest in the capital, one that had been loyal and filial for generations; in terms of social standing, he was a member of a distinguished family from Seoul's Samch'ŏng-dong, descended from the Yŏn'am Yi clan on his father's side and the Ch'ŏngp'ung Kim clan on his mother's. Yi Haejo was trying to relate a story of children of noble birth escaping from the bonds of traditional customs and learning the joys and importance of free love. Ch'unhyang's behavior, too, was no longer that of a refined and modest woman. She was changed into woman so fierce that, upon learning that Yi Mongnyong cannot take her with him when his father was transferred to Seoul, she threw and broke her mirrors and smashed her calligraphy brush and other writing implements.

The character of the governor was also portrayed in a completely different manner. In Sin Chaehyo's script, the new governor was initially given the name "Pyŏn Akdo," a name that suggests evil. Yi Haejo changed his name to "Pyŏn Hakdo," a name that suggests scholarly accomplishment, and portrayed him heroically. Pyŏn is a good singer who is handsome and refined; he is generous with his money and enjoys drinking liquor. Such a generous portrayal of the new governor minimized and even nearly nullified the critique of corrupt politics found in the original. Amazingly, in Yi Haejo's version, Ch'unhyang's mother Wŏlmae came to the defense of Pyŏn Hakdo, after the appearance of the secret government inspector, her son-in-law. Calling him a gallant man, she carried on about how it was natural for a man to desire a woman, how wise he was for not having Ch'unhyang killed for her abusive words against a government official, and how magnanimous he was for making her a woman of virtue.

The greatest changes to the story occurred in the scene where Yi Mongnyong, now a secret royal inspector, met Governor Pyŏn face to face. Saying that he had "heard of his fame," Yi Mongnyong told Pyŏn that it was common for a hero to covet a beautiful flower and therefore was not something to be harshly criticized. Mongnyong even thanked him for his harsh treatment of Ch'unhyang, which revealed how virtuous she was. Instead of punishing Pyŏn for his misadministration, Yi Mongnyong just asked him to govern wisely in the future.

In the *ch'anggŭk* versions of "The Tale of Ch'unhyang" that began to appear around the time of Japan's forced annexation of Korea, it is possible to hear the sounds of the complete collapse of Koreans' value system, which was based on Confucianism. Korea is now witnessing a shift to a value system that regards the unlimited play of natural instincts, rather than ethical restraint, as virtuous. Right before our very eyes, we can see that the loss of sovereignty resulted not only in political disgrace but also in cultural embarrassment. Only now is it possible to understand why the advocates of *tongdo sŏgi* worked so hard to preserve native things. In a woodblock print version (*wanp'an*) from 1909 (in the possession of Professor Im Hyŏngt'aek), the calligrapher wrote an afterword containing the epigram that "men must follow the example of Ch'unhyang's fidelity and not serve two kings." These words enable us to feel what *p'ansori* was trying to accomplish. What is sad is that even today, people continue to look down on Confucian culture without understanding this authentic tradition.

CONCLUSION

The objective of this chapter has been to examine the origins of the negative perceptions of yangban culture. This examination has shown that views on yangban culture and tradition began to become problematic during the mid-nineteenth century when Korea was forced to adopt Western technological civilization. However, these issues were not cultural but political in nature. They were closely connected to the search for a way to maintain the country's sovereignty.

The main response to Western civilization was the argument that Korea should adopt Western technology only, while reforming and maintaining native things as its spiritual foundation. The notion of *tongdo sŏgi* (Eastern ways, Western technology) was supported by the king and therefore was the official position of the government. However, reform efforts based on *tongdo sŏgi* faced many dangerous challenges because of the opposition of simple-minded reactionaries and because Korea was caught between the machinations of China and Japan. While China tried to keep Chosŏn within the old Sinocentric world order, Japan sought to sacrifice Chosŏn in its program of imperial expansion.

Even though the king and the government had decided to pursue *tongdo sŏgi*, they did not have the opportunity to implement reforms until after the queen was assassinated and the king had to move to a foreign legation. The Great Han Empire's reforms for national self-strengthening produced significant results within a short period of time, demonstrating clear potential for success. Alarmed at this potential, Japan decided to block the reforms before they could develop any further. If Korea were left alone to continue its development, the Japanese feared it would become much more difficult, if not impossible, to achieve their longstanding dream of seizing the Korean peninsula. The subsequent denunciation of yangban culture was the result of a deliberate effort by advocates of *sŏdo sŏgi*, who were engaged in a struggle with the Great Han Empire's reforms for *tongdo sŏgi*. Promoted mainly by Japan, the notion of *sŏdo sŏgi* shook the very foundations of the Great Han Empire. But while the Japanese sought to preserve their nation through the adoption of Western civilization under the idea of "Japanese spirit, Western materials," the same ideas in Korea led people to abandon their roots and traditions.

During the Japanese occupation period, denunciations of yangban culture became almost habitual. No one doubted any more that the failings of the yangban were the cause for the decline of the country. As such notions became more prevalent, the Government-General's propaganda about administrative reform became more effective, and the Japanese were better able to cultivate the submissiveness of the Chosŏn people. On the other hand, the Chosŏn people become mired in a state of mind that was unfilial and disloyal, blaming their ancestors for their shortcomings. Intangible cultural treasures were denounced as old-fashioned and abandoned. Intellectuals who realized the error of such thinking were extremely few in number. Though the intellect of the Korean people was being insulted, sadly, virtually no one realized it.

The habit of blaming one's ancestors for current problems remained even after the liberation of the country in 1945 and during the cold war that followed. Even if it could be said that Japan succeeded at achieving sŏdo sŏgi, it was more of a "model student" of the idea, not its main advocate. The newly rising U.S. and the Soviet Union were the true embodiments of sŏdo sŏgi, and Koreans, accustomed to the dominance of Western civilization, found it difficult to resist the influence of these great powers. With the division of the country, each side followed its own path; Soviet-style communism was adopted in the North, and American-style liberalism was adopted in the South. In the process, denunciations of yangban culture continued. An awareness of the importance of tradition was not completely lacking, but it did not go much beyond a superficial level. What then has been the result of blindly following Western civilization for the past one hundred years?

The North chose Marxism, a system of thought that emerged in the mid-nineteenth century as an effort to resolve the contradictions of Western capitalism, and it is now on the verge of collapse, its misery hidden from view. Though it could be said that the South has achieved economic development, mutual distrust is high, and social chaos and cultural confusion are prevalent. As a result, people have become desensitized even to immorality and unethical behavior. What must we do in a situation where the future is unclear? It is time for the Korean people to clear the confusion in their minds by going back to the time when the paths of *tongdo sŏgi* and *sŏdo sŏgi* were still options. At the present time, it is urgently necessary to undertake a fundamental reexamination of the understanding of modern Korean history.

*translated by Scott Swaner*

CHAPTER 13

# Was Early Modern Korea Really a "Hermit Kingdom"?

EARLY MODERN KOREA HAS often been labeled a "hermit kingdom." This designation is admittedly accurate in describing Korea during the rule of the Taewŏngun (1863-1873). Because of his isolationist policy, Korea experienced several outside intrusions including the "Foreign Disturbance of 1866" (France) and the "Foreign Disturbance of 1871" (United States). However, even beyond this period, Korea has been unable to rid itself of the "hermit" label. Even though it signed the Treaty of Kanghwa with Japan in 1876 and similar treaties with the United States (1882) and England (1883) and thereby entered into friendly trade relations, Korea at that time was still considered a "hermit kingdom." In fact, some even feel that Korea's forcible annexation by Japan in 1910 was the natural result of Korea's reclusive and isolationist nature. Based on this view, scholars have concluded that Korea failed at modernization through its own efforts.

Even today, whenever Koreans face a major international difficulty, most of them point to Korea's "failed modernization." They tend to single out Korea's early modern history to ascribe the blame to others or to awaken themselves to their circumstances. The same happened during the early stages of the recent International Monetary Fund (IMF) bailout. There is nothing wrong with looking back at history and reflecting on past mistakes to learn a lesson.[1] However, it

---

1. Korean people have a strong tendency to look back on history and reflect on past mistakes, almost as a form of punishment or penance, in the belief that recognizing past mistakes will straighten things in the future.

326  Chapter Thirteen

is self-destructive to try to learn lessons with an incorrect understanding of history. Countless people in Korea today talk about reflecting on Korea's failed modernization, but in the end, such reflection seems to have no effect. For all the supposed self-reflection, the Korean people do not seem to have improved at all in diplomatic sensitivity or in their ability to deal with the outside world. It would not be wrong to say that the ultimate cause of Korea's recent economic crisis was Korea's ignorance of international society and inability to respond properly to international circumstances. Could it be that singling out Korea's failed modernization has been not so much an act of self-reflection as an act of self-contempt?

It is a solemn fact that Korea's early modern history ended in disaster. However, it is important to evaluate carefully whether this ruin was caused by the incompetence of the Korean people as some people insist. When reflecting upon a certain historical period, it is necessary to avoid the preconception that Korea lacked ability; instead, it is important to analyze what efforts were toward modernization and what was lacking. Historians laying blame on the "isolationist" policy do not recognize the efforts and progress made by Koreans during the early modern period. Could this flawed perception of history be the reason why Koreans have not developed their ability to respond to international events? Koreans still lack a detailed or systematic understanding of this period of "failed modernization," which they are trying to reflect upon. Given the superficial understanding of this period, it is hard to expect such self-reflection to be effective. I will examine how Korea came to be viewed as a "hermit kingdom," which led to this perception of Korea's failed modernization. My goal, of course, is to help Koreans to develop their adaptability and responsiveness to the outside world.

GRIFFIS'S COREA, THE HERMIT KINGDOM

William Eliot Griffis's book *Corea, The Hermit Kingdom* may be the main reason why people consider Korea a hermit kingdom; even just the title could not help but leave this impression. The book was first published in October 1882 by AMS Press in New York and proved so popular that eighth (1906) and ninth (1911) editions were printed. In the preface to the eighth edition, the author commented on the popularity of the book and wrote, "For twenty-four years, this book, besides enjoying popular favor, has been made good use of by writers and students, in Europe and America, and has served even in Corea itself as the first book of general information to be read by missionaries and other newcomers." However, no one has yet seriously examined how accurately this book examines Korea's situation at the time.

William Eliot Griffis (1843-1928) was born in Philadelphia and graduated from Rutgers University in 1869 with a degree in the natural sciences. In December 1870, he traveled to Fukui, Japan, as an American Reformed missionary to teach at Hanko Meishinkan.[2] While at Rutgers, he met Saheita and Taihei Shonan, the nephews of Yokoi Shonan (1809-1869), who was the teacher of Matsudaira Shungaku, the *daimyo* of Echizen.[3] While there, he taught biology, chemistry, and the natural sciences. However, with the reform of the provincial system (*haikan-shiken*) on July 18, 1871, he finished teaching in Fukui. In 1872, he was hired by the Meiji government and went to Tokyo to teach chemistry and the natural sciences at Nanko, the predecessor to present-day Tokyo University. From February to July 1874, he worked as a chemistry professor at the Kaisei-gakko and helped set up the chemistry department. During this time, he had several opportunities to meet with the Meiji Emperor. After almost four years of living in Japan, he returned to the United States in July 1874 and entered the Union Seminary in New York. Afterward, he was active as a pastor and wrote often on Japan, while occasionally writing also about Korea.

In the preface to the first edition of *Corea, The Hermit Kingdom*, he described his motivation for writing the book as follows:

> In the year 1871, while living at Fukui, in the province of Echizen, Japan, I spent a few days at Tsuruga and Mikuni, by the sea which separates Japan and Corea. The thought often came to me as I walked within the moss-grown feudal castle walls—old in story, but then newly given up to schools of Western science and languages—why should Corea be sealed and mysterious, when Japan, once a hermit, had opened her doors and come out into the

---

2. A more detailed description of Griffis's background can be found in the section on William Eliot Griffis in the Showa Women's University's *Kindai bungaku kenkyu sosho* (vol. 28), and also the postscript of Professor Kamei Shunsuke's *Mikado* (Tokyo: Iwanami Bunko, 1995), which was originally published as William Eliot Griffis, *Mikado—Institution and Person* (Princeton, New Jersey: Princeton University Press, 1915).

3. Kamei Shunsuke, *Mikado: Nihon no uchinaru chikara* (Tokyo: Iwanami shoten, 1995), p. 340.

world's market-place? When would Korean awakening come? As one diamond cuts another, why should not Cho-ka (Japan) open Chosen (Corea)?

According to this passage, when he was in Fukui in 1871, he had already become interested in Korea. While spending a few days in Tsuruga and Mikuni, the regions facing Korea across the sea, he asked himself, "Why should Corea be sealed and mysterious?" and "When would Corea's awakening come?" It would be eleven years before he published what would be one of the first Western books on Korea. Without ever having directly visited Korea, he managed to produce a 520-page work on the country.

However, the main focus of his interest in Korea was its relationship with Japan and a relative comparison between the two nations. In the preface, he wrote, "Turning with delight and fascination to the study of Japanese history and antiquities, I found much that reflected light upon the neighbor country. On my return home, I continued to search for materials for the story of the last of the hermit kingdoms." In 1876, Griffis published his major work on Japanese history and culture, *Mikado's Empire*. It was after this that he began writing *Corea, The Hermit Kingdom*. In his preface, he notes that the bulk of the book was written between 1877 and 1880.

As he was writing this book, he was greatly aided by John Ross's *Corea, its History, Manners, and Customes* (1880) and Charles Dallet's *Histoire d'Eglise de Corée*, which he admits to in his preface. In fact, he borrowed heavily from Dallet's work, particularly in the chapters on folklore, social life, and Christianity. As he published this book about a country that he had never visited, he defended himself by pointing out the difference between a "traveller" and a "compiler." While a traveller only sees a part of the country at one time, he bragged that a compiler could produce a handbook of information more valuable to the general reader. The problem is that Griffis chose to compare Korea—again, a place he had never visited–with Japan, which he naturally praised, in an effort to explain Japan's success.

To learn more about Griffis's view of Japan, it is instructive to look at the analysis of Professor Kamei Shunsuke, who translated Griffis's other work, *The Mikado: Institution and Person*, into Japanese. In his translator's notes, Professor Kamei writes that Griffis evaluated the Japanese people and their mentality according to Western rationalism and welcomed their Westernization and modernization. Griffis thought that Mikadoism was of central importance to

Japan's successful modernization. However, he thought that the Japanese people's belief in unbroken lineage of the imperial dynasty was a political fabrication, and he criticized the fact that such a fiction was still accepted in spite of Japan's remarkable modernization and that Japan was unable to outgrow its intellectual and moral primitiveness. He highly regarded Mikadoism as the manifestation of the collective spirit of the Japanese people to join together to create a dynamically developing unified country, as evidenced during the rule of Emperor Meiji at that time.

With his deep trust in Western civilization, his Christian faith, his respect for individuality, and his confidence in democracy, Griffis was trying to help Japan's modernization and came to love modernized Japan. He was a firm believer in modernism, which was in vogue among Western intellectuals of the time. When he saw how the Meiji government was actively pursuing Westernization, he praised Japan from a modernist viewpoint. To him, any country refusing or slow to adopt Western civilization was a "hermit kingdom." He believed that Japan, which originally also was a hermit kingdom, had begun walking on the "road to civilization" with its opening by Commodore Matthew Perry, whereas China and Korea were still hermit kingdoms that lacked these positive signs.

The book is divided into three parts entitled "Ancient and Medieval History," "Political and Social Corea," and "Modern and Recent History." In the first part, there are twenty-two chapters: one on geography, six on ancient history, one on ancient Korea-Japan relations, one on Koryŏ or united Corea, one on Koryŏ's outside relations, one on the founding of the Chosŏn dynasty, nine on Japan's invasions of Chosŏn, and two on the coming of the West. As can be seen, most of this section is devoted to Korea's relationship with Japan and outside nations. Regarding China, he emphasizes the early Han Chinese commandary and the tributary relationship, and he also writes about the supposed Japanese colony Mimana (K. Imna) as postulated by the Japanese, which shows that he was heavily influenced by the ultranationalist historical views of contemporary Japanese intellectuals. In fact, he spelled the names of the Korean kingdoms of Koguryŏ, Paekje, and Silla according to their Japanese pronunciation—Korai, Hyakusai, and Shinra.

The second part consists of eighteen chapters: an introduction to the eight provinces, four chapters on the political system, and thirteen chapters on social life and customs, religion, and education. Since much of this section was borrowed from Dallet's *Histoire d'Eglise de*

330  Chapter Thirteen

*Corée*, his viewpoints in this section must be analyzed in detail. In the section on politics, he focused on despotism and factional strife, and in the section on traditional culture and beliefs, he described Korea as a "land of paganism, bigotry, superstition," which reveals his strong modernist views. In part three of the first edition, he started with the introduction of Catholicism in 1784, followed by chapters on the Catholic persecution, the resulting French naval expedition, Korea-American relations, and the United States naval expedition, Korea's opening by Japan, and the initiation of commerce with Western nations in the early 1880s.[4]

In chapter forty-eight, the last chapter of the first edition, he wrote about the chain of events that occurred in 1882 and made some future predictions. In 1882, Korea signed a treaty of amity and commerce with the United States; a military mutiny broke out in June and troops from Qing China intervened; and the Treaty of Chemulp'o (Inch'ŏn) was signed to compensate Japan for damages incurred during the mutiny. Griffis decided to entitle this chapter, "The Year of the Treaties." However, even though there were numerous indications that Korea's hermit-like ways were ending, his view of Korea at the time was still not positive. While acknowledging that Korea was ending its isolation and becoming the focus of the world's attention, he painted a dark picture of Korea as a future battleground among China, Japan, and Russia. Furthermore, he avoided mentioning Japan's aggressive intent toward Korea but instead predicted that the Korean valleys will be the site of collision between the "hoary empire" (China) and the "young northern giant" (Russia), and a war between "the dragon and the bear" is a possibility. Regarding the outcome of this battle, his outlook for Korea was cold and bleak. While trusting that the integrity of the "little kingdom" Chosŏn will be preserved, he hoped that "paganism, bigotry and superstition in Corea, and in all Asia, may disappear; and that in their place, the religion of Jesus, science, education, and human brotherhood may find an abiding dwelling place."[5]

---

4. In the preface of the first edition, he writes, "For lack of space, the original manuscript of "Recent and Modern History," part III, has been greatly abridged, and many topics of interest have been left untouched," which shows he was unable to write about everything he wanted to.

5. This same attitude is found in the dedication of *Corea, The Hermit Kingdom:* "To All Corean Patriots: who seek by the aid of science, truth, and pure religion, To Enlighten themselves and their fellow-countrymen, To Rid their land of superstition, bigotry, despotism, and priestcraft—both native and foreign—and To preserve the integrity, independence, and honor, of their

## Was Early Modern Korea Really a "Hermit Kingdom"? 331

In the eighth edition published in 1906, he added five chapters to describe the events that occurred after 1882 ("The Economic Condition of Corea, Internal Politics"; "Chinese and Japanese, The War of 1894"; "Corea an Empire"; "Japan and Russia in Conflict"; "Corea a Japanese Protectorate"). With Japan making Korea a protectorate in November 1905, he could not help but add new material. At that time, he recognized that the "center of the world's politics has shifted from the Atlantic and the Mediterranean to the waters surrounding Corea" and also praised Japan's rapid rise as follows:

> The rise of Japan, within half a century of immediate contact with the West, to the position of a modern state, able first to humiliate China and then to grapple successfully with Russia, has vitally affected Corea, on behalf whose independence Japan a second time went to war with a Power vastly greater in natural resources than herself. The present or eighth edition shows in both text and map, not only the swift, logical results both of Japan's military and naval success in Manchuria and on the Sea of Japan and of her signal diplomatic victory at Portsmouth, but more. It makes clear the reasons why Corea, as to her foreign relations, has lost her sovereignty (Preface to the eighth edition).

For Griffis, Korea's loss of sovereignty was due to Japan's rapid growth to become a modern nation and Japan's successive victories over China and Russia, who were trying to expand their influence over Korea; the loss was not just a diplomatic victory but the logical conclusion of Japan's having shed its isolationism early. Furthermore, he clearly stated his belief on the reason for Korea's loss of its sovereignty: the leaders of the kingdom were pursuing "intrigue" instead of "education" and "class interests" instead of "national welfare." He puts forth the harsh judgment that Korea's loss of sovereignty was directly the result of the "final failure of intriguing Yangbanism" and also the "moral trial before the world."

In the ninth edition, he added a chapter on Japan's annexation of Korea entitled "Chosen: A Providence of Japan." He justified Japan's takeover of Korea, writing, "I doubt not that the hopes of twelve millions of people will be increasingly fulfilled under the new arrangement." Whether it was because of his staunch modernist beliefs

country; This unworthy sketch of their past history and present condition is dedicated."

or his pleasure in seeing his predictions fulfilled, he came to praise Japan's aggressions.

After returning to the United States in July 1874, he continued his theological studies and then worked as a pastor. In 1884, he received his D.D. from Union Seminary, and in 1900, he was awarded an L.H.D. from his *alma mater*, Rutgers. In 1903, he left the clergy and continued with his writing, completing a total of 178 works by the time of his death in 1928. Most of his works were on Japan, but nine were on Korea.[6]

In 1908, he was awarded the Asahi Order of the Fourth Degree Merit by the Japanese government, in gratitude for his lifelong efforts to positively help and evaluate Japan's modernization. In December 1926, at the age of eighty-three, he returned to Japan for a visit, at the urging of his son, working at a New York bank, and also at the invitation of Shibusawa Eiichi (1840–1931), a famous banker. During the visit, he was awarded the Asahi Order of the Third Degree Merit and allowed to stay six months at the Imperial Hotel. During this extended stay in Japan, he finally visited Korea for the first time in 1927. Afterward, he returned to Fukui and Tsuruga in April and traveled in Japan. He passed away on February 5, 1928, at the age of eighty-five in Winter Park, Florida. He was at work writing an imperial biography of the Meiji Emperor and a work on "the Newly-born Japan."

The view of Korea expressed in *Corea, The Hermit Kingdom* was not unique to Griffis. In the bibliography of his book, there are references to two articles with a similar title: "Corea, the Last of the Hermit Kingdoms" (*Sunday Magazine*, New York, May 1878), and "Corea, The Hermit Kingdom" (*Bulletin of the American Geographical Society*, no. 3, New York, 1881). It seems highly likely that Griffis took his title from these articles. These similar titles also suggest that the idea of Korea as the last of the hermit kingdoms was common

---

6. According to *Kindai bungaku kenkyu sosho* vol. 28, William Eliot Griffis wrote *Corea, Without and Within* (Philadelphia: Presbyterian Board of Publication, 1885); "Jack and the Giant in Korea," *Outlook* (1894); "China and Japan at War in Korea," *Chatanquan* (1894); "Korea and Koreans: In the Mirror of Their Language and History," *Bulletin of the American Geographical Society* 27, no. 1 (1895); "Korea, the Pigmy Empire," *New England Magazine* (1902); "Japan's Absorption of Korea," *North American Review* (1910); *A Modern Pioneer in Korea* (New York: Fleming H. Revell Company, 1912), "The Opening of Korea," *The Korea Magazine* (1917); "Women of Chosen," *Missionary Review of the World* (1918); and "Japan's Debt to Korea," *Asia* (1919).

among Westerners at the time. He writes in the preface that many people think of Korea as "no more than a seashell" or they ask, "What's in Corea?" and "Is Corea of any importance in the history of the world?" In many ways, Griffis's book best represents this Western view.

THE HERMIT IMAGE PROMOTED BY JAPAN

The Japanese also promoted the perception of early modern Korea as a hermit kingdom. No one has really examined how much of an influence Griffis's works had on the Japanese, but judging from the fact that his major work on Japan, *The Mikado's Empire,* was in its thirteenth edition by 1913, it appears that his influence was significant. Furthermore, the fact that the Japanese government bestowed on him the Asahi Order of the Third Degree and Fourth Degree Merit medals indicates how much they valued his work on East Asia and Japan. There are also several direct records indicating that the Japanese were also interested in Griffis's *Corea, The Hermit Kingdom.*

In January 1895, the Suikosha Society in Tokyo published a work entitled *Chosen kaika no kigen* (The Origin of Korean Civilization), which was a summarized translation of Part Three of Griffis's book.[7] In the preface, the editor wrote that this book was printed for the members to read because "it contains many interesting events and precious stories we have never heard before, and we believe this is a valuable source in trying to discover the truth behind the origins of Chosŏn's modernization." Six years later, there was also a reference to Griffis's book in Shinobu Junpei's *Kanhando* (The Korean Peninsula) (1901, Tokyodo-shoten). One of the reviews of the book mentioned that Griffis's book was one of the major Western books on Korea. In his own preface, Shinobu wrote, "In their studies on the Korean peninsula, Westerners sometimes look down on the Koreans. Even though I may not be totally qualified, I have written this partly under their influence," which implies that he referred to Griffis's book. In fact, there are many places within his book where he quotes from Griffis.

7. The chapters of Part Three translated were as follows: "The Beginning of Christianity 1784-1794"; "Persecution and Martyrdom 1801-1834"; "The Entrance of the French Missionaries 1835-1845"; "The Walls of Isolation Sapped"; "The French Expedition"; "American Relations with Corea"; "A Body-Snatching Expedition"; and "Our Little War with the Heathen."

As just mentioned, Griffis's *Corea* had a direct influence on Japanese intellectuals, whom he obviously liked. At the same time, his book was also influenced considerably by Japanese intellectuals, particularly the section on history in Part One and the section on politics and customs in Part Two. Since he did not have any sources of information—especially in these areas—outside those in Japan, the influence of Japanese intellectuals inevitably must have been strong. Thus his relationship with Japanese intellectuals was one of mutual influence.

Japan's view of Korea started to adopt an aggressive attitude in Japanese historical studies during the Edo period (1603–1867).[8] Perhaps because the two Hideyoshi Invasions (1592, 1598) failed to achieve their objectives, a feeling of antagonism toward Chosŏn became widespread in Japanese society during the Edo period, even among common people. Intellectuals at first tended to admire and respect Chosŏn civilization, but by the eighteenth century, a strong ultra-nationalism had emerged in historical studies, and Japan's sense of superiority over Chosŏn began to grow. Japanese historians regarded foundation myths or legends in which ancient Japanese emperors ruled over Chosŏn as historically true, fostering Japan's sense of superiority over Chosŏn. Articles stating that Japanese gods or emperors ruled Chosŏn or that the Chosŏn kings and nobility submitted to Japan were printed as historical truths without any criticism, which fanned the sense of antagonism against Chosŏn growing in Japanese society.

This sense of superiority over Chosŏn fostered by Japanese historians developed into various forms of expansionism after the opening of Japan. In *Sankoku-tsuran-zusetsu*, written in 1785, Hayashi Shihei wrote that Chosŏn, along with the Ryukyu and Emish (Ainu) islands, had close ties to Japan's defense, and he emphasized the urgent need to study Chosŏn. After Japan's opening, those worrying about the West might argue, based on this logic, that Japan should preempt the Western powers and take over Korea and other Asian countries for the sake of Japan's overall defense. After the Meiji Restoration, the general position of Japanese intellectuals toward Korea this position was that Japan must invade Chosŏn in order to survive; i.e., the so-

---

8. The following section is mainly based on Hatada Takahashi "Chosen kanno tendo," in *Nihonjin no chosenkan* (Takakusa, 1969); Pak Yŏngjae, "Kŭndae Ilbon ŭi chimnyakjuŭijŏk taeoeron kwa Han'guknon" (Modern Japan's expansionist foreign policy and its Korea policy), *Han'guksa simin kangjwa* 19 (August 1996).

called Seikan-ron (the theory of conquering Korea). In fact, in 1873, one faction of leaders officially discussed subjugating Chosŏn to the Imperial Court. This faction was defeated by an opposing faction; however, the opponents were not against the idea of conquering Chosŏn but instead had different opinions on the timing, method, and the question of leadership.

By the early Meiji Restoration period, all Japanese intellectuals and social leaders supported the policy of "Conquering Korea." The proponents can be called the Greater "Conquer Korea" faction, while the more aggressive faction who proposed conquering Korea in 1873 can be classified as the Lesser "Conquer Korea" faction. In actuality, this distinction remained valid through the early 1900s.[9] The annexation of Korea in 1910 was the complete realization of the greater "Conquer Korea" school's vision; with this event, there was no longer any need for this term. Afterward, Japanese leaders were absorbed in trying to legitimize its colonization of Korea, based on the notion of "Giving Blessing," and the Greater faction concealed itself behind this notion, leaving the Lesser School as only a remnant in history books.

The "Conquer Korea" faction of the 1860s and 1870s opened Chosŏn's doors by instigating the Kanghwa Island Incident in 1875. However, with the Soldiers Riot of 1882 (*Imo kullan*) and the advance of Qing troops into Korea, the situation became unfavorable for Japan in various ways. As a result, advocates for invading Korea in Japan were forced to retreat from their position and changed their emphasis to "solidarity." The new position claimed that Asian nations were all possible targets of invasion by the Western powers and that solidarity was necessary for them to survive. However, this was based on the assumption that Japan was to be the leader of Asia. They regarded Qing China as a "rigidly ignorant, ultra-conservative country" and Chosŏn as the "most inflexibly bigoted country in East Asia." For their "enlightenment," Japan needed to intervene in their domestic affairs and, if necessary, be prepared to invade them.

There were also calls for "Greater East Asia Unification," advocating that Japan unify with Korea. This was one of the more indirect forms of the "Conquer Korea" discourse that emerged when it became clear it would be difficult to overcome Qing China's superiority. This faction argued that Japan and Korea, as equals, should form a unified

---

9. Kemiyama Sentaro, *Seikanron jisso* (The real state of the Conquer Korea school) (Tokyo: Waseda University, 1907), p. 3. He calls the "Conquer Korea" proponents who were defeated at the Imperial Court in 1873, the Lesser "Conquer Korea" faction.

country and maintain close ties with China to withstand Western advances into Asia, particularly that of Russia. The proponents of this school even produced a book in classical Chinese expounding this view for Korean and Chinese intellectuals. However, this position too could not hide Japan's self-righteous expansionism. They believed that Korea showed symptoms of lagging behind: the Korean people, having maintained *sadae* (serving the great) relations with China for so long, were lacking in autonomous spirit, suffered from political disarray due to Korea's autocracy, and had lost their vitality. On the other hand, this faction argued that Japan possessed a unique imperial state structure, superior natural beauty, a fully autonomous populace, wealth and power, enlightenment, etc.—all in all, a nation of which one could be truly proud. They argued that as Chosŏn came closer to Japan, it would become infused with Japan's *ki* or spirit and develop considerably; therefore, merging with Japan would benefit Chosŏn greatly and produce substantial rewards. After Japan's victory in the Sino-Japanese War (1894), this self-righteousness developed into the logic that Japan must become the leader of Asia.

Prior to the Sino-Japanese War, Japanese intellectuals did not write any worthwhile introductory books or writings on Korea in spite of their strong belief in the necessity of conquering Korea. When major events occurred such as the battle between Korean shore batteries and a Japanese ship (*Unyang* Incident of 1875), the Treaty of Kanghwa (1876), the Soldiers Riot of 1882, they printed and distributed many leaflets and booklets describing the event. With names like *Chosen kunki* (Record of the Military Incdient in Chosŏn), *Chosen jiken* (The Chosŏn Incident), and *Chosen shobun sanron* (Discussion on the Treatment of Chosŏn), these booklets were very demagogic in nature, even though they were published by private groups. More serious work on Korea began appearing in Japan in the 1890s, and until the Sino-Japanese War in 1894, these too were limited to writings on Korea's ancient history.[10] It was only in 1896 that books which examined the contemporary period finally started to appear. The three major works were: (1) Kikuchi Genjo's *Chosen okoku* (The Chosŏn Kingdom; Minyusha, 1896); (2) Tsuneya Seifuku's *Chosen kaikashi* (The History of Enlightenment in Chosŏn; Toa tobunkai, 1901); and (3) Shinobu Junpei's *Kanhando* (The Korean Peninsula;

---

10. For example, see Hayashi Taisuke's *Chosen-shi* (1892), Yoshida Shogo's *Nikkan koshi dan* (1893), and Nishimura Yukata's *Chosen shiko* (1895).

Tokyodo shoten, 1901).[11] The first book introduced Korea in three parts—geography (158 pages), society (120 pages, from a historical perspective), and history (279 pages). The history section affirmed the existence of Kija Chosŏn, a Chinese sub-state, and the Japanese colony Mimana. The part on early modern history covered the major developments relating to Japan, including the Taewŏngun's isolationist policy, the Kapsin Coup of 1884, the Sino-Japanese War, and the assassination of Queen Min. Kikuchi also emphasized Chosŏn's liberation from Qing China with Japan's victory in the Sino-Japanese War. In the section on society, he wrote that Chosŏn was on the verge of decline due to corruption and depravity. His criticism of Chosŏn was severe, going so far as to say that the thousand years starting from the Koryŏ dynasty (918–1392) was an immoral period. In the second book, a section on geography also affirmed Korea's supposed past colonialist history through examples such as Mimana and Kija Chosŏn. In a section on ethnography, he wrote that the Japanese and the Koreans have similar ancestors. In a section on culture, he criticized the Korean people, saying that they have no customs worthy of maintaining. Their hearts are filled with jealousy, suspicion, and lies; they all try to cheat each other; they have no sense of aggressiveness or independence, and they frequently have to depend on others. Furthermore, he emphasized that Chosŏn was fortunate in being able to become an independent nation through the help of the Japanese (p. 316) and that Japan's objective in the Sino-Japanese War was to give Chosŏn its independence. This idea that Chosŏn finally gained its independence through Japan's opening and victory in the Sino-Japanese War came to be the prevailing view on early modern Korean history by Japanese historians, which first appeared in a book by Tsuneya Seifuku. He also wrote, "Why has acceptance of the new civilization been so different in Japan and Korea? This has been the difference between accepting it naturally and accepting it forcefully." This view is exactly same as Griffis's.

The third book was mainly about human geography, economics, and international relations. Shinobu began by writing about the major cities, palaces, and the financial status and organizational structure of the Korean government and covered topics pertinent at the time of his writing. He also wrote about Korea's relations with Japan, China,

11. For more about these books, please refer to Cho Tonggŏl, "Singmin sahak ŭi sŏngnip kwajŏng kwa kŭndaesa sŏsul" (The establishment of colonial historiography and the writing of modern history), *Yŏksa kyoyuk nonjip* 13-14 (1993).

Russia, and other Western countries again up to the time of writing, but he did apologize for not knowing more about the internal situation of the Korean government and for writing more about Korea's relations with the West than those with Japan and China. Nonetheless, he also expressed the same perspective as the Japanese intellectuals of the time. When writing about the close ties between Japan and Korea dating back to ancient times, he used Griffis's exact words: "It is as nearly impossible to write the history of Corea and exclude Japan, as to tell the story of medieval England and leave out France" (Griffis p. 51, Shinobu p. 382). He then referred in succession to the supposed Mimana colony, the theory that Empress Jingu conquered Korea, the Hideyoshi invasions, and ends up with the Convention of T'ientsin, coming to the conclusion that "the Korean peninsula in general has developed as a tributary of Japan." Looking back at the relationship from ancient times, he concluded that Korea was basically a vassal of Japan which sometimes paid tribute.

Shinobu divided Korea's relationship with China into four periods according to changes in its relationship of dependency. During the first period (from the reign of King Injo (1623–1649) to 1866), Korea was truly dependent on the Qing, but in the second period (1866–1876), even though Korea was nominally a vassal, Qing China acknowledged Chosŏn's independence in its domestic and foreign affairs to the Western powers. In the third period (1876–1882), Japan regarded Chosŏn as an independent nation, and the same period saw China's influence declining. But in the fourth period (1882–1894), after the Soldiers Riot of 1882 and intervention of Qing troops, China's control strengthened, and Korea was once again dependent. Korea's dependent relationship with China was the biggest problem for the Japanese, who wanted to conquer Korea. They feared that if they tried to invade Korea, China would intervene and come to the aid of its vassal. The book addresses this issue in order to show that Japan ended the dependent relationship by defeating China in the Sino-Japanese War.

Through its examination of Korea's outside relations, Shinobu's book clearly emphasized Japan's primacy of interest over Korea in an effort to legitimize Japan's rule of Korea. In the section on Korea's trade relations, he wrote, "Between the nineteenth and twentieth centuries, a new trend has developed among the Western powers. Their primary ambition toward primitive or partially modernized nations is to increase their room for profit by expanding their markets, while controlling the territory is secondary." He added, "Given the

Was Early Modern Korea Really a "Hermit Kingdom"? 339

special relationship Japan shares with Korea not only in terms of geography and history, but future diplomacy, Japan has the natural right and natural responsibility of expanding its room for profit by including this market" (p. 662).

What the three books have in common is that they all support the idea of "Conquering Korea." In 1902, when the third book came out, Korea was not yet occupied by Japan. Korea was inevitably to become a target for conquest as the "Conquer Korea" faction advocated. This is why Japanese historians emphasized Japan's preemptive rights over Korea since ancient times, and why they showed inordinate interest in Korea's independence in order to eliminate China's existing preemptive rights. After Japan's victory in the Russo-Japanese War of 1904, the conception of "Conquering Korea" changed considerably. With its military victory, Japan was finally able to forcibly annex Korea, and historical accounts of Japan's relationship with Korea took on the form of a "victor's" history. As if to celebrate the annexation of Korea, a number of books appeared at the time, the first of which was Ikeda Tsunetaro's *Nikkan gappo shoshi* (A Bibliographical Work on Japan-Korea Relations).[12] The book consisted of the following chapters:

Chapter 1: Period of Tribute and Isolation
Chapter 2: Sino-Japanese War Period
Chapter 3: Negotiation and Maneuvering between Russia and Japan
Chapter 4: Russo-Japanese War Period
Chapter 5: Period of Advisory Politics
Chapter 6: Period of Protective Politics
Chapter 7: Korea's Annexation

The structure of the chapters was based on the "Conquer Korea" view of Korea and could have misled readers into believing that Japan fought for Korea's independence and protection. What is striking is the attitude toward Korea, the target of protection and annexation, in this process. In Chapter 1, the author wrote that the reason why Japan began to intervene actively in Korean affairs was the fault of Korea to some extent. After the Meiji Restoration, Japan wanted to initiate a new diplomatic relationship with Korea, but "arrogant Chosŏn... refused Japan's diplomatic message." There was no choice but to

12. Ikeda Tsunetaro, *Nikkan gappo shoshi* (A bibliographical work on Japan-Korea relations) (Tokyo: Yomiuri shinbun Nisshusha, 1910).

develop plans to conquer Korea, which is why the *Unyang* Incident (*Unyo* in Japanese) and the subsequent Treaty of Kanghwa were used to open Korea. With the "Conquer Korea" plan now having been achieved, Japan sought to legitimize and whitewash its conquest by categorizing Korea as the "most inflexibly bigoted country in East Asia" and Korea's isolationism as a historical mistake that needed to be remedied at the heavy cost of "annexation." Many of the books that appeared after Tsunetaro's *Nikkan-gappo-shoshi* have a similar structure and content.

## THE BURIED HISTORY OF KOREA'S OPEN-DOOR POLICY

Griffis and Japanese intellectuals played a major role in creating the impression that Korea resisted the global trend toward openness in the latter half of the 1800s and that the direct result of which was Korea's annexation by Japan in 1910. This view of history was greatly reinforced by the harsh reality of Korea's loss of sovereignty. Furthermore, as the circumstances did not permit Koreans to study the true nature of Korea's modern history, it became difficult to mount a scholarly challenge to this view. As a result, the conception of Korea as a "hermit kingdom" came to be accepted as the truth. However, as was shown before, the writings which gave birth to this conception were either biased from the start, had ulterior motives, or were not backed up by primary historical records or sources. It is urgent that efforts be made to examine the issue closely using primary sources. Regardless of the outcome, it is unacceptable that such an important issue has not been addressed.

Important research on Korea's opening of its ports was published in the 1970s.[13] These studies cover the period from the Treaty of Friendship signed with Japan at Kanghwa (1876) to the Treaty of Amity and Commerce signed with the United States (1882). This research showed that after much effort by Korean diplomats to ensure international equality, mainly focusing on tariff duties on Japanese and American goods, Korea became the first country in Asia to obtain the right to determine its own customs duties in the Treaty of Amity

13. Kim Kyŏngt'ae, "Kaehang jikhu ŭi kwansegwŏn hoebok munje" (The question of tariff compensation after the opening of Korea), *Han'guksa yŏn'gu* 8 (1972); "Pulp'yŏngdŭng choyak kaejŏng kyosŏp ŭi chŏn'gae" (The progress of negotiations over the revision of the unequal treaties), *Han'guksa yŏn'gu* 11 (1975).

Was Early Modern Korea Really a "Hermit Kingdom"? 341

and Commerce with the United States. This research also showed that the successful negotiations were the result of the king's leadership and the determined efforts of a few enlightened bureaucrats. However, because of the longstanding bias toward Korea's early modern history, the results of this study did not receive much attention. This research could have swept away traditional misconceptions, but instead our understanding of the early modern period remains clouded by the preponderant bias toward this period. There are many similar issues where the sources are readily available to test questionable assumptions about the past and possibly come up with entirely different explanations from a different perspective. Here I will discuss a couple of examples where new interpretations may be in order.

First, let us examine the rule of the Taewŏngun. As everyone knows, Korea's foreign policy during the Taewŏngun's rule (1864–1873) is generally categorized as a *swaeguk* (seclusionist) policy. The term *swaeguk* was first used by the Japanese historian Shitsuki Tadao in his translation *Geschichte und Beschreibung von Japan* by the German naturalist Engelbert Kämpfer. It appeared in the section heading describing how Japan would not let its citizens leave or foreigners enter the country. The first time the term was applied to Korea was in the previously mentioned *Chosen okoku* by Kikuchi Kenjo.[14] In the section on the Taewŏngun's second reign, Kikuchi wrote that the Taewŏngun strengthened the nation's defenses, fought with intruding French warships, clashed with American warships, and severed diplomatic relations with Japan after a demonstration by a mob of Japanese at the *waegwan* (the Japanese residence area) in Pusan in 1872. Kikuchi shifted all the blame on Chosŏn and described the period as an "age of seclusion" (*swaeguk sidae*). After the term *swaeguk* first appeared in Kikuchi's book, later books, including *Chosen kaikashi* and *Kanhanto*, also used the term in a similar manner. They felt that the Taewŏngun had strengthened national defenses in order to repel the advancing tide of Westerners and labeled this as a *swaeguk* or isolationist policy.

The French navy attacked Kanghwa Island because of Chosŏn's suppression of Catholicism. In response to Chosŏn's official persecution of French missionaries and their believers, a French *division navale* captured Kanghwa Island. From a foreigner's perspective,

---

14. Yŏn Kapsu, "Taewŏngun chipgwŏngi (1863–1873) sŏyang seryŏk e taehan taeŭng kwa kunbi chŭnggang" (Military expansion and responses to the Western powers during the Taewŏngun's reign) (Ph.D. diss., Seoul National University, 1998), pp. 2–3.

Chosŏn's prohibition of Catholicism in itself could be regarded as an isolationist policy. However, there are many ways in which Chosŏn was not fully responsible for the diplomatic clash with Japan that occurred shortly after this. It is common knowledge that toward the end of 1867, the Japanese emperor regained power from the Tokugawa Bakufu, and imperial rule was restored. On January 15, 1868, the new government informed the various ministers from other countries of this change and accepted their diplomatic credentials. However, an exception was made in the case of Chosŏn. As in the past, the Lord of Tsushima was invested with the full authority for foreign affairs and to act as a proxy for the new government. On June 28, a delegation called the *Daishu daisashi* was organized to inform the Chosŏn government of the imperial restoration. The delegation arrived at Tongnae on December 19, and copies of the diplomatic documents were sent to the Chosŏn side. The Chosŏn government did not receive them because of issues such as the delegation's unilateral changing of official posts and titles used to refer to each country, the usage of a seal newly made by the Japanese government instead of the official seal given to them by Chosŏn, and also the use of the term *hwangje* (emperor).[15] As is well known, this was a pending diplomatic issue between Korea and Japan for the next six years. Japan put the blame entirely on Chosŏn and began to call Chosŏn an "isolationist" or a "hermit" nation.

It is true that the Taewŏngun government initially rejected Japan's request to establish new diplomatic relations, but there was sufficient reason for this. First, Japan's diplomatic actions were overly unilateral and arbitrary. Normally, if a major political change occurred such as the Imperial Restoration, the appropriate sequence of action would have been to take steps to properly inform the other party of the news and then to enter into consultations on how the diplomatic style and procedures would be affected by the changes in the form of the state. However, Japan chose its own method of informing Chosŏn of the imperial restoration and its own diplomatic procedures to reflect the changed polity, and it expected Chosŏn to accept them. Expecting Chosŏn to accept such actions calmly and completely was, of course, entirely one-sided.

Second, an incident occurred a year or two before Japan sent its delegation that had made Chosŏn wary of Japan. On December 12,

---

15. Until then, documents between Japan and Korea came in the name of the Japanese Shogun translated as *taegun* or "great prince."

1866, one year before the Meiji Restoration, a Japanese self-claimed Confucianist named Hachinoe Junshuku wrote the following in the Chinese newspaper *Zhongwai xinbao* in Guangdong: at the call of the shogun, 260 Japanese feudal lords gathered in Edo concluded that there was no choice but to take up arms and enhance Japan's national prestige by launching a major military undertaking to conquer Chosŏn since Chosŏn refused to pay tribute every five years. In an article in a different newspaper, he also claimed that since the Silla period, the Samhan states in Korea had paid tribute to Japan and that from the time of the Hideyoshi Invasions, the Chosŏn king sent an envoy to Edo every five years to have an audience with the shogun. This was a direct manifestation of the "Conquer Korea" thinking common within samurai society at the time in Japan and cannot be explained as a mere rumor as the Japanese later claimed. The Chinese government sent word of this article to Chosŏn, who took this matter seriously. Chosŏn sent a message demanding an explanation to the Japanese government through Tsushima under the name of the Chief-of-Staff of the Ceremonies Board.[16] A year later, when Japan arbitrarily changed the form and style of its delegation, and suddenly started using the term *hwangje* without prior notice, Chosŏn's rigid stance seems only appropriate. To put it simply, Japan must also bear a large part of the responsibility for the diplomatic stalemate after the Meiji Restoration. The reason why Chosŏn has shouldered all of the blame until now is that historical analysis has always been from the Japanese perspective. Faced with enormous pressure from China and Japan in its early modern history, Korea had no opportunity to set the record straight at the time.

It is undeniable that the Taewŏngun government's response to Japan's request was extremely problematic. According to a detailed account of the events,[17] Chosŏn sent the *hundo* (the first-line diplomat for relations with Japan) and Tongnae county magistrate to negotiate. After they pointed out the problems with the Japanese documents, they did not attempt any sort of compromise. Because of this, negotiations stood at a standstill for three years. Finally, since Chosŏn would

16. Tabohashi Kiyoshi, *Kindai nissen kankei no kenkyu* (Studies on the relations between Japan and Chosen during the modern period), vol. 1 (Keijo [Seoul]: Chosen sotokufu chusuin, 1940), pp. 121–24.

17. The following account is taken from the above-mentioned Tabohashi Kiyoshi's book. While there may be some problems in terms of viewpoint or bias, overall his account seems accurate and well-detailed in describing the progress of events which took place at that time.

not budge from its rigid stance, the delegation withdrew from Korea in January 1872. In late May of that year, the Tsushima-born head of the *waegwan* announced that he wished to meet with the Tongnae county magistrate and left the Japanese compound to enter Tongnae, which caused a disturbance lasting five days. This event did not benefit Japan in any way and only served to worsen the bilateral relations. Japan's unilateral actions did not end there. Japan's Foreign Ministry took this incident as evidence that the people of Tsushima were no longer capable of conducting diplomacy with Chosŏn. They used this event to assume direct control over foreign relations with Chosŏn, and they secretly took measures to take over the *waegwan*. The *waegwan* was originally built by the Chosŏn government, and the Japanese only possessed the right to use the facilities, not own them. Therefore, any changes in the situation needed to be discussed with the Chosŏn government. However, the Japanese started in May and completed the following February the unilateral measures to take over the *waegwan*, even going so far as to rename it the *Dai Nippon kokan* ("The Official Residence of Great Japan"; hereafter, the "Japanese Residence").

The Japanese Foreign Ministry's occupation of the *waegwan* was just another manifestation of their aggressive "Conquer Korea" thinking. The so-called Lesser "Conquer Korea" faction's proposal at the court in late May 1873 was a more active expression of the same attitude. In light of these events, it is improper to say that all the blame should be placed on Chosŏn for being isolationist or seclusionist.

The diplomatic confrontation stemming from the issue of establishing bilateral relations dragged on for about five years since June 1868, and it finally took its toll and led to changes in the power structure of both governments. However, the original situation, represented by Japan's offensive stance and Chosŏn's defensive stance, remained unchanged. In Japan, the Lesser "Conquer Korea" faction fell out of grace in October 1873, while in Korea, the Taewŏngun fell from power in late December, directly showing how much of a burden this diplomatic clash was. One common denominator in the power shift of each country was that it was the hard-liners or "hawks" which lost power. In the case of Japan, the faction that replaced the Lesser "Conquer Korea" faction did not relinquish the idea of conquering Korea; rather, their views differed in terms of timing and leadership. On the other hand, the monarch who deposed the Taewŏngun, King Kojong, adopted a policy of complete openness. He firmly believed that the only way to save Chosŏn was through openness, and by establishing diplomatic relations with foreign countries. In late December 1873, the Chosŏn monarch appointed a close, trustworthy official, Pak Chŏngyang (1841–1904), as a special investigator and sent him down to Tongnae to examine why diplomatic relations had become deadlocked. In addition, he replaced all the officials, including the Tongnae county magistrate, who had been involved in diplomatic matters with Japan. From this point onward, the attitude of the Chosŏn king and government toward Japan made an almost 180-degree turn. In April 1874, Japan launched a military expedition against Taiwan. The Chosŏn government learned about it from the Chinese Ministry of Rites on August 4. In contrast with the past, the Chosŏn government did not harden its attitude toward Japan. They came to the conclusion that too much reliance had been placed on the words of the *hundo* to the point where bilateral relations were in danger. Therefore, in the middle of August, all the relevant officials were punished, and a negotiator was sent to the Japanese Residence in Pusan to discuss the basic direction of future bilateral relations. The Japanese side suggested a direct-exchange system where the Chosŏn Minister of Rites would interact with the Foreign Minister, the Chosŏn Vice Minister of Rites would interact with the Japanese Vice Foreign Minister, and so on, to which the Chosŏn side agreed. In addition, Chosŏn also agreed not to raise any objections to Japan's use of the term *hwangje* in its diplomatic documents, but Chosŏn had the right not to use the term in its responses according to circumstances. A preliminary agreement was formally proposed on September 3, and on September 19, the Chosŏn government convened a ministerial meeting. They accepted the proposal, saying that the Japanese government clearly had "friendly and amiable intentions," and received the king's approval. The Chosŏn government demonstrated without a doubt its commitment to openness. Now, everything was up to the Japanese.

That October, the head of the Japanese Residence in Pusan, Moriyama Shigeru, went back to Tokyo to report on the latest developments. His actual mission had been only to report on the state of affairs, but because events had transpired so quickly, he also signed the agreement. The Japanese Foreign Ministry took steps to promote him and make him the official head of the Residence. On December 28, he was promoted to the rank of vice-minister and dispatched as the *isagwan* (executive director) of the Japanese Residence in Pusan. However, because the Foreign Ministry was preoccupied with the military expedition in Taiwan, the issues concerning Korea were placed on the backburner, and Moriyama did not arrive at his new post until the following year on February 24, 1875.

Starting from March 2, the Tongnae country magistrate began preparations to formally welcome the Japanese Residence Executive Director as an official diplomat. The magistrate asked for copies of the diplomatic papers and also the diplomatic-passage authorization. Upon receiving the copies, he noted that the original diplomatic papers were written in Japanese (instead of Chinese), carried the stamp of the Foreign Ministry (instead of the head of state), and used terms such as "Great Japan" and "the present Emperor"; therefore, he asked the central government to make the final decision. On March 12, King Kojong held a meeting with his three Ŭijŏngbu ministers (High State Councillors), who advised returning the documents for correction. But the king said that "it is clear there is nothing suspicious about Japan's intentions," and since the Japanese had brought the diplomatic papers as was agreed upon, "it would not be in good faith if we did not accept them." He also said that if there were any problems after receiving the documents, it would not be too late to reject them. There were some officials who, still holding anti-Western sentiments from the past, took issue with the fact that the Japanese official had arrived in Pusan on a steamship. But the king rejected this, saying that Qing China was also using steamships because of their convenience and speed, and so there was no problem with the Japanese doing the same. Since the king showed such a progressive attitude, no one could argue and the procedures were quickly implemented. Future obstacles to rapid progress in bilateral relations came from the Japanese side.

On March 27, working-level officials entered into detailed discussions on the protocols for the meeting between the Tongnae county magistrate and the Japanese executive director. The Japanese side announced that Moriyama would be arriving at a banquet ceremony for guests of state through the central front gate wearing a Western evening coat.[18] The flustered Chosŏn officials reported this to the county magistrate, who then asked the court to deal with the matter. On April 9, the court decided that in terms of this matter alone, the traditional ways should be observed and informed the Japanese Residence as such on May 9. Moriyama's attempt to impede the

---

18. Until then, diplomats would enter through one of the front gates to the side of the central front gate in traditional attire.

smooth progress in resuming diplomatic relations over such a trifling matter had an ulterior motive. On April 15, he sent the assistant executive director to Tokyo to report that judging from various incidents, the current Chosŏn political situation was unstable and that the most effective method of diplomatic relations would be to threaten Chosŏn by dispatching a warship to the waters off its coast, and asked for instructions from Tokyo to proceed in this direction. This clearly shows that Japan's attempts to initiate foreign relations with Chosŏn were from the beginning based on the policy of "Conquering Korea." Their true intent was to establish new diplomatic relations with Chosŏn to their advantage through a demonstration of military might. Judging from the attitude of the Japanese diplomats, it was no accident that the *Unyang* Incident off Kanghwa Island occurred only four months later.

While recognizing the validity of Moriyama's request, the Japanese Foreign Ministry ordered that diplomatic means be tried to achieve their earlier objective. On May 15, the Tongnae county magistrate again tried to persuade the director, saying that Chosŏn wanted to hold a banquet in the traditional style since the director and his subordinates had traveled from afar and that Chosŏn wanted a special celebration of the resumption of relations after an approximately ten-year stalemate. However, Moriyama criticized the move as a mere stalling tactic and even detained the Korean officials within the Japanese Residence. On May 17, the Japanese executive director issued a public statement saying that Chosŏn was trying to intervene in another country's internal affairs, even going so far as to say that this was a matter of national disgrace. Given his status as a diplomat, this was akin to issuing a final ultimatum. The Tongnae county magistrate criticized the statement as a damaging insult to the Chosŏn state, to which Moriyama issued another rebuttal in writing on May 19. On May 21, the Korean magistrate ended negotiations with the Japanese diplomat and asked the court for help.

At the meeting of ministers of the second rank and higher held on June 9 (10th day of the fifth lunar month), the moderate camp prevailed. The main groups were those advocating compromise, saying that a break in relations with Japan should be avoided, and those emphasizing accommodation, saying that neighboring countries had no right to resist changes in Japan's polity. The king also said the first priority should be to avoid a head-to-head collision. But at the meeting of Ŭijŏngbu ministers, the hard-line view won out once again. On August 6 (9th day of seventh lunar month), the Ŭijŏngbu (High

348  *Chapter Thirteen*

State Council) announced that as long as the Japanese executive director insisted on entering through the central front gate wearing Western attire, the ceremony could not be held. The king, searching for a way out, replaced the Tongnae magistrate and ordered the new magistrate to make the Japanese understand Chosŏn's situation and ensure the ceremony would be held. However, on September 20, Moriyama received an order from the Japanese government to return home and left that very day. September 20 was the day when the *Unyang* Incident occurred near Kanghwa Island.

CONCLUSION

Until now, the prevailing view on Korea's foreign relations in the early modern era has been that Korea was "hermit-like" or "exclusionist." This chapter first examined the origins of this attitude and then the accuracy of this perception. In particular, my focus was on the period starting from 1868, right after the Meiji Restoration when Japan sent a delegation to Korea to request the initiation of new diplomatic relations, and up to 1875, right before the *Unyang* Incident. This examination showed that Chosŏn's rejection of Japan's proposal to initiate new diplomatic relations was not because of Chosŏn's overall exclusionary attitude but because of Japan's aggressive intentions toward Korea. This chapter also demonstrated that Chosŏn's attitude shifted rapidly toward openness after the restoration of King Kojong and that to call Chosŏn "hermit-like" or "seclusionist" at the time is not accurate. In fact, the Chosŏn government was even more active than the Japanese government in trying to establish diplomatic relations. This was probably done in an effort to recover from the decline caused by Chosŏn's delay in opening its ports.

The Japanese were perplexed by the Chosŏn government's stance, and so when they requested the reestablishment of new diplomatic relations, they did so in a manner that Chosŏn could not accept. They expected—and wanted—Chosŏn to reject their proposal. Their actual aim was to create an opportunity to use military force or pressure and eventually conquer Korea. The reason why Japan decided to end the negotiations over the state-dress issue in the final stage of setting up diplomatic relations was that the negotiations were not going the way they desired because of Korea's open stance. Normal negotiations were thrown aside and, using that fact as a pretense, Japan instigated the *Unyang* Incident, a threat of military force. In reality, early modern Korea was not seclusionist but rather a nation that was opening itself of its own accord. Japan was not a "messiah" trying to save a "hermit" nation but instead an aggressor. By calling early modern Korea a hermit kingdom, Griffis was only acting as a spokesperson for Japan's expansionists.

The Chosŏn government maintained its open stance after the *Unyang* incident when it signed the Treaty of Friendship with Japan in 1876. The Japanese again had made plans to respond with force in the event the talks broke down, but these plans were made useless by Chosŏn's willingness to establish relations.[19] After signing the treaty of friendship with Japan, Chosŏn gathered many materials to prepare for signing a treaty of amity and commerce with the United States. When it did so in April 1882, Chosŏn became the first country in Asia with the right to determine its own customs duties.[20] However, Korea was then hampered by China, which was trying to reassert its authority over Korea.

The Taewŏngun, who fell out of power with the restoration of King Kojong, rallied the forces opposing the policy of openness and caused the Soldiers Riot of 1882 in an effort to regain power. This event gave Qing China an opportunity to regain control over Chosŏn, which seemed to have escaped from its sphere of influence through its treaty with the United States. China, after confirming that the soldiers riot was indeed against the king, sent troops into Chosŏn under the pretext that it was the protector country of the Chosŏn dynasty. After the Qing troops captured the Taewŏngun and sent him by force to China, they remained in Chosŏn and began to directly intervene in Chosŏn's domestic affairs. Among the progressive-minded bureaucrats appointed by the king, a faction of them tried to use the strength of Japan and initiated the Kapsin Coup of 1884 (Kapsin chŏngbyŏn), but in the end, this only further weakened the monarch's influence.

China unilaterally imposed an agreement on trade and commerce that guaranteed Chinese merchants the unlimited right to do business on the Korean peninsula and placed the Chosŏn Tax Office directly under the Chinese Tax Office in Shanghai. As a result, the Chosŏn government slipped into financial poverty. Under the king's guidance,

---

19 . Please refer to "Kuroda benridaishi Chosen shikosimatsu" (Minister Kuroda's reports on activities in Chosŏn) and "Kuroda benridaishi chosen shikonikki" (Minister Kuroda's diary on activities in Chosŏn), in *Nihon gaiko bunsho* vol. 9 (Tokyo: Gaimusho), document #26, p. 139.

20. Kim Kyŏngt'ae, "Pulp'yŏngdŭng choyak kaejŏng kyosŏp ŭi chŏngae," pp. 198–99.

intermittent progress was made in pursuing an open-door policy, but in the end, the efforts proved ineffective because of the lack of finances. In his book *China and Korea* (1888), Owen N. Denny (?–?), an American who was Advisor to the Chosŏn King and Director of Foreign Affairs, wrote that Korea's determination to open itself was clearly proven, as evidenced by its conclusion of treaties with various Western nations and its firm declaration of being an independent nation. While having been appointed as advisor to the Chosŏn monarch on the recommendation of the powerful Chinese official, Li Hongzhang (1823–1901), Denny became a firm admirer of King Kojong once he came to understand more about the situation in Chosŏn. Even though he and William Eliot Griffis were both Americans, they had entirely different views on Korea. Having actually been to Korea during that period, Denny was able to witness Korea's efforts to open itself to the West.

The failure of Korea's modernization was not necessarily its own fault, as is generally believed. On the contrary, Korea was actively trying to enter into the international society, albeit late, but was impeded by the selfish interests of its neighbors, aggressive Japan and egoistic China. It is true that Chosŏn had weak national defenses and could not overcome its difficulties, but it is not historically accurate to say that Chosŏn lacked the will to modernize. Korean historians should move quickly to rectify these mistaken historical perceptions by rethinking their research agendas from new perspectives.

Not only has this flawed understanding or awareness of Korea's early modern history caused a great loss of pride among most Koreans today, but it has also made it difficult for them to reflect on and learn from history. This greatly hampers the ability of Korean people today in all areas, particularly in their international activities and relations. Faulty knowledge and shallow thinking preclude effective judgment and analytical ability. It would be futile to try to expand one's international activities and raise one's international competitiveness without a proper understanding and recognition of one's own history.

translated by Edward Park

CHAPTER 14

# Korean Historiography's Escape from Modernism

RECENTLY, THE FIELD OF KOREAN history has been in a state of confusion, with calls for change coming from all directions. Compared to other fields of scholarship, Korean historiography has accomplished much since the country's liberation in 1945. However, critiques insisting on change have been louder than any recognition of these achievements. These critiques are not simply calling for qualitative improvement; in many cases, the demand is for a fundamental change in orientation. In other words, past accomplishments are regarded as an old form of scholarship that does not suit the needs of the new era. Beginning in the 1980s, there was much talk about rapid industrialization and, in the 1990s, about the shift to an information society. As inclinations and perspectives have changed tremendously because of these rapid socioeconomic changes, it seems that the public is demanding a historiography suited to the changing times.

The demands for a change in Korean historiography fall roughly into two types. The first are the silent demands of the general public, and the second are the more academic critiques and exhortations coming from the field of history itself and related fields. For instance, a publishing company recently produced a CD-ROM containing the Korean translation of the *Chosŏn Wangjo Sillok* (Veritable Records of the Chosŏn Dynasty), an indispensable resource for research on Chosŏn period history. Even nonspecialists now have in their hands the ability to search easily for information on any item they are interested in. Using the CD-ROM, an amateur historian wrote the book *Han'gwŏn Ŭro Iknŭn Chosŏn Wangjo Sillok* (The Veritable

Records of the Chosŏn Dynasty in a Single Volume),[1] and it instantly became a bestseller. Professional historians familiar with the records would not even think of writing such a book as they contain a massive amount of information covering five hundred years of history. Regardless of its content, what does it mean that a book with such an ambitious title became a bestseller? The only explanation seems to be that the general public wants a different kind of history book. Further evidence is the fact that even television programs based on the CD-ROM are popular.

For many years, Korean scholars of Western history have been quick to introduce the latest trends in historiography. There was an implicit expectation that Korean historiography would be influenced by the introduction of these trends. Examples include the new historiography of the *Annales* School in France, structuralist history, and the history of daily life from Germany. The recent shift in focus in Western historiography from structure to culture has also been introduced to Korea.

Another recent trend in Korea is the popularity of postmodernism, which has affected all fields of the humanities and social sciences, and it has also had an effect on Korean historiography. As the term suggests, postmodernism is a critique of modernism, whose influence has been predominant since the nineteenth century. The Western intellectual world in the nineteenth century put absolute faith in the power of reason and regarded the European experience as applicable to the entire world, emphasizing its universality. Postmodernism has indicated the limitations of this absolute faith in reason and criticized its indiscriminate application to the experience of the non-West. According to this critique, this application of reason resulted in the concealment of numerous meaningful realities and truths. Since postmodernism began as a total critique of intellectual history of the past few centuries, historiography too has been subjected to the same critique. There is no reason to dismiss postmodernism in the non-Western world, including Korea, since, unlike modernism, it has shown a great concern for the experience of the non-West.

The demands of the general public and of scholars for a change in Korean historiography may differ in their focus. It is likely, however, that there is some connection between the two since both emerged at the same time. Modernism influenced all areas of scholarship in both

---

1. Pak Yŏnggyu, *Chosŏn wangjo sillok (han'gwŏn ŭro iknŭn)* (Seoul: Ungjin tat k'ŏm, (1996) 2004).

the East and the West during the past century, and Korean historiography is no exception. Up to now, Korean historiography has developed under the auspices of modernism. But has modernism fallen out of favor with both scholars and the general public? To ascertain the meaning of these widespread criticisms, it is necessary to examine the emergence of modernism and its forms. Only after such an examination is it possible to take the next step of discussing alternatives.

The objective of this chapter is to examine existing methodologies of Korean historiography and to discuss new methods for writing history. The major approaches to Korean history that historians have used up to now can be classified as colonialist, nationalist, positivist, and socioeconomic. These approaches were all influenced by modernism. Because of the country's tumultuous history, Korean historiography has been strongly ideological. The dominant ideologies of the twentieth century were outgrowths of modernism.

The negative influence of modernism has been a major reason for the problems Korea has faced. With all scholarship and knowledge enslaved to modernism, it was nearly inevitable that Korea should become ill. Historians under the sway of modernism have also contributed to the spread of this malady. I propose that we move away from past practices and devote our energies to diagnosing more accurately the origins and history of Korea's illness.

THE MODERNIST CHARACTERISTICS OF TWENTIETH-CENTURY KOREAN HISTORIOGRAPHY

(1) **Strong Ideological Nature**
The history of Korean historiography as a modern form of scholarship falls entirely within the past century. Although modern Western historiography was first introduced into Korea in the late nineteenth century, it was not until the twentieth century that Korean history began to be written from a modern historical perspective. Scholars generally agree that the major approaches to Korean historiography that emerged at this time were Japanese colonialist historiography, nationalist historiography, socioeconomic historiography, and positivist historiography.[2]

---

2. On colonialist historiography, see *Han'guksa simin kangjwa*, no. 1 (1987). On nationalist historiography, socioeconomic historiography, and positivist historiography, see Yi Kibaek, "Kŭndae Han'guk sahak ŭi paljŏn," *Han'guk sahak ŭi panghyang* (Seoul: Ilchogak, 1978).

Colonialist historiography was an effort by the Japanese to reinterpret and rewrite Korean history from their perspective in order to justify their rule over Korea. Though their efforts had already begun before the "annexation" in 1910, their research was conducted more systematically when Keijo Imperial University[3] was founded after the March First Movement (1919) as part of the colonial government's "Cultural Policy" (Bunka Seiji). By locating within Korean history the causes of Korea's decline to a colony, the Japanese sought to justify their rule and make it acceptable to the Koreans. According to the Japanese view, it was historically inevitable for Korea to come under Japanese rule because Koreans were a people without dynamism.

Nationalist historiography was established by Korean intellectuals who opposed Japan's colonial rule and colonialist historiography. Though this form of historiography encompassed a variety of positions, what they had in common was the objective of achieving independence and promoting a spirit of independence. Similarly, socioeconomic historiography also opposed colonialist historiography but was based on a materialist view of history that began to emerge in the 1920s. Though there were nonmaterialist forms of socioeconomic historiography, it produced far fewer works and was much less influential than those based on historical materialism. Lastly, advocates of positivist historiography argued that in order for Korean historiography to become established as a discipline, it was more important to focus on empirical research than on ideological issues.

In short, Korean historiography developed in the context of two opposing positions toward colonial rule. Korea's liberation in August 1945 promised to bring about changes in Korean historiography. However, things did not develop as expected. Although colonialist historians returned to Japan after liberation, colonialist historiography itself still remained. After World War II, many scholars of Korean history in Japan criticized the colonialist perspective of their predecessors; however, there were also scholars who still clung to the colonialist view. Most of all, the negative prejudices that the Japanese held about Koreans and their history could not be corrected since school textbooks at all levels were not immediately rewritten. The recent revival of Japan's aggressive attitudes toward Korean history with the growth of Japan as a major power is a troubling development.

Socioeconomic history based on historical materialism rose in prominence after liberation. Before 1945, it was generally read and

---

3. This institution is the predecessor of Seoul National University.

discussed secretly in reading clubs, but with the establishment of a communist state in the North after liberation, historical materialism performed a central role in the establishment of its ideology. Historical materialism was also influential in the south where a liberal democratic government was formed. Up to the outbreak of the Korean War in 1950, socialists in the south continued to engage in political struggle, and one part of their struggle was to conduct work on Korean history based on historical materialism.

With the intensification of the struggle against military dictatorship from the 1960s, leftist historiography as a new form of socioeconomic historiography held tremendous appeal among young intellectuals. During the successive military dictatorships of the Third, Fifth, and Sixth Republics, the leftist interpretation of Korean history in terms of class struggle struck young students as a "penetrating" critique of their own situation. The critiques of the corruption of the dictatorship and the contradictions of capitalism became more persuasive as political oppression became more severe.

Nationalism and positivism served as the two foundations for the development of Korean historiography after liberation. Neither had any significant connection with the left. However, this difference with the left was not sufficient to establish a historiography that could contribute to the development of liberal democracy. In fact, it was through an examination of nationalism and the utilization of positivism from a liberal democratic perspective that both were able to develop into a historiography supporting the development of liberal democracy.

In South Korea after liberation, historiography developed gradually through such efforts. In the South, the search for a nationalist history based on the principles of liberalism trained many researchers and produced new works as interest in national identity grew in the 1960s. Despite the quantitative growth in research, many limitations in methodology and the organization of data also became apparent. Historians were aware of problems of a leftist historiography that rigidly adhered to principles of historical development, but their overemphasis on understanding historical facts produced situations in which they were unable to string together the facts that they unearthed. Work on a systematic understanding of Korean history was lacking, leading to doubts about whether such historiography was the right way to proceed. Leftist scholars remarked disdainfully that these problems were a natural result of a historiography without an ideology.

Korean historiography was born in the early twentieth century and developed over the course of the century. A century is certainly not a short period of time for the growth of an academic discipline. Although it is true that Korean historiography experienced many vicissitudes during this period, the major approaches that emerged early in the century have all remained to this day and continue to occupy prominent positions. Why, then, have the major approaches to Korean historiography not undergone significant change during the past one hundred years?

In the early twentieth century, the imperialist powers were involved in a fierce competition for colonies. The opposing world historical trend was the rise and spread of socialist revolution with its focus on class issues. In twentieth century world history, the competition for colonies brought about a world war, and its aftermath led to a division of the world into liberal and socialist camps. Korea was a flash point for the collision of these world historical trends. After a thirty-six year occupation by Japan, the country was tragically divided after the end of World War II. In a place where major trends of the age are in intense conflict, it is not unusual for the dominant ideologies of the period to have a deep influence. Korean historiography was shaped by these ideologies since it developed under such conditions. Without a change in these ideologies, it is unlikely that the major approaches of Korean historiography will undergo change as well. The major approaches that emerged in the early twentieth century—colonialist, nationalist, socialist—still remain dominant at the turn of the century.

In conclusion, Korean historiography in the twentieth century became strongly ideological in orientation because of the situations that Korea faced in that period. The dominant ideologies of the century were the outgrowth of modernism; that is, the ideologies from the nineteenth century that upheld the superiority of Western civilization. Unfortunately, modernism's hold on Korean historiography is the strongest and the most lasting. Even the positivist school cannot be considered free of modernism's influence since it is based in liberalism and nationalism. When academics and the general public demand changes in Korean historiography, it seems to be because it has been under the sway of modernism for so long.

## (2) Particularity Obscured by Universality

One of the main characteristics of modernism is that it emphasizes universality over particularity. Modernism has little concern for particularity since it pursues historical development and world historical universality through the power of reason. If Korean historiography developed under the influence of modernism, then it cannot be free of this aspect of it. The principal task of historiography has been to uncover a host of particularities and then either compare them to other histories or measure them against world historical universals. If historiography becomes strongly influenced by modernism, then would it not impair the search for particularities? Depending on one's perspective, this problem can be considered a crisis of historiography or a fatal flaw. If a historian were strongly influenced by modernism, would not his or her obligation to seek individuality be impaired? This is the central problem, even the fatal flaw, of modern history studies.

Even before Korea came into contact with Western culture, it had long been exposed to the cultural universality and particularity of East Asia. In Korean history, the transition from Buddhism to Confucianism was a major turning point that marked the transition from an age of religion to one of ideology. In general, history begins with the emergence of religion. Tribes and states established their rule and underwent development through the power of religion. In the case of Korea, primitive religions and later Buddhism helped to establish ancient states and contributed to the development of medieval society. However, in the late fourteenth century, the limitations of a statecraft based on religion became apparent, and Korea underwent another major turning point, adopting Neo-Confucianism as its ruling ideology. Compared to religions of the time, Neo-Confucianism was greatly concerned with bettering the secular world. Its adoption as state ideology thus signified the strong desire of the state to improve the lives of the commoners. It is striking that such a change occurred in Korea at a time when religion still played a central role in statecraft in Europe.

A main premise of Confucian thought was that the will of heaven (*ch'ŏndo*) is to encourage all living things to flourish. The duty of the monarch was thus to provide amply for his subjects' basic needs: food, clothing, and shelter. Under the influence of this political ideology, the rulers of the Chosŏn dynasty oversaw great changes in the agricultural economy that overcame the limitations of fallow-field farming. Because their efforts were successful, they did not question the fundamental universality of Confucianism. However, it was not until the late Chosŏn period that intellectuals began to feel the necessity of studying the particularities of Chosŏn's situation in order to realize the universality of Confucianism more fully. A new form of thought called Silhak (practical learning) emerged within Neo-Confucianism. Silhak scholars felt that it would be difficult to develop an effective response to the changes in state and society using only the orthodox policies of Confucian thought.

Intellectuals of the Chosŏn dynasty came into contact with the new universalism of the West in the late nineteenth century. This foreign universalism was based on a strong faith in the power of human reason, and it was very different from Confucian universalism, which was based on the notion of *ch'ŏnin habil* (harmony between heaven and humankind).

What perplexed Chosŏn intellectuals was not just Western universalism itself but also Western steamships with their powerful cannons. These inventions were the products of this ideology, and they had not seen such things when they first learned about Western civilization (under the name of *sŏhak* or "Western learning") over a century earlier. Chosŏn intellectuals felt they could not ignore this Western civilization that had become so completely different; in response, they developed the notion of *tongdo sŏgi* (Eastern Ways, Western Technology). The concept of *tongdo sŏgi* referred to a fundamental mindset toward life and statecraft in which the technology of Western civilization would be adopted but only if tradition were preserved. Around the time that Korea was opened in 1875, support for *tongdo sŏgi* spread among reformist officials through the initiative of King Kojong.

The policy of *tongdo sŏgi* can be viewed as a descendant of Silhak thought, which emerged in the late Chosŏn period out of the need to focus on the particularities of Chosŏn's situation. The difference between the two was that the search for a method of focusing on particularity now extended to the West, but both were similar in that they both upheld the universality of Confucianism. The king and reformist officials advocated the notion of *tongdo sŏgi* as their program for *kaehwa* (enlightenment) and began to take concrete steps to implement it in the early 1880s.

However, their efforts were not successful because of resistance from conservatives and Qing China's interference in Chosŏn's affairs. In the mid-1890s, Qing China withdrew from Korea as a result of the Sino-Japanese War, but Japan forced Chosŏn to undertake an entirely different kind of reform. Japan claimed that only a policy of "Western Ways, Western Technology"—i.e., complete Westernization—could bring stability to Chosŏn. This claim created a way for Japan to interfere in Chosŏn's internal affairs.

Modernization through the *tongdo sŏgi* policy finally gained an opportunity for implementation with the establishment of the Great Han Empire (Taehan Cheguk) and the Kwangmu Reforms. From 1896 to February 1904, just before the outbreak of the Russo-Japanese War, the government successfully implemented an impressive number of projects within a short period of time as part of its effort to increase the nation's wealth and build its military strength. These projects included the beginning of construction on the northwest railway line (the Kyŏngŭi line), the building of facilities for Seoul's electric tramway, the construction of a munitions factory, and plans for a military conscription system. However, Japan could not merely sit by and let the Great Han Empire pursue these reforms. Fearful of losing an opportunity to take over the peninsula if Korea continued with its modernization program, Japan instigated the Russo-Japanese War, thereby creating an opportunity to seize Korea's sovereignty by force.

Although the *tongdo sŏgi* reforms were cut short by Japan, they constituted a self-strengthening program for modernization that was grounded in Korea's realities and was historically significant. Nonetheless, modern Korean historiography has never given due credit or recognition to this reform. Japanese colonialist historiography established the framework for modern Korean historiography and deliberately concealed Korea's achievements. Since Japan's objective was to seize Korea's sovereignty, the Japanese could not acknowledge the *tongdo sŏgi* policies for modernization that the Great Han Empire was implementing under the leadership of the emperor. If it had done so, it would have negated the Japanese justification for its takeover of Korea. There was only one possible interpretation of modern Korean history for Japan. According to this interpretation, Korea was able to modernize only as a result of Japanese policies. The notion of *tongdo sŏgi* was the most important theory of modernization in Korea, but it fell victim to Japan's imperialist aggressions.

Immediately after Japan forcibly annexed the Korean peninsula in 1910, Japanese writers produced various books on Korea's history following the opening of its ports in order to celebrate the annexation. These accounts portrayed Kojong—who was in fact an enlightened monarch dedicated to the modernization of his country—as a weak-willed, ineffectual leader under the control of his queen and his father, the Taewŏngun. The reforms implemented under his leadership were instead attributed to pro-Japanese members of the Enlightenment Faction (Kaehwap'a). The conquerors were able to rewrite history without any opposition. Since Japan ruled Korea at the time, the Japanese were able to achieve their goals even by emphasizing the pioneering role played by the Enlightenment Faction as pioneering and progressive.

Japan's suppression of the *tongdo sŏgi* policy did not end with its distorted portrayal of the leading force for modernization. This was also an act of cultural violence that robbed Koreans of their pride in the uniqueness of their culture and history. While Japan ruled Korea, Japan's strategy was to put forth negative views of Chosŏn's culture and history by comparing them to those of the West. In fact, Japan used Western modernism to trample on Korean pride and self-esteem. On the other hand, Japan emphasized that it was unique in East Asia since it was able to become a colonizer by following a historical path similar to the West. The notion of *datsu-A* (separating from Asia) as formulated by Fukuzawa Yukichi signified Japan's effort to enter the leading ranks of modernism. As Japanese imperialism suppressed the policy of *tongdo sŏgi*, modernism was the bait in the trap set for Korea. It was a trap well suited to undermine the resistance of the small number of nationalist intellectuals.

Historical materialism also played a role in undermining the identity of Korean history. Marx saw history as progressing from ancient slave society to the feudal manor system (serfdom) to modern capitalism and finally to socialism. Since Marx's principles of historical development were, as is well known, based primarily on European history, many exceptions emerge when these principles are applied to situations outside of Europe. The fact that he created the separate category of the Asiatic mode of production suggests that Marx himself was aware of this problem. Later Marxists devoted much effort to explicating the Asiatic mode of production in order to demonstrate the universality of proletarian revolution. Under Stalinism, the five-stage model of development, which was supposed to be applicable to all world history, gained ascendancy by political decree. The principles of world history were taken as orthodoxy though they lacked scientific proof because of the political objective of spreading proletarian revolution internationally.

Whether based on Marx's original formulation of historical development or on Stalin-era historical materialism, the application of historical materialism to Korea produced a version of Korean history that only reflected the viewpoint of historical materialism. It did not present the true picture of Korean history or even its key aspects. Even though the Stalinist model of historical development claimed to reduce inequalities in development among countries, it required each country to conform to this paradigm, rather than seeking the true nature of each country's history. The individuality of each country's history became buried in the world historical theory of revolution. When Korea was divided after liberation, the modernist ideology of historical materialism became dominant in North Korea, as is well known. The winds of a different form of universalism, Western capitalism, surged into South Korea. Under the cold war system, the Eurocentric modernism utilized by Japanese imperialism came to be replaced by American culture. After liberation, social scientists in the South came into contact with new scholarship mainly through America. They learned theories of industrialization and modernization in the U.S. and then applied them to Korea, believing that adoption of these theories was the country's only path to survival. Within these theories and ways of thinking, there was no consideration for the unique aspects of Korean society and culture. In fact, native Korean characteristics were regarded merely as an obstacle to the new development policies.

Liberation in 1945 could not bring Korea back to the path of *tongdo sŏgi* that had been lost before the occupation. Both North and South Korea were overwhelmed by a cold war modernism centered on the U.S. and the Soviet Union, whose foundation was the belief in the omnipotence of "Western Ways, Western Technology" established by Japanese imperialism.

For purposes of comparison, let us examine Japan's situation briefly. After World War II, Japan was successful in achieving rapid industrialization and became an economic superpower. Was its success the result of a policy of "Western Ways, Western Technology"? While Japan outwardly called for complete Westernization, Japanese traditions were actually maintained. Japan is the only country in the non-European world that has best preserved its traditional culture. While the Japanese were urging Koreans to become completely Westernized, they themselves upheld the virtues of *wakon-yŏsai* (blending Japanese spirit with Western materialism). It is clear that the notion of "Western Ways, Western Technology" was merely used by Japan as a pretext for interfering in Korea's modernization.

What about Korea's situation? Because of Japanese propaganda and coercion, all things Western or Japanese were exalted, while native Korean things were discarded. From the time of the Japanese occupation, all traditional order and authority in Korea became undermined. After liberation, the situation remained the same, and although the economy has become developed, it is clear that Korea lacks the ability to maintain social order. With the complete disintegration of social authority, people have become atomized like grains of sand and are unable to unite. Japan stands in stark contrast with Korea; under the notion of *wakon-yosai*, it preserved traditional order and authority. As a result, the notion of *tongdo sŏgi*, which is similar to the idea of *wakon-yosai*, can be seen as the proper course for modernization. Because the path of *tongdo sŏgi* was closed to Koreans, they have suffered an irretrievable loss. One cannot help but wonder how much Korea has suffered as a result of the damage done to its cultural roots because of the negative influence of modernism.

THE PATH TO ESCAPING MODERNISM

It is necessary to overcome the evils of modernism since its influence inflicted significant damage on Korean culture and historiography. One of modernism's characteristics is its strong ideological orientation, but it is also one of its vices. Given its inherently subjective viewpoint, ideology often commits falsities.[4] It is all the more important for historiography to avoid ideology since it must pursue objectivity. It is virtually impossible for humans to abandon ideology, but it is clearly necessary to be aware of the dangers of viewing the past from a specific ideological viewpoint. For instance, there is a high probability of deliberately overlooking or concealing facts that are opposed or unrelated to one's ideology.

In their research, historians should always keep in the mind the following three considerations:

1. From what position should history be seen?
2. What explanatory framework should be used?
3. How should history be analyzed?

These three questions are related to issues of viewpoint (view of history), paradigm, and methodology. The term "position" refers to the viewpoint for comprehending history, to the standpoint of

---

4. Edward Shils, "Ideology: The Concept and Function of Ideology," in David L. Sills, ed., *International Encyclopedia of the Social Sciences*, vol. 7 (New York: Macmillan and the Free Press, 1979), p. 73.

interpretation, and to the convictions, beliefs, and preconceptions that privilege certain interpretations or interpretive stances. The term "paradigm" denotes the research framework adopted to understand the history of a specific period. While a position can be applied to all periods of history, a paradigm is much more effective when its application is limited to a shorter time period. Finally, the term "methodology" refers to the various analytic tools of historical research such as textual exegesis, statistics, and archaeological methods.

Of the three principal issues in historical research, only the first and the third were viewed as crucial under modernism. In the mid-twentieth century, Thomas Kuhn (1922–1996) was the first to pay attention to the second issue in his explanation of the structure of scientific revolutions. Thereafter, it was the social sciences, rather than historiography, that utilized paradigms as a means of overcoming the limitations of modernism.

It is generally difficult to distinguish between the first and third issues in the case of Marxist historiography because of its ideological nature. In socialism and historical materialism, historical research is only about the application and verification of the laws of historical development since these laws serve as the foundation for the establishment of this ideology. One characteristic of Marxist historiography is the fact that other individuating or unique factors are hardly considered.

Similarly, nationalist historiography does not place much importance on methodology since its main objective is to uncover a history that glorifies the nation. In imperialism, totalitarianism, and other ideologies of violence, there is also a strong tendency for research methods to be compromised to serve ideological goals. Since each of these ideologies has been overly focused on establishing its own legitimacy, modernism contains the danger of distorting the truth of history.

Because of the inherent problems of modernism, its historiography could not remain unaffected. Not only has the truth been distorted, but history itself has been degraded into a means of legitimizing a specific ideology. It is important to be aware of the negative tendency to simplify history and to promote oppositions in historical understanding. The main purpose of historiography should be to depict the forms of life characteristic of a particular people in each age of history more fully and more accurately. To do so, historiography must discard or minimize its ideological orientation. In the past, modernism looked down upon historiography that lacked a viewpoint (issue 1). However, this disdain had more to do with being faithful to an ideology than to being concerned with the true purpose of historiography. This reflection on modernist historiography is concerned with this very issue. My conclusion is that in order to overcome modernism historical research should refrain as much as possible from directly reflecting issue 1 (From what position should history be seen?).

Historians are free to choose socialism as their ideology. They also have the right to focus their research on issues in line with their ideological viewpoint, such as peasant uprisings. However, all history is not about a process of continuous class struggle, as argued by Marxist historians in the past. The social existence of humans is marked by discord; however, each age has its own method for resolving this conflict. The further we look back in time, the greater the reliance was on faith or religion, and life in ancient times was characterized by the weakness of people's class consciousness against their rulers. It was not that people were completely obedient; rather, there was a way to resolve conflict through faith or religion. Such resolution of conflict can be regarded as the flowering of culture. These are the issues that historians should examine. It would be a tremendous error to view ancient peoples as possessing the strong consciousness of class struggle felt by workers after the Industrial Revolution.

It is no easy task to uncover the conditions of life of the people in each age since their traces are difficult to find in written records. Such tasks require the specialized abilities of historians. Historians must cultivate their grasp of the atmosphere of a period through a long examination of historical materials. By developing such abilities, historians will come to possess a special insight into the process of history, enabling them to piece together the conditions of life in each age even from the few remaining traces. This ability is one of the basic characteristics distinguishing historians from social scientists and other humanists. For a historian, working with a paradigm can be the most effective way of cultivating such abilities and pursuing the task of historiography.

Kuhn first used the term "paradigm" to describe the manner in which the scientists of a certain age conducted scientific research.[5]

---

5. On Kuhn's concept of paradigms, see Thomas S. Kuhn, *The Structure of Scientific Revolutions* (Kwahak hyŏngmyŏng ŭi kujo), trans. by Kim Myŏngja (Seoul: Tonga ch'ulp'ansa, 1992; originally published in 1970).

Originally, the term "paradigm" signified an exemplar used in language acquisition. In his research on the history of science, Kuhn discovered that the workings of science were similar to the process of students generating variations from an exemplar in the process of learning a language. Prior to Kuhn, scientists and historians of science thought that scientific progress was made through a process of accumulation, but Kuhn found this thinking to be wrong. According to him, scientific revolutions occurred through a non-cumulative change in which a paradigm was partially or completely replaced. In other words, the science of an age would remain valid for a certain period, but it would face a crisis when the limitations of its explanatory power began to generate serious anomalies. The crisis would lead to a revolution that completely changed the explanatory framework.

Kuhn's use of the concept of the paradigm originally represented the discovery of a model for the rise of scientific revolutions. However, after the publication of his work, social scientists began to utilize his findings to explain the workings of their own field. Historians expected that the application of Kuhn's methods to their choice of subject matter would be useful in escaping from the yoke of modernism. Kuhn's conception of the paradigm has some similarities with the *Annales* School's concept of "*la longue durée.*" The way of life of people differs in each age. The temporal unit of the "age" is not fixed, but it is applicable in referring to cultural changes. Whenever the cultural foundation of an era changes, it leaves a mark. The historian must find these marks and describe the ways of life belonging to each age.

Let us examine cases where it is possible to determine the existence of a paradigm using existing scholarship on Korean history. First, in the ancient and medieval periods, the relationship between religion and the functioning of society can be regarded as a paradigm. It can be surmised that the social and political role of religion in this period was extremely large. Religion may even have had a greater influence than Confucianism did during the Chosŏn period. However, since scholarship on religion is confined to explaining matters such as changes in Buddhist sects or philosophical thought, it has been unable to clarify religion's influence on the lives of people in those periods. The conditions of life in an age when religion was dominant would certainly constitute an important paradigm since they were completely different from the relation between religion and society in the modern period.

Second, another major paradigm was the agricultural economy and the lives of the peasantry under the conditions of fallow-field farming that prevailed until the end of the Koryŏ period. In terms of productivity and the process of implementation, fallow-field cultivation differed from the intensive farming methods established in the early Chosŏn dynasty that enabled continuous cultivation. Therefore, the way of life in rural villages up to the Koryŏ period was probably very different from that of the Chosŏn period. During the dynastic change from Koryŏ to Chosŏn, there was a great transformation in agricultural techniques, and the ruling ideology changed from Buddhism to Confucianism. The factors behind these changes were certainly not unrelated. If there was a mutual relationship between these factors, then Kuhn's concept of the paradigm can easily be applied to the framework of life in the Koryŏ and Chosŏn periods.

Third, another relevant issue that could be considered a paradigm is the strong inclination in Korean history for a powerful state. In modernist scholarship, the general trend has been to regard the strong state as a consequence of Korea's backward and abnormal development. According to this view, the late-Chosŏn period should have been the time when capitalism began to emerge and develop, but the strong presence of the state in the circulation of goods went against capitalist principles. Such a state has generally been regarded as a unique and backward aspect of Korean history. However, this interpretation might only be a biased view based on modernism.

In Korean history, the state or the monarch often played a mediating role in social conflicts in both the age of religion and the age of ideology. As a result, Korea has a longer history of centralized authority compared to other countries. This history is significant because it gave rise to cultural traditions that emphasized harmony over conflict. The devaluing of this tradition from the perspective of class struggle or Western feudalism can only be seen as an act of destruction.

The modernist view of Korean history also contains strong preconceptions about the relationships among the monarch, the *sadaebu*, and the common people. The class-centered approach to history conceived of the monarch as merely the leader of the *sadaebu*, regarding him as an enemy of the people. However, an in-depth examination of the historical reality can easily show that this view of history is completely wrong. During the Chosŏn period, particularly in its later years, monarchs were well aware that backing the class interests of the *sadaebu* would alienate the people, ultimately undermining the foundation of the dynasty. As a result, monarchs sided with the people and developed the new political doctrine of *min'guk* (republic), which held that the people were the foundation of the state.⁶ The emergence of this concept was an important moment in the development of a modern political consciousness in Koreans.

Ignoring such unique aspects of Korean history, modernism saw its proper role as the establishment of a Western-style framework for history, in which only the victory of the masses could secure the rise of modernity. No matter how enlightened the masses may be, modernity at the state level cannot be established in a society where the center of state administration has collapsed. It is also rare in history for the masses to become enlightened so early. In short, during the late-Chosŏn period, the general populace had direct contact with the king, and some of the privileges of the yangban⁷ *sadaebu* were eliminated. Such a political development can serve as a paradigm for modernization for a country with a long history of centralized authority.

An examination of Japanese imperialism in terms of paradigms can also better reveal its true nature. The history of Japanese aggression toward Korea has generally been explained within the general framework of theories of imperialism. In other words, this issue had been examined within the explanatory frameworks of modernism. The history of resistance to Japanese imperialism has also been examined using theories of class struggle. It was thought that only such an approach had the world historical universality that was a necessary condition of objective historiography.

However, Japan's aggressions toward Korea were not achieved on a foundation of imperialism but were carried out in order to gain the strength necessary to join the ranks of the imperialist powers. The nature of Japan's aggressions can be properly analyzed through the paradigm of its aggressive views of international affairs in the early modern era, rather than through general theories of imperialism. When the traditional aspects of Japanese expansionism are sufficiently understood, the reasons for Korea's demise can be more accurately explained. General theories of imperialism are better understood as theories of Western imperialism. If they are used to explain Japan's takeover of Korea, there is a danger that the results of such research will legitimize Japanese expansionism.

---

6. In general, the state was taken to be the monarch.

7. The term *yangban* refers to members of the upper class who were eligible to sit for the government service examinations.

The strong ideological orientation of twentieth-century Korean history is itself a historical phenomenon and is thus not wholly without significance. This characteristic of Korean intellectuals during the past century was the consequence of their desire to overcome Korea's history of "defeats" and the "backwardness" caused by Japan's occupation. Even though each ideology has its own weaknesses and contradictions, it is undeniable that all ideologies share the goal of achieving development and modernization. Historiography also felt that its important duty was to contribute to this goal, and it similarly came to possess a strong ideological orientation. Now that an entire century has passed, it can be said that the goals of development and reform advocated by modernist ideologies have been achieved. At least, this is true of South Korea. If Koreans do not acknowledge the limitations of the current situation and continue to approach matters the same way as in the past, it is possible to commit mistakes that will cause significant damage. North Korea is perhaps an extreme example of what can result from such mistakes.

The focus of this age is shifting from modernization to raising the quality of life. To contribute to this goal, Koreans should not be bound to ideological dogma but must strive to obtain more accurate information about their situation. If Korean historiography is to become a discipline responsive to the changing times, then it cannot follow the ways of the past. It should at least provide an accurate account of life under the particular conditions of each age. Historical information is not just knowledge of the past but also a potential source of wisdom for people as they try to develop new modes of living. What will be useful in accomplishing this task is not research based on universal laws of world historical development but research conducted through new paradigms or the methods of comparative history. What is needed is not a crude Korean historiography created under the gaze of Western modernism. A new age is opening in which sophisticated knowledge about the historical forms and traces of the actual lives of the Korean people contributes to the building of their future.

CONCLUSION

Currently, Korean society has fallen into a state of confusion. Even though there have been many achievements in economic modernization, Korea has fallen behind in social and cultural matters. There is no need to go over the argument that this situation is a consequence of "Western Ways, Western Technology" thinking, which held that economic development would solve all problems. However, what is commonly called the "Korean disease" cannot be easily remedied by adopting *tongdo sŏgi* thinking. Koreans will have to pay a heavy price for this distorted history. In the coming years, every branch of academia in Korea must devote its energies to eradicating this disease. Historiography must play the role of diagnosing this disease, and the fields of social science must develop prescriptions for its cure.

Like any other nationality, the Korean people have their own distinctive characteristics. For instance, Koreans can be characterized as being emotional or fond of singing. Records from ancient China noted that Koreans loved to sing and dance, and today, the existence of countless *noraebang* (*karaoke* rooms) throughout the country attests to the truth of this observation. The problem is the culture of singing; i.e., how are songs being enjoyed. Until a few decades ago, group singing was common. However, a major generational change has occurred, and now solo singing is prevalent. Group singing, which was grounded in the ethics of social coexistence, has disappeared because of the dominance of *noraebang* today. Is this not an accurate reflection of the flaws in Korean social relations today?

In pre-modern Korean society, the main arena for songs was places where Koreans labored. Through their affinity for song, Koreans were able to develop a spirit of cooperation and to relieve the pain and drudgery of farming, fishing, and other kinds of work. In rituals to mark the beginning of the farming season and to celebrate the harvest, songs were sung together in order to honor the guardian deities and to foster communal unity. Officials, aware of this social context, even promoted the development of music to promote harmony.

With industrialization and urbanization, Koreans have completely lost touch with this tradition. In *noraebang*, people grab microphones and sing individually as if seeking to confirm their existence. It is a lonely sight to see Koreans today who only know how to sing individually; they have long forgotten the *samgang oryun*, the ethical relations governing family and social life.[8] However, no new set of social ethics has been adopted. Such a society can only be described as grains of sand. In such a society, is it possible for the strength needed

---

8. The *samgang oryun* were the three bonds and five moral rules governing familial and societal relationships in Confucianism.

to withstand globalization to arise? Can something beautiful enough to be called culture emerge from this environment?

My argument has been that the negative influence of modernism is greatly to blame for the problems that Korea is facing today. As all knowledge and scholarship have become slaves to modernism, Korean society has become susceptible to such illnesses. It is impossible to deny that Korean historiography, enraptured by modernism, has also been a contributing cause of the disease. My proposal is for Korean historiography to escape from modernism and to undertake the new mission of devoting all its energies to diagnosing more accurately the origins of Korean society's illnesses. This new mission is of critical importance since it will help to develop new prescriptions to cure these illnesses; accordingly, I have stressed the necessity of searching for new research methods in order to diagnose the disease properly.

Since one of the causes of the disease was an excessive infatuation with modernism, searching for a cure within modernism is akin to strangling a patient already dying. Korea must now decisively break away from modes of thought that take theories developed in the West as absolute or that sees class struggle as the only messiah that can resolve the contradictions of modern industrial society.

Korea's traditional culture emphasized harmony in all areas. Since this emphasis on harmony is deeply embedded in the Korean temperament, Koreans would only need to become self-aware to turn this into a great strength. During the past century of modernization, this potential became buried under the influence of Western scholarship, which emphasized discord over harmony. Korean historiography by its very nature must play a leading role in the transformation of this mindset of Koreans, though it will be very difficult to achieve. While playing an active role in this transition, Korean historiography must develop to a level where it is not a follower of a certain school of Western historiography but is recognized by the international community of historians for its originality. The confusion that Korean historians are feeling now will dissipate naturally through such development.

translated by Edward Park

# Notes on Original Appearance

Chapter 1 appeared in *Chindan hakbo*, no. 55 (July 1983). An earlier version of the English translation appeared in *Korea Journal* 23, no. 5 (1983).

Chapter 2 appeared in *Kyujanggak* 5 (Dec. 1981). An earlier version of the English translation appeared in *Seoul Journal of Korean Studies* 2 (1989).

Chapter 3 appeared in *Tongbang hakji*, no. 64 (Dec. 1989).

Chapter 4 appeared in *Chindan hakbo*, no. 76 (Dec. 1993). An earlier version of the English translation appeared in *Korea Journal* 37, no. 2 (1997).

Chapter 5 can be found in *Chosŏn yugyo sahoe saron* (Seoul: Chisik san'ŏpsa, 1989), chapter 5. An earlier version of the English translation appeared in *Seoul Journal of Korean Studies* 4 (1991).

Chapter 6 appeared in *Chindan hakbo*, no. 78 (Dec. 1994). An earlier version of the English translation appeared in *Sahoe kwahak kwa chŏngch'aek yŏn'gu* 16, no. 3 (1994).

Chapter 7 appeared in *Yŏksa hakbo*, no. 181 (2004).

Chapter 8 appears in Yi T'ae-jin, ed., *Han'guk pyŏnghap sŏngnip haji anattda* (Seoul: T'aehaksa, 2001). An earlier version of the English translation appeared in *Korea Journal* 36, no. 4 (Winter 1996).

Chapter 9 appeared in *Han'guksa simin kangjwa*, no. 13 (1993). An earlier version of the English translation appeared in *Korea Journal* 40, no. 4 (Winter 2000).

Chapter 10 appeared in *Sŏulhak yŏn'gu* 4 (1995). An earlier version of the English translation appeared in *Korea Journal* 35, no. 3 (Autumn 1995).

Chapter 11 appeared in *Han'guk saron*, no. 37 (Department of History, Seoul National University; June 1997). An earlier version of the English translation appeared in *Korea Journal* 39, no. 3 (Autumn 1999).

Chapter 12 appeared in *Han'guksa simin kangjwa*, no. 29 (2001). An earlier version of the English translation appeared in *Sungkyun Journal of East Asian Studies* 3 (2003).

Chapter 13 was first published in English translation in *Korea Journal* 38, no. 4 (Winter 1998). The original Korean version was published in *Han'guk saron* no. 41-42 (1999).

Chapter 14 appeared in *Han'guksa simin kangjwa*, no. 20 (1997).

# Translators

Milan Hejtmanek is assistant professor of Korean history at the University of Pennsylvania. His research focuses on Chosŏn Korea and encompasses the social, political, and cultural history of local educational institutions; the institution of slavery; Confucian thought; and magic and ritual in the royal court.

Todd A. Henry is a Ph.D. candidate in History at University of California Los Angeles.

Hong Soon-kwon (Hong Sun'gwŏn) is a professor in the Department of History at Dong-A University in Busan, South Korea. He received his Ph.D. from the Department of Korean History at Seoul National University in 1991. His research focuses on modern Korean history.

Edward Park graduated with an A.B. in East Asian Studies from Harvard University. He worked for many years in Seoul, where he also worked as a part-time translator. He credits the generosity of mentors and colleagues and his extremely patient parents and sister for their help in completing the translations.

Scott Swaner was an assistant professor of Korean literature at the University of Washington. His research focused on modern Korean poetry, and he was also an active translator. He received his M.A. from Cornell University in 1997 and his Ph.D. from Harvard University in 2003.

# Glossary of Names

An Hyang (1243–1306) 安珦

Ch'ae Chegong (1720–1799) 蔡濟恭
Chang Shih-ch'en (1321–1367) 張士誠
Chang Yunhwan (?–?) 張允煥
Crown Prince Changhŏn (1735–1762) 莊獻世子
Chen Fu (?–?) 陳敷
Cho Chondu (?–?) 趙存斗
Cho Kwangjo (1482–1519) 趙光祖
Cho Pyŏngho (1847–?) 趙秉鎬
Ch'ŏljong (r. 1849–1863) 哲宗
Chŏng Mongju (1337–1392) 鄭夢周
Chŏng Pyŏngha (?–1896) 鄭秉夏
Chŏng Sŏn (1676–1759) 鄭敾
Chŏng Yag'yong (1762–1836) 丁若鏞

Ding Ruchang (1836–1895) 丁汝昌

Fang Guo-zhen (1319–1374) 方國珍
Fukuzawa Yukichi (1834–1901) 福澤諭吉

Han Kyujik (1845–1884) 韓圭稷
Hasegawa Yoshimitsu (1850–1924) 長谷川好道
Hayashi konsuke (1860–1939) 林權助
Hayashi Shihei (?–?) 林子平
Hong Chunp'yo (?–?) 洪俊杓
Hong Kukyŏng (1748–1781) 洪國榮
Hong Nak'an (?–?) 洪落安

Hong Ponghan (1713–1778) 洪鳳漢
Hŏnjong (r. 1834–1849) 憲宗
Hwang Hyŏn (1855–1910) 黃玹
Hyŏn Sanggŏn (1875–1926) 玄尙建

Ikeda Tsunetaro (?–?) 池田常太郎
Im Kkŏkchŏng (?–1562) 林巨正
Inoue Kaoru (1835–1915) 井上馨
Inoue Ryokei (?–?) 井上良馨
Ito Hirobumi (1841–1909) 伊藤博文

Kang Hsi (1662–1722) 康熙
Kikuchi Genjo (?–?) 菊池謙讓
Kil Chae (1353–1419) 吉再
Kil Yŏngsu (?–1919) 吉永洙
Kim Chongjik (1431–1492) 金宗直
Kim Chongsŏk (?–?) 金正錫
Kim Hongjip (1842–1896) 金弘集
Kim Hwak'u (?–?) 金鶴羽
Kim Kajin (1846–1922) 金嘉鎭
Kim Koengp'il (1454–1504) 金宏弼
Kim Okkyun (1851–1894) 金玉均
Kim Yangmuk (?–?) 金良默
Kim Yunsik (1835–1922) 金允植
Kim Yusin (595–673) 金庾信
King Ch'ungsŏn (1275–1325) 忠宣王
King Kongmin (1330–1374) 恭愍王
Kojong (r. 1863–1907) 高宗
Komura Jutaro (1855–1911) 小村壽太郎
Ku Pŏmsŏ (?–?) 具範書
Kwon Han'gong (?–1349) 權漢功

## Glossary of Names

Lady Hong of the Hyegyŏng palace
  (1735–1815) 惠慶宮洪氏
Li Hongzhang (1823–1901)
  李鴻章    (Li Hung-chang)
Lo Tai-fang (1027–1098) 呂大鈞

Maema Kyosaku (1868–1942)
  前間恭作
Min Ŭngsik (1844–?) 閔應植
Min Chongmuk (1835–1916)
  閔種默
Min Kŭngsik (?–?) 閔肯植
Min Yŏngch'an (1873–?) 閔泳瓚
Min Yŏnghwan (1861–1905)
  閔泳煥
Min Yŏngik (1860–1914) 閔泳翊
Moriyama Shigeru (?–?) 森山茂
Murayama Tomiichi (b. 1924)
  村山富市

Ŏ Yunjung (1848–1896) 魚允中
Ŏm Seyŏng (1831–1899) 嚴世永

Paek Munbo (?–1374) 白文寶
Pak Chŏngyang (1841–1904)
  朴定陽
Pak Chega (1750–1815) 朴齊家
Pak Chesun (1858–1916) 朴齊純
Pak Ŭnsik (1859–1925) 朴殷植
Pak Yŏnghyo (1861–1839)
  朴泳孝

Queen Dowager Kim (1745–1805)
  貞純王后
Queen Min (1851–1895) 閔王后

Sejong (r. 1418–1450) 世宗
Shinobu Junpei (?–?) 信夫淳平
Shitsuki Tadao (?–?) 志忠雄
Sim Sunt'aek (1824–?) 沈舜澤
Sim Uisŏk (1854–1924) 沈宜碩
Sin Chaehyo (1812–1884) 申在孝
Sŏ Chaep'il (1864–1951) 徐載弼
Sŏ Sang'u (1831–?) 徐相雨
Sunjong (r. 1907–1910) 純宗

Taewŏngun (1820–1898)
  興宣大院君

Takezoe Shinichiro (1842–1917)
  竹添進一郎
Terauchi Masatake (1852–1919)
  寺內正毅
Toyotomi Hideyoshi (1536–1598)
  豊臣秀吉
Tsuneya Seifuku (?–?) 恒屋盛服

Wang Yang-ming (1472–1529)
  王陽明

Yi Ch'aeyŏn (?–?) 李采淵
Yi Chaemyŏn (1845–1912)
  李載冕
Yi Chaesun (1851–1904) 李載純
Yi Chaeu (?–?) 李載禹
Yi Chehyŏn (1287–1367) 李齊賢
Yi Chongha (?–?) 李宗夏
Yi Haejo (1869–1927) 李海朝
Yi Hakgyun (?–1909) 李學均
Yi Hwang (1501–1570) 李滉
  (Yi T'oegye)
Yi I (1536–1584) 李珥   (Yi
  Yulgok)
Yi Kwangsu (1892–1950) 李光洙
Yi (Ri) Kyep'il (?–?) 李啓弼
Yi Mansu (1752–1820) 李晩秀
Yi Sŏgu (1754–1825) 李書九
Yi Sangjae (1850–1927) 李商在
Yi Wanyong (1858–1926) 李完用
Yi Yong'ik (1854–1907) 李容翊
Yokoi Shonan (1809–69)
  横井小楠
Yŏnsan'gun (r. 1494–1506)
  燕山君
Yoshida Shigeru (1878–1967)
  吉田茂
Yu Kiljun (1856–1914) 俞吉濬
Yuan Shih-kai (1859–1916)
  袁世凱
Yun Ch'iho (1865–1945) 尹致昊
Yun Haengim (1762–1801)
  尹行恁

Zhen Dexiu (1178–1235) 眞德秀
Zheng He (1371–1435) 鄭和
Zhu Xi (1130–1200) 朱熹
   (Chu Hsi)
Zhu Yuanzhang (1328–1398)
   朱元璋

# Glossary of Terms

Agwan p'ach'ŏn 俄館播遷
  the King's flight to the Russian legation
bao-ch'ao (C.) 寶鈔
  paper currency
bingyuan houlun 病源候論
  Discussions on Examination of Nature of Disease
caoshi (C.) 草市
  a type of market in China (ts'ao-shih)
cha 尺
  unit of measurement about one foot in length
chaein 才人
  class of people who worked as butchers
chaeyŏk-chŏn 再易田
  fallow land
chagang 自強
  national self-strengthening
chahyul chŏngch'ik 字恤典則
  a welfare law for abandoned children or the needy in years of famine
ch'anggŭk 唱劇
  a type of singing drama
changmun 長文
changmun 場門
  periodic market
Changyongwi 壯勇衛
  Command of Grandeur and Bravery
Changyongyŏng 壯勇營
  Garrison of Grandeur and Bravery
chapnan 雜亂
  general immorality
chayŏnch'on 自然村
  natural village
chayu yŏnae 自由戀愛 free love

ch'e 體
  very constitution of all creation
cheŏn 堤堰
  method in which mountain streams would be dammed up to gather water for use in farming
chekiang (C.) 浙江兵法
  Chekiang military tactics
chiao-ch'ao (C.) 交鈔
  paper currency
ch'iin 治人 to ideally govern others
ch'ik 勅 imperial
chikp'a 乾畓直播法
  direct dry seeding
chikp'a-pŏb 直播法
  direct sowing of seeds
ch'in'gang 親講
  special lecture
Chinhyulch'ŏng 賑恤廳
  Office of Relief Works
ch'inmin 親民
  being close to the people
Chiphyŏnjŏn 集賢殿
  Hall of Worthies
chiyŏkch'on 地域村
  communal village
Cho-Chung sangmin suryuk changjŏng 朝中商民水陸貿易章程
  Regulations for maritime and overland trade between Chosŏn and China
ch'ogye munsin 抄啓文臣
  the most promising civil servants under the age of thirty-seven working in administrative bureaus were handpicked for intensive study at the Kyujanggak for a set length of time
chŏhwa 楮貨 mulberry currency
chokbo 族譜 clan genealogies
ch'ŏkhwabi 斥和碑
  anti-Western monuments

*ch'ŏksa wijŏng* 斥邪衛正
    reject heterodoxy and defend orthodoxy
*ch'ŏksin* 戚臣 royal in-law families
*ch'ŏnbang* 川防 water fence
*ch'ŏndo* 天道 the Will of Heaven
*chŏng* 精 purity
*Ch'ong'a kugŭpbang* 村家救急方
    First-Aid Medicine for Villagers
*Chonggak* 鐘閣
    Tower of Bell located at the center of wall
*chŏnggwan* 貞觀
    to view the world honestly
*chŏnggyo* 正敎 orthodoxy
*Chŏngjo sillok* 正祖實錄
    The Veritable Records of King Chŏngjo
*chŏngmyŏng* 貞明
    to shine righteously
*chŏngnan* 賊亂 bandit rebellions
*Ch'ongni naemubusa* 總理內務府事
    Minister of Department of the Interior
*chŏngp'o* 正布
    standard cloth currency
*chŏngsa* 正史 official history
*ch'ŏnin habil* 天人合一
    harmony between heaven and humankind
*chosa kyŏnmundan* 朝士見聞團
    a mission to Japan
*Chosen jiken* (J.) 朝鮮事件
    Chosŏn Incident
*Chosen kaika no kigen* (J.) 朝鮮改化之起源
    The Origin of Korean Civilization
*Chosen kaikashi* (J.) 朝鮮開化史
    History of Enlightenment in Chosŏn
*Chosen koryakron* (J.) 朝鮮攻略論
    Theory of Invasion Chosŏn
*Chosen kunki* (J.) 朝鮮軍記
    Record of Military Accident in Chosŏn
*Chosen okoku* (J.) 朝鮮王國
    Chosŏn Kingdom

*Chosen shobun sanron* (J.) 朝鮮處分纂論
    Discussion on Disposal of Chosŏn
*chosŏ choyak kŭp pŏmnyŏng* 勅書條約及法令
    Royal Edicts, Treaties, and Laws
*Chosŏn* 朝鮮
    kingdom that existed from 1392–1910
*Chosŏn mulsan kongjinhoe* 朝鮮物産共進會
    Chosŏn Industrial Exposition
*chuch'ŏng* 奏請
    petitions to the throne
*chugyosa* 舟橋司
    Institute of Boat Bridge
*Chuhamnu* 宙合樓
    the pavilion where all the principles of the universe gathered
*Chungch'uwŏn* 中樞院
    Privy Council
*Ch'unhyangjŏn* 春香傳
    The Tale of Ch'unhyang
*Ch'unjŏrok* 春邸錄
    Record of the Days of the Crown Prince
*ch'uswaegwan* 推刷官
    system for finding runaway slaves
*chwayŏngsa* 左營使
    Left Garrison Officer
*Cohong* 公行
    a guild of licensed monopoly merchants
*Cunqiu* 春秋
    The Spring and Autumn Annals
*cunshi* (C.) 村市
    a type of market in China (*ts'un-shih*)

*Da Qing huidian* (C.) 大淸會典
    Collected Statutes of the Great Qing
*Dai Nippon kokan* (J.) 大日本國公館
    The Official Residence of Great Japan
*Daishu daisashi* (J.) 大修大差使
    The Great Dispatched Envoy for the Great Amity

Daito gapporon (J.) 大東合邦論
  Theory of Annexation of the
  Greater East Asia
Daitoa senso sokatsu (J.)
  大東亞戰爭總括
  A Survey of Wars in Greater East
  Asia
dajokan (J.)　太政官　prime minister
datsu-A (J.)　脫亞
  separating from Asia
datsu-A-ron (J.)　脫亞論
  Theory of Escaping from Asia
Daxue (C.)　大學
  The Great Learning
daxue yanyi (C.)　大學演義
  Further Explication of the *Daxue*
daxue yanyibu (C.)　大學演義補
  Supplement to the *Daxue yanyi*
do　道　provinces

haengsang　行商
  a type of merchant
haesang　海商　maritime merchant
haet'aek　海澤　coastal marsh
haikan-shiken (J.)　廢藩置縣
hai-tang (C.)　海塘
  type of field developed in Song
  China as part of the Jiangnan
  agricultural techniques
Hakkyu sillon　學規新論
  New Theory of Academic Rules
Han'gyong chiryak　漢京識略
  Summarized Records on Seoul
Han-Ch'ŏng choyak　韓淸條約
  The Korea-Qing Treaty
Hanko Meishinkan (J.)　藩校明新館
Hansŏng　漢城　Seoul
Hansŏng chubo　漢城周報
  name of a weekly newspaper
Hansŏng sunbo　漢城旬報
  name of a newspaper issued every
  ten days
Hansŏng-bu　漢城府
  Seoul prefecture
Hanyangga　漢陽歌
  Song of Seoul
Hojo　戶曹　Ministry of Taxation
hojŏk　戶籍　household registers

Glossary of Terms　381

Honggŏnjŏk　紅巾賊
  Red Turbans
Hongikchŏnggong chugo
  洪翼靖公奏稿
  volume of records compiled under
  Chŏngjo's orders and completed
  in 1800
Hongmun'gwan　弘文館
  Office of the Royal Secretariat
hsu-shi (C.)　集場　a type of market
  in China (*hsu-shih*)
hua-i (C.)　華夷
  the civilized and the barbarian
hŭmhyul chŏnch'ik　欽恤典則
  exacting standard for determining
  the guilt of prisoners
hundo　訓導
  the first-line diplomat for relations
  with Japan
Hunginjimun　興仁之門　East Gate
hŭnghaksŏl　興學設
  A theory of emerging learning
hun'gu ch'ŏksin　勳舊戚臣
  royal in-law allies
hunsin　勳臣　merit subjects
husi　後市
  Private trade in the Sino-Korean
  border region
hwach'ŏk　禾尺
  a group of people who made a
  living by selling products made of
  dried willow twigs
hwang　皇　emperor
Hwangguk hyŏphoe　皇國協會
  Imperial Association
Hwanggŭkp'yŏn　皇極編
  Book of Emperors
hwangje　皇帝　emperor
Hwasŏng　華城
  the present-day city of Suwŏn
Hwasŏnt'on-gi　華盛頓記
  On Washington, D.C.
hyangdo　香徒
  communal village organization
hyangdogwan　嚮導官　guides
hyangni　鄕吏
  local functionaries
hyangsadang　鄕射堂
  communal archery pavilion

*hyangsarye* 鄉射禮
    community archery ritual
*hyangŭmjurye* 鄉飲酒禮
    community wine-drinking ritual
*hyangyak* 鄉約
    community compact
Hyangyak chipsŏngbang 鄉藥集成方
    The Compilation of Native
    Korean Prescriptions
Hyangyak kugŭbpang 鄉藥救急方
    First-aid Prescriptions Using
    Native Ingredients
Hyangyak ponch'o 鄉藥本草
    Native Herbal Medicines
*hyangyak ŭisul* 鄉藥醫術
    native Korean prescriptions
Hyŏllyungwŏn 顯隆園
    name of tomb for Crown Prince
    Changhŏn
Hyŏmnyulsa 協律社
    a Western-style amphitheater
*hyŏn* 縣 district
*hyŏnshi* 州縣市
*hyŏpsanggwan* 協商官
    negotiation officer
Hyŏpp'an naemubusa 協辦內務府事
    Vice-Minister of Department of
    Internal Affairs

Ihyanggak 移香閣
    a center for airing the books
*ijŏng* 里正 village chief
*ijang* 里長 village chief
*ikki* 一揆 peasant rebellions
Ilsŏngnok 日省錄
    Records of Daily Reflection
*ilyŏk-chŏn* 一易田
    term indicating the existence of
    the practice of fallow farming
Imo ch'ŏbun 壬午處分
    the act by which the Crown Prince
    was stripped of his title and
    reduced to commoner status in the
    38th year of Yŏngjo's reign
Imo kullan 壬午軍亂
    Military Mutiny of 1882
Imunwŏn 摛文院
    Bureau of Beautiful Expression of
    Writings

*in* 仁 benevolence
Inbo-pŏp 隣保法
    the "neighborhood protection"
    system
Insŏrok 人瑞錄
    Records of Auspicious Events
*inŭi* 仁義 benevolence and justice
*iran* 移亂 refugees
*isaje* 里社制 village shrine
*isagwan* 理事官 executive director

Jiangnan (C.) 江南
    region immediately to the south of
    the lower reaches of the Yangzi
    River (Chiang-nan)
Jurakutei (J.) 聚樂第
    palace built by Hideyoshi
Jinsilu (C.) 近思錄
    Book of Thoughts

*kŏnkyŏng chikp'a* 乾耕直播
    dry-direct sowing
*ka* 家 family
Kabo kaehyŏk 甲午改革
    Kabo Reforms of 1894
*kaehwa* 開化 enlightenment
*kaehwa chŏngch'aek* 開化政策
    enlightenment policy
Kaehwap'a 開化派
    Enlightenment Faction
Kaeyuwa 皆有窩
    storehouse for all books
Kaisei gakko (J.) 開成學校
    school of higher education
    founded in 1873; precursor of
    Tokyo University
Kangsangryŏn 江上蓮
    A Lotus Flower on the River
Kanhando (J.) 韓半島
    The Korean Peninsula
*kanjongbŏp* 間種法
    intermediate sowing
Kankoku chusatsugun (J.)
    韓國駐箚軍 Resident Army in
    Korea
Kankoku gaiko itaku joyaku
    韓國外交委託條約
    Treaty to Transfer Korea's
    Diplomatic Rights

## Glossary of Terms 383

Kankoku heigo jyoyaku (J.)
　韓國併合條約
　Treaty regarding the Annexation of Korea to the Empire of Japan
Kankoku rinji hakentai (J.)
　韓國臨時派遣隊
　Temporary Military Contingent to Korea
Kapsin Chŏngbyŏn　甲申政變
　Coup of 1884
kata-arashi (J.)　片ありじ
　lying fallow in part
Keijo hattatsu shi (J.)　京城發達史
　A Developmental History of Keijo (Seoul)
Keijo shiku kaishu yotei keikaku rosen-zu (J.)
　京城市區改修豫定計劃路線圖
　Draft Plan to Restructure Kyongsŏng's [Seoul's] City Roads and Streets
Keijo-fu shi (J.)　京城府史
　A History of Keijo Prefecture
Kimyo sahwa　己卯士禍
　Literati Purge of 1519
kinai (J.)　畿內
　five provinces near the capital in Japan
Kiroso　耆老所
　Superannuation Bureau
kisaeng　妓生
　a female artist-entertainer
Koguryŏ　高句麗
　one of the Three Kingdoms; 37 B.C.–668 A.D.
Kojong sillok　高宗實錄
　Veritable Records of King Kojong
Kokugaku (J.)　國學
　National Studies
kong　空　emptiness
kongsa nobi　公私奴婢
　public and private slaves
Koryŏ　高麗
　kingdom that existed from 918–1392
Koryŏ togyŏng　高麗圖經
　a description of Koryŏ agriculture by a Song envoy who visited Korea in the first half of the twelfth century

Koryŏsa　高麗史
　The History of Koryŏ
kubon sinch'am　舊本新參
　the belief that innovations must be based on established foundations
Kugŭpbang　救急方
　First-Aid Medicine
kuk　國　state or country
kukga　國家　state
kukje　國制　State System
Kukjo hak'an　國朝學案
　title of book compiled by Pak Ŭnsik
kun　郡　county
Kun'guk kimuch'ŏ　軍國機務處
　Office for Military and State Affairs
kunja　君子
　superior men; men of cultivation
kunmin ilch'i　君民一體
　unity between the ruler and the people
kusŭp　舊習　old customs
Kusŭp kaeryang　舊習改良
　Reforming Old Customs
kwagŏ　科擧
　civil service examination
kwanbo　官報　Official Gazette
Kwangmu　光武
　Year appellation of Emperor Kojong, 1897–1907
kyesa　啓辭
　submissions to the throne
kyŏkjaeng　擊錚
　a petition system in which a person could strike a gong during a royal procession and then file a grievance
kyŏl　結
　unit of measurement for land
Kyŏng-Ŭisŏn　京義線
　railway line between Seoul and Ŭiju
Kyŏng'ungung　慶運宮
　Kyŏng'un Palace; modern-day Tŏksu Palace

384  Glossary of Terms

Kyŏngguk taejŏn 經國大典
　Grand Code for State
　Administration; the new legal
　code of the Chosŏn state
kyŏnggwa 慶科
　the national examination
kyŏngjaeso 京在所
　capital liaison offices
Kyŏngsa kangŭi 經史講義
　lecture on the Classics
kyŏngyŏn 經筵
　classics mat or royal lectures
kyomok sega 喬木世家
　These families derived their
　authority from having generations
　of members in high-ranking
　offices
Kyŏnggang 京江　Han River
Kyoiku chokugo (J.)　教育勅語
　Imperial Edict on Education
kyoyumun 教諭文　edict
Kyujanggak 奎章閣　Royal Library
kyunyŏkbŏp 均役法
　the Equalized Tax Law

lei-shu-xue (C.)　類書學
　"encyclopedic" learning
li 理　principle
Longtuge (C.)　龍圖閣
　Tower of the Drawings of
　Dragons

manch'ŏn myŏngwŏl chuin'ong
　萬川明月主人翁
　The master of ten thousand rivers
　and the bright moon
man'guk kongbŏp 萬國公法
　international law
Man'gwŏndang 萬卷堂
　Library of Ten Thousand Volumes
Manmin kongdonghoe 萬民共同會
　Convocation of Ten Thousand
　People
mansaku (J.)　滿作
　continuous cultivation
minbon 民本　people as foundation

minguk 民國
　a new theory of kingly rule which
　emphasized the unity of the king
　and his people
Minjok kaejoron 民族改造論
　On national reconstruction
Misok sŭp'yu 美俗拾遺
　Brief Observations on American
　Customs
muban 武班　military
munban 文班　civilian
munbon ŏngmal 務本抑末
　striving for agriculture,
　suppressing commerce
munhak 文學
　promotion of learning
munjip 文集　anthology
Muo sahwa 戊午士禍
　Literati Purge of 1498
Muyedobo t'ongji 武藝圖譜通志
　Comprehensive Illustrated Manual
　of Martial Arts
myŏngdŏk 明德
　explain virtuous conduct
myŏngmyŏngdŏk 明明德
　brightening man's inherent
　virtuous nature
myŏnju 綿紬
　unpatterned silk

Naemubu 內務府
　Department of the Interior
namch'ang Ch'unhyangjŏn
　男唱春香傳
　a version of the Tale of
　Ch'unhyang for a male singer
Namwŏn kosa 南原古詞
　Old Song of Namwŏn
Nanko (J.)　南校
　precursor to Tokyo University
nenko (J.)　年荒
　lying fallow yearly
Ni-Kan giteisho (J.)　日韓議定書
　Japanese-Korean Protocol
Ni-Kan kyoyaku (J.)　日韓協約
　Japanese-Korean Agreement

Glossary of Terms 385

Nikkan gappo shoshi (J.)
　日韓合邦小史
　A Bibliographical Work on Japan-
　Korea Relations
Nongga chipsŏng　農歌集成
　Compilation for Farmers
Nongsa chiksŏl　農事直說
　Straight Talk on Farming
noraebang　노래방　karaoke rooms
Noron　老論　Old Doctrine faction
nung-sang chi-yao (C.)　農桑輯要
　Collection of Agricultural and
　Sericultural Practices
nung-shu (C.)　農書
　Book of Farming

ogat'ongbŏp　五家統制
　the "five-family supervision"
　system
Ogunyŏng　五軍營
　Five Army Garrisons
ŏjejon'gak　御製尊閣
　a storehouse containing tens of
　thousands of books
Okjunghwa　獄中花
　Imprisoned Flower
Onin no nan (J.)　應仁의亂
　Onin Rebellion
ŏnjŏn　堰田　diked field
oran　五亂　five confusions
osŭng-p'o　五升布　five-ply cloth
Owi toch'ongbu　五衛都摠府
　Five Military Commands
　Headquarters

p'abungdang　破朋黨
　Anti-factionalism
p'ach'ŏn　播遷
　flight from the royal palace
p'ansori　판소리
　dramatic story-singing; one-person
　opera
p'yŏngdŭngnye　平等禮
　an equal footing
pangga　邦家　country and family
pi-A-hang-Il ch'aek　備俄抗日策
　policy of countering Russia and
　Japan

Pibyŏnsa　備邊司
　the Border Defense Council
Piwŏn　秘苑　the Secret Garden
po　洑　banked river
pu　府　prefectures or districts
puguk kangbyŏng　富國強兵
　rich country and powerful army
Pukhak'ŭi　北學議
　Discourse on Northern Learning
punbal chagang　奮發自強
　to devote great effort to national
　self-strengthening
pungdang chŏngch'i　朋黨政治
　factional politics
p'ungsujiri　風水地理　geomancy
punsin　分身　incarnation
Pyŏljubujŏn　鼈主簿傳
　The Tale of the Water Palace
Pyŏnghakt'ong　兵學通
　Manual of Military Science
pyŏngnong-ilch'i　兵農一致
　the principle of soldier-farmer
　equivalence

Qianjinfang (C.)　千金方
　Thousand Gold Prescriptions

rakushi rakuza (J.)　樂市樂座
ri　里
rokusai-si (J.)　六齋市
　the prototypical form of Japanese
　rural market
ronin (J.)　浪人　masterless samurai

sa　士　literati
sach'ang　社倉
　village granary system
sadae　事大　serving the great
sadaebu　士大夫
　literati, scholar-officials
sadaebuga　士大夫家
　families of the sadaebu
sadaejuŭi　事大主義
　serving the great
sain　士人　man of literature
sajanghak　詞章學　literary style
sajok　士族
　hereditary aristocratic families

*samaso* 司馬所
Association of Licentiates
*samdae chich'i* 三代至治
ideals of the rule of the Three Dynasties
*samgang* 三綱
Three Ethical Bonds
*samgang oryun* 三綱五倫
Three Bonds and Five Moral Rules of human relationships
*samp'o* 三浦  three Korean ports
*sangŏn* 上言
a petition system in which people would wait until the royal carriage reached a designated stop and petition the king either as an individual or as part of group by presenting an official document
*sangp'yŏngch'ang* 常平倉
Ever-Normal Storehouses; an office to regulate the prices of goods
*Sankoku-tsuran-zusetsu* (J.) 三國通覽圖說
book written by Hayashi Shihei in 1785
*sa-nong-kong-sang* 士農工商
scholars, farmers, artisans, and merchants
*sallan* 山亂
lawsuits about graveyards
*sarim* 士林  Neo-Confucian literati
*sedo chŏngch'i* 勢道政治
government by royal in-law families
*sei-Kan-ron* (J.) 征韓論
the theory of conquering Korea
*sengoku* (J.) 戰國
the Warring States period (middle 15th–early 17th centuries)
*sengoku daimyo* (J.) 戰國大名
*shi-ji* (C.) 市集
a type of market (shih-chi)
*shoen* 莊園制
*shugo daimyo* (J.) 守護大名
part of class of high feudal lords
Siganggwan 侍講官
Bureau of Prince Lectures

*siji yŏsang* 視之如傷
meaning that Chŏngjo's concern for them extended to the point that he worried about whether they would come to harm
*sijŏng kaesŏn* 施政改善
improvement of administration
*silhak* 實學  practical learning
Silla 新羅
*sillok* 實錄  Veritable Records
*Simch'ŏngjŏn* 沈淸傳
The tale of Simch'ŏng
*sin hangmun* 新學問  new learning
*sinhŭng sadaebu* 新興士大夫
newlyrising literati
*sinmin* 新民
renovating or making new the people
*sinmun'go* 申聞鼓
petitioners' drum
*sinsaenga samang* 新生兒死亡
death of those who died within one month of their birth
Sinyu saok 辛酉邪獄
The Purge of 1801
*sip'o* 市舖  market stalls
*soin* 小人  inferior men
*soa samang* 小兒死亡
early-childhood death
Sŏdaemun 西大門  West Gate
*sŏdo sŏgi* 西道西器
Western ways, Western technology
Sŏgo 西庫
West storehouse of books
*sŏhak* 西學  Western learning
Sŏhyanggak 書香閣
a building for reading and writing
*sŏjae* 書齋  village school
*sŏmin* 庶民  common people
*sŏnch'ŏnjŏk tanhap* 先天的團合
the inherent unity
*sŏnduan* 宣頭案
the official register of public slaves owned by the government
*sŏnggun* 聖君  virtuous ruler
Sŏnggyun'gwan 成均館
Koryŏ's Royal Confucian Academy

# Glossary of Terms 387

*sŏnghak* 聖學
   the study of the (Chinese) sages
Sŏngnihak 性理學
   Neo-Confucianism
Sŏngshi chŏndo shi 城市全圖詩
   a poem about life within the walled city
Sŏnhyech'ŏng 宣惠廳
   Agency to Bestow Blessings; in charge of collecting the Uniform Land Tax
*sŏnjŏn'gwan* 宣傳官
   the elite royal heralds also in charge of guarding the king
*sŏran* 西亂 Catholicism
*sŏri* 胥吏 village clerks
*sŏwŏn* 書院
   local private Confucian academy
*sowŏn* 訴冤 petition
Sŏyu kyonmun 西遊見聞
   Observations while Traveling in the West
*such'aek* 水車 a kind of water pump
*such'aek* 水柵
   embankments built of earth and often bamboo
*sugi* 修己 self-cultivation
*sugi ch'iin* 修己治人
   one who could govern himself and thus govern others
*sugwiso* 宿衛所 a night guard
Suikosha (J.) 水交社
   Suikosha Society
*sugyŏng chikp'a* 水耕直播
   wet-direct sowing
Sungnyemun 崇禮門 South Gate
*susang* 水商 a type of merchant
*susin taesa* 修信大使
   delegation that went to Tokyo in September 1882
*susinjega ch'igukp'yŏngch'ŏnha* 修身齊家治國平天下
   to cultivate oneself, to put one's house in proper order, to rule the country, and to bring peace to the world
*swaeguk* 鎖國 seclusionism

Taedongbŏp 大同法
   Uniform Tax Law
Taedonggyo 大同敎
   name of a religion
*taedongmi* 大同米
   rice collected under the Taedongbop
T'aegŭk 太極 the Great Ultimate
Taehak 大學 Great Learning
*taehak ryuŏi* 大學類義
   a complication of key passages from three texts
Taehan Cheguk 大韓帝國
   the Great Han Empire
Taehan Minguk 大韓民國
   Republic of Great Han; Republic of Korea
Taejŏn t'ongp'yŏn 大典通編
   Comprehensive National Code of Laws
T'aesan yorok 胎産要錄
   Summary of Obstetrical Medicine
*tai-Kan hosin* (J.) 對韓方針
   Policy toward Korea
Taiping (C.) 太平天國亂
   Taiping rebellion in China
Taiping shenghuifang (C.) 太平聖惠方
   Remedies Given by the Grace of Heaven
T'akjibu 度支部
   Ministry of Finance
*t'angp'yŏng* 蕩平
   impartiality that had existed during the rule of the Three Dynasties
*t'angp'yŏngch'aek* 蕩平策
   policy of impartiality
T'ongni kimu amun 統理交涉通商事務衙門
   Office for Extraordinary State Affairs
Tosŏng samgunmun pun'gyejido 都城三軍門分界之圖
   The map of three army garrisons' assigned to defensive districts of the capital wall
Tianzhangge (C.) 天章閣
   Tower of the Writings of Heaven
*to* 道 moral principle

*To ŭi kan* 兎의肝
 The liver of the rabbit
*tongdo sŏgi* 東道西器
 Eastern Ways, Western Technology
*T'ongni amun* 統理衙門
 Office of Foreign Affairs
*Tongnip hyŏphoe* 獨立協會
 Independence Club
*tongran* 東亂 Tonghak
*tonyu* 唐入 entry into China
Tong-zhi (C.) 通志
 General Treatise (T'ung-chih)
Tung-lin (Academy) (C.) 東林
 aka, Donglin Academy; founded during the Song dynasty
*tunjŏn* 屯田 garrison land

Ŭibang yuch'wi 醫方類聚
 Classified Collection of Medical Prescriptions
*ŭich'ang* 義倉
 government granaries
Ŭijŏngbu 議政府 State Council
Unyang sagŏn 雲揚號事件
 Unyang Incident
*uyŏngsa* 右營使
 Right Garrison Officer

*waegwan* 倭館
 the Japanese residence area
*wako* (J.) 倭寇 Japanese pirates
*wakon-yŏsai* (J.) 和魂洋才
 blending Japanese spirit with Western materialis
*wangga* 王家 royal family
*weimin* 爲民 serving the people
Wen-hsien-t'ung-kao (C.) 文獻通考
 Comprehensive Inquiry into Recorded Institutions
*wioe kyŏkchaeng* 衛外擊錚
 strike a gong during the procession, thus creating an opportunity to file a grievance

*Xiaopinfang* (C.) 小品方
 Small Book of Prescriptions

*xiaoshih* (C.) 小市
 a type of market in China (*hsiao-shih*)
*Xiaoxue* (C.) 小學
 Elementary Learning (Hsiao-hsüeh)
*Xinjing* (C.) 心經
 Heart Classic; The Way of the Mind (Hsin Ching)

*yangjŏl* 兩截 dual system
*yehak* 禮學 the study of ritual
yemun'gwan 藝文館
 Office of the Royal Decrees
*Yiji* (C.) 易繫
 The Twisting of Divinations
*Yijing* (C.) 周易 Book of Changes
*yixue qimeng* (C.) 易學啓蒙
 Enlightenment through Divination
*yŏlgogwan* 閱古觀
 library for old books
Yomei gakkai (J.) 陽明學會
 Wang Yang-ming Neo-Confucian Society in Japan
*Yŏn ŭi kak* 燕의脚
 Leg of a Swallow
*yonaoshi* (J.) 世直し
 rebellion in Japan
*yong* 用 use of all creation
*yŏng'a samang* 嬰兒死亡
 death of those who died within one year of birth
Yŏngjongjin 永宗鎭
 an island near Kanghwa Island
*yŏngsŏnsa* 領選使
 a high-ranking official stationed in Tianjin
*yŏpkun* 獵軍
 the hunting brigade that caught pheasants on royal lands to present to the king
Yu-hai (C.) 玉海 Jewel Sea
*yuhyangso* 留鄕所
 local self-governing organizations
*yuksang* 陸商
 a type of merchant in Korea
Yongle Emperor 永樂帝
 aka, the Yung-lo Emperor

*yusuja* 遊手者
    the wandering dispossessed
*yuŭi yusik* 遊衣遊食   idle and lazy

Zhongwai xinbao (C.)   中外新報
    a Chinese newspaper in
    Kuangtung
*Zhongyong* (C.)   中庸
    Doctrine of the Mean
*Zhouli* (C.)   周禮
    Rites of the Zhou
Zongli yamen   總理各國事務衙門
    the Office for Foreign Affairs

# Index

Agwan p'ach'ŏn, 163, 168, 248, 270–75, 280, 285, 287, 308
Allen, Horace N., 186, 257, 282
An Hyang, 25
Andong Kwŏn, 75–77
annexation, 141, 167, 301, 322, 325, 331, 335, 339–40, 354, 359
Asiatic mode of production, 360
Aston, William George, 162

bao-chao, 99, 101
bingyuan houlun, 79–80
Brown, McLeavy, 247, 250, 254, 257, 277, 279, 281, 283, 285, 287
Buddhism, 81, 357

caoshi (C.), 95
Catholicism, 230, 301, 307, 330, 341–42
cha, 250, 271, 277
Ch'ae Chegong, 242–43, 245
Chaein, 62
chaeyŏk-chŏn, 97
chagang, 318
chahyul chŏngch'ik, 227
Chang Yunhwan, 277
ch'anggŭk, 319–21
changmun, 96, 116
Changyongwi, 217–19
Changyongyŏng, 217–19, 230
chapnan, 312
chayŏnch'on, 33
chayu yŏnae, 320
ch'e, 302, 315
Cheju Island, 227
chekiang, 112, 124
Chen Fu, 27
cheŏn, 27, 31, 54
chiao-ch'ao, 99
ch'iin, 222, 232
ch'ik, 142
ch'in'gang, 214–15
ch'inmin, 298, 315–16
Cho Chondu, 160
Cho Kwangjo, 42

Cho Pyŏngho, 154
Cho-Chung sangmin suryuk, 149
ch'ogye munsin, 215–16, 221
chŏhwa, 101
chokpo, 75
ch'ŏkhwabi, 304
ch'ŏksa wijŏng, 316–17
ch'ŏksin, 38
Ch'ŏljong, 245, 311
ch'ŏnbang, 31–32, 41, 44–46
ch'ŏndo, 296, 316
Chŏng Mongju, 40
Chŏng Pyŏngha, 248
Chŏng Sŏn, 242
Chŏng Yagyong, 245, 313
Ch'on'ga kugŭpbang, 84
Chŏngch'i togam, ix
Chonggak, 242
chŏnggyo, 303
Chŏngjo: abolition of slavery, 225, 228–32; criminal justice, 227; kyŏngyŏn, 214–15, 220–21; Kyujanggak, 207–08, 212–16, 218; military reform, 216–19; petition system, 211–12, 226; theory of monarchy, 220, 224–25
chŏngmyŏng, 222
chŏngnan, 113
Ch'ongni naemubusa, 159
chŏngp'o, 103–4
chŏngsa, 68
ch'ŏnin habil, 358
chosa kyŏnmundan, 145
Chosen jiken, 336
Chosen kaika no kigen, 333
Chosen kaikashi, 336
Chosen koryakron, 168
Chosen kunki, 336
Chosen okoku, 336
Chosen shobun sanron, 336
chosŏ choyak kŭp pŏmnyŏng, 183
Chosŏn: capital of, 236–37, 241; currency, 106; founding of, 34, 36 75, 81, 83, 329; Great Han Empire, 163, 254, 269; markets, see markets; medicine, 56;

Chosŏn (continued)
  Neo-Confucianism (Sŏngnihak), vii, xi, 3–4, 68, 94, 115, 220, 232, 298, 315, 357–58; population, 55, 69, 75–77, 128–29; relations with China, 102, 107–08, 121, 125, 128, 130, 139–41, 146–57, 160–64, 302, 305–06, 336; relations with Japan, 108–11, 125–27, 131, 142, 144, 168, 301, 334, 342–45, 347–49; trade, see trade; treaty, 109, 141–47, 149–55, 162, 164, 274, 301–02, 305; tribute (tributary system) see tribute; yangban, 296–301, 310–11, 319, 322; Chosŏn agriculture: books on agriculture, 27; irrigation, 28
Chosŏn mulsan kongjinhoe, 290
chuch'ŏng, 228
chugyosa, 244
Chuhamnu, 213
Chungch'uwŏn, 258
Ch'unhyangjŏn, 310, 320
Ch'unjŏrok, 221
ch'uswaegwan, 226, 228
chwayŏngsa, 158
Cleveland, Grover S., 187
cloth currency, 102–104
Cohong, 132, 135
Collbran-Bostwick Development Company, 186, 284–85
Convention of 1905, 166, 170, 172–74, 176–81, 184, 186–90, 192–93
Convention of Tianjin, 306
cotton, 63, 103–04, 108–11, 126–27
Crown Prince Changhŏn, 210, 217–19
cunshi, 95
currency, 62, 64, 99–104, 116–17, 126

Da Qing huidian, 150
Dai Nippon kokan, 344
Daishu daisashi, 342
Daito gapporon, 168
Daitoa senso sokatsu, 166
dajokan, 144
datsu-A, 360
Datsua-ron, 168
Davidov, 159, 157
Daxue, 220–22, 224
daxue yanyi, 221–22
daxue yanyibu, 221
de Speyer, Alexis, 154, 155, 157
Denny, Owen N., 158, 161–62, 350
Ding Ruchang, 157
do, 250
Dowell, William, 156
Dye, William M., 276, 279

England, 146, 151–52, 155–57, 161–62, 183, 185, 233, 325, 338

fallow (fallow farming; fallow-field cultivation), 4, 6–12, 14, 16–19, 28–29, 49, 51–53, 61, 97–98, 127, 357, 366
Fang Guo-zhen, 124
five-day market, 60
Foote, Lucius H., 149
France, 153, 168, 233, 301, 338, 352
Fukuzawa Yukichi, 317, 360

Germany, 146, 151–52, 162, 164, 254, 352
Government-General, 251, 258–59, 322
grave epitaph, 55
Griffis, William Eliot, 326–34, 337–38, 340, 349–50

haengsang, 96
haesang, 96
haet'aek, 53
haikan-shiken, 327
hai-tang, 32
Hakkyu sillon, 314
Han Kyujik, 153
Han'gyŏng chiryak, 242
Han-Ch'ŏng choyak, 164
Hanko Meishinkan, 327
Hansŏng, 237, 270, 282
Hansŏng chubo, 284
Hansŏng sunbo, 284
Hansŏng-bu, 240–42, 247, 250–51, 270–73, 275–76
Hanyangga, 242
Hasegawa Yoshimitsu, 176
Hayashi Gonsuke, 172
Hayashi Shihei, 334
hermit nation / hermit kingdom, 342, 349
historiography, 351–57, 359, 362–64, 367–70
hojo, 238–39

hojŏk, 300
Hong Chunp'yo, 277
Hong Kukyŏng, 214, 217
Hong Nak'an, 230
Hong Ponghan, 228
Honggŏnjok, 78
Hongikchŏnggong chugo, 228, 230
Hŏnjong, 242, 244-45
hsu-shi, 95
hua-i (C.), 106
Hulbert, Homer B., 186
Hŭnghaksŏl, 313
hun'gu ch'ŏksin, 114
hundo, 343
Hŭnginjimun, 250
Hunsin, 38
husi, 130, 134
hwach'ŏk, 62
hwang, 142
Hwang Hyŏn, 171
Hwangguk hyŏphoe, 258
Hwanggŭkp'yŏn, 225
hwangje, 342-43, 345
Hwasŏng, 218, 244
hyangdo, 12-14, 33-34, 26, 39, 58-59
hyangdogwan, 149
hyangni, 11, 34, 59-60
hyangsadang, 47
hyangsarye, 38, 40-43
hyangŭmjurye, 42-44, 116
hyangyak, 24, 35, 38, 40-47, 59, 62, 116
Hyangyak chipsŏngbang ,58-59, 78, 84-85
Hyangyak kugŭbpang, 78-80
Hyangyak ponch'o, 84
hyangyak ŭisul, 78
Hyŏllyungwŏn, 219
Hyŏmnyulsa, 319
hyŏn, 10, 14, 60
Hyŏn Sanggŏn, 185
hyŏnshi, 195
Hyŏpp'an naemubusa, 158
hyŏpsanggwan, 149

Ihyanggak, 213
ijang, 36
ijŏng, 36
Ikeda Tsunetaro , 339
ikki, 94, 113-14
Ilsŏngnok, 212
ilyŏk-chŏn, 97
Im Kkŏkchŏng, 113
Imo ch'ŏbun, 209
Imo kullan, 150, 335

Imunwŏn, 214
in, 297, 315
Inbŏbŏp, 59
Inoue Ryokei, 142
Insŏrok, 219
inŭi, 312
iran, 312
isagwan, 345
Ito Hirobumi, 178-81,270, 314

Japan: agriculture, 62 71, 111, 113;
 Anglo-Japanese alliance, 175;
 annexation of Chosŏn (see
 annexation); books on Korea,
 335-37, 339-41; colonialist
 historiography, 353-54, 359;
 Hideyoshi Invasion, 112, 167,
 237, 334, 343; imperialism,
 167-68, 360-61, 363, 367;
 market, 95; Meiji Japan, 139,
 141, 272, 310-311, 314, 338;
 pirates (wako), (see wako);
 Russo-Japanese War, (see
 Russo-Japanese War); Sino-
 Japanese War, (see Sino-
 Japanese War); trade, 64-65,
 108-10, 127-28; treaty, 139,
 141-44, 150, 162, 164, 166,
 170, 174, 176-78, 181-83,
 190-194, 301, 305, 325, 336,
 340, 349; Triple Intervention,
 168-69, 274, 308
Jiangnan, 26-33, 35-36, 44, 83, 98
Jinsilu, 214
Jurakutei,112
Jurchen, 47, 64 125, 129, 237-38

ka, 292
Kabo Reform, 270, 272, 274, 304-05, 307
kaehwa, 358
kaehwa chŏngch'aek, 163, 302
Kaehwap'a, 153, 359
Kaeyuwa, 213
Kaisei gakko, 324
Kangsangryŏn, 319
Kanhando, 333, 336
Kanjong, 52
Kankoku chusatsugun (J.), 169
Kankoku gaiko itaku joyak, 178
Kankoku heigo jyoyaku, 170
Kankoku rinji hakentai, 169
Kapsin chŏngbyŏn, 349
kata-arashi, 52, 97
Keijo hattatsu shi, 235

# 394 Index

Keijo shiku kaishu yotei keikaku rosen-zu, 190
*Keijo-fu shi*, 235
Kija, 228
Kikuchi Genjo, 336–37, 341
Kil Chae, 40
Kil Yŏngsu, 185
Kim Chongjik, 40–41
Kim Chongsŏk, 277
Kim Hongjip, 248, 271
Kim Hwak'u, 160
Kim Kajin, 160
Kim Koengp'il, 43
Kim Okgyun, 152–54, 270–73, 304–06, 317
Kim Yangmok, 160
Kim Yunsik, 148–49, 155, 157, 159–60
Kim Yusin, 318
kinai, 100
King Ch'ungsŏn, 5, 25–26
King Kongmin, 4–5, 16, 19
Kiroso, 281
kisaeng, 310–11
Koguryŏ, 121, 335, 329
Kojong: abdication, 180, 188; Agwan pach'ŏn, (see Agwan pach'ŏn); Convention of 1905, 166, 170, 172, 174, 177–81, 184, 186–90, 192–93; diplomacy, 301, 344; Great Han Empire, 167–68, 184, 188–90, 252–54, 257, 317; military reform, 252–53; modernization, 259, 273–74, 306, 308; relation with China, 301–02; The Hague, 180, 187; United States, 186–87, 190, 274; urban development, 289
*Kojong sillok*, 248
Kokugaku, 167–68
Kŏmun Island, 156–57, 161
Komura Jutaro, 249
kong, 81
kongsa nobi, 299
kŏn'gyŏng chikp'a, 54
Koryŏ :administration, 82; agriculture, 14, 17, 19, 27, 33–34, 51, 366; currency, 101; hyangdo, (see hyangdo); inheritance, 57; King Kongmin,4, 16, 19; market, 96; medicine, 55–56, 78–79; Military Coup of 1170, 73; Neo-Confucianism, 19, 40; population, 55, 71, 75, 78;
scholar-officials, 4, 15, 18–19; social structure, 34; tomb inscriptions, 71–72, 76–77; trade, 60 ; tribute system, 124–25
*Koryŏ togyŏng*, 17, 51
*Koryŏsa*, 10, 13, 15, 51
Ku Pŏmsŏ, 277
kubon sinch'am, 288
*Kugŭpbang*, 78–80, 84–85
kuk, 299
kukga, 299
kukje, 163
*Kukjo hak'an*, 316
kun, 10, 14, 34, 60
Kun'guk, 274
kunja, 225
kunmin ilch'i, 311
*Kusŭp kaeryang*, 315
kwagŏ, 296
kwanbo, 172, 175
Kwangmu, 168, 253, 257, 308–09, 314
Kwŏn Han'gong, 26
kyesa, 228
kyŏkjaeng, 212, 225–26
kyŏl, 6–9, 86
kyomok sega, 218
Kyŏng'un Palace, 247, 249–52, 257, 259, 271, 275–79, 282–83, 290–91
Kyŏnggang, 241
*Kyŏngguk taejŏn*, 102, 163
kyŏnggwa, 217
kyŏngjaeso, 37–38, 41–42, 47
*Kyŏngsa kangŭi*, 221
Kyŏng'ŭi, 285
kyŏngyŏn, 214–13, 220–21
Kyoiku chokugo, 310
kyoyumun, 303
Kyujanggak, 182–83, 207–08, 212
kyunyŏkbŏp,209

Lady Hong of the Hyegyŏng palace, 208, 215, 219, 230
Ladygensky, 161
lei-shu-xue, 24
li, 222
Li Hongzhang, 145, 149–53, 155–60, 161, 302, 350
liberalism, 323
literati purge, 94, 115, 117
Little Ice Age, 129–30
Longtuge, 213
Maema Kyosaku, 179
man'guk kongbŏp, 302

Man'gwŏndang, 25
manch'ŏn myŏngwŏl chuin'ong, 219
Manchu (Manchuria), 117, 130,–31, 133, 331
Manmin kongdonghoe, 253, 258
mansaku, 97
market, 94–98, 100, 104–05, 115–16, 127, 137, 209, 243, 255, 259, 276, 538–39
Marx, Karl, 360
Marxism, 323
Matiunin, N.G., 153
medicine, 55–56, 126, 313
Meiji Restoration, 307
Military: Chŏngjo's reforms, 218–19; coup, 73, 191; Five Military Commands, 214, 253; Japanese military, 112, 258–59, 317, 331; Koryŏ period (military regime), 5, 13, military advisors, 155, 157; military draft (conscription), 170, 185; military service, 59, 63; military services, 105
Military Coup of 1170, 73
Min Chongmok, 158
Min Kŭngsik, 158
Min Ŭngsik, 158
Min Yŏngch'an, 174
Min Yŏnghwan, 158
Min Yŏngik, 152, 158
minbon, viii, 19, 299
Ming, 94–95, 100, 102, 105–06, 108, 112, 114, 122–25, 127–132
minguk, viii, 256, 299
Minjok kaejoron, 318
*Misok sŭpyu*, 283
Modernism, 329, 352–53, 356–57, 3620–64, 366–68, 370
modernization: Chŏngjo, 208; Japan, 167; Kabo Reforms, 305; Kwangmu Reforms, 308–09, 314; Seoul, 235–37, 260, 270; tongdo sŏgi, (*see* tongdo sŏgi)
Mongol, 5, 55, 101, 133
Moriyama Shigeru, 345–48
muban, 296
munban, 296
munbon ŏngmal, 117
munhak, 313
munjip, 316
Murayama Tomiichi, 166
*Muyedobo t'ongji*, 216

myŏngdŏk, 297–298, 315
myŏngmyŏngdŏk, 220–21
myŏnju, 108–09

Naemubu, 160
namch'ang Ch'unhyangjŏn, 319
Namwŏn kosa, 320
Nanko, 327
Neinstead, F., 287
nenko (J.), 52, 97
Ni-Kan giteisho, 169–70
Ni-Kan kyoyaku, 169, 175
*Nikkan gappo shoshi*, 339–40
*Nongga chipsŏng*, 32
*Nongsa chiksŏl*, 6, 7, 12, 27–32, 52, 86
noraebang, 369
Normalization Treaty, 190–194
Noron, 230
nung-sang chi-yao, 27, 30
Nungxu, 27

Ŏ Yunjung, 147, 149
O'Connor, Nicholas R., 156
ogat'ongbŏp, 59
Ogunyŏng, 218
ŏjejon'gak, 213
Okjunghwa, 319
Ŏm Seyŏng, 157
Onin Rebellion, 95
ŏnjŏn, 32, 44–45
oran, 312
osŭngp'o, 103, 104
Owi toch'ongbu, 214

p'abungdang, 225
p'ach'ŏn, 248
Paek Munbo, 19, 26–27, 30
Pak Chega, 242
Pak Chesun, 179
Pak Chŏngyang, xiii, ix, 187, 247, 271–75, 268–84, 353
Pak Ŭnsik, 312–17
Pak Yŏnghyo, 152–53
pangga, 256, 270–73
p'ansori, 310–11, 319–21
paradigm, 231
Parkes, 151
petition, 37–38, 187, 211–12, 226, 228, 245, 255–56, 258
Pibyŏnsa, 218, 245
Piwŏn, 213
Plenipotentiary, 143, 145, 148, 153, 176, 179–82
po, 31, 54
population, 50, 54–57, 59–60, 62

396   *Index*

population (continued)
    67–71, 74–75, 77–78, 82–83,
    85–88, 97, 129, 227, 231, 276,
    285, 318
Port Hamilton, 156
Postmodernism, 352
puguk kangbyŏng, 134
*Pukhak'ŭi*, 242
punbal chagang, 315
pungdang chŏngch'i, 297
pungsujiri, 279
punsin, 299
Purge of 1801, 229–30
*Pyŏljubujŏn*, 319
p'yŏngdŭngnye, 148
*Pyŏnghakt'ong*, 217
pyŏngnong-ilch'i, 59

*Qianjinfang*, 79
Qing: Korea-Qing Treaty, 164;
    markets, 95 ; Qianlong emperor,
    225; relations with Chosŏn
    (Korea), 150, 162, 302, 305,
    335, 349, 358; sea-trade
    restrictions, 130–32
Queen Dowager Kim, 229–30
Queen Min, 158–59, 163, 248–49,
    271, 274, 279, 290, 306, 308

radial-road (plan), 251, 271, 277–
    79, 281, 282, 290
rakushi rakuza, 111
reversal effect, 50, 60, 62–63
Rey, Francis, 172, 189–90
ri, 13, 237, 244
rice transplantation, 27–28, 30, 32,
    40, 54, 64
rokusai-shi, 95
ronin, 306
Roosevelt, Theodore, 187
Root, Elihu, 174, 186
Rosen, Roman Romanovitch, 152
royal tomb, 208–11, 219, 239, 244–
    45
Russia: secret agreement, 151, 158,
    160–61; treaty with Chosŏn,
    153
Russian legation, 160–61, 163, 168,
    247–50, 253
Russo-Japanese War, 163–64, 168–
    69, 175–76, 184, 187–88, 236,
    258, 260, 275, 286, 309, 314–
    15, 317–18, 339, 359

sa, 298
sach'ang, 24, 35, 38–40

sadae, 148–49, 336
sadaebu, 3–4, 245, 296–300, 310–
    11, 313, 315, 366–67
sadaebuga, 299
sadaejuŭi, 318
sain, 300
sajanghak, 25
sajok, 296
sallan, 312
samaso, 42
samdae chich'i, 298
samgang, 310
samgang oryun, 310
samp'o, 109
sangŏn, 211–12, 225–26
sangp'yŏngch'ang, 239
*Sankoku-tsuran-zusetsu*, 334
sa nong kong sang, 304
sarim, 315
sedo chŏngch'i, 231, 233–34, 311
seikan-ron, 335
Sejo, 39–40
Sejong, 6–8, 12, 17, 20, 25, 31, 39,
    41, 107, 208
sengoku, 95, 111, 113
sengoku daimyo, 111
shiji, 95
shiji yŏsang, 226
Shinobu Junpei, 333, 336–38
Shitsuki Tadao, 341
shoen, 97
shugo daimyo, 113
Siganggwan, 221
sijŏng kaesŏn, 318
silhak, 313, 358
Silla, 329, 343
sillok, 7, 68, 212, 213, 263
silver, 99–102, 104–05, 107–08,
    111, 118, 126–27, 129, 131–32,
    134
Sim Sunt'aek, 159
Sim Uisŏk, 278–79, 281
Simch'ŏngjŏn, 313
Sin Chaehyo, 319–20
sin hangmun, 313
sinhŭng sadaebu, 3–4, 71
"single whip" tax system, 105
sinmin, 297–299
sinmun'go, 211
Sino-Japanese War, 152–163, 168,
    175–76, 248, 253, 272, 274,
    307, 317, 336–38, 358
sinsaenga samang, 72
*Sinyu saok*, 229
sip'o, 96
slavery, 256

Smith, P., 175
Sŏ Chaep'il, 280, 288
Sŏ Sang'u, 155
soa samang, 72
Sŏdaemun, 251
sŏdo sŏgi, 317–18, 322–23
Sŏgo, 213
Sŏhak, 358
Sŏhyanggak, 213
soin, 225
sŏjae, 46
sŏmin, 223
sŏnch'ŏnjŏk tanhap, 315
sŏnduan, 226, 228
Song, 19, 24, 26–28, 32, 35, 51, 60, 68–69, 79–80, 82–83, 86, 213–17, 297, 310, 320
Sŏnggyun'gwan, 26
sŏnghak, 215, 220, 232
Sŏngnihak, 115–17
*Sŏngshi chŏndo shi*, 242
Sŏnhyech'ŏng, 238–39
sŏran, 312
sŏri (village clerk), 37
sŏwŏn (private Confucian academy), 46–47
sowŏn (petition), 211
*Sŏyu kyŏnmun*, 139–40
sprouts of capitalism, 236
Stalin, Josef, 360
such'aek (water pump), 26, 28
sugi, 220, 232
sugi ch'iin, 220, 232, 313
sugwiso, 216
sugyŏng chikp'a, 54
Sui, 121
Suikosha, 333
Sungnyemun, 271
Sunjong, 311
susang, 96
susin taesa, 152
susinjega ch'igukp'yŏngch'ŏnha, 297
suzerain, 147, 149, 156–57, 161, 302
swaeguk, 341

Taedongbŏp, 117
Taedonggyo, 315
taedongmi, 239
T'aegŭk, 222–224
Taehak, 327
taehak ryuŭi, 221–22
Taehan Cheguk, 167, 359
Taehan Minguk, 188
*Taejŏn t'ongp'yŏn*, 233

*T'aesan yorok* (Summary Obstetrical Medicine), 84
Taewŏngun, 142, 158–59, 245, 256, 274, 290, 301–02, 304, 311, 317, 359
Tai-Kan hosin, 175
Taiping, 118
*Taiping shenghuifang*, 79, 83
Takezoe Shinichiro, 305
T'akjibu, 247
Tang, 29, 82, 97, 99–100, 105, 121, 310, 318
t'angp'yŏng, 298–99, 311
t'angp'yŏngch'aek, 218, 220, 231–32
T'apol Park, 254–55, 257
tariff, 144–46, 151–52, 162, 302, 340
Terauchi Masatake, 182
Tianzhangge, 213
Tibet, 133
To ŭi kan, 319
tomb inscription, 71–72, 76–77, 236, 253, 273, 288
tongdo sŏgi, 236, 251, 273, 288, 314, 316–18, 321–23
Tonghak peasant army, 307
T'ongni amun, 160
T'ongni kimu amun , 145
Tongnip hyŏphoe, 247
tongnan, 312
*Tong-zhi*, 25
tonyu, 110
*Tosŏng samgunmun pun'gyejido*, 242
Toyotomi Hideyoshi, 167
trade, 49–50, 60, 64–65, 122–37, 144, 146–51, 154, 226, 248, 303–04
tribute (tributary system), 123–25, 128–36, 138, 147–48, 227, 239–40, 243, 329, 338, 343
Tribute Tax Law, 20
Tsuneya Seifuku, 336–37
*Tŭnggwarok*, 15–16
Tung-lin, 113, 115
tunjŏn, 32

*Ŭibang yuch'wi*, 56, 84–85
Ŭijŏngbu, 164, 249
United Nations, 189–90, 192–93
United States: and Japan, 169, 176, 178, 185, 191; minister to, 151, 272, 274–75, 283–84; treaty, 145–47, 151, 246, 301–02, 330, 340–41, 349

# 398  Index

Unyang Incident, 336, 340, 347–48
urbanization, 269–70, 280, 283–84, 286, 369
uyŏngsa, 153, 158
von Möllendorff, Paul G., 153–55, 157–58

Waeber, Carl, 153, 158–60
waegwan, 341, 342
wako, 11, 55, 78, 106, 110, 112
wakon-yŏsai, 361–62
Wang Yang-ming (Wang Yangming), 115, 298–99, 315, 316
wangga, 299
Washington, D.C., 247, 257, 278, 283
waterwheel, 19, 26–28, 31
winmin, 226, 234
*Wen-hsien-t'ung-kao*, 25
wioe kyŏkchaeng, 212

*Xiaopinfang*, 79
xiaoshih, 95
*Xiaoxue*, 43
Xinjing, 43, 214

yangjŏl, 139, 150
Yech'ŏn, 12
yehak, 44, 47
yemun'gwan, 214
Yi (Ri) Kyep'il, 277, 279
Yi Ch'aeyŏn, 247, 251, 255, 257, 271–73, 275–78, 281, 284–85
Yi Chaemyŏn, 248
Yi Chaesun, 282
Yi Chaeu, 277
Yi Ch'aeyŏn, 7, 247, 251, 255, 257, 271–73, 275–78, 281, 284–85
Yi Chongha, 275, 277
Yi Haejo, 319–20
Yi Hakgyun, 185
Yi Hwang (Yi T'oegye), 43
Yi I (Yi Yulgok), 46, 316
Yi Kwangsu, 318–19
Yi Mansu, 210, 226–27
Yi Sangjae, 275, 277
Yi Sŏgu, 245
Yi Wanyong, 180, 182
Yi Yong'ik, 185
*Yiji*, 223
*Yijing*, 223
yixue qimeng, 223
Yokoi Shonan, 327
yŏlgogwan, 213
Yomei gakkai, 316

Yŏn ŭi kak (leg of swallow), 319
yonaoshi, 118
yong (use of all creation), 298
yŏnga samang, 72
Yŏngjongjin, 142
Yongle Emperor, 100
yŏngsŏnsa, 149
yŏpkun (hunting pheasant), 276
Yoshida Shigeru, 165
Yu Kiljun, 139–40, 150
Yuan, 5, 24, 26–27, 30, 81, 99, 101, 123–25, 310
Yuan Shikai, 158–60, 305–07
Yu-hai, 25
yuhyangso, 37–38, 41–42, 44–45, 47
yuksang, 96
Yun Ch'iho, 193
Yun Haengim, 228
yusuja, 114
yuŭi yusik, 318

Zhang Shicheng, 124
Zhen Dexiu, 43
Zheng He, 123
*Zhongwai xianbao*, 343
*Zhongyong*, 220
*Zhou-li*, 41
Zhu Xi, 35, 37, 39, 43, 115, 220–21, 223, 225
Zhu Yuanzhang, 124–25
Zongli yamen, 147–48, 160

# CORNELL EAST ASIA SERIES

4 Fredrick Teiwes, *Provincial Leadership in China: The Cultural Revolution and Its Aftermath*
8 Cornelius C. Kubler, *Vocabulary and Notes to Ba Jin's Jia: An Aid for Reading the Novel*
16 Monica Bethe & Karen Brazell, *Nō as Performance: An Analysis of the Kuse Scene of Yamamba*
18 Royall Tyler, tr., *Granny Mountains: A Second Cycle of Nō Plays*
23 Knight Biggerstaff, *Nanking Letters, 1949*
28 Diane E. Perushek, ed., *The Griffis Collection of Japanese Books: An Annotated Bibliography*
37 J. Victor Koschmann, Ōiwa Keibō & Yamashita Shinji, eds., *International Perspectives on Yanagita Kunio and Japanese Folklore Studies*
38 James O'Brien, tr., *Murō Saisei: Three Works*
40 Kubo Sakae, *Land of Volcanic Ash: A Play in Two Parts,* revised edition, tr. David G. Goodman
44 Susan Orpett Long, *Family Change and the Life Course in Japan*
48 Helen Craig McCullough, *Bungo Manual: Selected Reference Materials for Students of Classical Japanese*
49 Susan Blakeley Klein, *Ankoku Butō: The Premodern and Postmodern Influences on the Dance of Utter Darkness*
50 Karen Brazell, ed., *Twelve Plays of the Noh and Kyōgen Theaters*
51 David G. Goodman, ed., *Five Plays by Kishida Kunio*
52 Shirō Hara, *Ode to Stone,* tr. James Morita
53 Peter J. Katzenstein & Yutaka Tsujinaka, *Defending the Japanese State: Structures, Norms and the Political Responses to Terrorism and Violent Social Protest in the 1970s and 1980s*
54 Su Xiaokang & Wang Luxiang, *Deathsong of the River: A Reader's Guide to the Chinese TV Series* Heshang, trs. Richard Bodman & Pin P. Wan
55 Jingyuan Zhang, *Psychoanalysis in China: Literary Transformations, 1919-1949*
56 Jane Kate Leonard & John R. Watt, eds., *To Achieve Security and Wealth: The Qing Imperial State and the Economy, 1644-1911*
57 Andrew F. Jones, *Like a Knife: Ideology and Genre in Contemporary Chinese Popular Music*
58 Peter J. Katzenstein & Nobuo Okawara, *Japan's National Security: Structures, Norms and Policy Responses in a Changing World*
59 Carsten Holz, *The Role of Central Banking in China's Economic Reforms*
60 Chifumi Shimazaki, *Warrior Ghost Plays from the Japanese Noh Theater: Parallel Translations with Running Commentary*
61 Emily Groszos Ooms, *Women and Millenarian Protest in Meiji Japan: Deguchi Nao and Ōmotokyō*

62 Carolyn Anne Morley, *Transformation, Miracles, and Mischief: The Mountain Priest Plays of Kōygen*
63 David R. McCann & Hyunjae Yee Sallee, tr., *Selected Poems of Kim Namjo*, afterword by Kim Yunsik
64 Hua Qingzhao, *From Yalta to Panmunjom: Truman's Diplomacy and the Four Powers, 1945-1953*
65 Margaret Benton Fukasawa, *Kitahara Hakushū: His Life and Poetry*
66 Kam Louie, ed., *Strange Tales from Strange Lands: Stories by Zheng Wanlong*, with introduction
67 Wang Wen-hsing, *Backed Against the Sea*, tr. Edward Gunn
69 Brian Myers, *Han Sōrya and North Korean Literature: The Failure of Socialist Realism in the DPRK*
70 Thomas P. Lyons & Victor Nee, eds., *The Economic Transformation of South China: Reform and Development in the Post-Mao Era*
71 David G. Goodman, tr., *After Apocalypse: Four Japanese Plays of Hiroshima and Nagasaki*, with introduction
72 Thomas Lyons, *Poverty and Growth in a South China County: Anxi, Fujian, 1949-1992*
74 Martyn Atkins, *Informal Empire in Crisis: British Diplomacy and the Chinese Customs Succession, 1927-1929*
76 Chifumi Shimazaki, *Restless Spirits from Japanese Noh Plays of the Fourth Group: Parallel Translations with Running Commentary*
77 Brother Anthony of Taizé & Young-Moo Kim, trs., *Back to Heaven: Selected Poems of Ch'ŏn Sang Pyŏng*
78 Kevin O'Rourke, tr., *Singing Like a Cricket, Hooting Like an Owl: Selected Poems by Yi Kyu-bo*
79 Irit Averbuch, *The Gods Come Dancing: A Study of the Japanese Ritual Dance of Yamabushi Kagura*
80 Mark Peterson, *Korean Adoption and Inheritance: Case Studies in the Creation of a Classic Confucian Society*
81 Yenna Wu, tr., *The Lioness Roars: Shrew Stories from Late Imperial China*
82 Thomas Lyons, *The Economic Geography of Fujian: A Sourcebook*, Vol. 1
83 Pak Wan-so, *The Naked Tree*, tr. Yu Young-nan
84 C.T. Hsia, *The Classic Chinese Novel: A Critical Introduction*
85 Cho Chong-Rae, *Playing With Fire*, tr. Chun Kyung-Ja
86 Hayashi Fumiko, *I Saw a Pale Horse and Selections from Diary of a Vagabond*, tr. Janice Brown
87 Motoori Norinaga, *Kojiki-den, Book 1*, tr. Ann Wehmeyer
88 Chang Soo Ko, tr., *Sending the Ship Out to the Stars: Poems of Park Je-chun*
89 Thomas Lyons, *The Economic Geography of Fujian: A Sourcebook*, Vol. 2
90 Brother Anthony of Taizé, tr., *Midang: Early Lyrics of So Chong-Ju*
92 Janice Matsumura, *More Than a Momentary Nightmare: The Yokohama Incident and Wartime Japan*
93 Kim Jong-Gil tr., *The Snow Falling on Chagall's Village: Selected Poems of Kim Ch'un-Su*

94 Wolhee Choe & Peter Fusco, trs., *Day-Shine: Poetry by Hyon-jong Chong*
95 Chifumi Shimazaki, *Troubled Souls from Japanese Noh Plays of the Fourth Group*
96 Hagiwara Sakutarō, *Principles of Poetry (Shi no Genri)*, tr. Chester Wang
97 Mae J. Smethurst, *Dramatic Representations of Filial Piety: Five Noh in Translation*
98 Ross King, ed., *Description and Explanation in Korean Linguistics*
99 William Wilson, *Hōgen Monogatari: Tale of the Disorder in Hōgen*
100 Yasushi Yamanouchi, J. Victor Koschmann and Ryūichi Narita, eds., *Total War and 'Modernization'*
101 Yi Ch'ŏng-jun, *The Prophet and Other Stories*, tr. Julie Pickering
102 S.A. Thornton, *Charisma and Community Formation in Medieval Japan: The Case of the Yugyō-ha (1300-1700)*
103 Sherman Cochran, ed., *Inventing Nanjing Road: Commercial Culture in Shanghai, 1900-1945*
104 Harold M. Tanner, *Strike Hard! Anti-Crime Campaigns and Chinese Criminal Justice, 1979-1985*
105 Brother Anthony of Taizé & Young-Moo Kim, trs., *Farmers' Dance: Poems by Shin Kyŏng-nim*
106 Susan Orpett Long, ed., *Lives in Motion: Composing Circles of Self and Community in Japan*
107 Peter J. Katzenstein, Natasha Hamilton-Hart, Kozo Kato, & Ming Yue, *Asian Regionalism*
108 Kenneth Alan Grossberg, *Japan's Renaissance: The Politics of the Muromachi Bakufu*
109 John W. Hall & Toyoda Takeshi, eds., *Japan in the Muromachi Age*
110 Kim Su-Young, Shin Kyong-Nim, Lee Si-Young; *Variations: Three Korean Poets;* trs. Brother Anthony of Taizé & Young-Moo Kim
111 Samuel Leiter, *Frozen Moments: Writings on Kabuki, 1966-2001*
112 Pilwun Shih Wang & Sarah Wang, *Early One Spring: A Learning Guide to Accompany the Film Video* February
113 Thomas Conlan, *In Little Need of Divine Intervention: Scrolls of the Mongol Invasions of Japan*
114 Jane Kate Leonard & Robert Antony, eds., *Dragons, Tigers, and Dogs: Qing Crisis Management and the Boundaries of State Power in Late Imperial China*
115 Shu-ning Sciban & Fred Edwards, eds., *Dragonflies: Fiction by Chinese Women in the Twentieth Century*
116 David G. Goodman, ed., *The Return of the Gods: Japanese Drama and Culture in the 1960s*
117 Yang Hi Choe-Wall, *Vision of a Phoenix: The Poems of Hŏ Nansŏrhŏn*
118 Mae J. Smethurst and Christina Laffin, eds., *The Noh* Ominameshi*: A Flower Viewed from Many Directions*
119 Joseph A. Murphy, *Metaphorical Circuit: Negotiations Between Literature and Science in Twentieth-Century Japan*

120 Richard F. Calichman, *Takeuchi Yoshimi: Displacing the West*
121 Fan Pen Li Chen, *Visions for the Masses: Chinese Shadow Plays from Shaanxi and Shanxi*
122 S. Yumiko Hulvey, *Sacred Rites in Moonlight: Ben no Naishi Nikki*
123 Tetsuo Najita and J. Victor Koschmann, *Conflict in Modern Japanese History: The Neglected Tradition*
124 Naoki Sakai, Brett de Bary, & Iyotani Toshio, eds., *Deconstructing Nationality*
125 Judith N. Rabinovitch and Timothy R. Bradstock, *Dance of the Butterflies: Chinese Poetry from the Japanese Court Tradition*
126 Yang Gui-ja, *Contradictions,* trs. Stephen Epstein and Kim Mi-Young
127 Ann Sung-hi Lee, *Yi Kwang-su and Modern Korean Literature:* Mujŏng
128 Pang Kie-chung & Michael D. Shin, eds., *Landlords, Peasants, & Intellectuals in Modern Korea*
129 Joan R. Piggott, ed., *Capital and Countryside in Japan, 300-1180: Japanese Historians Interpreted in English*
130 Kyoko Selden and Jolisa Gracewood, eds., *Annotated Japanese Literary Gems: Stories by Tawada Yōko, Nakagami Kenji, and Hayashi Kyōko* (Vol. 1)
131 Michael G. Murdock, *Disarming the Allies of Imperialism: The State, Agitation, and Manipulation during China's Nationalist Revolution, 1922-1929*
132 Noel J. Pinnington, *Traces in the Way: Michi and the Writings of Komparu Zenchiku*
133 Charlotte von Verschuer, *Across the Perilous Sea: Japanese Trade with China and Korea from the Seventh to the Sixteenth Centuries,* Kristen Lee Hunter, tr.
134 John Timothy Wixted, *A Handbook to Classical Japanese*
135 Kyoko Selden et al, eds., *Annotated Japanese Literary Gems: Stories by Natsume Sōseki, Tomioka Taeko, and Inoue Yasushi* (Vol. 2)
136 Yi Tae-Jin, *The Dynamics of Confucianism and Modernization in Korean History*

Order online: www.einaudi.cornell.edu/eastasia/publications
or contact Cornell University Press Services, P.O. Box 6525, 750 Cascadilla Street,
Ithaca, NY 14851, USA. Tel toll-free: 1-800-666-2211; Fax: 1-800-688-2877;
E-mail: orderbook@cupserv.org or ceas@cornell.edu